BIOFEEDBACK
AND MINDFULNESS
IN EVERYDAY LIFE

"This book is simply brilliant! Inna Khazan is the world's leading expert on mindfulness and biofeedback. She combines these fields in a remarkably clear and insightful manner, grounding all she writes in solid science and clinical wisdom. The book is at once a reliable guide for managing common problems such as insomnia, pain, anxiety, or shame, and an invaluable resource for behavioral health professionals. The author shows us how to work with our human physiology using easily accessible technologies—mindfulness and biofeedback—to live happier and healthier lives. Highly recommended!"

—Christopher Germer, Ph.D., Lecturer on Psychiatry,
Harvard Medical School, author of *The Mindful Path to
Self-Compassion*, co-editor of *Mindfulness and Psychotherapy*

"Inna Khazan brilliantly integrates two approaches, mindfulness and biofeedback. A truly readable book—anchored in science—that explains how biofeedback enhances the self-regulation of the body and how mindfulness is the cognitive emotional approach for acceptance and resilience. This approach integrates the concept that mind/emotions/body are one. It is skills, NOT pills. This is a MUST book for students, therapists, and anyone interested in reducing symptoms, optimizing health, and promoting resilience. It provides pragmatic practices that anyone can do at home or at work to increase well-being; since health is the integrating of learned health-promoting skills into daily life."

—Erik Peper, Ph.D., Professor at San Francisco State University,
author of *Biofeedback Mastery: An Experiential Teaching and Self-Training
Manual* and *Fighting Cancer*, produces the blog www.peperperspective.com

"Dr. Khazan is a master at taking complex subject matter and turning it into a readable, step-by-step manual that can be valuable for almost anyone interested in self-improvement. This book, *Biofeedback and Mindfulness in Everyday Life*, covers recent developments in fields as diverse as applied psychophysiology and biofeedback to mindfulness-based interventions, and translates scientific findings into useful daily skills. A wonderful resource for both clinicians and patients."

—Richard Gevirtz, Ph.D., BCB, Distinguished Professor, California School
of Professional Psychology, Alliant International University

"Dr. Khazan provides an intuitive step-by-step guide for building resilience and emotional flexibility. She demystifies biofeedback and mindfulness, systematically teaches invaluable skills that don't require equipment, and explains how we can apply these new skills to challenges like anger, depression, and pain. If you've always wanted a clearly written and engaging introduction to biofeedback and mindfulness for clients or students, your wait is over! This amazing book has earned my highest recommendation."

—Fredric Shaffer, Ph.D., BCB, BCB-HRV, Professor of Psychology, Truman State
University, and Director of the Center for Applied Psychology

BIOFEEDBACK AND MINDFULNESS IN EVERYDAY LIFE

Practical Solutions for Improving

Your Health and Performance

INNA KHAZAN, Ph.D.

W. W. NORTON & COMPANY

Independent Publishers Since 1923

BIOFEEDBACK AND MINDFULNESS IN EVERYDAY LIFE is intended as a general information resource for readers. It is not a substitute for medical care and should not be used in lieu of treatment of any diagnosed condition or any symptom that may require the personal attention of a physician. The vignettes that serve as chapter openers, and other references to individuals incorporating or seeking to incorporate the techniques described in the book, are composite portraits, designed to illustrate the experiences of people who may be helped by biofeedback and mindfulness. None of the individuals described represents an actual person, living or dead, and any apparent resemblance is purely coincidental.

As of press time, the URLs displayed in this book link or refer to existing Internet sites. The author is not responsible for, and should not be deemed to endorse, any content that appears on third-party websites. Likewise, the publisher is not responsible for and cannot endorse any website or content other than its own.

For information about permission to reproduce selections from this book, write to Permissions, W. W. Norton & Company, Inc., 500 Fifth Avenue, New York, NY 10110

For information about special discounts for bulk purchases, please contact W. W. Norton Special Sales at specialsales@wwnorton.com or 800-233-4830

Manufacturing by Sheridan Books
Book design by Joe Lops
Production manager: Katelyn MacKenzie

Library of Congress Cataloging-in-Publication Data

Names: Khazan, Inna Z., author.
Title: Biofeedback and mindfulness in everyday life : practical solutions for improving your
    health and performance / Inna Khazan.
Description: New York : W.W. Norton & Company, [2019] | Includes bibliographical
    references and index.
Identifiers: LCCN 2018059612 | ISBN 9780393712933 (pbk.)
Subjects: LCSH: Biofeedback training. | Mindfulness-based cognitive therapy.
Classification: LCC RC489.B53 K44 2019 | DDC 615.8/514—dc23
LC record available at https://lccn.loc.gov/2018059612

W. W. Norton & Company, Inc., 500 Fifth Avenue, New York, N.Y. 10110
www.wwnorton.com

W. W. Norton & Company Ltd., 15 Carlisle Street, London W1D 3BS

1 2 3 4 5 6 7 8 9 0

To my father, Simon Zaslavsky, for always believing.

Contents

Acknowledgments

The book you hold in your hands would not have been possible without the many wonderful and supportive people in my life whose contributions have been invaluable and to whom I am forever grateful.

First, I'd like to thank the amazing team of editors at W. W. Norton. To Deborah Malmud, Vice President and Editorial Director at Norton Professional Books, thank you for encouraging me to undertake this project and your wise and thoughtful guidance in making it come to fruition. Thank you to Mariah Eppes and Sara McBride for your keen attention in making sure all the details of the book were well taken care of. To Trish Watson, thank you for your masterful editing of the book. Thank you to everyone else at Norton working behind the scenes.

I owe an immense debt of gratitude to Christopher Germer who has been my mentor and friend for many years. Chris, thank you for introducing me to mindfulness and self-compassion and guiding me in practice, for patiently helping me work through the nuances of how mindfulness and biofeedback fit together, for providing inspiration, and most of all, for your unwavering support and belief in my ideas.

I am grateful to my biofeedback mentors and colleagues who have shared their knowledge, expertise, and friendship with me over the years. To Fredric Shaffer, thank you for everything you have taught me, for giving me opportunities to grow and contribute to the field, and for your trust and friendship—they mean more to me than words can express. To Donald Moss, thank you for sharing your passion for writing, for encouraging me to write more on the subject of biofeedback and mindfulness, and for your ever-present support. Christopher Gilbert, thank you for our deep enlightening conversations, your willingness to review and improve chapters of this book, and tireless encouragement. Richard Gevirtz, Paul Lehrer, and Erik Peper—so much of what I know about biofeedback I've learned from you. Thank you for your generosity in sharing your expertise, materials, and passion for the science and practice of biofeedback.

I am grateful to my friends and colleagues at Biofeedback Certification International Alliance: Randy Lyle, Leslie Sherlin, Dave Hagedorn, Don Moss, Fred Shaffer, Denise Graf, and especially Judy Crawford. Judy, thank you for your wisdom and friendship over the years.

I am honored to work with incredibly talented scientists and clinicians at the Association for Applied Psychophysiology and Biofeedback, many of whom I call my friends. A special thank you to Michelle Cunningham, Ethan Benore, Katie Fleischman, Tracy Heller, Heather King, Urszula Klich, Leah Lagos, Brad Lichtenstein, Diana Martinez, Ainat Rogel, Christine Sanchez, and Patrick Steffen.

I am grateful to my colleagues at the Institute for Meditation and Psychotherapy, and especially to Susan Pollak, who was also one of my first meditation teachers. Susan, I have learned so much from your kind and compassionate presence. Thank you for helping me deepen my practice and for your support and encouragement throughout this process.

To my colleagues at the Biofeedback Federation of Europe and Thought Technology LTD—thank you for your support of my work and for the many years of fruitful collaboration, and especially to Carol Meyers, Hal Myers, and Jon Bale. A special thank you to Lawrence Klein for his unending enthusiasm in advocating for mindfulness-based biofeedback and my work in particular.

I am grateful to my early biofeedback mentors Saul Rosenthal, Satya Bellerose, Leslie Borne, and Amaro Laria, as well as local friends and colleagues Elizabeth Gagnon, Vikki Brown, and Rebekah Montgomery for supporting and fostering this work. I am grateful to Judy Krulewitz for her wisdom and guidance over many years.

My international colleagues and friends—David Arroyo and Claudia Coronel-Arroyo, Hiroko Demichelis, Yuval Oded, Federico Pedrabissi, Arnon Rolnick, and Jan Vagedes—thank you for your friendship, collaboration, and enthusiasm for bringing biofeedback and mindfulness together. To my colleagues at Meru Health—Kristian Ranta, Albert Nazander, Outi Hilgert, and

Disha Roy—thank you for your wisdom and ingenuity in bringing mindfulness and biofeedback together.

I am grateful to my students who have helped me refine ideas presented in this book and to my clients who have sought me out and allowed me to learn from them on their journey to improving their health and performance.

I owe a profound debt of gratitude to my family and friends, who have supported me throughout this project in every possible way. To my husband Roger—this book would not have happened without you. Thank you for being a sounding board, a tireless editor, and a steadfast supporter. Thank you for the sacrifices you've made in order to give me time to write. Thank you for always being there. To my children Robert, Aaron, and Eliana—thank you for your laughter, smiles, and a limitless supply of hugs. Thank you for your patience and understanding when I had to work late to meet a deadline. To my father, Simon Zaslavsky, who passed away 5 years ago—even though you are no longer here, I am forever grateful for the lessons you've taught me and for the encouragement to follow my passion. To my mother, Sima Zaslavsky, thank you for being just a phone call away, your unconditional support, and always being willing to help with the kids to allow me to write. I am fortunate to have an amazing extended family who have always believed in me and supported me. I am grateful to Leonard Khazan and Lana Brodsky, Irina, Alex, and Dana Dubovis, Izolda Lishansky and Jacob Fink, Marina and Mark Lishansky. And finally, I couldn't have done this without the support of my friends: Lucy and Igor Lubashev, Buket and Dan Grau, Anya and Eugene Dashevsky, Anna and Mark Gurevich, Gami and Seth Maislin, Marina Shtern and Grant Heard, Dan and Marianna Utin, Katya and Leonid Taycher, and Maria and Leo Mirkis.

Thank you all! I could not have done this without you.

Introduction

Imagine you are learning to fly an airplane and someone covers up the instrument panel—you are learning to fly with only what you see outside the window for feedback; you don't know what's going on inside the plane. Then, the instrument panel is opened, and you can suddenly see all the instruments. You no longer have to guess what the plane's altitude is by looking out the window; you know exactly how high you are flying. You no longer have to guess the plane's direction, or fuel level, or air pressure. How different would your experience be flying with full information about the external and the internal environment of the plane? Having full information from the instruments, you can now adjust your altitude and direction to get exactly to where you need to go, rather than guess and hope you get close enough without crashing in the process.

Has there been a time in your life when you've attempted to make changes to the way you feel or do things and felt like you were flying blind, not knowing which changes to make and how to make them, or whether they would even help? Perhaps you've tried to control your anxiety, stop feeling depressed, fix your pain, or reduce stress? Perhaps you've wanted to do better at your job, in a sport, or in artistic performance? Or maybe you've wanted to do better in your personal life, be a better partner, parent, or friend? Did you ever feel like you had a general idea of what you needed to do to make changes but had a hard time doing it or getting the results you wanted?

Often, in our attempts to fix ourselves—get rid of anxiety, sadness, or pain or fix whatever gets in the way of performing at our best—we end up making those things worse and then "beat up" on ourselves for being unable to achieve our desired goals. For example, in our professional lives, we as human beings often bring a great depth of skill and knowledge to our work. We excel in many areas of expertise and lead successful lives and careers. And yet, we are not always able to bring our knowledge and skills to bear in high-stress situations, leaving us dissatisfied with our performance. Similar situations happen in our personal lives too. We might know how we want to act but are unable to act in accordance with this knowledge because automatic reactions from our minds and bodies override our intentions.

These challenges are not related to a lack of any professional or academic skill or experience and require a set of skills not typically taught anywhere. Our mind's and body's abilities to regulate our physiological and emotional activation are at the core of how we handle stressful situations. Ideally, we want our brains and our bodies to work in ways that foster a resilient response to stress, and we want them to recover quickly once the stressful event is over. For most of us, the only way to get there is to specifically train our brains and bodies to self-regulate at all times, and especially when the stakes are high. This is what this book is about.

This book is intended to help you find simple, practical solutions for improving the way you respond to life challenges and increasing your resilience and emotional flexibility. Simply put, this book is about helping you do what you do, but better. Many books have been written about ways to fix what's wrong with people. This book is not about fixing yourself—it is not helpful to see yourself as broken. Rather, this book is about using the powers of your mind and body to their fullest potential.

The purpose of this book is to guide you in training your body and your brain to perform at their best to meet whatever challenges come your way. It addresses three components of training—physiological, emotional, and interpretive. The *physiological component* is the ability of your body to self-regulate, or adjust your physiological activity to be most helpful at each moment throughout your day, whether facing a challenge, recovering from a challenge, or engaging in everyday life. In this book I discuss physiological concepts vital to your ability to self-regulate and ways to use this knowledge in everyday life. I introduce the technology of biofeedback and suggest practical skills using this powerful tool to train self-regulation. With biofeedback, you learn to activate or power up your body to just the right level for the task or challenge you face and then, once that challenge is over, to recover quickly and fully.

The *emotional component* is the ability of your mind to respond in the most helpful way to emotions that arise moment to moment, without getting stuck in difficult emotions, while cultivating compassion and fostering resilience. Mindfulness and compassion training are central to our ability to regulation emotion. I discuss these concepts in detail and provide you with practical skills aimed at cultivating mindfulness and compassion in training emotional regulation.

The *interpretive component* is the ability to integrate the physiological and emotional training you have done. With physiological and biofeedback-based training, you train your body to find the sweet spot of activation needed to meet the challenge and to recover fully. With mindfulness training you train your brain to activate in just the right way to allow clear thinking, decision making, and emotion regulation.

Now your brain and your body are able to do what they do best to support you during a challenge. Sounds great, right? Except that's not enough. What you also need is the ability to recognize the signs of physiological and emotional activation as being helpful and adaptive and not fight against them with attempts to calm down. This book will help you to tell the difference between helpful and unhelpful activation, both physiological and emotional, to provide you with skills to allow helpful activation to stay and to respond to the unhelpful activation. In other words, this book will allow you to take the cover off the instrument panel and stop flying blind.

You will benefit from reading this book and incorporating the skills discussed here if you would like to achieve any of the following goals:

- Improve your professional performance
- Improve your athletic performance
- Improve your academic performance
- Better regulate your emotional reactions
- Improve your ability to make quick decisions
- Improve flexibility in responding to difficult situations
- Improve ability to cope with stress, anxiety, sadness and depression, pain, shame and anger

- Improve your sleep
- Improve communication with important people in your life
- Find ways to better take care of yourself

This book contains three parts. The first part is dedicated to psycho-physiological biofeedback-based skills. You will learn about the concept of biofeedback and five modalities of physiology that you may be able to improve by using the skills described in each chapter, as well as ways in which these skills may be helpful to you in your everyday life. You will learn ways in which you may be able to train your physiology using biofeedback devices, as well as things you can do by using psychophysiological knowledge without the use of devices. All skills are described in a clear, step-by-step manner, enabling you to begin practicing right away.

The second part addresses mindfulness and compassion. You will learn ways to introduce meditation into your life or deepen your existing meditation practice. You will also learn mindfulness and compassion-based skills that you may be able to use in moments of increased challenge or distress. The third part of the book is dedicated to applying biofeedback and mindfulness-based skills to specific challenges you may encounter: sleep difficulty, stress, anxiety, sadness and depression, pain, anger, and communication with important people in your life.

As you move through each chapter and section of the book, you will be able to formulate your own training plan. You will decide whether your plan will include biofeedback and, if so, which modalities. You will decide whether to include a biofeedback device or follow the guidelines without one, or whether to enlist the help of a biofeedback therapist, as well as how to choose one. You will decide how to practice mindfulness: Will you meditate? If so, which meditation will you start with? Will you use mindfulness-based skills, and if so, which ones seem the most helpful to you? Will you practice compassion, gratitude, and appreciation, and how might they fit into your life? You will decide how to apply these skills to any of the issues described in part 3—stress, anxiety, anger, sadness, depression, pain, shame, sleep difficulty, and communication challenges.

At the end of the book the appendices provide a collection of medita-tion scripts that you will find useful in your practice.I have made recordings of these meditations available on my website at www.innakhazan.com/ meditation_recordings.html. And throughout the book I've placed notes to additional scientific sources, if you would like to dig deeper into the evidence for the concepts and techniques I describe.

Finally, I would like to offer a few tips that may make it easier for you to make good use of this book:

- I suggest many different exercises and practices to guide your training. I encourage you to do the practices—don't skip over them. You will benefit a lot more from doing the practice than from just reading about the concepts.
- Many of the concepts introduced in one chapter are intertwined with concepts in other chapters. Refer back and forth between chapters as you need to.
- Skills I discuss in the context of one application are not exclusive to that application; they can be applied to other situations as well. For example, anxiety skills can be applied to sadness/depression, shame, or pain.
- I encourage you to keep a notebook to write down thoughts that occur to you as you read, to do some of the exercises in the book, and to keep track of what's important. Writing things down as you go will help you process them and remember them much better than if you just read them.

I hope you enjoy the book and find the practical skills useful in improving your health and performance. If you have questions or comments, you can reach me through my website at www.innakhazan.com.

BIOFEEDBACK
AND MINDFULNESS
IN EVERYDAY LIFE

PART I

Physiological Principles

CHAPTER 1

Biofeedback

As David sat on the train on the way to work, he silently ran through the mental checklist of everything he had to do that day. He had a very important meeting with his boss as soon as he got to work, followed by a team brainstorming meeting for a new project he was heading, and then a lunch date with Kate, whom he recently met online, and he really wanted to make a good impression. The rest of the afternoon he would spend making phone calls and answering e-mails, and maybe getting some of his own work done as well. The train suddenly came to a stop. Startled, David looked around. They were in a tunnel. The train engineer's voice came on the intercom announcing that there is a medical emergency at the stop ahead and they would be standing by for a while. David's stomach tied itself in knots—this could not have happened on a worse day! Now he'll be late for the meeting with his boss, and since there was no cell reception in the tunnel, he didn't even have a way to let him know. By the time the train started moving, David was fidgeting in his seat, feeling sweaty and anxious. He checked the heart rate monitor he wore on his wrist—his heart rate was in the nineties! Once he was off the train, David ran all the way to work, bursting into his boss's office, panting. The meeting was short, and David could barely remember what happened. He could not focus during the brainstorming session with his team. All he could do was think about whether this meeting with his boss was going to affect his promotion and feel his heart pounding in his chest. His wrist monitor confirmed that his heart was beating too fast. He met Kate for lunch, but his stomach was tense and he was feeling nauseous. It was hard to keep a smile on his face and have a conver-

sation. David spent the rest of the afternoon beating up on himself for what must have been a terrible impression he made on Kate. She'll never want to talk to him again. He checked his heart rate monitor again—still nineties, but he didn't know what to do about or how to bring it down.

Like David, you've probably heard the advice, Listen to your body. You often hear it when you exercise, play sports, perform, make lifestyle changes, or try to find ways to improve your health. Your body is constantly sending you signals—through your heart rate, your breath, your muscles, your skin, and so forth. Unfortunately, many of those signals are subtle, and either you are not aware of them, don't recognize their importance, or don't know what to do with them. At some point, your body will turn up the volume of its messages to get your attention. Pain, high blood pressure, headaches, stomach aches—all those are your body's way of turning up the volume to get your attention. You definitely hear those, but do you know how to respond to them?

Biofeedback gives you the clearest and most effective way to understand the messages your body is sending you, learn to recognize them before the signals intensify, and know what kinds of changes you need to make and how to make them. This chapter discusses what biofeedback is, scientific evidence for its effectiveness, how you may be able to use it in your own life, and the process of biofeedback training.

Biofeedback is a learning process that helps you develop greater awareness and ability to influence your physiological, emotional, and cognitive activity by using signals from you own body to improve your health and performance. Sensors are placed on the surface of your skin to read the signals your body is sending—your breathing, heart rate, muscle tension, finger temperature, and skin conductance. I say more about these modalities shortly.

Biofeedback software picks up these signals and displays them for you on a computer screen in a clear, easy-to-understand way. You can see what happens to your heart rate when you make changes to your breathing. You can see what happens to your muscle tension when you change positions or release your muscles. You can see what happens to your breathing and heart rate when you meditate. You can see what happens to your finger temperature when you imagine yourself sitting on a beautiful, warm beach. You get the point—you can observe subtle changes in your body's functioning in response to your thoughts, feelings, and actions. This feedback allows you to "hear" the signals from your body in a different way and learn how to interpret them and how to respond to them. In other words, biofeedback allows you to truly listen to your body.

BIOFEEDBACK IS NOT A RELAXATION TOOL

Many people believe that biofeedback is a way to learn to relax. While it is true that you can learn to relax using biofeedback, relaxation is not the main goal. The main goal is *self-regulation*, which means being able to activate your nervous system most optimally for action and being able to relax and recover after the action is complete.

The goal of biofeedback is to increase your body's ability to regulate itself. Self-regulation is the ability of your nervous system to respond adaptively to changes in your environment, both internal and external. Much of the regulation in your body happens automatically, without conscious awareness on your part. For example, your brain monitors and adjusts your body temperature and pH levels to keep them stable. Your brain also monitors your heart rate, breathing, and blood pressure and adjusts them based on the needs of your body at that moment. This kind of self-regulation is necessary for your mind and body to switch gears smoothly while going from one state to another. For example, self-regulation is necessary to transition from an intense argument with a spouse to being able to sleep. It is necessary to transition from running late to a meeting to being able to lead it. It is necessary to quickly access your physiological and emotional resources to attend to an unexpected crisis.

Your ability to self-regulate in these complex ways can get disrupted and lead to difficulty in adjusting to changes in your environment and meeting daily life challenges, as well as undermine your resilience. In the example above, David had trouble with self-regulation as he waited on the train, transitioned from a difficult meeting with his boss to brainstorming with his team, and attempted to be present during his lunch with Kate. Your body's ability to self-regulate can get disrupted by circumstances such as trauma, chronic stress, physical, or mental illness. It can also get disrupted when you have a hard time understanding the signals your body is sending you.

WHAT IF YOU DON'T HAVE A BIOFEEDBACK DEVICE?

You may use the principles of psychophysiology underlying biofeedback to strengthen your self-regulation and improve your health and performance without the use of biofeedback. I encourage you to use the most easily accessible devices (such as a heart rate variability app on your phone, or a thermometer or even a piece of chocolate) if at all possible. The feedback these simple devices provide will give you benefit above and beyond training without it. However, if using biofeedback is simply not possible, or if your device measures some but not all modalities you'd like to train, you may use psychophysiological principles outlined in each chapter without measurement and still derive benefit.

Biofeedback provides you with the information you need to train and strengthen your ability to self-regulate. Biofeedback works by measuring parameters of your body's physiological functioning and displaying that information back to you for use in making appropriate adjustments. *Biofeedback training* is learning how to make adjustments to your physiological functioning based on the feedback you receive. Biofeedback and biofeedback training can be done using various devices, from very simple to very sophisticated:

- Biofeedback can be done without technology, such as by using a mirror to observe your breathing patterns and make adjustments to it, or by using a piece of chocolate to give you information about finger temperature (see Chapter 5 for more on this).
- You can use simple technology, such as a thermometer to measure finger temperature.
- You can use sophisticated but simple-to-use self-training devices, such as heart rate or heart rate variability (HRV) measurements using

your smartphone's camera or small devices that connect to your mobile device and measure skin conductance or HRV.

- You can use sophisticated, multimodality devices using advanced graphics and software. These devices are typically used by biofeedback therapists.

Biofeedback Modalities

Biofeedback devices can measure several parameters of your body's physiological functioning—these are called *biofeedback modalities*. Each one gives you important and unique information about the way your body functions. Each modality can help you listen to different signals your body is sending and help you train your ability to self-regulate in different ways. I review various biofeedback modalities in this section and then discuss scientific evidence for how each modality is best used.

Biofeedback modalities include the following:

Breathing. Some biofeedback devices measure rate and pattern of your breath using a belt that goes around your waist. Other devices measure concentration of oxygen and/or carbon dioxide in your blood using a finger oximeter to measure oxygen or a nasal cannula of an instrument called the capnometer to measure levels of carbon dioxide.

Heart rate. These biofeedback devices measure heart rate using a finger photoplethysmograph, a device that sends a red light through your finger and determines your heart rate based on how much red light is absorbed, or an electrocardiogram sensor that detects electrical signals from your heart.

Heart rate variability (HRV). This measurement is done with software from your heart rate signal. HRV is the difference in time that passes from heartbeat to heartbeat and is determined through statistical calculations using the heart rate measurements.

Muscle tension. These biofeedback devices measure electrical activity of the muscles using *surface electromyography (sEMG)*, which detects electrical impulses sent out by the muscles as they activate.

Temperature. These biofeedback devices measure finger and sometimes toe temperature using a thermistor, which transforms warming of the sensor into electrical information that is displayed on the screen as your temperature.

Skin conductance. These biofeedback devices measure activity of sweat glands on your fingers or the palm of your hand. As your sympathetic nervous system (the one responsible for the stress response) is activated, sweat glands become more active and produce more sweat. The sensor sends a very small electrical current through your finger to determine how conductive your skin is—the more moisture there is, the more conductive your skin is. Higher skin conductance indicates increased stress activation. (You don't need to worry about being electrocuted by the electrical current—it is a very small current that you don't even feel.)

Brain waves. This type of biofeedback, called *neurofeedback* or EEG (electroencephalogram) biofeedback, measures electrical activity of the brain. Because this book is dedicated to body biofeedback, I do not discuss neurofeedback.

Research Evidence for Biofeedback Success

Biofeedback has been scientifically shown to be an effective tool for improving many areas of your health and performance. Keep in mind that it is not a panacea, not a fix for everything. Think about what kind of changes you'd like to make, and then decide whether the research evidence supports the use of biofeedback for these areas. To help you decide, I include a list of conditions for which biofeedback has been scientifically shown to be helpful.[1] This list does not include conditions best treated with neurofeedback. Please keep in mind that self-training in biofeedback is not intended to be a substitute for treatment with a biofeedback therapist. If any of these conditions listed present a significant problem in your life, consider seeking out a biofeedback therapist to help you with training.

- Asthma
- Anxiety

- Chronic back pain
- Depression
- Diabetes (for glucose control)
- Fibromyalgia
- High blood pressure
- Insomnia
- Irritable bowel syndrome (IBS)
- Migraine headaches
- Noncardiac chest pain
- Posttraumatic stress disorder (PTSD)
- Preeclampsia
- Repetitive strain injury
- Raynaud's disease, a condition in which fingers and/or toes, and sometimes nose and ears, temporarily lose circulation (because of blood vessel constriction), turn colors (white, blue, and red), and feel very painful
- Temporomandibular joint (TMJ) disorders
- Tension headaches
- Tinnitus
- Traumatic brain injury

Biofeedback has also been shown to be an effective tool in enhancing performance in professional fields, music, and athletics. Specifically, biofeedback is helpful in enhancing the following qualities:

- Overall self-regulation ability
- Athletic performance, endurance, and reaction time
- Performance in dance and music
- Ability to interpret manifestations of stress in helpful ways
- Ability to sustain attention
- Decision making
- Emotion regulation
- Goal-directed behavior
- Memory capacity and retrieval
- Situational awareness

All of these qualities establish an important foundation for optimal performance in multiple professional and athletic arenas.

Self-Training Versus Working With a Biofeedback Therapist

Given the availability and improving quality of low-cost biofeedback devices, you have a lot of excellent options for self-training. Appendix B gives examples of self-training devices you can use for each biofeedback modality. Following the guidelines provided in Chapters 2–6, dedicated to each of the biofeedback modalities, will equip you with the ability to train yourself. You may consider working with a biofeedback therapist if you have complex medical or psychological needs or if self-training is not producing the benefits you are hoping for.

How to Find a Biofeedback Therapist

As with any medical or mental health professional, it is important to ensure that the biofeedback therapist you choose is properly credentialed and trained. There is no license to practice biofeedback, but there is biofeedback board certification for those who are licensed in a related field and are trained to practice biofeedback. Biofeedback therapists are typically licensed in medical or mental health fields, such as psychology, medicine, social work, occupational or physical therapy, dentistry, nursing, or counseling. Biofeedback therapists not licensed in a medical field, who provide only optimal performance training without treating any medical or mental health conditions, may also be board certified in biofeedback.

Biofeedback practitioners may hold one or more of four certifications: biofeedback (BCB), neurofeedback (BCN), heart rate variability biofeedback (BCB-HRV), and pelvic floor biofeedback (BCB-PMD). Biofeedback-certified therapists (BCB) are trained in all the biofeedback modalities described in this book. Those certified in HRV biofeedback are trained in heart rate and respiratory biofeedback only. Neurofeedback-certified therapists are trained in neurofeedback, a modality I do not cover in this book. Pelvic floor biofeedback therapists are typically occupational or physical therapists who work with pelvic floor pain and incontinence.

The Biofeedback Certification International Alliance (BCIA) can help you find a board-certified biofeedback therapist. BCIA is the certification body for biofeedback practitioners in the United States and around the world. Visit the BCIA website at BCIA.org and click on Find a Practitioner. If you would like to find a therapist who can help advance your biofeedback training using the guidelines in this book, look for BCB- or BCB-HRV-certified practitioners.

What Biofeedback Is and Is Not

As you decide how to use biofeedback training in your own life, it is important to recognize what biofeedback can and cannot do, and also what it is and what it is not.

WEARABLE DEVICES

The popularity of wearable devices has been remarkable. Lots of people are walking around with various devices that measure steps, sleep, movement, and heart rate, and some that also measure blood pressure, temperature, calories, muscle tension, and heart rate variability. Much of the information these devices give us would be considered biofeedback, because they measure physiological parameters and give us feedback about it. However, not all of the information these devices give you can be easily used for biofeedback training.

Several components are necessary to call something *biofeedback* and for that biofeedback to help you with self-regulation training. First, biofeedback provides information about physiological functioning of your body, such as breathing or heart rate. This component of biofeedback is called *psychophysiological monitoring*. It is necessary, but not sufficient, for the process of biofeedback. The second component is the *feedback* about your physiological functioning. An example of physiological monitoring is the nurse at your doctor's office measuring your blood pressure and heart rate during your physical exam. When she tells you what your heart rate and blood pressure are, giving you feedback, the information becomes biofeedback. The feedback is necessary for you to be able to make helpful changes to your physiological functioning. Making these changes based on the feedback you receive is *biofeedback training*. For example, as you change your breathing rate and pattern, you observe the changes in your breathing and heart rate displayed on the screen, giving you the ability to refine the change to what you need it to be.

Many apps are available on mobile devices that deal with some aspects of physiology. Some apps measure your heart rate, which is a form of biofeedback. David's heart monitor is that kind of biofeedback device. Some apps measure your HRV, mostly with the use of an external device that measures your heart rate and HRV and sends information to your phone. There are also a few apps that measure HRV using the phone camera. These apps are inexpensive and easily accessible forms of biofeedback. Keep in mind that not all biofeedback devices allow you to train the physiological parameter they measure. For example, some HRV apps measure and give you feedback about your HRV but do not offer training using feedback. Just knowing what your HRV is over some period of time is not enough to know how to make changes. Choose an app or device that gives you live, real-time feedback about the moment-to-moment changes in your HRV. See Appendix B for examples of biofeedback devices that measure your HRV and allow you to train it, as well as examples of devices for other biofeedback modalities.

There are also numerous apps that guide and pace your breathing in some way. These breathing pacing apps are not biofeedback because they do not measure anything about your physiology and do not provide feedback. Some of these apps, however, are quite useful in facilitating your biofeedback training and can be used to guide your self-practice if you have chosen not to use a biofeedback device. Examples of these apps are also listed in Appendix B.

I've seen cases where, under the guise of biofeedback, people were offered a recording with a relaxation exercise or a meditation. That is not biofeedback, although recordings are often used as part of biofeedback training. Breathing training without some sort of physiological measurement and feedback is also not biofeedback.

People sometimes see biofeedback as something that is done to them as a way of curing whatever ails them. It is important to remember that biofeedback is not something that is done to you. Biofeedback is a tool that helps you take an active part in your own training to improve your health and well-being. Your willingness to be an active participant is crucial. The next section outlines steps you can take to maximize the effectiveness of your biofeedback practice.

Biofeedback Training Plan

1. Choose Your Modalities

Decide which modalities of biofeedback are most likely to be useful to you. Choose modalities based on the goals you'd like to achieve. The following is a concise list of modalities and areas for which each modality may be helpful.[2] Please refer to chapters devoted to each modality for more details.

- Breathing (Chapter 2)—breathing dysregulation, especially over-breathing; also asthma, anxiety, chronic pain, headaches, anger, IBS, Raynaud's disease, stress, and performance improvement.
- Heart rate variability (Chapter 3)—asthma, anxiety, anger, depression, headaches, high blood pressure, IBS, chronic pain, preeclampsia, posttraumatic stress disorder, stress, and performance improvement.
- Muscle tension (Chapter 4)—muscle-related pain, chronic back pain, anxiety, tension headache, TMJ disorders, repetitive strain injury, and muscle-related areas of performance, such as learning to use correct muscles to perform certain movements.
- Temperature (Chapter 5)—Raynaud's disease, high blood pressure, migraine headaches, stress, and performance improvement.
- Skin conductance (Chapter 6)—anxiety, stress, motion sickness, and performance improvement.

If you choose to work with a biofeedback therapist, he or she will be able to conduct stress and relaxation assessments, which will further guide your choice of training modalities. These assessments will pinpoint which areas of your physiology need to be trained and how.

2. Make a Plan for Practicing Biofeedback Skills

Once you've chosen your modality or modalities to train, think about good practice times. Having a regular time to practice will help you establish a routine, which is crucial for developing new habits. Pick a time when you are able to practice most days of the week, when you are less likely to be disturbed or be tired or hungry. Practicing at bedtime can often be a good way to end the day and establish a consistent routine. However, if you fall asleep while practicing your skills (which are often relaxing), consider picking a different time when you are able to follow through with the practice and is predictable day to day. Helpful times may be when you first wake up in the morning, right when you get to work or to school, before or after lunch, before you leave work or school, or when you first get home.

Regular practice is crucial to biofeedback success. Practicing a skill once or twice or every once in a while is unlikely to benefit you. Once your biofeedback practice is established, practicing your skills 7 days a week for 20 minutes a day is ideal. Set realistic goals for practice until it becomes a habit. For example, you may start with 5 minutes 3 times a week and then increase to 5 minutes every day, then 10 minutes every day, then 15, and finally 20 minutes a day.

It is often difficult to figure out how to fit all the good things you can be doing for yourself into your day—biofeedback, meditation, exercise, walking, massage, acupuncture, physical therapy, meetings with a mental health therapist, and so on. Biofeedback and meditation can often be combined into one practice time—you initially learn biofeedback and mindfulness skills separately and then combine them. This makes it a little easier to make time for two important components of health and well-being. Twenty minutes a day may be possible to find in addition to everything else that is important for you to do. There will be days when something else takes precedence—that's expected and understandable. Just make sure that if you have decided to devote time to biofeedback (and mindfulness) practice, the practice happens as regularly as possible.

Don't over-practice. Limit each session of biofeedback practice to 20 minutes. Twenty-minute sessions are sufficient to make progress and will limit boredom and frustration if things are not going as you'd like them to. If you'd like to practice more to reap greater benefit, set aside two 20-minute time periods each day, one in the first and one in the second part of the day.

3. Monitor Your Progress

Before starting your biofeedback skills training, choose areas of functioning where you would like to see improvement. It could be your blood pressure readings, the way you perform under pressure, your endurance in athletic training, your test-taking ability, your performance in your professional arena, frequency, duration, and intensity of pain or headaches you experience, or anything else you choose to track.

Decide on your markers of progress, and rate how well you are doing in that area before starting biofeedback training. Then check in with yourself after 4–6 weeks of consistent training (consistency is key!). It will take a few weeks for signs of progress to become apparent. Then continue checking in every 4–6 weeks to keep track of continued progress.

It is hard to keep track of so much information yourself. At the end of this chapter I provide two worksheets you can use to keep track of your progress. The first worksheet is designed to track continuous ratings of symptoms or performance goals, which you can rate on a scale from 0 (low) to 10 (high). These ratings may be for symptoms of anxiety, pain, gastrointestinal distress, mood, or level of stress or for performance and self-regulation goals such as ability to shift from situation to situation, perceptions of your ability to speak in public, or your rating of your sports or artistic performance.

The second worksheet is designed for specific physiological scores, such as your blood pressure readings or number of headaches, or specific performance goals, such as the score on your tennis matches, the number of goals you scored in soccer, and so forth. Each worksheet has a blank version for you to copy and use and an example of one already filled out.

It is not helpful to be constantly on the lookout for ratings of how you feel or how you are doing, and it is often not realistic to keep track of anything for very long, so I suggest rating your progress for one week at a time, every few weeks (one week at baseline, one week at week 5 of training, one week at week 10 of training, etc.)—this will give you sufficient data to track progress without overwhelming you.

4. Begin Training

Follow protocols outlined in Chapters 2–6, depending on the specific modality you've chosen to work with.

Biofeedback and Mindfulness

Biofeedback is often described as a way to control how you feel, emotionally and physically. As I describe in detail in Chapter 9 on mindfulness-based skills, extensive research shows that efforts to control your internal experience are unlikely to be helpful. In fact, these efforts are much more likely to be counterproductive rather than helpful to your biofeedback training. Instead of attempts to control what is out of your control (your feelings and emotions), I suggest using a mindfulness-based approach to biofeedback. Chapter 7 provides background information about mindfulness and Chapter 9 describes specific mindfulness-based skills that you may use in life in general, as well as in your biofeedback practice to achieve the best results from your practice. Please be sure to review chapters 7 and 9 as you begin biofeedback training. As you read more on mindfulness and mindfulness-based skills, compassion (chapter 10), as well as applications of biofeedback and mindfulness to specific conditions (chapters 11–18) such as anxiety and pain, you will learn more skills to integrate into your initial biofeedback practice.

BIOFEEDBACK AND MINDFULNESS: STORY OF THE MIDDLE WAY

The synergy of biofeedback and mindfulness is reflected in the Parable of the Lute, a famous Buddhist story describing the concept of the middle way. The parable tells the story of Sona, the son of a rich businessman in ancient India who became a monk. Sona meditated diligently all day long, attempting to experience nonattachment to worldly desires and the happiness that comes with it. But despite his diligence and persistence, Sona was frustrated by his lack of progress toward happiness and the persistent craving for worldly things. Sona went to the Buddha and asked him why he was not successful in his practice. The Buddha replied with a question: "Sona, are you not a skilled player of the lute?" "Yes," answered Sona. The Buddha then asked Sona: "When you played the lute, and its strings were too tight, was the lute tuneful and easy to play?" "No," answered Sona. The Buddha went on: "And when the strings of the lute were too loose, was the lute tuneful and easy to play?" "No, it was not," answered Sona once again. "But when the strings of your lute were adjusted just right, not too tight and not too loose, was your lute tuneful and easy to play?" "Yes," answered Sona. "So, Sona, just like the strings of the lute, if you strain too hard or try to achieve your goal by force, you will fail, and if you don't try at all, you will fail, too. Therefore, Sona, you should find a balance between having a sense of purpose and moving toward it and exploring the moment the way it is."

Biofeedback and mindfulness together provide us with that middle way, finding the balance between goal-directed action and letting go, like tuning the strings of a lute—not too tight, not too loose.

One question I sometimes get from my clients is whether mindfulness and biofeedback are fundamentally incompatible because biofeedback is all about making changes, while mindfulness is about letting things be. I see biofeedback and mindfulness to be extremely compatible and complementary to each other. Biofeedback is indeed about making changes. The best way to make changes is to do so mindfully, focusing on what is under your control (actions), rather than unsuccessful attempts to change what is not under your control (thoughts and feelings). *Mindfulness allows you to tell the difference between what is and is not under your control and to focus on mindfully changing what you can.* Mindfulness, the way it is used in the West for purposes of improving health and well-being, has a goal of making helpful changes, mindful changes, through letting go of what is not under your control and focusing on what is. Biofeedback enables you to make mindful changes by strengthening your physiological ability to self-regulate in moments of challenge and providing you with helpful ways to respond to what is not under your control. Fundamentally, goals of biofeedback and mindfulness are the same. They achieve those goals by providing balance between goal-directed action and letting go.

Mindfulness enhances biofeedback in the following ways:

- Brings biofeedback training to its full effectiveness
- Enables you to make mindful changes without getting stuck in an unhelpful struggle with things that are not under your control
- Enhances your awareness of and ability to attend to physiological and emotional experiences
- Improves learning, planning, and decision making
- Improves emotion regulation
- Allows you to work with what gets in the way of biofeedback success:
  — Automatic reactions to thoughts, feelings, and physiological sensations
  — Attempts to control or resist
  — Judgment

Biofeedback enhances mindfulness in the following ways:

- Increases ability to self-regulate and reduces intensity of suffering without a struggle
- Makes it easier to accept experiences that may otherwise be fundamentally unacceptable, for example, learning to regulate your breathing physiology during a panic attack, making it easier to accept the presence of panic and not struggle against it
- Increases body awareness
- Illustrates connection between physiological and emotional states
- Decreases physiological arousal to facilitate quiet awareness

- Reduces physiological symptoms at times of distress to allow mindful awareness
- Provides real-time feedback on the effects of meditation

Biofeedback Safety and Contraindications

Biofeedback is generally quite safe. A biofeedback device itself is not doing anything to you; it is only recording signals from your body so that you can use the feedback to make helpful changes. However, there are circumstances when you need to be cautious in using biofeedback:

- Biofeedback is not a substitute for other medical treatment in severe or life-threatening conditions, such as cancer or heart disease. Biofeedback may be an excellent addition to traditional medical treatment.
- If you have severe mental illness, such as schizophrenia or another psychotic disorder, be sure to consult with your mental health provider before using biofeedback.
- If you use medications for conditions that may be improved with bio-feedback, be sure to consult with your health care provider about medication dosage. Your need for medication may decrease as your condition improves. Conditions for which medication adjustments are most likely to be needed are high blood pressure, diabetes, asthma, pain, and headaches. If you are taking thyroid replacement medica-tions or anticonvulsants, consult with your health care provider as well.
- It is possible that some of the subjective experiences that occur during biofeedback training, such as physiological sensations, images, thoughts, or feelings, may be unexpected or startling to you. For example, you might feel lightheaded, experience faster heartbeat, feel sleepy, or be reminded of unpleasant experiences from your past. These unwanted effects are almost always tem-porary and virtually never dangerous. If such experiences are per-sistent, consult with a biofeedback professional for the best way to manage them.

Chapters 2–6 review underlying psychophysiology for each biofeedback modality and offer step-by-step guidelines for training: breathing, heart rate variability, muscle tension, temperature, and skin conductance, to help you select your biofeedback modalities for training. Parts II and III offer guidance in mindfulness (part II) and applications for common challenges you may encounter (part III). Once you've selected the biofeedback modalities you would like to train, and reviewed Chapters 7 and 9 on mindfulness and mindfulness-based skills to help your biofeedback practice be most effective, start your practice. As you progress further through the book, integrate the new skills you learn into your practice.

Outcomes Tracking Worksheet 1: Continuous Goals

This tracking worksheet is for outcomes that can be rated on the scale from 0 to 10. You can track symptoms you'd like to reduce, performance goals, or your perception of your resilience or ability to self-regulate. Decide whether you are looking to lower your scores (symptoms) or raise your scores (performance, self-regulation). Then rate your outcomes on the scale from 0 (lowest) to 10 (highest).

Examples of symptoms you can track with this worksheet: anxiety, pain, muscle tension, anger, stress, mood

Examples of performance goals you can track: athletic endurance, quality of public speaking, communication skills, ability to focus on a task

You can also track resilience, overall self-regulation, emotion regulation, and adaptability to change.

Rate how you did on your measure at the end of each day for 1 week at a time—a week before starting biofeedback and mindfulness training, to establish a baseline, and then at weeks 5, 10, and 15 to track progress. Starting at week 5, you would also write down the number of minutes of biofeedback and/or mindfulness practice you did that day.

Table 1.1 is a blank tracking worksheet for you to use, and Table 1.2 is an

TABLE 1.1 OUTCOMES TRACKING WORKSHEET 1

Write down your choice for outcome tracking here: _____

Decide whether you are looking to lower your scores (symptoms) or raise your scores (performance, self-regulation). Indicate your ratings on a scale of 0 (low) to 10 (high).

Day	Pretraining rating (0–10)	WEEK 5 OF TRAINING		WEEK 10 OF TRAINING		WEEK 15 OF TRAINING	
		Duration of practice (min/day)	Outcome rating (0–10)	Duration of practice (min/day)	Outcome rating (0–10)	Duration of practice (min/day)	Outcome rating (0–10)
1							
2							
3							
4							
5							
6							
7							
Average							

TABLE 1.2 OUTCOMES TRACKING WORKSHEET 1: FILLED OUT EXAMPLE

Write down your choice for outcome tracking here: _____ Anxiety _____

Day	Pretraining rating (0–10)	WEEK 5 OF TRAINING		WEEK 10 OF TRAINING		WEEK 15 OF TRAINING	
		Duration of practice (min/day)	Outcome rating (0–10)	Duration of practice (min/day)	Outcome rating (0–10)	Duration of practice (min/day)	Outcome rating (0–10)
1	5	5 min	4	20 min	2	20 min	1
2	6	10 min	5	20 min	4	20 min	0
3	4	20 min	2	20 min	3	20 min	3
4	5	10 min	5	20 min	0	20 min	1
5	8	20 min	4	10 min	5	20 min	0
6	7	15 min	5	20 min	2	20 min	2
7	6	20 min	7	0 min	1	20 min	1
Average	5.85	14.28 min	4.57	15.75 min	2.42	20 min	1.14

example of a worksheet already filled out. You can download electronic copy of the worksheet at www.innakhazan.com/resources.html.

Outcome Tracking Worksheet 2: Discrete Goals

This tracking worksheet is designed for outcomes that are expressed as a discrete measurement rather than a rating. You can track symptoms you'd like to reduce or performance or athletic goals. Decide whether you are looking to lower your scores (symptoms) or raise your scores (performance, self-regulation).

> Examples of symptoms you can track with this worksheet: blood pressure readings, number of headaches, episodes of unhelpful behavior (e.g., anger outbursts)
>
> Examples of performance goals you can track: time spent running, swimming, biking, etc.; scores in a sports game/match; performance scores

Track how you did on your measure at the end of each day for one week at a time—a week before starting biofeedback and mindfulness training to establish a baseline, and then at weeks 5, 10, and 15 to track progress. Starting at week 5 you would also write down the number of minutes of biofeedback and/or mindfulness practice you did that day.

Table 1.3 is a blank tracking worksheet for you to use, and Table 1.4 is an example of a worksheet already filled out. You can download electronic copy of the worksheet at. www.innakhazan.com/resources.html.

TABLE 1.3 OUTCOMES TRACKING WORKSHEET 2

Write down your choice for outcome tracking here: _____

Day	Pretraining score/time	WEEK 5 OF TRAINING		WEEK 10 OF TRAINING		WEEK 15 OF TRAINING	
		Duration of practice (min/day)	Training score/time	Duration of practice (min/day)	Training score/time	Duration of practice (min/day)	Training score/time
1							
2							
3							
4							
5							
6							
7							
Average							

TABLE 1.4 OUTCOMES TRACKING WORKSHEET 2: FILLED OUT EXAMPLE

Write down your choice for outcome tracking here: _____ Blood pressure _____

Day	Pretraining score/time	WEEK 5 OF TRAINING		WEEK 10 OF TRAINING		WEEK 15 OF TRAINING	
		Duration of practice (min/day)	Training score/time	Duration of practice (min/day)	Training score/time	Duration of practice (min/day)	Training score/time
1	190/110	15 min	173/96	20 min	154/87	20 min	140/76
2	159/98	0 min	184/90	15 min	152/78	20 min	135/78
3	176/95	20 min	164/84	20 min	160/90	20 min	132/80
4	184/104	10 min	173/92	20 min	165/84	20 min	153/86
5	163/90	5 min	152/89	10 min	145/83	20 min	129/84
6	173/90	15 min	160/85	20 min	149/83	20 min	132/79
7	155/89	15 min	183/89	10 min	178/80	20 min	135/76
Average	171/96.5	11.42 min	169.85/89.28	16.42 min	157.57/83.57	20 min	163.57/77.14

CHAPTER 2

Breathing

Margaret, a thirty-five-year-old vice president in a financial firm, was preparing for a meeting with an important client. She felt a bit nervous, felt her heart beating faster, her breathing becoming heavier. A coworker walking by asked her how she was doing. Margaret answered, "Feeling nervous, I am not even sure why." The coworker responded: "Don't worry, you'll do great. Just take some deep breaths and calm down." Margaret did just that: sat down and took some deep breaths. But the more she breathed, the more aware she became of her heart pounding, the more lightheaded and nervous she felt.

Margaret's experience is a common one—her attempt to use a well-known skill that is supposed to be helpful in a stressful situation made things worse instead of better. The idea of taking deep breaths to calm down is one we hear all the time. "Take a deep breath" is a suggested remedy when we feel anxious or uncertain about the future, when we are in pain, when we are angry, or when we are having trouble resisting an unhelpful urge, such as smoking, drinking, or consuming illicit substances. Most of us don't realize how easily deep breathing can lead to unintended unpleasant consequences, making us feel worse rather than better. This chapter addresses the following topics related to breathing and biofeedback:

- Some of the physiological principles underlying healthy breathing and ways in which breathing may get disrupted
- Common problems that happen because of breathing dysregulation
- Healthy breathing skills and ways you may be able to use them in everyday life

Carbon Dioxide and the Physiology of Healthy Breathing

You may be wondering what carbon dioxide has to do with healthy breathing. After all, isn't carbon dioxide something we are supposed to get rid of? Turns out, that's not it at all. In fact, we need to retain most of our carbon dioxide (about 85 percent). Carbon dioxide is crucial to healthy breathing, because it is responsible for distribution of oxygen. Without sufficient carbon dioxide, the oxygen that we have remains in the blood stream and does not go into our tissues, where it is most needed.

Let's talk about what is supposed to happen in healthy breathing and how things can go wrong. Breathing serves several functions in our body:

- Adequate saturation of blood with oxygen
- Adequate saturation of blood with carbon dioxide (CO_2), which is dissolved in the blood as carbonic acid
- Maintenance of pH level of the blood and other bodily fluids between 7.35 and 7.45
- Removal and retention of alkaline and acidic products by the kidneys through pH regulation
- Maintenance of the breathing drive

pH REGULATION

pH stands for "power of hydrogen" and refers to the acid-base balance in any solution. A neutral solution, such as distilled water, has a pH of 7.0. A decrease in pH indicates greater acidity of the solution, while an increase in pH indicates greater alkalinity. The human body needs to maintain pH levels between 7.35 and 7.45, meaning that normal pH for humans is slightly alkaline.

Derivation of pH as a measure of acidity and alkalinity is described by the Henderson-Hasselbalch equation, which in simplified form looks like this:

$$pH = [HCO_3-]/pCO_2$$

where $[HCO_3^-]$ is the concentration of bicarbonate ions (regulated by the kidneys) and pCO_2 is the partial pressure of carbon dioxide (regulated by moment-to-moment breathing).

When you breathe air in through your nose or mouth, it makes its way into your lungs, through the bronchi and bronchioles, eventually dissolving in the lining of the alveoli. From the alveoli, oxygen from the air is absorbed into the blood. In the blood, oxygen binds to hemoglobin, a protein in your red blood cells that transports oxygen, carbon dioxide and other gases. Hemoglobin releases oxygen to organs and tissues that need it. Your cells consume oxygen (and glucose) for energy, and release carbon dioxide in the process. In the human body, carbon dioxide is a byproduct of metabolism, and at the same time, is extremely important for the release of oxygen from hemoglobin, its delivery to organs and tissues that need it, as well as maintenance of the drive to breathe.

Figure 2.1 summarizes normal respiratory chemistry. Carbon dioxide is responsible for oxygen getting to the various tissues and organs in the body, through its effect on the pH level of your blood. Distribution of oxygen in the human body is determined by the Bohr effect, a physiological phenomenon first described by the Danish physiologist Christian Bohr. The Bohr effect describes the way in which hemoglobin releases oxygen from the bloodstream to the rest of the body. Oxygen is released based on metabolic activity. As metabolic activity of the body increases, cells release more CO_2 into the blood, and pH level of the blood decreases (becomes more acidic). This change in pH level signals hemoglobin to release more oxygen. Conversely, as metabolic activity decreases, cells release less CO_2 into the bloodstream, and pH increases (becomes more alkaline). *An adequate level of CO2 in the blood is necessary for the oxygen circulating in your bloodstream to get released in sufficient quantities to the organs and tissues that need it.*

In addition to oxygen, hemoglobin also carries nitric oxide, a gas that in the human body regulates dilation and constriction of the blood vessels. (Nitric oxide (NO) should not be confused with nitrous oxide (NO_2), a sedative gas also known as laughing gas.) Nitric oxide is released by hemoglobin

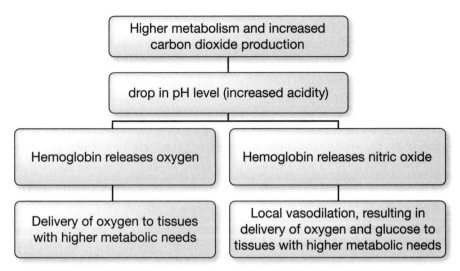

FIGURE 2.1: Normal respiratory physiology   *Source: the author*

from the blood into body tissues and organs at the same time as oxygen. As nitric oxide is released, blood vessels dilate. When less nitric oxide is released, blood vessels constrict. Therefore, *carbon dioxide is necessary for sufficient amounts of nitric oxide to be released to dilate blood vessels enough to deliver oxygen and glucose to various tissues and organs.*

Our drive to breathe is regulated by the medulla oblongata, a part of the brain located in the brainstem, at the base of the skull. The medulla contains chemoreceptors that detect pH (acid-base) changes in the cerebrospinal fluid. Carbon dioxide, which is acidic and is dissolved in the blood as carbonic acid, plays a major role in determining pH in the body. When pH decreases (becomes more acidic due to the increase in CO_2), chemoreceptors in the medulla send out a signal for the body to breathe. This means that *our carbon dioxide levels have to rise to a sufficiently high level for our brain and body to know that it is time to take the next breath.*

Imagine you are going for a run. As your activity level rises, so does your metabolism. Your body consumes more oxygen. Your breathing reflects that increased need for oxygen, becoming faster and deeper, allowing you to take in the extra oxygen you need. As your metabolism increases, so does your production of carbon dioxide. As more carbon dioxide enters your bloodstream, the pH of your blood drops (becomes more acidic). The drop in pH signals hemoglobin to release more oxygen and nitric oxide, thereby ensuring delivery of proper amount of oxygen and glucose to tissues and organs that are working harder as you run and therefore have higher metabolic needs.

Now let's imagine that you are sitting in your chair worrying about an important meeting you have the next day or preparing for an unpleasant conversation you have to have with your spouse. Anxiety can often send your body into the fight-or-flight response, meaning that your body starts preparing you for running or fighting. If you were actually about to run or fight, you would need more oxygen. So, your breath becomes deeper and faster as your body prepares for running and fighting. But, you are not actually going anywhere—you are sitting in your chair worrying. You are taking in more air, but you don't need it, since your metabolism is not changing. If you breathe in more, you have to breathe out more, and as a result you breathe out more carbon dioxide than your body is making. Levels of carbon dioxide in your blood

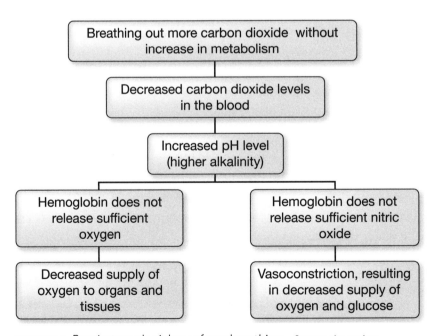

FIGURE 2.2: Respiratory physiology of overbreathing   *Source: the author*

drop, and your blood pH rises (becomes more alkaline). To hemoglobin, the rise in pH signals that your metabolism has decreased (pH typically rises when carbon dioxide levels drop due to decrease in activity). Therefore, hemoglobin releases less oxygen and less nitric oxide, resulting in less oxygen and glucose being delivered to your body and brain. However, your metabolism has not changed—you are still sitting in the chair worrying. As a result of a normal, but under the circumstances unhelpful, change in your breathing, your carbon dioxide levels have dropped, and your body is now receiving less oxygen and less glucose than it needs. This kind of unhelpful breathing change is called overbreathing (summarized in Figure 2.2).

Overbreathing

Overbreathing is a behavior of breathing out too much carbon dioxide, which results in a physiological condition called hypocapnia, or lack of carbon dioxide. When you overbreathe, the acid-base balance of your bodily fluids (pH balance) becomes disrupted, and so does oxygen delivery. As a result, oxygen is not getting to your brain, muscles, and other organs.

In addition, overbreathing and the resulting pH dysregulation also lead to electrolyte imbalances. Electrolytes, such as sodium (Na^+), calcium (Ca^+), and potassium (K^+), are responsible for communication between cells through electrical impulses. When your pH becomes too alkaline, electrolytes migrate into muscle and brain cells instead of staying in the fluid outside of those cells. As a result, you may experience muscle spasms, weakness, and fatigue. Since your intestines, blood vessels, and bronchi are made up of smooth muscle, overbreathing often results in gastrointestinal distress and constriction of the blood vessels and the bronchi (as happens during an asthma attack). In the brain, electrolyte imbalances increase activation of brain cells, therefore increasing their demand for oxygen. However, since the body overall is experiencing a reduction in available oxygen, this can lead to oxygen insufficiency in the brain.

As a result of overbreathing, people experience such symptoms as

- Lightheadedness or dizziness
- Pounding heart

- Shortness of breath
- Muscle tension
- Feelings of agitation or restlessness
- Tingling in fingers, hands, or feet
- Nausea or "butterflies" in the stomach
- Difficulty focusing or thinking straight
- "Fuzzy" or "foggy" mind
- Difficulty making decisions
- Difficulty regulating emotions
- Feeling of unreality, disconnectedness from the body

Take a closer look at these symptoms. What do they remind you of? Perhaps a panic attack or severe anxiety? If that was your thought, you are entirely correct. All of these symptoms of overbreathing are also symptoms of a panic attack, and many of them are symptoms of anxiety in general. In fact, research shows that panic attacks almost always involve overbreathing. The tricky part about overbreathing is that, because it so closely resembles anxiety, its symptoms are often interpreted as anxiety, whether or not anxiety is actually present. Of course, once you think you are anxious, you become anxious. Sometimes anxiety does indeed provoke overbreathing. This is what happened to Margaret from the earlier example, as she worried about an important meeting.

In addition to anxiety, overbreathing may trigger, cause, or exacerbate a whole host of problems:

- Asthma
- Anger
- Anxiety of various kinds, including panic attacks
- Attention and concentration difficulty
- Chronic pain
- Difficulty regulating emotion
- Heart problems
- Irritable bowel syndrome and other digestive problems and stomach discomfort
- Insomnia
- Raynaud's disease

Overbreathing may also interfere with performance: athletic, artistic, business, musical, public speaking, and so forth.

Why Do We Overbreathe?

Overbreathing may result from a momentary breathing dysregulation, such as running up the stairs too quickly or being startled by a loud noise. Overbreathing may also result from habitual ways of responding to various situations. Possible reasons for overbreathing include the following:

Response to stress, anxiety, or fear. When you feel anxious, your body prepares for running or fighting. As described earlier, in anticipation of needing more oxygen for those activities, your body starts taking in more air. If you are not actually increasing your activity level, then you take in more air than you need, and you breathe out more carbon dioxide than you produce, resulting in lower levels of carbon dioxide in the blood. For example, if you are afraid of flying, being at the airport and preparing to board a plane may trigger a fight-or-flight response, with the corresponding increase in breathing rate and depth. However, your activity level, and therefore, your metabolism, would not actually change. As a result, you would take in more air than you need and breathe out more carbon dioxide than your body makes. In other words, you would overbreathe.

Response to pain, including chronic pain. Breathing is often a prescribed remedy for pain. Many people believe that certain ways of breathing will relieve pain. This is true. However, when attempting to alleviate pain with breathing, it is very easy to inadvertently slip into overbreathing. Most people take big, deep, effortful breaths, taking in more air than they need and breathing out too much carbon dioxide. (See the section on deep breathing later in this chapter for a more detailed explanation of the problem.) Symptoms produced by overbreathing may mask the pain, which will produce temporary relief and reinforce future overbreathing. Finally, people often brace in response to or in anticipation of pain, tensing muscles, including the muscles used for breathing. Tense respiratory muscles also tend to promote overbreathing.

Mouth breathing. Some people develop a habit of breathing with their mouths, perhaps through a history of sinus infections, which make breathing through the nose difficult. Mouth breathing results in exhaling too much carbon dioxide too quickly, simply because an open mouth allows a lot more air, and therefore more carbon dioxide, to escape.

Fear of breathing awareness. Fear of breathing sensations can result from experiences of having trouble catching one's breath—asthma attacks, panic attacks, other medical situations when breathing was difficult. Fear of not being able to catch your breath may cause you to rush your inhalations and cut your exhalations short. This overrides your breathing reflex, promoting taking in more air than you need and breathing out too much carbon dioxide. This chain of events results in overbreathing and hypocapnia, lack of carbon dioxide in the blood.

Many people develop a habit of overbreathing as a protective response in difficult situations. Taking a big deep breath through the chest may make you feel powerful and in control. Overbreathing happens as a result of taking in more air that you need and breathing out more carbon dioxide than your body makes. One or two breaths like that are not likely to cause a significant problem, but some people breathe this way, and overbreathe, frequently.

OVERBREATHING VERSUS HYPERVENTILATION

You have probably heard the term *hyperventilation* to describe disordered breathing, and you may be wondering how hyperventilation is different from overbreathing. Physiologically, they are the same. Overbreathing and hyperventilation both involve a drop in carbon dioxide levels, which results in the symptoms described in this chapter. Hyperventilation has a certain behavioral presentation. When you think of hyperventilation, what do you think about? A person visibly panting, huffing and puffing, showing a lot of distress, right? This is one presentation of overbreathing. Most of the time, however, you can't tell when someone is overbreathing—it is much more subtle behaviorally. Therefore, it is easier to use the broader term *overbreathing*, which encompasses hyperventilation.

Chronic Overbreathing

Overbreathing may be acute, meaning that it happens only in certain moments, or chronic, meaning that it happens much of the time, with overbreathing becoming the baseline. If you overbreathe at baseline, your levels of carbon dioxide are habitually low. However, your body cannot tolerate a chronically alkaline pH level. Once you've been overbreathing for several hours, your kidneys start expelling bicarbonates, which are alkaline. You might remember that your pH is regulated by two functions in your body: your breathing and your kidneys. Breathing regulates your pH through carbon dioxide levels, and kidneys regulate your pH through bicarbonate levels. If your breathing produces chronically low levels of carbon dioxide, which is acidic, your kidneys will start compensating by expelling bicarbonates, which are alkaline. This restores your pH levels back to normal levels. The problem, however, is that those bicarbonates serve a purpose—they buffer acid produced in the process of metabolism and take it out of the body. If your activity level remains stable, lower levels of bicarbonates may not bother you. However, if you increase level of activity—say, go for a walk or run—your body will produce more acid (such as lactic acid), but there will not be enough bicarbonates to take it out of your body. This may result in muscle pain and loss of endurance. You may also end up overbreathing more to reduce acidity, continuing the unhelpful cycle.

How to Tell If You Are Overbreathing

At this point, you may be wondering how to recognize overbreathing. The only way to know for certain is through the use of a device called a capnometer, which measures levels of carbon dioxide retained in your lungs. Capnometers are used in hospitals during surgery and in intensive care units, as well as on ambulances, where monitoring carbon dioxide levels is directly relevant to patients' physiological state. In addition, capnometers are now more and more frequently being used by biofeedback therapists to assess their patients' breathing and recognize overbreathing. Unfortunately, there are currently no consumer-focused, inexpensive capnometers on the market.

But even without a capnometer, there are behavioral signs that you may be overbreathing. These are not as precise, but if you frequently experience a number of signs on the list below, there is a good chance that you may be overbreathing some of the time. As you read through the list, make a note of whether or not you experience each of these behavioral signs, as well as situations in which you are likely to experience it.

- Tendency to breathe through your mouth
- Yawning or sighing frequently
- Running out of air while speaking
- Aborting your exhalations
- Rushing to inhale
- Breathing fast and shallow or fast and deeply
- Holding your breath
- Need to take a deep breath after every few breaths

In addition, the Nijmegen questionnaire was developed specifically to evaluate people for overbreathing. Take a few minutes and go through the questionnaire below to see whether you may be overbreathing.

Nijmegen Dysfunctional Breathing Questionnaire

Rate how often you experience each one of the sensations below. If you never experience the sensation, give yourself a score of 0. If you experience that sensation rarely, give yourself a score of 1. If you experience the sensation sometimes, give yourself a score of 2. If you experience the sensation often, give yourself a score of 3. If you experience the sensation very often, give yourself a score of 4. Add up the scores for all the sensations. If you end up with a score higher than 19, it is likely that you overbreathe at least some of the time.

If your score on the Nijmegen questionnaire shows a high likelihood of overbreathing (19 or above), take a few moments to think about situations in which you have experienced these symptoms. Here is a list of possible situations when you might experience overbreathing:

- At work
- Interacting with people of authority
- While talking

TABLE 2.1 NIJMEGEN DYSFUNCTIONAL BREATHING QUESTIONNAIRE

SENSATION	NEVER 0	RARELY 1	SOMETIMES 2	OFTEN 3	VERY OFTEN 4
Chest pain					
Feeling tense					
Blurred vision					
Dizzy spells					
Feeling confused					
Faster or deeper breathing					
Shortness of breath					
Tight feeling in the chest					
Bloated feeling in stomach					
Tingling fingers					
Unable to breathe deeply					
Stiff fingers or arms					
Tight feelings around mouth					
Cold hands or feet					
Heart palpitations					
Feeling of anxiety					

- While taking deep breaths to calm down
- When doing something relaxing
- While meeting new people or interacting with large groups of people
- Before and/or during a test, performance, or presentation
- While doing or seeing something you are afraid of
- When feeling stressed or anxious
- While exercising or exerting yourself physically
- During arguments with other people
- When feeling or expressing any intense emotion
- When experiencing pain or physical discomfort

- Preparing for sleep or upon waking up
- Taking part in challenging activities

Any situation where you have experienced symptoms of overbreathing presents a good opportunity to practice breathing skills discussed in the rest of this chapter. It is also very important to recognize and name the symptoms of overbreathing for what they are, rather than lumping them together with anxiety. Ability to separate purely physiological overbreathing from anxiety is important because responses to overbreathing and anxiety are different. When overbreathing, changing your breathing will stop the physiological cascade that produces unpleasant sensations. Anxiety, on the other hand, is not something you can just stop. Mindful breathing changes will help make the experience of anxiety easier, but they will not make anxiety go away, and attempts to do so are likely to result in making things worse. I say a lot more about this in Chapter 9 on mindfulness-based skills and in Chapter 13 on anxiety and fear.

Now, let's switch gears and talk about ways to rebalance your breathing, bring helpful changes, and reduce or stop overbreathing.

Deep Breathing

You've probably heard or said some variation of the phrase, "Just take a deep breath and calm down," hundreds of times. At first glance it seems completely reasonable—deep breathing is supposed to be good for us, right? Well, not so fast. Let's come back to the physiology of healthy breathing for a moment. In order for oxygen to be distributed properly, we need to retain sufficient carbon dioxide. What happens with a deep breath? Try taking one now—big deep breath in and out. A large volume of air goes in, and the same volume of air goes out. What do you get in that large inhalation? More oxygen. Sounds good, except do you actually need it? At sea level there is 21 percent oxygen in the air you breathe in and 16 percent oxygen in the air you breathe out. You are only using about a quarter of the oxygen you take in. You have plenty of oxygen! You need extra oxygen only when your activity level, and therefore your metabolism, increases. When you take a deep breath to calm down, your metabolism stays the same. You do not need to bring extra oxygen into your bloodstream. You do, however, need to make optimal use of the plentiful oxygen that is already circulating in your blood.* For that, you need to retain sufficient carbon dioxide. With a deep breath, and an exhalation that is not long enough, you are expelling too much carbon dioxide, raising alkalinity of your blood, and preventing the oxygen that is circulating in your bloodstream from being released in sufficient quantities to your brain, organs, and muscles. As a result, an attempt to calm down produces the exact opposite effect. This was Margaret's experience described in the beginning of this chapter—she attempted to take deep breaths in order to calm down and ended up feeling more anxious as a result.

BREATHING AT ALTITUDE

At higher altitudes, atmospheric pressure is lower and the oxygen molecules are spread further apart. Even though the percentage of oxygen in the air around you does not change, you take in fewer oxygen molecules with each breath. The higher you go, the less oxygen is effectively available for you to use. When adjusting to higher altitude, people compensate for lack of oxygen by taking larger faster breaths. This can be helpful: since less oxygen is available in the air, you need to take more of it in. However, it is still possible to overbreathe if you exhale too much carbon dioxide too quickly. *Low-and-slow breathing* is helpful at altitude to reduce overbreathing and enable you make the best use possible of the oxygen you have. Follow the low-and-slow breathing guidelines in this chapter, but allow yourself to take deeper breaths in and breathe out as slowly as possible. In addition, practicing low-and-slow breathing at your resonance frequency breathing rate, as described in Chapter 3, will further maximize oxygen absorption. As you become accustomed to breathing at altitude, the amount of hemoglobin in your blood will increase, delivering more oxygen.

---

* This is the case when your lungs and heart are generally healthy. If you have heart or lung disease, the concept of overbreathing still applies, but the practice is a little different. See section on medical conditions later in this chapter for more.

Let me be clear: it is OK to take a deep breath. But it is not actually necessary for the purpose of calming down or any other purpose that does not involve an increase in activity and metabolism. The problem is not the depth of the breath itself—it is the way in which most of us take it: a large inhalation and an exhalation that is too short. With a short exhalation, you expel too much carbon dioxide over a short period of time, thereby reducing the levels of carbon dioxide in your bloodstream and leading to the symptoms of hypocapnia described earlier. For a deep breath to be healthy, the exhalation has to be very slow, which can be hard for people to do. If you are one of those people, just remember that, to calm yourself, a deep breath is not actually necessary.

Healthy Breathing

The key to overcoming and preventing overbreathing is to learn healthy breathing skills. If you don't overbreathe, the breathing skills described in this section will still be helpful to you in learning self-regulation. For breathing to be healthy, you need your metabolic needs, levels of CO_2 production, and size and rate of breath to match. You need to maintain proper breathing chemistry at all times, with any activity, and at any rate of breathing. You don't pay much attention to your breathing most of the time. If you tend to overbreathe, suddenly trying to make changes to your breathing can be quite challenging, and these attempts are likely to bring on struggle and frustration. This struggle is in turn likely to produce further overbreathing. Therefore, to make helpful changes to your breathing, start with practicing mindful breathing. Mindful breathing training will help you let go of the struggle and make helpful changes to your breathing. Please refer to Chapters 8–10 for more details on the practice of mindfulness.

Mindful Breathing

Mindfulness is a way of being in the present moment, with nonjudgmental awareness and an ability to choose the most helpful ways to respond to your moment-to-moment experience. When breathing mindfully, allow your breath to be just as it is; let go of expectations of how you should feel and judgments you might have about the experience, and most important, let go of the struggle to change your breath in that moment. To make helpful breathing changes, you first learn to allow yourself to breathe just the way you do without a struggle. Letting go of the struggle to breathe differently allows you to make changes without exacerbating the problem. The following are steps in mindful breathing awareness (based on Christopher Germer's mindful breathing exercise[3]). Also, see a full mindful breathing script in Appendix A (also available as a recording at www.innakhazan.com/meditation_recordings.html).

1. Begin with settling into your body, noticing physical sensations, particularly sensations of touch or pressure where your body is in contact with the chair or the floor.
2. Bring gentle focus to the sensations of the breath. Allow your breath to be just as it is. Let go of the need to fix anything or make any changes.
3. Attend to the sensations of the inhalation, noticing where you feel the sensations of the inhalation most easily and most strongly—perhaps noticing sensations as the air comes into your nostrils, or the sensations of the chest or belly rising with each inhalation. Notice and allow these sensations to be, just as they are.
4. Attend to the sensations of the exhalation, noticing where you feel the sensations of the exhalation most easily and most strongly—perhaps noticing the sensations as the air comes out of the nostrils, or the sensations of the chest or belly falling with each exhalation. Notice and allow these sensations to be, just as they are.
5. Allow yourself to transition naturally from an inhalation into an exhalation and from an exhalation into an inhalation. There is no need to rush the inhalation or the exhalation. Allow your breath to easily move from the inhalation into an exhalation, and from the exhalation into an inhalation.
6. Notice any thoughts, emotions, or physiological sensations that arise. Acknowledge their presence, and return your attention back to the breath, just as it is. When you notice any distress or discomfort, difficult thoughts, emotions, or sensations, allow yourself to notice and acknowledge them with kindness and compassion. Allow the discomfort to stay, and gently bring your attention back to the breath. If you notice yourself getting engaged with any of those thoughts or emotions, whenever your mind wanders off, bring kindness and acceptance

into the moment, and then gently return your attention back to the breath, just as it is.

7. Widen your attention to the sensations of the breath in the whole body, just as they are, making no changes, accepting all sensations with kindness and compassion.

This exercise, as any new skill, may initially feel challenging. Your mind will wander away from the breath, and it will do so frequently. This is normal and human. All you need to do is return your attention back to the breath, with kindness, whenever you notice that it has wandered off. Begin with 5 minutes of practice, and as it becomes more familiar, gradually increase the amount of practice time to about 10 minutes each day.

LISTENING TO YOUR BREATH WITH EARPLUGS

If it is difficult to attend to your breathing because it creates anxiety or another kind of discomfort, try doing a mindful breathing practice while plugging your ears with earplugs (or your fingers). Try it now: plug your ears with your fingers, and then take two or three breaths and just listen to the sound of the inhalation and exhalation. This exercise will help you experience your breathing in a slightly different way and may make it easier to attend to your breath.

If you have a history of asthma, panic attacks, or other conditions that impact breathing, attending to your breath may feel uncomfortable. For you, going slowly is key. Start with just a few mindful breaths, focusing on accepting whatever sensations come along the way. Lengthen practice time in very small increments, a few breaths at a time.

Mindful Low-and-Slow Breathing

Once mindful breathing with no changes becomes more comfortable and familiar, the next step is to introduce mindful change. Low-and-slow breathing, described by Robert Fried in his book *Breathe Well, Be Well,*[4] allows for breathing to be calming without overbreathing, by matching the size and rate of the breath to the metabolic needs of a resting state. I have modified the technique to include elements of mindfulness.

This practice is easiest to start while laying down or reclining. This position allows your diaphragm, the muscle that controls breathing, to move most easily.

1. Begin with taking in a normal-size breath, through your nose. There is no need for a deep or large breath. Just a comfortable, normal inhalation. Bring mindful attention to your breath the way you did in the previous exercise.

2. Now exhale slowly and fully, until your lungs feel comfortably empty. Allow your exhalation to be slightly longer than your inhalation (about 40 percent of your breath for the inhalation, and about 60 percent of your breath for the exhalation). You may breathe out through your nose or through pursed lips, as if you are blowing out a candle. Pursed-lips exhalation is particularly helpful if it is difficult to slow down your exhalation through the nose. Make sure to *never* breathe out through a widely open mouth—that is a sure way to overbreathe.

3. As you breathe in, gently shift your breath from your chest to the abdomen. Allow your abdominal muscles to expand as you breathe in and contract when you breathe out. If you like, you may imagine a balloon in your belly. As you breathe in, gently inflate the balloon. As you breathe out, gently let the air out of the balloon. While a new practice will always require a conscious decision to make a change, and therefore some cognitive effort may be required, there should not be a physical effort when you breathe. In other words, don't pull the air in, don't push the air out. Just allow the air to come in and out of your lungs.

4. Practice low-and-slow breathing for about 5 minutes, just noticing the sensations of your breath coming in and out of your nose (or pursed lips).

5. Remember that breathing practice may not always feel relaxing. If you find yourself worried about not feeling relaxed, or struggling to

relax during breathing practice, let go of the intention to relax and bring your focus to the process of breathing itself.

OVERBREATHING FOR SWIMMING OR DIVING

Have you ever seen competitive swimmers or free divers breathe out several times forcefully before going under water? They are overbreathing (or hyperventilating) in order to extend their ability to stay under water longer before needing to surface for air. How does that work?

Remember that our breathing center is sensitive to rising levels of CO_2. Once CO_2 levels rise high enough, the medulla oblongata sends a signal to breathe. Blowing out a lot of CO_2 by overbreathing means that it will take longer for the CO_2 levels to build back up and trigger the need for next breath. A deep breath prior to going under water provides adequate oxygen during that time. This allows swimmers and divers to stay underwater longer.

A word of caution here—don't try this without supervision or experience, since it is possible to pass out under water.

Continue practicing 5 minutes a day for the first week, then increase your breathing practice time to 7 minutes a day for another week, then bring the practice time up to 10 minutes a day, and finally 10 minutes twice a day. Choose a time of day when you are the least likely be disturbed or to be in a hurry to be somewhere or to do something else. For some people the best time to practice is first thing in the morning, before they get out of bed. For others, the best time to practice is in bed when they are preparing for sleep. For yet others, it is right before leaving their office for lunch during the day.

Often people ask me if it is OK to do their breathing practice on a train or bus or in the car during their commute. Practicing breathing on the train or bus is not ideal, because the noise may be distracting, and you may not be able to find a seat. However, it is better to practice on the train or bus than not at all. You could use the commute option on days when you have trouble dedicating another 5–10 minutes to breathing practice. (Yes, it is often surprisingly hard to find 5 or 10 minutes a day to breathe!) I do not recommend practicing breathing while driving. This practice is often quite relaxing and may make you feel sleepy, especially if you are sleep deprived. It is OK to take a couple of low-and-slow breaths at a red light or when stuck in traffic, but reserve the actual practice time for when you are not operating dangerous machinery.

Overcoming Overbreathing

Once you are comfortable with mindful low-and-slow breathing, it is time to move on to learning how to respond to moments of overbreathing. A skill foundational to overcoming overbreathing is finding your breathing reflex, which I adapted from the skill described by Peter Litchfield.[5] In my experience, this skill is almost always successful in helping people move from overbreathing into healthy breathing. When you overbreathe, you often override your natural breathing drive and breathe in before your body needs the next breath. As I described in the beginning of this chapter, your breathing drive is regulated by the medulla oblongata in the brain stem. As carbon dioxide levels rise at the end of the exhalation, the change in pH levels in the cerebrospinal fluid signals the chemoreceptors in the brainstem that it is time to take a breath. When you overbreathe, you inhale before your carbon dioxide levels have risen sufficiently. The goal of finding your breathing reflex is to allow your natural breathing drive to take over.

To practice this skill, begin at a time when you are feeling well and not likely to be overbreathing. The practice has the following steps:

1. Begin with taking a few mindful low-and-slow breaths.
2. When settled, take a normal-size, comfortable inhalation.
3. Exhale as slowly as you are comfortable doing.
4. Pause your breath at the end of the exhalation and wait while mindfully observing your internal experience.
5. Notice any thoughts or emotions telling you to breathe—fear of running out of air, anxiety, temptation to rush to the next breath, or thoughts of "it's time to breathe." Mindfully observe those thoughts or emotions and, do not rush to inhale again.
6. Once you feel a physiological signal to breathe, inhale again. I can-

not describe for you how the physiological signal will feel, but you will know it once you feel it. That physiological signal is your breathing reflex.

7. The pause in breathing may only be 2 or 3 seconds. It may be longer if you've been overbreathing before the exercise. If your carbon dioxide levels were low, it will take much longer for them to come up high enough to trigger the breathing reflex (could be 20 or 30 seconds, or possibly even a bit longer). The goal is not to hold your breath until you are gasping and blue in the face (don't do that!) but, rather, to wait for the physiological signal to breathe, which will happen as soon as your carbon dioxide levels have risen sufficiently.

8. Continue breathing like this—comfortable, normal-sized inhalations, slow exhalations, pause and wait for the breathing reflex to signal the next breath. Practice for 5 or 6 breaths initially, and then gradually extend the practice time to about 5 minutes. You will notice that the pause between the end of the exhalation and the physiological signal to breathe in again will get shorter as you practice and may disappear completely, with your exhalation smoothly moving into the physiologically driven inhalation. This exercise is helpful in rebuilding trust that your body will be able to breathe properly on its own.

Once finding your breathing reflex becomes comfortable, you may start using this skill in moments of overbreathing in order to reestablish healthy breathing chemistry. Below is a summary of the steps to take when you notice signs of overbreathing, such as shortness of breath, lightheadedness or dizziness, nausea, tingling, or any of the other signs of overbreathing:

1. Label the sensation as "overbreathing" (I say more about labeling in Chapter 9 on mindfulness-based skills).
2. Bring mindful attention to your breath, allowing mindful change without struggling.
3. Take some low-and-slow breaths.
   a. Shift the breath to the belly.
   b. Take a normal-sized inhalation.

   c. Extend your exhalation, breathing out fully, through the nose or pursed lips. Slow down the very beginning of the exhalation (most people breathe out too much right at the beginning of the exhalation).

4. Pause at the end of the exhalation to allow your natural drive to breathe to signal the next inhalation. Inhale when you feel the physiological need to do so.

5. Continue breathing low-and-slow until the signs of overbreathing subside, usually within a few minutes.

THE PAPER BAG AND HYPERVENTILATION

You are probably familiar with the infamous paper bag given to people to breathe into when they hyperventilate (a severe form of overbreathing). The paper bag works to stop overbreathing because you breathe out carbon dioxide and then breathe it back in on the next breath. This raises your CO_2 levels, normalizes your pH, and stops the symptoms. However, I do not recommend using the paper bag because you may end up actually depriving yourself of oxygen—you have no idea how much carbon dioxide you are breathing in from the bag, and after a few breaths into the bag, the oxygen content may be low. In cases of severe overbreathing, instead of the paper bag, just hold your breath for a short time (could be 10, 20, or 30 seconds) until your breathing reflex kicks in and sends a physiological signal to breathe in again. Do this for 5 or 6 breaths, or until you feel calmer, and then return to low-and-slow breathing.

A Word of Caution With Medical Conditions

Some medical conditions that involve a problem with liver or kidney function, such as diabetes, when not adequately controlled lead to increased acidity in the body, a condition called *acidosis*. In these situations, overbreathing may be a way to compensate for acidosis—overbreathing reduces the amount of acid in the blood by reducing levels of carbon dioxide, which is acidic, thereby increasing pH back to normal levels. Stopping overbreathing in such cases could be harmful. If you have diabetes or any other medical condition that affects kidney function, please get in touch with your health care provider to make sure that the medical condition is adequately managed.

If you have chronic lung or heart conditions, such as emphysema, chronic obstructive pulmonary disease (COPD), or heart failure, you may not be getting sufficient oxygen into the bloodstream. The discomfort you feel as a result may trigger overbreathing, which will further reduce the amount of oxygen available for your body to use. The skills described in this chapter may still be helpful, with some modifications. When practicing low-and-slow breathing, you may need to take deeper breaths and focus more on using your abdominal muscles, allowing the air to go all the way down to the bottom of your lungs. Your lungs are "fatter" at the bottom, with greater surface area available for oxygen absorption. In addition, low-and-slow breathing at your resonance frequency breathing rate (see Chapter 3) will further increase your respiratory efficiency. Finally, because of the possibility of inadequate intake of oxygen, it is important to monitor oxygen saturation during breathing training. The easiest way to do this is with a pulse oximeter, an inexpensive device that is easy to get. It goes on your finger and measures oxygen saturation. Make sure that your oxygen levels are staying between 94 and 99 percent. If your oxygen levels fall below 93 percent, consult your health care provider.

CHAPTER 3

Heart Rate Variability and Self-Regulation

Laura, an experienced trial attorney, was on her way to a court appearance. She was driving along her usual route to the courthouse when another car cut her off, almost causing an accident. If Laura hadn't hit the brakes, the other car would have driven right into hers. Laura was shaken. She kept thinking of what could have happened if she hadn't seen the other car in time to hit the brakes. She felt sweaty and agitated and had trouble bringing her mind back to the arguments she had prepared. She didn't have much time before the court session began, and the more she tried to relax, the more agitated she felt. She knew exactly what she wanted to say, her arguments were well crafted, she had been in front of this judge many times before— she was supposed to have this down. And yet, she did not feel quite like herself. When the time came, she argued the case, but instead of speaking strongly and confidently, Laura felt that her voice was weak and her speech lackluster. She could have done better.

Have you ever had a similar experience when you were facing a challenge? A time when you felt prepared to meet your challenge, you knew exactly what you were supposed to do, and yet when it came time for the task itself, you got thrown off and could not perform at your best? You are not alone—we have all had this experience. And it likely did not happen because you did not prepare enough or because you did not know enough or because you simply weren't good enough, no matter what the voice inside your head insisted on.

It happened because your body did not have the skill of coping with whatever happened to throw you off your game. Your body was not able to properly regulate its level of activation and reset after being thrown off. Your physiology got in the way of being able to do your best.

Thankfully, self-regulation is a skill anyone can learn. You can train your body to properly regulate itself in situations like these, thereby allowing you to make full use of the learning and experience you have. HRV training is a big part of learning self-regulation. In fact, heart rate variability, or HRV, is the physiological mechanism underlying self-regulation. This chapter briefly reviews some of the physiology underlying HRV, discusses its importance in physical and emotional health, and then describes several ways you may be able to increase your HRV in order to increase self-regulation and resilience.

Underlying Physiology

Self-regulation, when applied to humans, refers to your ability to monitor your physiological and emotional states and alter them in accordance with the demand of the situation or the environment you are in. Physiological regulation happens at the level of your autonomic nervous system, the part of your nervous system responsible for functions that are considered to be "automatic" and do not require conscious control on your part (see figure 3.1). Keep in mind, this does not mean that you don't have the ability to make changes in your autonomic function, you just don't need to make conscious effort in order for the autonomic nervous system to do its job.

You don't need to make an effort to control the autonomic nervous system, but you can make helpful changes nonetheless. Why would you want to make changes, if the nervous system is capable of functioning without interference from you? While the autopilot functions well enough for your heart to beat and your lungs to take in oxygen, with a few conscious adjustments, your nervous system may become more resilient and more adept at functioning at your best. This is similar to a DSLR camera that has an auto function, which will allow you to take pictures. However, if you want to take really good pictures, you need to learn to make adjustments to many of the camera's settings. HRV training gives you the ability to make adjustments to the settings of your nervous system in order to allow for most optimal functioning.

The autonomic nervous system is subdivided into sympathetic and para-sympathetic branches (see Figure 3.1). Sympathetic branch is responsible for the so-called stress response, or the fight-or-flight response. In other words, the sympathetic nervous system drives your physiological activation. That is, the sympathetic nervous system is responsible for the increased heart rate, faster breathing, sweaty, clammy hands, "butterflies" in the stomach, and increased energy that you experience when you are physiologically activated.

The parasympathetic branch is responsible for relaxation and recovery. It slows down your heart and breathing rate, calms your stomach, relaxes your muscles, and allows your hands to warm up. The parasympathetic nervous system is also responsible for regulating activation of the sympathetic branch. It does so by putting on the brakes when sympathetic activation has reached the desired level. The parasympathetic nervous system is therefore sometimes referred to as the parasympathetic brake. While the sympathetic nervous system consists of numerous nerves, the parasympathetic nervous system essentially comprises one pair of cranial nerves—the vagus, also known as the vagal nerve. This pair of nerves wind their way through your body from the neck down to the hip, innervating every organ except for the adrenal glands. The function of the vagal nerve is to regulate the level of your physiological activation by putting the brakes on to sympathetic activation.

The analogy of a car accelerator and brake is often used to describe the sympathetic and parasympathetic branches of the nervous system: the sympathetic branch is the accelerator, and the parasympathetic branch is the

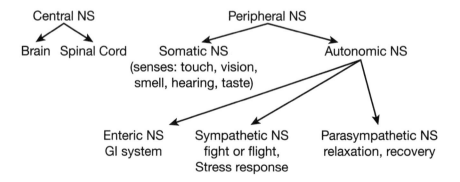

FIGURE 3.1: Structure of the human nervous system (NS)   *Source: the author*

brake. In order for you to regulate the speed of the car, you need to use the brake to bring acceleration to its optimal level. The same thing happens in the human body: the parasympathetic branch puts on the brakes to the sympathetic branch in order to bring the overall activation to its optimal level.

Just like a car that requires the brake to shut off acceleration, the sympathetic nervous system does not have a shutoff other than the one provided by the parasympathetic nervous system. When the parasympathetic nervous system is not strong enough to put on the brakes to sympathetic activation appropriately, your ability to self-regulate suffers.

This is where HRV assessment and training come in. HRV reflects the parasympathetic nervous system's ability to put on the brakes to sympathetic activation. Increasing HRV with training strengthens the parasympathetic brake.

This section discusses the physiology of HRV in order to fully explain its function. *Heart rate variability* refers to the change in time from heartbeat to heartbeat (see figure 3.2). As Fred Shaffer from Truman State University says: "A healthy heart is not a metronome."[6] Your heart does not beat at the same rate all the time. The time that passes from heartbeat to heartbeat is constantly changing. The greater this change, the higher your HRV and the healthier and more resilient you are.

This may seem counterintuitive. After all, you have probably heard that your heart rate is supposed to be steady. It is indeed true—your average heart rate should be regular and steady, staying somewhere around 60–80 beats

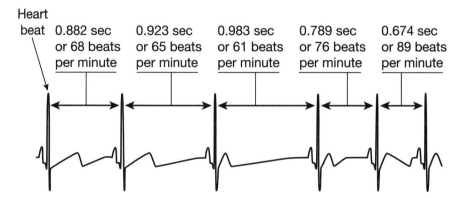

FIGURE 3.2: Heart rate variability—the difference in time from heartbeat to heartbeat   *Source: the author*

per minute. However, your heart rate within each minute varies, speeding up (intervals between heartbeats shortening) and slowing down (intervals lengthening) all the time (figure 3.2). Your average heart rate may be at 72, but your heart rate may vary from 61 to 89 beats within that minute, as it does in the example in Figure 3.2. It is this kind of variability that we want to increase as much as possible.

Importance of Heart Rate Variability

Higher HRV is related to better cardiac and overall health, better emotional health, and better mental and physical performance. The concept of HRV is a very old one—the known first mentions of a heart rate rhythm are in the writings of Greek physician Herophilos around 300 BC and then another Greek physician, Galen, around 170 AD. Galen used his observations of the variations in pulse to diagnose diseases and predict their outcomes. The first description of beat-to-beat pulse variability and the beginning of the modern definition of HRV were made by English clergyman Stephen Hales in 1733, followed by the first recording of heart rate fluctuations in 1847 by the German physician and physiologist Carl Ludwig. These findings occurred before the development of the electrocardiogram by Willem Einthoven in 1903, used to produce a continuous recording of the electrical activity of the heart.

The early twentieth century saw a further development of the concept of HRV and much controversy regarding its origins and function. It was not until the 1960s that HRV was first used clinically. In 1965, Edward Hon and Stanley Lee noted that a reduction in a baby's HRV during labor was the first sign of fetal distress, before any other symptoms could be observed.[7] This discovery remains a cornerstone in obstetrics to this day. Through the late 1960s and 1970s, scientists learned more and more about the physiology of HRV and the role it plays in cardiac health and the overall health of the nervous system, and this research has grown exponentially since then. We now know that HRV is a strong predictor of outcomes after a heart attack. It is also a strong predictor of the likelihood of currently healthy people developing heart disease and high blood pressure, as well as having a heart attack down the road.

The association of HRV with our health was examined by the Framingham Heart Study, the longest running heart health study in the world.

This study began in 1948 with 5,209 participants. In 1971, 5,124 children and spouses of the original participants were added to the study. The study continues today with regular examinations of the original and subsequent participants. Hisako Tsuji and her team at Lahey Medical Center in Massachusetts reexamined the electrocardiogram data of 2,501 participants (1,101 men and 1,400 women, with a median age of 53), looking specifically at the predictive value of HRV for future cardiac events.[8] Researchers also examined participants' blood pressure, cholesterol levels, and resting heart rate. All the participants were free of heart disease at the time of the first HRV measurement. Researchers then examined data from a 3.5-year follow-up, looking for onset of heart disease. They found a very strong relationship between baseline HRV and future heart disease. Of all the participants who experienced a cardiac event, two-thirds had the lowest HRV (bottom third of the full HRV distribution). Only 10 percent of cardiac events occurred in participants with high HRV (top third of the full HRV distribution). After controlling for possible confounding factors, the researchers concluded that *HRV is a better predictor of future cardiac events than blood pressure, cholesterol levels, and resting heart rate.*

Moreover, we now know that low HRV is associated with disorders like high blood pressure, chronic pain, anxiety, depression, posttraumatic stress, irritable bowel syndrome (IBS), and asthma.[9] HRV is also strongly associated with our ability to perform at our best during times of increased stress or challenge. In fact, HRV is one of the best metrics of psychophysiological health and ability to perform we currently have. Research has shown that HRV underlies our ability to regulate our physiological and emotional activation. For example, a 2015 study by DeWayne Williams and his colleagues at Ohio State University showed that lower HRV is associated with greater difficulty with day-to-day emotion regulation, ability to understand our own emotions, and impulse control.[10] Jacob Holzman and David Bridgett of Northern Illinois University specifically examined the relationship between HRV and our so-called top-down self-regulation, meaning our ability to regulate behavioral, cognitive, and emotional processes.[11] They conducted a thorough meta-analysis of 123 studies that reported associations between HRV and various aspects of self-regulation and concluded that HRV is indeed a robust indicator of our ability to regulate our emotions and behavior.

One way in which HRV influences our ability to self-regulate is through the bidirectional connection between the parasympathetic nervous system (vagus nerve) and areas of the prefrontal cortex, which is involved in both emotion regulation and behavior control. An imaging study by Richard Lane at the University of Arizona and his colleagues demonstrated the association between HRV and activity of the prefrontal cortex in the context of emotion regulation.[12] Another imaging study conducted by Michiko Sakaki at University of Reading in the United Kingdom and her team in 2016 revealed an association between higher HRV and stronger functional connectivity between the amygdala and the prefrontal cortex.[13] This means that high HRV is associated with better ability of the prefrontal cortex to regulate activation of the fight-or-flight amygdala response.

The connection between HRV and the prefrontal cortex is highlighted by the neurovisceral integration model put forth by Julian Thayer of Ohio State University and Richard Lane of the University of Arizona.[14] This model examines the neural circuits that link the heart with cortical and subcortical brain structures via the vagus nerve. Thayer and Lane and their team have conducted numerous studies examining the relationship between the brain and HRV. A 2012 meta-analysis of such studies revealed a significant relationship between HRV and blood flow to areas within the ventromedial prefrontal cortex, as well the left amygdala.[15] These findings are also consistent with the polyvagal theory formulated by Stephen Porges, discussed in more detail in Chapter 10.

In addition to emotion and behavioral regulation, the connection between HRV and the brain is also evident in the role HRV plays in executive function of the brain, further highlighting the importance of HRV in optimizing performance. Studies have shown that higher HRV is associated with better memory retrieval, working memory, sustained attention, situational awareness, and goal-directed behavior.[16]

Given the high promise of HRV, extensive research has also been conducted on the effectiveness of HRV biofeedback in improving health and performance. This research has demonstrated the effectiveness of HRV biofeedback in reducing symptoms of anxiety, depression, chronic pain, IBS, posttraumatic stress disorder, asthma, high blood pressure, coronary heart disease and heart failure, COPD, and preeclampsia.[17] Moreover, HRV biofeedback is also effective in increasing HRV, respiratory efficiency, and athletic endurance and enhancing performance in academic testing, music, dance, golf, soccer, basketball, and baseball.[18]

HRV biofeedback training increases our physiological and emotional regulation and our flexibility and resilience, as well as reducing the risk of future health problems. The following sections are devoted to HRV training, starting with choosing a biofeedback device.

HRV Devices

There has been a proliferation of various devices for HRV training, with some designed specifically for athletes, and others, for us "regular people" interested in improving health, well-being, and performance. Many of these devices provide good options for HRV training. Choose one that best suits your needs and budget. Note that, while a lot of wearable fitness trackers measure heart rate, not all of them measure HRV—the ability to measure HRV has to do with the sampling rate of the sensor; not all devices get enough data to be able to determine HRV. If you are planning to use a fitness tracker, make sure it can measure HRV. In addition, free or low-cost mobile apps are now available for measuring and training HRV. Appendix B includes a sample list of several HRV training apps and devices; it is not an exhaustive list and I do not endorse a particular device—new HRV devices are coming out all the time.

While HRV training is best done with a biofeedback device that measures HRV, you would still benefit from HRV training guidelines discussed in this chapter even if you don't have one.

How HRV Is Measured

Different HRV monitors may give you feedback about your HRV in different ways, because there are many different ways to measure HRV. Essentially, all those measurements provide you with the same information: how well your nervous system is able to regulate itself and adapt to the changes in your internal and external environment. That said, you may be interested in knowing what kind of measurements your device is giving you. I review a few of the common ways to measure HRV that you are most likely to encounter. If you would like to learn more about measuring HRV, please refer to the excellent paper by Fred Shaffer and Jay Ginsberg published in 2017 in *Frontiers in Public Health*.[19]

- *SDNN* is the standard deviation of the time that passes between heartbeats over a certain period of time (see Figure 3.2 for an illustration of the heartbeat intervals). It is the simplest to perform and most common method of measuring HRV in research. The greater the SDNN, the higher the overall HRV. This measurement is expressed in milliseconds.

- *rMSSD* is the square root of the mean of the squares of the differences between adjacent heartbeat intervals. While still measuring overall HRV, this measure particularly reflects your vagal tone and the strength of your parasympathetic nervous system. This measurement is also expressed in milliseconds.

- *Max-min* (or peak-to-trough) is difference between the maximum and minimum (max-min) heart rate that occurs during a full breath cycle, measured over many breath cycles. The bigger the max-min difference, the higher the HRV. See Figure 3.3 for an illustration of max-min HRV. This measurement is expressed in beats per minute.

- *Power spectral analysis* is a frequency-domain measure that uses an algorithm called the fast Furrier transform (FFT) to decompose the heart rate signal into its individual frequency components. Think about looking at white light through a prism—you would see the rainbow, because white light is a composed of the seven color frequencies mixed up together. The prism separates the seven frequencies, so you

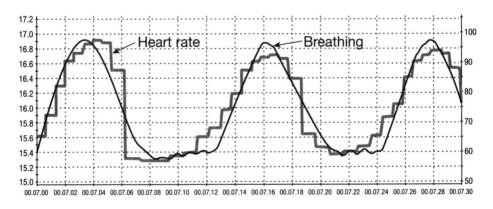

FIGURE 3.3: High HRV illustrated by synchronous oscillations of the heart rate and the breath. This also illustrates the max-min (or peak-to-trough) HRV measure   *Source: Screenshot from Mindfulness Suite Software by Biofeedback Federation of Europe using Thought Technology ProComp Infiniti Hardware, with permission*

can see each of the colors separately. Power spectrum analysis of HRV works the same way: Your heart rate signal is composed of several individual frequencies mixed together. FFT allows us to see each of the component frequencies separately. And we know what each of these frequencies stands for. There are three frequencies that we can identify and make sense of:

— *High-frequency (HF)* signal reflects the influence of the parasympathetic (relaxation) nervous system on the heart. This component also reflects vagal tone and the ability of the parasympathetic nervous system to put on the brakes to sympathetic activation. HRV training strengthens this component of HRV in particular.

— *Low-frequency (LF)* signal reflects the sympathetic and parasympathetic influences on the heart. This is the frequency that reflects resonance frequency breathing (discussed later in this chapter): when you breathe at your resonance frequency, you increase the LF signal, as if you are training the ability of your sympathetic and parasympathetic nervous systems to work well together. This ultimately strengthens your HF HRV (vagal tone) when you return to normal breathing rates.

— *Very low frequency* signal is primarily influenced by the sympathetic (stress) nervous system.

HRV Biofeedback Training

The most direct way to train your HRV is through breathing. Your respiratory and cardiovascular systems are designed to work in synchrony. As you breathe in, your sympathetic nervous system activates and your heart rate increases. As you breathe out, your parasympathetic nervous system activates and your heart rate decreases. Your breathing acts as a stimulus for the heart. In physics, this kind of relationship between your breathing and your heart rate is called *resonance*, a property of a system where two oscillating components interplay with each other, producing increases in oscillation amplitude. In our case, both breathing and heart rate are oscillating systems—inhalation/exhalation, heart rate increases/heart rate decreases. Breathing stimulates heart rate in an interplay feedback relationship: your heart rate increases as you breathe in and decreases as you breathe out. See Figure 3.3 for an illustration.

Training HRV increases heart rate oscillations as much as possible. That is, you learn to maximize heart rate increases and decreases with each breath cycle (inhalation and exhalation). To do this, you can determine your so-called resonance frequency (RF) breathing rate. Regular practice at your RF breathing rate increases HRV and trains your physiological and emotional flexibility and resilience.

An easy way to understand RF is to think about a swing. Have you ever pushed a child on a swing? If so, you may remember that for maximal delight of the child you need to find a way of regularly pushing the swing to produce the highest amplitude. If you push too frequently, the swing won't go very high. If you get distracted and don't push frequently enough, the swing slows down and you get brought back to reality by reproachful squeaks. In this scenario, you are the stimulus for the swing, just like your breath is the stimulus for the heart. When you find the ideal frequency to push the swing, swing amplitude increases, and your child is maximally happy. When you find your ideal breathing rate—your RF breathing rate—the amplitude of your heart rate oscillations increases, and you train your physiological and emotional well-being in the most optimal way.

To determine your RF breathing rate, you need a biofeedback device that can measure HRV. If you do not have one, you can train at a breathing rate that gets close enough for most people—6 breaths per minute—and still experience most of the benefits of HRV training.

Before determining your RF breathing rate and/or starting RF breathing training, be sure to review Chapter 2 on breathing. Skills discussed in that chapter will help minimize the chances of overbreathing during RF training. Practicing low-and-slow breathing described in Chapter 2 and becoming comfortable with this breathing skill before moving on to RF breathing determination and training is particularly important.

The protocol I present here for determining your RF breathing rate and training HRV is based on the work of Paul Lehrer, Eugene Vaschillo, Bronya Vaschillo, and their team at the Robert Wood Johnson Medical School.[20]

For most people over the age of thirteen, RF breathing rate falls somewhere between 4.5 and 7 breaths per minute (children under the age of thirteen breathe faster than adults, so their RF frequency is higher). You can use your HRV biofeedback device to determine your particular RF frequency. Some, but not all, HRV biofeedback devices are set up to determine your RF breathing rate. If your device is not set up to determine your RF, you can do it yourself by using the feedback about your HRV from the device. Here are the steps to follow in determining your RF breathing rate:

1. Find a breath pacer to use for this assessment. Your device may come with a pacer that can be adjusted to different breathing rates. If it does not, use one of the free mobile breath pacer apps to pace yourself (see Appendix B for suggestions).

2. Set your pacer to 7 breaths per minute (bpm), and breathe at that rate for 2 minutes while recording your HRV. Note your average HRV measurement during the 2 minutes.

3. Now set your pacer for 6.5 bpm and breathe at that rate for 2 minutes, while recording your HRV. Note your average HRV during the 2 minutes.

4. Continue the assessment by setting the pacer to the remaining breathing rates for 2 minutes each: 6 bpm, 5.5 bpm, 5 bpm, and 4.5 bpm. Note your average HRV during each of the 2-minute intervals.

5. Compare your HRV measurements for each of the 2-minute breathing intervals. The breathing rate that produces the highest HRV is your RF rate. Different devices provide different ways of measuring HRV; use whichever measurement your device provides. If your device provides feedback in more than one way, the best determinants of HRV are highest max-min measurement and highest LF peak on the spectral analysis.

6. If your measurements indicate two adjacent breathing rates as being equally good, your RF breathing rate is likely somewhere between the two. In this case, use the range between those two breathing rates to train with. For example, if your measurements indicate that 5.5 and 6 breaths per minute are equally good, train to breathe between 5.5 and 6 breaths per minute.

HOW IMPORTANT IS IT TO PRECISELY
DETERMINE RF BREATHING RATE?

Research shows that people increase their HRV to a greater extent and experience greater reduction in symptoms when they practice breathing at their RF breathing rate compared to breathing at a rate one breath away from RF. Patrick Steffen and his team at Brigham Young University examined the effect of breathing at RF, at a rate one breath per minute away from the RF, and just quiet breathing at a normal rate.[21] They found that breathing at RF rate produced the highest improvement in HRV, greatest increase in mood, and greatest decrease in blood pressure.

RF Breathing Training

Once you are comfortable with low-and-slow breathing (Chapter 2) and have determined your RF breathing rate (or have decided to train at 6 breaths per minute), you can move on to RF breathing training. I describe the process in detail below, and at the end of the chapter is a step-by-step guide to HRV training—including RF training—for your reference.

Begin by pacing your breathing at your RF breathing rate to train awareness of the sensations of that breathing rate and eventually learn to breathe at your RF rate without a pacer. As described earlier in this chapter, many HRV biofeedback devices have built in adjustable breathing pacers. If your device does not have an adjustable pacer, or if you are not using a device, you can get a free or low-cost pacer for your phone/tablet or PC (see Appendix B for suggestions).

Once you've picked and installed your breathing pacer, you will need to set it up in accordance with your RF breathing rate. First, figure out how many seconds each of your breaths will last. To do that, divide 60 seconds by your RF breathing rate. For example, if your RF breathing rate is 6 breaths per minute, you divide 60 seconds by 6 breaths, which equals 10. This means that each of your breath cycles will last 10 seconds. If your RF breathing rate is 5.5 bpm, you divide 60 by 5.5 to get 11 seconds per breath.

Next, determine how many seconds of each breath cycle will be allocated for inhalation and how many for exhalation. I recommend reserving about 40 percent of each breath cycle for inhalation and about 60 percent for exhalation, to minimize chances of overbreathing (see Chapter 2). Some experts recommend a 50-50 percent split between inhalation and exhalation. Purely for HRV training, a 50-50 percent split is just fine. If there is any concern about overbreathing, a 40-60 percent split for inhalation and exhalation will decrease the probability of overbreathing. In this step, take the total duration of the breath cycle you have just determined and multiply it by 0.4 to get your inhalation length. The rest of the time is the 60 percent exhalation. For example, with an RF breathing rate of 6, you have a 10 seconds breath cycle, with 4 seconds for the inhalation and 6 seconds for the exhalation. See Table 3.1 for quick view of determining your RF breathing rate cycle duration and inhalation/exhalation ratio.

Many pacers allow a pause during the transition from inhalation to exhalation and from exhalation to inhalation. It is entirely up to you whether to utilize pauses. If your body naturally pauses during those transitions, then include one or both pauses in your breathing cycle. If you tend to overbreathe or have trouble fully extending your exhale, a pause after the exhalation may be particularly helpful. If you decide to include a pause after the inhalation, set it for somewhere between 0.3 and 0.5 seconds. The time for this pause will come out of your total inhalation time. For example, if your RF breathing rate is 6.5 bpm, and your total inhalation time is 3.7 seconds, you will need to set the inhalation to 3.4 seconds in order to include a 0.3 second pause. If you decide to include a pause after the exhalation, set it to 0.3–0.5 seconds, with this time coming out of your total exhalation time. Similarly, an RF rate of 6.5 indicates an exhalation of 5.5 seconds. If you'd like to add a 0.5 second pause after the exhalation, you will need to set the exhalation time to 5 seconds, for a total of 5.5 seconds.

Once your pacer is set up, follow the pacer for a few minutes, while mindfully attending to the sensations of breathing at your RF rate. Use your low-and-slow breathing skills from Chapter 2—take a comfortable slow breath in and then exhale slowly and fully, either through your nose or through pursed lips (as if you are blowing out a candle). If it is hard to complete the exhalation and you feel like you are running out of air too soon, slow down your exhalation at the very beginning—that's where people breathe out the most air, and

TABLE 3.1 BREATH CYCLES AND INHALATION/EXHALATION DURATION FOR RESONANCE FREQUENCY BREATHING RATES

Breathing rate (breaths per minute)	Total duration of each breath (rounded to nearest decimal)	Duration for inhalation	Duration for exhalation
7 bpm	8.6 sec	3.4 sec	5.2 sec
6.5 bpm	9.2 sec	3.7 sec	5.5 sec
6 bpm	10 sec	4 sec	6 sec
5.5 bpm	11 sec	4.4 sec	6.6 sec
5 bpm	12 sec	4.8 sec	7.2 sec
4.5 bpm	13.3 sec	5.3 sec	8 sec

Source: adapted with permission from The Clinical Handbook of Biofeedback (Khazan, 2013)

there may not be enough left to complete the exhalation. Pursing your lips, as if you are blowing out a candle, will help slow down your exhalation.

You may need to make a few adjustments to your paced breathing practice early on in your training. You may decide to adjust the inhalation/exhalation ratio for greater comfort—perhaps making the inhalation slightly shorter while lengthening the exhalation, or making the inhalation slightly longer while shortening the exhalation. If you do this, I don't recommend making adjustment of more than 0.5 seconds either way.

As you follow the pacer, bring your attention to the sensation of the breath: What does the paced inhalation feel like? What does the pause feel like (if you take one)? What does the exhalation feel like? See Chapter 8 on mindfulness meditation for more on mindful breathing. This is a time to start developing internal pacing cues, so that you are not always dependent on the pacer. Your internal cues may be one of the following:

- Count, using the number of seconds for inhalation and exhalation as a guide. For example, counting to 4 for the inhalation and to 6 for the exhalation if your RF breathing rate is 6; or counting to 4.5 for inhalation and 6.5 for exhalation if your RF rate is 5.5 (refer to Table 3.2 for a guide).

- Choose a phrase, a verse from a song, or just two words that you can sing-song in a rhythm that matches your breathing rate. For example, one of my clients used the words *Encyclopedia Britannica* that she sang in a way to match her breathing rhythm—*Encyclopedia* on the inhalation and *Britannica* on the exhalation. Another client used the words *blue* (inhalation) *ocean* (exhalation), in a rhythm to match his breathing rate. It is best to choose words that are either pleasant or neutral in meaning, and it is best to stay away from words that directly encourage certain outcomes from breathing, like *relax* or *be calm*.
- Attend to the physiological sensations themselves, like the feeling of your heart rate speeding up and slowing down, or the way the air feels on the inhalation and on the exhalation.

Once you find a cue you like, practice using it together with the pacer, to fine-tune the rhythm of your cue. When the cue feels familiar, cover or turn away from the pacer and continue breathing using your cue and paying mindful attention to how the breathing feels. Breathe on your own for a few breaths, and then return to the feedback screen or the pacer for a few breaths to check how you are doing. Continue doing this, allowing yourself to breathe without a pacer longer and longer, eventually checking in with the pacer only when you feel like you have gotten off pace and have trouble getting back on. The goal is to use the pacer less and less, reducing it to only occasional use after a few weeks of practice.

Why can't you use the pacer all the time? Well, you could. Physiologically there is no harm, and you will be training your HRV. But what happens in the future when you don't have your device with you or are unable to use it at the moment of need? For example, you might find yourself in a stressful meeting, anticipating needing to speak. That may be a good time to take a few RF breaths to optimize self-regulation. If you haven't had sufficient practice in RF breathing without a pacer, it is unlikely that you will be able to quickly bring yourself to that pace during a challenging time. If you've trained to breathe at RF rate without a pacer, that skill will be available to you anytime you need it.

Make a Breathing Training Plan

Making an RF training plan will allow your training to become a habit and will maximize efficiency of your training. Choose a time that will work for you most days of the week. (If you've already set aside time for low-and-slow breathing practice from Chapter 2, you can now dedicate that time to RF breathing, using your low-and-slow skills.) The goal is to practice RF breathing 20 minutes each day. When you first start your breathing practice, set aside 5 minutes each day for a week, then go up to 10 minutes for a week, up to 15 minutes for another week, and then finally get to the 20 minutes. It helps to ramp up your practice time gradually, since everyone's schedule is busy and finding 20 minutes for practice can be surprisingly challenging. At the same time, you don't want to practice too little and miss out on the full benefits of training.

Choose a time when you are the least likely to be disturbed or be in a rush, hungry, or overly tired. For some people, ideal training time is first thing in the morning, before they get out of bed. For others, ideal time is when they get into bed at night. Yet others prefer to practice breathing right before lunch, provided that they are not starving at the time. There is no general right time for practice—whatever time works for you and your needs is the best time.

People often ask me whether it is OK to practice RF breathing while doing something else, like during their commute or while reading or watching TV. Ideally, your RF breathing time would be dedicated to breathing only. If that does not seem possible, doing your breathing while you are on a bus or a train is OK, as long as you are not talking to someone and not doing something else at the same time. I caution you against doing your breathing practice while driving. While the purpose of RF breathing is not to relax, it can often feel relaxing and may make some people sleepy—this may create a dangerous situation on the road. It is OK to take a few RF breaths when you are at a red light or stuck in traffic, but don't do your regular breathing practice while driving. I also don't recommend doing your breathing practice while reading, watching TV, or similar activities. It is not possible to attend to the sensations of your body in guiding your breathing or fully pay attention to a pacer while your attention is occupied somewhere else. Your breathing rate will likely be suboptimal much of the time when you are also doing something else, making your practice much less effective.

When hearing about RF breathing rate, many of my clients worry that they will need to breathe that slowly all the time. That is not the case at all. RF breathing is reserved for your training times and for challenging occasions when you need to take a few breaths to maximize your body's self-regulation abilities. You can think of breathing training in the same way as strength training at the gym. You do your strength training workout three times a week for an hour, and you don't need to drag your dumbbells or kettlebells around with you in order to continue making progress and maintain your strength gains. This applies to your breathing training as well. As long as you do your 20 minutes of training a day, you will strengthen your autonomic nervous system's ability to regulate itself; you don't need to keep breathing at your RF all the time in order to maintain and continue making gains. With continued practice, better ability to self-regulate will remain with you at all times.

Regular RF breathing practice under neutral conditions will provide your nervous system with a stronger foundational ability to self-regulate. Once RF breathing feels comfortable and familiar under neutral conditions, you could also use it just before or during challenging situations to further facilitate self-regulation. Taking a few RF breaths as you go into a difficult meeting or as you notice yourself worrying about an upcoming trip will remind your body to self-regulate. In combinations with skills described in other chapters of this book (such as mindfulness-based skills in Chapter 9), RF breathing practice in difficult situations will allow you to navigate those situations with greater ease and success.

Observing Progress

You can tell that all that training you've been doing is achieving results in two ways. First is your own experience. Before starting your training, note the areas of functioning where you would like to see an improvement. It may be the way you respond in challenging professional situations, interact with your partner in emotionally charged conversations, feel when studying and taking exams, or your sports performance, blood pressure readings, number of headaches you experience, or level of back pain. Whatever the situation is, note your experience before the training. You can use Outcomes Tracking Worksheets 1 and 2 in Chapter 1 (see Tables 1.1–1.4) to track progress.

You can expect to notice early changes after about 4 weeks of regular 20-

minute a day training. *Regular training is key!* You are unlikely to experience positive change if you are not sticking to the training plan. You can expect to continue improving after the 4-week mark. The longer you train, the more benefit you will observe. If you stop training, its benefits will gradually decrease.

As a result of your HRV training, you might notice a change in the way you react to challenging situations. It may become easier to compose yourself and choose the best course of action when emotions are running high. Your sports performance may improve (e.g., increased endurance in running, lower golf scores, higher hit rate in baseball). You might find it easier to focus under pressure during exams. Or you may find it easier to wind down and recover at the end of the day. Symptoms of a physiological condition you might have may improve—your blood pressure readings may be lower, you might experience fewer headaches, less anxiety, and less pain.

Keep in mind that if you are taking medication for issues like high blood pressure, asthma, diabetes, or a heart or lung condition, it is important to check in with your health care provider. It is best to let your health care provider know that you are starting HRV training before you start, and then check in as your training progresses. While the exercises described in this book are not a substitute for medical treatment, regular HRV training may change your need for medication. For example, your blood pressure may stabilize, and you may not need as much blood pressure medication. It is a good idea to keep a record of your blood pressure at home to notice changes.

The second way to observe changes as a result of HRV training is through monitoring HRV itself. You can observe these changes only if you are using an HRV biofeedback device, which will enable you to track your HRV scores and note improvement. When you track HRV, be sure to measure your baseline HRV prior to training while breathing normally for 2–5 minutes. Then measure HRV again at 4–5 week intervals, again while breathing normally (not at your RF). You cannot compare HRV while breathing at RF to HRV at normal breathing rates.

In summary, HRV is a strong indicator of your ability to regulate your physiology at all times, including times of increased stress and challenge, and times of rest and recovery. Training your HRV benefits your health and performance.

Below is a step-by-step summary of the HRV training I outline in this chapter.

1. Decide which areas of functioning you would like to improve.
2. Choose measurable criteria for evaluating effects of training, such as number of headaches each week, blood pressure readings, or running distance (use Outcomes Tracking Worksheet 2, Table 1.3), or your assessment on a scale from 1 to 10 of your ability to handle challenging situations or overall level of anxiety (use Outcomes Tracking Worksheet 1, Table 1.1).
3. Choose an HRV biofeedback device, or decide to train at 6 breaths per minute with a pacer.
4. Practice low-and-slow breathing, as outlined in Chapter 2.
5. Determine your RF breathing rate (or stick with 6 breaths per minute), by pacing yourself for 2 minutes at each one of these breathing rates: 7 breaths per minute (bpm), 6.5 bpm, 6 bpm, 5.5 bpm, 5 bpm, and 4.5 bpm, and then choosing the breathing rate that produces the highest HRV.
6. Make your training plan—when and where you will practice.
7. Begin training at RF breathing, gradually building up to 20 minutes a day (practice for 5 minutes a day for the first week, 10 minutes a day for the second week, 15 minutes a day for the third week, and 20 minutes for the fourth and all subsequent weeks).
   a. Start with a pacer.
   b. Determine your internal pacing cue, and begin using it alongside the pacer.
   c. Use your internal cue more and more, gradually weaning off the pacer.
8. Train HRV at your RF breathing rate 20 minutes a day.
9. Observe changes in internal experience and markers of HRV starting after about 4 weeks of 20 minutes-a-day training.
10. Maintain your practice to continue benefits!

CHAPTER 4

Muscle Health

Kevin has been studying for hours, days, months—time has all blurred together. The bar exam is coming up in a week. He has to pass or his job offer may go away. Breaking away from the practice test on the computer, Kevin rubs his sore neck and shoulders, noticing a headache coming on, wishing he had time for a massage—too bad he doesn't. He returns back to the computer screen, clicking away at what he hopes are correct answers.

If you've ever had to spend time working on the computer, studying, reading, using a tablet or phone, or driving for a long time, you have probably had an experience similar to Kevin's—achy sore muscles, headaches, back pain that you wished would just go away. This chapter addresses common causes for muscle pain, the importance of muscle health for mood and performance, and biofeedback and mindfulness-based skills for improving muscle health.

Muscle Pain

Most people know what muscle pain feels like. It is one of the most common complaints in primary care physicians' offices, resulting in more than 30 percent of all primary care visits. Sixty-six percent of adults experience significant neck pain at some point in their lives. Ninety percent of college students experience muscle pain by the end of the semester, and at least 30 percent of people who regularly work at the computer experience neck, back, hand, and arm pain. You are not alone!

Much of the chronic pain and discomfort is due to one reason: *dysponesis,* or misplaced effort, a condition described by George Whatmore and Daniel Kohli in 1968.[22] Dysponesis results from the unhelpful ways in which you may use your muscle without realizing you are doing so. Whatmore and Kohli described four ways in which you could misuse your muscles:

Performance dysponesis happens when you use your muscles for appropriate activities, but with a lot more effort than is required to perform those activities. For example, you might chew with more force than is necessary for proper digestion, overusing the muscles of your jaw and contributing to jaw pain and conditions such as temporomandibular joint (TMJ) disorder. Or you might tense your forearms and shoulders while typing, contributing to neck, shoulder, and back pain.

Bracing dysponesis happens when you are preparing for quick action, such as running or fighting as part of the fight-or-flight response. Bracing efforts often result in rigid posture, with the body being "on guard" for danger, whether or not actual danger is present. This is particularly likely to happen when you brace for pain. Tightening your muscles in anticipation of or in response to initial signs of pain is something you may do automatically as a protective reaction. Unfortunately, repeated overactivation of the muscles that happens when you brace for pain is likely to make pain worse.

Erik Peper, professor at San Francisco State University, often illustrates dysponesis in this way: Close your eyes and imagine that you are threading a needle. Just imagine, don't try to do it. In your mind's eye, create a very clear picture of the eye of the needle, the thread, and your attempts to put the thread through the eye, trying over and over until you get it. Once you are done, observe what happened in your body— did your shoulders rise toward your ears? Did your forearms stiffen? Did your eyebrows rise? Did your jaw and forehead tighten? Did you hold your breath or stiffen your back and abdomen? You may be surprised to notice just how much unnecessary effort went into a simple act of imagining threading a needle.

Representing dysponesis happens when you inadvertently activate your muscles while thinking, remembering, anticipating, daydreaming, or worrying. These activities involve forming mental representations of events, situations, or sensations of the past or future, those that are not present at the moment the effort occurs. For example, you might notice yourself tightening your fists when remembering a situation when you felt extremely angry. Or you might tighten your shoulders and slouch when worrying about making a fool out of yourself at an upcoming work meeting.

Attention dysponesis happens when you are very focused, paying attention to something very specific. For example, you might notice yourself furrowing your brow when working on a difficult problem or squinting your eyes when staring at the computer screen.

Here are some common examples of muscle dysponesis. Which ones have you noticed for yourself?

- Clenched jaw
- Squinting eyes
- Furrowed brow
- Rigid tense neck with head held forward
- Raised, tense shoulders
- Clenched fists
- Tense or "sucked in" abdomen
- Stiff back

When you overuse your muscles on a regular basis, you may experience an increase in symptoms such as headaches, anxiety, TMJ disorders, repetitive strain injuries, and chronic back pain. Most people are unaware of overusing their muscles until pain and discomfort have already set in.

Biofeedback can help you become aware of dysponesis by monitoring your muscle function while you engage in activities that are likely to lead to muscle overuse, such as working at the computer and driving. You can then learn to use biofeedback and mindfulness skills to prevent and correct dysponesis, as discussed in the chapter.

Overbreathing and Muscle Health

Along with the unnecessary effort and muscle overuse resulting from dysponesis, you might also experience a dysregulation in breathing, resulting in overbreathing. Breath holding is a very common form of dysponesis (such as bracing dysponesis), which often results in overly large breaths to compensate, leading to overbreathing. Breathing faster and deeper than necessary may also result from representing dysponesis, when you remember or anticipate difficult situations in the past or future. This kind of dysponesis may trigger fight-or-flight response, with an increased possibility of overbreathing.

As described in Chapter 2, overbreathing is a behavior of breathing out too much carbon dioxide, which results in low levels of carbon dioxide in the blood, disrupting pH balance, electrolyte balance, and oxygen delivery to tissues and muscles. These physiological changes produce the following muscle-related problems:

- Insufficient oxygen going to the muscles interferes with the muscles' ability to activate and recover properly.
- Lactic acid accumulating in the muscles produces pain and discomfort.
- Electrolyte imbalances increase activity in muscle cells, producing muscle spasms and fatigue.

These physiological consequences point us to the importance for proper breathing training as part of attending to overall muscle health.

Muscle Immobility

Fun fact: Do you know why people who frequently used manual typewriters did not experience as much muscle pain as people who type on the computer nowadays? It is because those typewriters required users to frequently change the movement of their arms—every time you came to the end of the line, you had to move the carriage back to the beginning of the line. While one hand moved the carriage back, the other hand dropped for a break. If you made a mistake, you had to move your hands differently while correcting it. You had to change paper each time you typed up a sheet. All of these movements prevented your hands, arms, and shoulders from remaining in one tense position. Nowadays, when you work on a computer, your need for movement is greatly reduced. You could spend hours typing on the computer without significant movement in any part of your body other than your fingers. This immobility results in pain.

You have probably heard about muscle overuse as one of the reasons for muscle pain. Repetitive strain injury is considered to be a muscle overuse disorder, such as what happens when you type too much and develop pain in your wrist. A condition that people don't pay enough attention to is muscle immobility. Muscle immobility contributes to muscle pain as much, if not more, than repetitive strain. Think about it this way: You can walk for long periods of time without a problem. But what if you tried to stand on one leg for even a minute? That position is part of walking, and you do it multiple times while walking without a problem. But if you were to stop midmovement with one leg up and the other on the ground, you would start feeling tension and pain in that leg after a minute or two.

When muscles remain in one tension-producing position for long periods of time, tension continues to increase during that time, while blood supply to the muscle decreases. A 20 percent increase in muscle tension can decrease blood supply to the muscle by as much as 80 percent. When your muscles are tense, their metabolism is higher (tense muscles are more active) and therefore produce more metabolic by-products, such as lactic acid. When blood supply is reduced, these metabolic by-products do not get taken away. Accumulation of lactic acid causes pain. This is partly why your muscles might hurt after typing, driving, playing on your phone, or even just sitting and reading in a tension producing position.

Let's try something together. This is an exercise I learned from Erik Paper, professor at San Francisco State University, an expert on muscle health. Find a way to sit in your chair so that you may be able to move your head, shoulders, and arms without changing the position of your torso or the position of the chair you are in. Now turn your head over your right shoulder as far back as you comfortably can, and notice the spot behind you, marking the farthest you can see behind you. Without moving your torso or chair, put your left arm over your head to your right ear and gently move your head around, up and down, side to side. Do this for about a minute. Now, turn your head over your right shoulder again and note the farthest spot you can see behind you. Did you see a little farther? Most people do. You can try doing the same thing over your left shoulder, using your right hand to reach to your left ear. You will likely notice a similar effect. Movement reduces the stiffness created by immobility and increases your range of motion.

If you suffer from muscle or muscle-related pain (back, neck, or shoulder pain, headaches) and tend to spend time in one position while typing, driving, reading, knitting or crocheting, or playing the piano or another instrument, you would benefit from increasing your muscle mobility. There are two ways to do this:

> Cross-crawl, a favorite of Erik Peper: Jump up on the right leg with left knee high toward the chest, while swinging the left arm forward. Then jump up on the left leg with right knee high toward the chest, while swinging the right arm forward. Repeat lightheartedly several times. This is a great way to release tension from the whole body.

- Take microbreaks every few minutes for 2 or 3 seconds at a time. Microbreaks involve small movement or position changes, such as dropping your hands on your lap while typing, shaking and dropping your shoulders while driving, or changing position of your body while reading.
- Take large movement breaks every 20 or 30 minutes. You might get up from your chair, walk around, do gentle stretches, swing your arms around, jump up and down, or do cross-crawl (see box for a description). Setting a timer or a reminder/alarm on your phone or computer for every 20–30 minutes will help you remember to take those breaks.

Muscle Spindles and Chronic Pain

It is possible for people to experience muscle pain without an obvious elevation in muscle tension. This happens because of activity of stretch receptors
called *muscle spindles*, sensory organs located in the central part of the muscle.
Their main role in the muscle is to regulate muscle length and make postural
adjustments by monitoring the way the muscle stretches. Richard Gevirtz,
professor of psychology at Alliant International University in San Diego, and
David Hubbard, professor of neurology at the University of California in San
Diego, and their colleagues demonstrated another role of the muscle spindle
and its involvement in chronic pain. They showed that muscle spindles are
responsible for the pain produced by trigger points. By inserting a needle electromyographic (EMG) sensor into the muscle spindle, they showed that muscle spindles produce much higher electrical activity readings than nontender
tissue surrounding the trigger point.[23]

Moreover, they showed that muscle spindles are activated by a different
part of the nervous system than the rest of the muscle.[24] The muscle itself is
controlled by the somatic, or voluntary, nervous system. This means that you
can decide when and how to activate the muscles under somatic control—you
can decide to raise your arm or to walk or to chew. However, muscle spindles
are under the control of the sympathetic branch of the autonomic nervous
system, the one responsible for the fight-or-flight response. This means that
muscle spindles start sending out electrical impulses, activating trigger points,
and creating pain in response to worry, anxiety, anger, and other difficult emotions. Based on these findings, the researchers formulated the muscle spindle
trigger point model of chronic pain, which states that pain is caused by the
activity of muscle spindles, which are activated by the sympathetic nervous
system activity, including stress, anxiety, anger, and other emotional stimuli.[25]

In summary, there are four main causes of muscle pain: unnecessary effort
or dysponesis, muscle immobility, overbreathing, and activity of muscle spindles and trigger points. All of these causes can be addressed with biofeedback, described in the section below on biofeedback training for muscle pain.
I discuss the training you can do with a biofeedback device and ways you can
improve your muscle health without a biofeedback device.

Role of Biofeedback and Psychophysiology Training in Muscle Health

Three main biofeedback modalities are helpful in restoring muscle health. First is surface electromyography (sEMG), which measures muscle tension and is the main focus of the rest of this chapter. The second modality is breathing training. Overbreathing may create disruption to muscle function and lead to tension and pain. See Chapter 2 on breathing for a thorough review of overbreathing—if you think you may overbreathe some of the time, the detailed breathing training protocol described there may be helpful. I encourage you to do some breathing training before starting on muscle training. If you continue overbreathing, muscle training will be significantly less effective. Heart rate variability (HRV), described in Chapter 3, is the third modality to train if you experience muscle pain; this addresses muscle pain due to the activity of muscle spindles. It is not possible to tell with certainty with sEMG whether muscle pain is due to activity of muscle spindles or typical muscle tension. Much of the time muscle tension is due to both factors. If you have other reasons in addition to muscle pain to practice HRV biofeedback, such as desire for overall improvement in self-regulation, anxiety, depression, or another condition for which HRV training is recommended, start with HRV training. If that is not the case, then do EMG training first and see if that helps sufficiently. If not, add HRV biofeedback.

sEMG Biofeedback for Reducing Muscle Tension

Surface electromyography (sEMG) is a type of biofeedback that records and displays electrical activity of the muscle from the surface of your skin. This type of biofeedback can let you know when your muscle tension is elevated, when it is decreasing, and when it reaches normal levels. This is a good way to monitor for dysponesis and learn to release tension. See Appendix B for a sample list of portable EMG devices. Most of them allow you to work with one or two muscles at a time.

The first step in doing EMG biofeedback is to pick which muscle (or muscles) you are going to work with. The easiest way is to simply notice which muscles experience tension or pain—if you are thinking of doing muscle biofeedback, you probably already know which muscles give you trouble. If you are not sure which muscle are best to use, refer to Table 4.1 for a summary of most common muscle-related problems and which muscles are best to use in addressing them.

Once you've chosen which muscles you are going to use, there are a few issues to consider with using an EMG device. If you do not have a biofeedback device that measures muscle tension, you can still benefit from many of the skills described in this section. Without a device, skip the sensor placement section and go to the next section on muscle training.

TABLE 4.1 COMMON MUSCLE SENSOR PLACEMENT SITES AND DIRECTION OF MUSCLE FIBERS

Problem	Muscles to work with	Direction of muscle fibers
Headaches	Right and/or left upper trapezius (back of the shoulder) Frontalis (forehead) Right and/or left temporalis (temples)	Across the back of the shoulder Down the forehead Down the temple
Shoulder tension and pain	Right and/or left upper trapezius (back of the shoulder)	Across the back of the shoulder
Upper back pain	Right and/or left latissimus dorsi (large muscle in the middle of your back on both sides of the spine)	Wrapping around from your ribcage toward your spine
Low back pain	Right and/or left paraspinals (long muscles running down parallel to the spine, approximately 3 cm away from the midline on each side)	Down the spine
Jaw pain	Right and/or left masseter (muscle that runs down your cheeks; if you put the palms of your hands on both cheeks and clench your jaw, you'll feel the masseters)	Down the cheek
Neck pain	Right and/or left sternocleidomastoid (muscle that runs from behind your ears, down both sides of your neck to your clavicle)	Down the sides of your neck
Wrist pain	Wrist flexor (top side of the forearm) or extensor (underside of the forearm)	Down the forearm

Source: the author

If you have an EMG device, decide how you are going to place your sensors: parallel or across the muscle fibers. Muscle sensors pick up electrical signals (action potentials) from your muscles. These signals move along the length of the muscle fiber. Therefore, placing your sensors parallel to the muscle fibers will give you more precise information about that specific muscle. Placing your sensors across the muscle fibers, on the other hand, will give you information about several muscles in the general area of your sensor. See Figure 4.1 for an illustration of sensors placed across to the muscles fibers on the forehead and Figure 4.2 for sensors placed along the muscle fibers on the upper trapezius. Also, see Table 4.1 for a description of the direction of other muscle fibers to consider in sensor placement.

Since it may not always be easy to find the specific muscle you should work on, I recommend placing your sensors across the muscle fibers so you pick up information about muscles in that general area. This gives you the most room

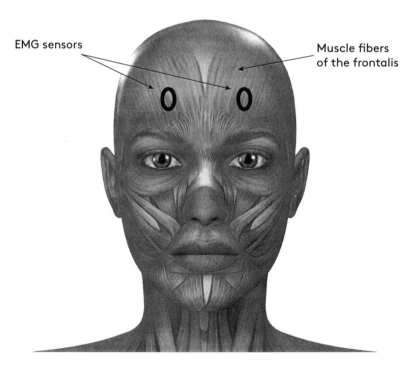

FIGURE 4.1: Illustration of EMG sensor position on the frontalis muscles, across the muscle fibers. Note the downward direction of muscle fibers. The EMG sensors are placed perpendicular to the direction of the muscle fibers (across the forehead). *Source: Shutterstock*

for error. For example, the frontalis muscle fibers go down your forehead, perpendicular to the ground. To place your sensors across the muscle fibers, place them across the forehead, above each eye, parallel to the ground (Figure 4.1).

Keep your sensors placed in the same way from training to training so that you can compare results from session to session. If your sensors are placed significantly differently, you'll be comparing apples to oranges.

Signal artifact from the heart is something to be aware of during muscle training. Your heart sends out an electrical signal, just like your muscles. Therefore, muscle tension sensors will pick up activity from the heart along with the activity of the muscles. The sensor would not know the difference between electrical signal it picks up from the heart and the electrical signal it picks up from the muscle. Sensor placements close to the heart, specifically those on the left side of your upper and lower back, will likely show you the pulsing heart activity mixed in with the muscle activity. Some types of EMG devices can

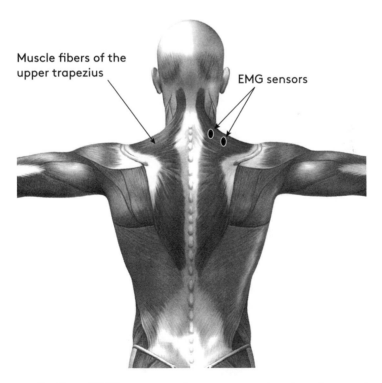

FIGURE 4.2: Position of EMG sensors on the upper trapezius along the muscle fibers. Note the direction of the muscle fibers—across the shoulders. EMG sensors are placed parallel to the muscle fibers. *Source: Shutterstock*

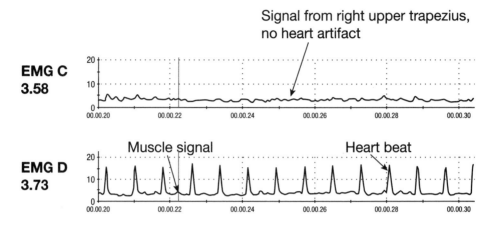

FIGURE 4.3: Muscle tension (EMG) signal with and without heart artifact
Source: Screenshot from Mindfulness Suite Software by Biofeedback Federation of Europe using Thought Technology ProComp Infiniti Hardware with permission

correct for that. If your device does not, just remember that the pulsing signal is the heart artifact and not the muscle (activity of the muscle is between the pulses). See Figure 4.3 for an illustration. Heart artifact is visible only when muscle tension is fairly low; once it gets higher, the heart signal gets lost in the muscle signal.

EMG Muscle Training

When you are ready to begin training, follow the guidelines in this section.

Goal of Training

The goal of training is to reduce muscle activation to 3 microvolts or below at rest. With activities such as typing, the goal is to reduce activation of the muscles that are not necessary for the activity (for example, your neck, back, and shoulders should not have increased muscle tension while typing) as close as possible to 3 microvolts, and to reduce activity of muscles that are involved (such as wrist flexor and extensor while typing) to as low as possible.

Mindful Awareness of Tension

Begin with training mindful awareness of tension. Awareness is crucial to muscle tension reduction, because you can't change something you are not aware of. If you suffer from muscle-related pain, you probably become aware of muscle tension only when pain has already set in. The goal of initial biofeedback training is to learn to recognize muscle tension much earlier in order to release it before pain sets in. You can do this practice with or without EMG sensors. To practice recognizing tension:

1. Find a comfortable place to sit or lie down.
2. Attach muscle tension sensors, if you are using them, and notice the baseline reading.
3. Bring your attention to the muscle(s) you have decided to train.
4. Gradually tense the muscle until you notice the sensation of tension. Mindfully observe the sensations of tension, just noticing what they feel like for a few moments, and then bring the tension back down. What did you notice about the sensations of tension? What does the biofeedback device tell you about your tension?
5. Tense the muscle a bit more, and mindfully observe the sensations of tension for a few moments and bring it down—how is this level of tension different from the lower one? What does the biofeedback device tell you about your tension?
6. Tense the muscle once more, again observing the sensations mindfully for a few moments, and then release tension. How is this level of tension different from the lower ones? What does the biofeedback device tell you about your tension?
7. Repeat steps 4–6 two or three times (if you felt significant amount of pain after the first time, stop there).
8. Practice mindful tension awareness on two or three other days. If you are not using biofeedback equipment, pause for a few moments four times a day and attend to your muscle tension. Rate the level of tension you feel on the scale from 0 (no tension) to 10 (highest tension you can imagine). Continued conscious awareness of muscle tension will help alert you to rising levels of muscle tension during the day and help you reduce it.

YOGA MEDITATION PRACTICE FOR MUSCLE HEALTH

Douglas Baker, a psychotherapist and yoga teacher in Cambridge, Massachusetts, shared a yoga meditation practice that I have adapted with his permission for mindful biofeedback practice.

Sit in a stable, balanced way on a firm chair, away from the back of the chair if you can. Place your feet firmly on the floor, knees over ankles, feet a little wider apart than the hips.

Allow your muscles to release tension, while remaining in upright position.

Guide your breath to your resonance frequency (RF) breathing rate, or to 6 breaths per minute, and take 10 low-and-slow breaths (review these techniques in Chapter 2). Then let go of effort and allow your body to breathe. When your attention wanders off from the breath, gently return it back to the breath, your posture, and your muscle activity.

Prepare to bring simple movements into the practice, synchronizing, as closely as possible, the movements with the breath pattern of inhalation and exhalation. The synchrony of breath and movement will help focus your attention. Continue breathing at your RF or at 6 breaths per minute.

As you begin the next exhalation, gently turn your head and neck to the right, moving slowly, bringing attention to the sensations in your muscles. When the exhalation is finished, pause the movement, and observe the inhalation. Once the next exhalation starts, continue turning your head and neck to the right, without forcing, synchronizing the movement to the breath as closely as you can. Pause the movement to inhale. Allow the face and shoulders to stay relaxed. On the third exhalation, continue turning your head to the right some more, without forcing, only as far as you can turn comfortably.

On the next inhalation, slowly return your head to the center. As you begin the exhalation, begin to turn your head to the left, mindfully attending to the sensations of the muscles. Pause to inhale, continue turning on the next exhalation, pause to inhale again, and turn some more on the third exhalation.

Return your head to the center on the inhalation. Take 2 or 3 mindful low-and-slow breaths at your RF or at 6 breaths per minute.

As you begin an exhalation, gently reach your right ear downward toward the right shoulder, stretching the side of the neck. Do not force the movement. Pause where you are for the inhalation. On the next two successive exhalations, lean slightly into the stretch of the neck toward the shoulder, without forcing. If you cannot lean anymore, just explore the sensations. Pause in between to inhale. Allow the face and shoulders to remain relaxed.

On the inhalation, let the head float back up to center. Take 2 or 3 mindful low-and-slow breaths at your RF or at 6 breaths per minute.

As you exhale, reach the left ear toward the left shoulder, and continue as you've done on the right side, stretching on the exhalations, pausing to notice and allow the inhalations. Allow your breath to coordinate with the movement.

As you inhale, allow the head to float back to the center. Take 2 or 3 mindful low-and-slow breaths at your RF or at 6 breaths per minute.

As you begin an exhalation, lean the torso over the hip to your right—lean as much as you'd like, a little or a lot. As you begin to inhale, lift back to the center, taking the whole inhalation to slowly move back to center. As you begin the next exhalation, lean over to your left. Continue this movement for at least three times on each side—as you exhale, lean over; as you inhale, float back to center. Synchronize your breath and the movement as closely as possible.

Allow your body to center itself. Take 2 or 3 mindful low-and-slow breaths. Notice the sensations in your muscles.

General Muscle Relaxation

Practice general muscle relaxation using traditional relaxation techniques, such as mindful progressive muscle relaxation, passive muscle relaxation, autogenic training, or guided imagery (see Appendix A for all). You can also practice mindful low-and-slow breathing (Chapter 2) to allow your muscles to relax. You can try each one of these and see which one(s) you like best. General relaxation training will allow you to mindfully release tension in all muscles, giving all your muscles a break. Tired muscles have a hard time releasing tension, so practicing longer relaxation skills will let those muscles rest and make it easier for them to release in the future. If you are using a biofeedback device, be sure to note the level of tension before and after practicing whichever relaxation skill you use. A mindfulness-based approach to relaxation is particularly helpful to adopt here. See Chapter 9 on mindfulness-based skills for more details. Pay specific attention to the "trying to relax" problem described there.

Muscle Deactivation Training

Once you've practiced general muscle relaxation skills and noticed improvement in levels of muscle tension after you practice, move on to targeted muscle deactivation training, which teaches you to quickly release tension in the muscle you've decided to train. If using an EMG biofeedback device, monitor initial tension level and tension level after release. Quick deactivation skills include three parts:

1. Postural adjustments, since muscle tension often results from unhelpful body posture. If you are using an EMG biofeedback device, experiment to see which postural adjustments help reduce muscle tension the most. See Table 4.2 for suggestions on postural adjustments.
2. Use gentle movement to relieve immobility and allow tension to release. See the previous section on muscle immobility for movement suggestions.
3. Use skills from the longer general muscle relaxation practices, described above, but performed over 30–60 seconds. See Table 4.3 for examples of quick skills you can use based on longer practices.

Once you've released muscle tension, pause for a moment and do it once more. Research shows that releasing twice, even if you feel that the first time was effective, produces further reduction in tension.

Down-Training During Activity

Muscle tension down-training during activity is helpful if you notice that your muscles tend to tense up during certain activities, such as typing, chewing, or washing dishes. With feedback, you will discover ways to reduce unnecessary activation of the muscle (dysponesis).

TABLE 4.2 POSTURAL AND POSITION CHANGES TO FACILITATE MUSCLE TENSION DEACTIVATION

Body part	Postural/position change
Shoulders	Drop the shoulders. Do not pull them back. You can imagine that someone attached a string to the top of your head and is gently pulling it up, so that the base of your skull is aligned with the spine, allowing the shoulders to drop.
Face	Close or half-close the eyes
	Tuck in your chin, so that it is not sticking out
	Part teeth, place tongue to the roof of the mouth
Arms	Drop arms on the lap
	Drop arms alongside the body
	Place elbows on armrest
Upper body (also useful for neck release)	Bend over at the waist, let your arms and upper body hang down. Make sure to release your neck and let it hang—do not use it to prop up the head.
Abdomen	Take some low-and-slow breaths, allowing your abdomen to gently expand on the breath in and gently deflate on the breath out.
Lower body	Put the feet up on a stool, with back supported.

Source: the author

TABLE 4.3 QUICK RELAXATION SKILLS BASED ON LONGER PRACTICES TO FACILITATE MUSCLE DEACTIVATION

Longer practice	Quick skill
Progressive muscle relaxation (Appendix A)	Tense and release target muscle or muscle group only, repeating a few times.
Autogenic training (Appendix A)	Visualizing body part containing target muscle, repeat to self, "My _____ is warm, comfortable, and relaxed."
Breathing (Chapter 2)	Take a few low-and-slow breaths, directing the breath toward the target muscle.
Visualization	Use the image you most associate with muscle relaxation to focus on and allow the muscle to relax.
Passive muscle relaxation (Appendix A)	Bring attention to the target muscle and allow the muscle to release.

Source: the author

If using an EMG biofeedback device, attach muscle tension sensors to the muscle of interest and note the initial tension. Without a device, rate your tension in your mind on the scale from 1 to 10, the way you did during awareness training. Then perform the activity, paying attention to posture, using less effort, and going slower than usual. Note the reduction in tension. Using less effort and going slower may often feel unfamiliar and therefore uncomfortable—you are so used to putting in more effort than necessary that using a more typical effort feels strange. Keep practicing, and you will get used to it. Your muscles will thank you.

Ergonomic Considerations

If you spend a significant amount of time working at the computer, and if you tend to experience muscle tension or pain during or after computer use, consider making changes to the ergonomics of your workstation. Many of us work in conditions that inevitably lead to muscle pain and tension because they place our bodies in suboptimal positions and encourage dysponesis. The guidelines I provide are based on those by Erik Peper and Katherine Gibney in their book *Muscle Biofeedback at the Computer*.[26] Also, see Figure 4.4 for an illustration of ergonomic positions while sitting and standing at your desk.

- *Arm position at the keyboard.* Your arms should be hanging straight down from the shoulder, bent at about a 90° angle at the elbow. You should not be reaching for the keyboard.
- *Forearms, wrists, and hand position at the keyboard.* Your forearms should be straight, wrists and hands straight or gently sloping downward (about 15° angle down), not bent upward at the wrist. If your keyboard has little legs that elevate the back portion of the keyboard, don't use them. The elevation of the back portion of the keyboard will force your wrist to bend upward, producing unnecessary tension.
- *Body position.* Your torso and head should be straight, shoulders down, chin tucked in. Do not lean forward or stick your head forward toward the monitor.
- *Back position.* Your back should be straight or slightly leaning back, supported at the lower back.

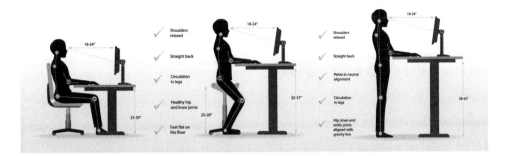

FIGURE 4.4: Ergonomic positions when sitting or standing at your desk   *Source: Shutterstock*

- *Leg position*. Your legs should be bent at 90° at the knees, not crossed. Thighs should be parallel to the floor, with sufficient space between the top of the legs and the bottom of the desk. Lower legs should be perpendicular to the floor.
- *Foot position*. Your feet should rest on the floor. If your feet do not reach the floor comfortably, use a foot rest—do not let your feet dangle in the air or rest on tiptoes.
- *Phone use*. Use a headset instead of pressing the phone to the ear with raised shoulder.
- *Vision issues*. If you need glasses, use them to prevent squinting. Use computer glasses instead of bifocals.
- *Computer screen position*. The screen should be at eye level, so that you are looking straight ahead.
- *Mouse position*. The mouse should be located centrally, so that you do not need to reach to the side for it.
- *Keyboard position*. The keyboard is best placed on an under-desk keyboard tray, not on the desk itself, if possible. The keyboard should be stable on the tray (or desk), not elevated by the little feet on the far corners of the keyboard.

Ergonomic aids, such as wrist rests, pen grips, and ergonomic mice and keyboards, may also be useful in facilitate biofeedback training.

CHAPTER 5

Temperature

Alex has been preparing for his final exam for weeks. He has mem-
orized all the formulas, gone through dozens of practice problems,
and reread the chapters he needed several times. And yet, as he was
standing in the hallway about to go into the classroom where his
physics exam was about to take place, Alex felt his hands getting
colder and his stomach tightening.

What Alex would learn, if he were to read this chapter, is that cold hands is one of the most common physiological responses to stress, part of the fight-or-flight response. This chapter discusses the foundations of finger temperature regulation as part of the fight-or-flight response, the role finger temperature plays in self-regulation and health, and biofeedback skills you can use to train finger temperature regulation.

Fight-or-Flight Response and Peripheral Temperature

The fight-or-flight response is an evolutionarily adaptive response that has enabled human beings to survive as a species. When your brain perceives danger, the fight-or-flight response kicks in, and your body starts preparing for running or fighting. In that process, along with your heart rate speeding up and your breathing becoming faster and deeper, your blood gets routed toward major organs and muscle groups most needed for running and fighting. This means that blood is going toward your heart, lungs, and muscles of the legs and upper arms. You don't really need your hands nearly as much as other parts of your body in order to run or fight, and therefore, blood vessels in your hands and fingers constrict, allowing more blood to go elsewhere. Moreover, your hands are the most likely to get injured in the event of a fight. Thus, limited blood flow to the hands decreases possible bleeding in the event of injury. This is another protective function of cold hands. The same thing often happens to feet, and people who get cold hands in response to stress often also have cold feet, and sometimes cold ears and noses as well.

In addition, when the fight-or-flight response is activated, your gastrointestinal (GI) system slows down or shuts down its function. The reason for this is the same: survival—a time when you are in physical danger is not a time to be digesting food. Your GI system shuts down in order for the most resources, including the blood supply, to go to organs vital for survival. This explains why cold hands and unpleasant sensations in your stomach often go together.

Chronically cold hands indicate chronic overactivation and dysregulation of the autonomic nervous system. Chronically cold hands are often associated with psychophysiological conditions like migraines, irritable bowel syndrome (IBS), Raynaud's disease (a condition in which fingers, toes, nose, and/or ears temporarily lose circulation), and high blood pressure. While cold hands are a normal part of the fight-or-flight activation, this response may be exaggerated and result in intensification of symptoms of these disorders.

Temperature Biofeedback

If you frequently experience cold hands, it may be an indication of autonomic nervous system dysregulation. Learning self-regulation strategies through temperature biofeedback will help deal with cold hands and, perhaps more important, with conditions associated with having cold hands. Temperature biofeedback involves learning to *allow* your finger temperature to rise. Notice that I did not say *make* your finger temperature rise. There is a good reason for that. It has to do with effort and stress activation.

The human mind forms strong associations with certain words. And often these words are associated with the way the body responds. Close your eyes for a moment and think of the word *jump*—do you feel your muscles tightening just a bit, as if preparing to jump? The same thing happens with words that suggest effort, words like *try* or *make* or *work*. These words are associated with physiological activation, preparing you for some kind of effort or action. When you exert effort, when you try to make your finger temperature go up, your body responds with sympathetic, or fight-or-flight, activation. Here is the problem: sympathetic activation constricts your blood vessels, as discussed in the beginning of this chapter. When you blood vessels constrict, your fingers become cold. This is the opposite of what you want.

But wait, it is even more complicated than that. Your blood vessels are innervated by sympathetic nerves only; there is no innervation from the parasympathetic or relaxation nervous system. This means that, in order for your blood vessels to dilate, it is not enough to relax—you have to actually turn down the sympathetic activation. The only way to do that is by letting go of any kind of effort. This means allowing or letting your finger temperature rise without effort on your part to do so.

How do you let your fingers warm up without effort? By letting go of struggle and attempts to control your finger temperature, while bringing mindful attention to your body. See Chapters 8 and 9 on mindfulness and mindfulness-based skills for a detailed description of what it means to be mindful and to let go of struggle and futile efforts to control.

If you have decided to include more than one biofeedback modality in your training, I suggest starting with something other than temperature. The reason is, again, effort. Temperature is the modality most vulnerable to effort. When you are new to something, you tend to exert effort in order to "get things right." In most cases, effort is exactly what's needed to acquire and excel at a new skill, but this is not the case with biofeedback in general, and temperature biofeedback in particular. Effort will get in the way of temperature training and will cause unnecessary frustration. Other biofeedback modalities are less vulnerable to effort. If you practice with another modality first, you may learn a new biofeedback skill that will be helpful in temperature biofeedback (such as breathing), while also giving yourself a chance to learn to let go of effort and control.

Temperature is the easiest biofeedback modality to find a device for. You just need a thermometer that can be taped to your finger or palm of your hand, or one that can be held. Please see Appendix B for a sample list of temperature biofeedback devices. Chocolate can also make for a fun temperature biofeedback "device" (see the side bar for details).

Temperature Training Skills

> **TRAINING WITH CHOCOLATE**
>
> If you prefer not to use a temperature device at all, you may follow a suggestion by Erik Peper, who recommends getting a small piece of chocolate and holding it between your thumb and index finger as an indicator of hand warming. Dark chocolate melts between 90°F and 93°F, while milk chocolate melts at a slightly lower temperature, between about 87°F and 90°F. If your hands are typically fairly warm, start with the dark chocolate. If your hands are typically rather cool, start with the milk chocolate and move up to dark chocolate as you get better at melting milk chocolate first.

Whichever device you choose, and whichever biofeedback skill you decide to practice, be sure to give yourself time—don't rush. Don't expect your finger temperature to go up very fast. If your hands are cold a lot of the time, allowing them to warm up will take a while. Initially, a change of 1°F is significant, so give yourself a pat on the back for that! Eventually, you finger temperature will increase to 95°F, which is your goal. Again, remember that effort will not help you get there. The idea is to focus on the biofeedback skill you are using, without looking at the thermometer or trying to figure out whether or not your finger temperature is going up.

Now, which biofeedback skill should you use? Before you look at the list of skills in the next section, take a moment to think of what you might do to allow your finger temperature to rise. Now grab your temperature device if you have one, or get a piece of chocolate, and see what happens when you do whatever comes to your mind as a way of allowing your finger temperature to rise. I strongly encourage you to do this before looking at the list I made. I always ask my patients to come up with their own idea first before giving them my suggestions. Very often my patients come up with something that is exactly what they need and would never have occurred to me. Go for it—take 2 or 3 minutes.

What happened when you used your idea for allowing your finger temperature to rise? Did the temperature change? Did it go up or down? Did you notice yourself trying to bring it up? Were you able to focus on your biofeedback skill and let the temperature rise on its own?

If your temperature rose even the tiniest bit, that's great—you now have a biofeedback skill you can use in the future. If you finger temperature did not rise or if it went down, don't despair—this is the outcome for most people at first.

Now take a look at the list of biofeedback skills. If your first skill was helpful, then you have more to add to your tool kit. If not, see what happens to your temperature when you use these skills:

- *Low-and-slow breathing.* An excellent way to allow your finger temperature to rise is low-and-slow breathing (see Chapter 2). It activates the parasympathetic (relaxation) nervous system and decrease activation of the sympathetic (stress) nervous system. This allows your blood vessels to dilate and temperature to rise. At the same time, low-and-slow breathing minimizes the chances of overbreathing (Chapter 2). If you were to overbreathe during this practice, your blood vessels would constrict due to the lack of nitric oxide, a neurotransmitter responsible for blood vessel dilation. When you breathe, allow your focus to gently rest on the sensations of your breath (see Appendix A for a script for mindful low-and-slow breathing) and not on what may or may not be happening to your finger temperature. Temperature will do whatever it is going to do, and you will be most successful when you allow it to rise on its own while you focus on your breath.
- *Image of warmth.* Close your eyes for a moment and think about warmth—see what image comes to mind. Let your own image come up first before you look at my suggestions:
  — A warm beach
  — Holding a hot cup of tea or hot cocoa
  — Sitting by the fire
  — Wrapping yourself in a warm blanket
  — Dipping into a warm bath or hot spring
  — Cuddling with a pet
  Once you've selected your image of warmth, allow your atten-

tion to focus on the image. Don't try to use the image as a way to increase your temperature. Just allow your mind to focus on the image itself and the experience it brings. Allow your finger temperature to do whatever it is going to do.

- *A sound you associate with warmth.* Again, close your eyes and see what sound comes to mind when you think of warmth. Once you've selected your sound, allow your attention to focus on that sound, and allow your finger temperature to do whatever it is going to do. Here are some suggestions:
  - A particular piece of music that evokes warmth
  - A lullaby from your childhood
  - The sound of jets in a hot tub
  - The sound of rain on the window, as you sit in front of a warm cozy fireplace
- *Sensations in your body as your fingers warm up.* An example would be the sensation of your muscles releasing and blood flowing down your arms toward your fingers. Again, allow your attention to focus on the sensations of warmth, and allow finger temperature to rise on its own.
- *Relaxation and meditation practices.* You can also use any relaxation or meditation practice in Appendix A. These are the ones I particularly like for temperature training:
  - Autogenic training
  - Beach imagery
  - Light meditation
  - Mettā practice (Chapter 10)

Here are a few general suggestions for practice, no matter which skill(s) you choose to use:

- Take note of your temperature before practicing your skill of choice, and don't look at your device again until you are done. Record your pre- and postpractice temperature.
- Remember that it may take a few practice times before your finger temperature goes up.
- For the first practice time, set your timer for 2 or 3 minutes.

- After that, increase the time to 5 minutes. Practice as many days of the week as possible for 5 minutes.
- After the first week, or when you are comfortable, start increasing the time until you reach 95°F within your practice time. Increase the time to 10 minutes each time for a week, then 15 minutes for another week, and finally 20 minutes. Don't practice for more than 20 minutes.
- Once you are able to reach 95°F at least 70 percent of the time, you can start reducing the time needed to get to 95°F. Eventually, you'll allow your finger temperature to rise in 1–2 minutes. This so-called speed training is useful in situations when you don't have more than a couple of minutes to increase your finger temperature, like Alex from the earlier example, who might use a quick warming skill to regulate his activation before going into an important exam.

CHAPTER 6

Skin Conductance

Let's do a simple exercise together for a few minutes. Below is a list of words—don't read them just yet. In fact, get a piece of paper and cover up the words. Then move the paper down, revealing one word at a time. As you read each word, say (out loud or silently to yourself) the first word that comes to mind in association with the printed word, and then spend 20 or 30 seconds observing how you feel. Then move on to the next word.

Mother
Car
Dog
Test
Scary
Friend

Did you notice any change in how you felt with any of the words? It is possible that you didn't, and that's OK. However, if you had been measuring your skin conductance, you would have seen a change in your physiological response to some of those words. This chapter discusses the concept of skin conductance, the way it relates to self-regulation, and ways you can measure it and use it to train self-regulation.

What Is Skin Conductance?

Skin conductance is a type of electrodermal activity measurement, also known as galvanic skin response, named after Luigi Galvani, an Italian scientist who famously discovered electrical nerve signals by making frog legs twitch. Skin conductance is an excellent marker of physiological and emotional activation. Carl Jung, a Swiss psychiatrist, psychoanalyst and close colleague of Sigmund Freud, was the first to utilize skin conductance (he called it galvanic skin response) in psychotherapy. Jung attached a galvanometer, a device that measures electrical activity, to his patients with finger electrodes and then presented them with a list of words and asked them to say the first word that came to mind in response (just like you did in the beginning of the chapter). The needle of the galvanometer moved each time the patients' physiological activation increased in response to an emotionally charged word.

To measure skin conductance, a tiny electrical current is passed through your skin, and the device measures the amount of electricity conducted by your skin. Don't worry, you don't get electrocuted—you don't notice the current at all.

Skin conductance depends on the amount of moisture produced by the sweat glands on your fingertips, palms of your hands, or soles of your feet. Fingertips are the typical place to measure skin conductance. As your body becomes more physiologically activated, either in response to an emotional stimulus or just because your physical activity increases, these sweat glands produce more moisture in the form of sweat. As your skin becomes moister, more electricity gets conducted, meaning that your skin conductance goes up.

So, if you were hooked up to a skin conductance sensor while doing the word association task in the beginning of this chapter, you would see the skin conductance go up whenever you came across an emotionally charged word. Skin conductance is a very sensitive measure: it goes up within seconds of physiological or emotional activation.

There are ways to use skin conductance in your own biofeedback training other than by having fun with word associations. Because skin conductance is a good measure of overall activation, it is particularly useful for the following:

- *Relaxation and recovery.* As you practice a relaxation or recovery skill, you can monitor your skin conductance to see your physiological activation decreasing.
- *Recognize your emotional reactions.* Monitoring your skin conductance when thinking or talking about important events in your life

can point you to particularly strong emotional reactions, of which you may or may not be aware. With this practice you can get to know the subconscious cues for what upsets or distresses you.

- *Demonstrate effects of meditation practice.* While the goal of meditation is not to relax, meditation practice does typically produce changes in your activation level, and skin conductance is an excellent way to observe them.
- *Notice effort during your temperature or other biofeedback skill practice.* As described in Chapter 5, allowing your fingers to warm up without effort is crucial to mastering the skill. Monitoring your skin conductance levels while focusing on your temperature skills will help you to notice and reduce effort.
- *Reducing activation intensity.* Monitoring your skin conductance levels may allow you to reduce the intensity of unhelpful activation, such as might happen from trying to get rid of stress or anxiety, or when simply feeling agitated. See the section below on biofeedback training skills for how to practice.

Skin Conductance Biofeedback Training Skills

The following is a list of biofeedback skills you can choose to reduce overall physiological activation and therefore bring down skin conductance

- *Mindfulness practice* is a helpful way to start skin conductance training. (See Chapter 8 for detailed explanations of mindfulness and meditation practice.) Briefly, mindfulness practices teach you to become aware of your thoughts and feelings without fighting with them and without getting stuck in them. Mindfulness allows you to respond to your thoughts and feelings in the most helpful way—giving up attempts to control the uncontrollable, disengaging from the content of your thoughts without following them to the worst possible scenarios, and responding to the presence of difficult thoughts and feelings with kindness. Three exercises particularly fitting to skin conductance training are the thoughts-on-leaves meditation, difficult emotion practice, and mindfulness of thoughts, feelings, and physiological sensations exercise (see Appendix A for scripts, or download recordings at www.innakhazan.com/meditation_recordings.html). However, you may use any other mindfulness practice that appeals to you.

- *Mindful low-and-slow breathing* (Chapter 2) activates the parasympathetic (relaxation) nervous system and is therefore almost always helpful in reducing physiological arousal, including bringing down skin conductance. Reducing skin conductance with low-and-slow breathing is particularly helpful for a quick recovery break, between meetings, or as a break from challenging activities of the day.
- *Any relaxation practice*, such as guided imagery, passive muscle relaxation, or autogenic training (see Appendix A for scripts, or download recordings at www.innakhazan.com/meditation_recordings.html), when practiced mindfully is a nice way to reduce skin conductance and give yourself a much needed recovery break.

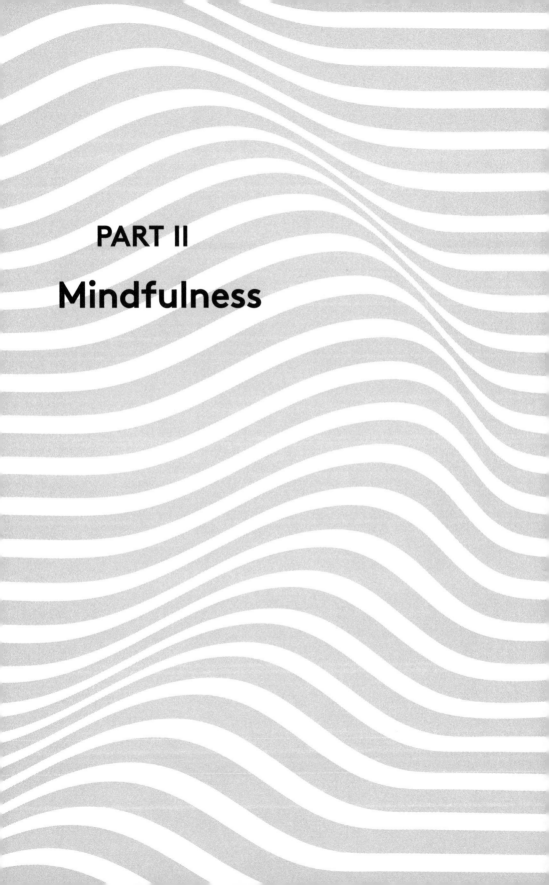

PART II

Mindfulness

CHAPTER 7

Foundations of Mindfulness

George left the doctor's office feeling dejected. His blood pressure was high for the third visit in a row. No wonder: he had been stressed out at work, he wasn't getting along with his wife, and he wasn't sleeping well. His doctor was insisting on giving him medication to reduce blood pressure. George kept trying to figure out something else he could do. His doctor suggested that mindfulness meditation may be helpful in reducing his stress and anxiety. George has heard a lot about mindfulness himself and had tried meditation in the past. The problem was that he just couldn't do it—his mind kept wandering off every few seconds, and he could not keep it still no matter how hard to tried to focus. It was too hard, and he felt kind of funny just sitting there doing nothing.

The word *mindfulness* has garnered a lot of attention and has become quite the buzz word. Many books have been written on the topic of mindfulness. I do not attempt to cover in a few chapters what many wise practitioners and researchers have written volumes on. Instead, I review some of the basics that will be most helpful to you in getting started with the practice of mindfulness, and I cover topics most relevant to self-regulation and resilience. Specifically, this chapter addresses the definition of mindfulness and the research demonstrating its effects on your brain, body, and ability to improve functioning, some myths and concerns people often have about mindfulness, as well as reasons for mind wandering, one of the most common complaints people have about meditation. Chapters 8 and 9 address the practical aspects of mindfulness: mindfulness meditation and mindfulness-based skills you can use in everyday life.

Defining Mindfulness

There are many definitions of *mindfulness*, all coming down to some version of being in the present moment, allowing it to be just as it is while letting go of judgment. My favorite definition is by Christopher Germer of Harvard Medical School. He describes mindfulness as "preverbal awareness of the present moment with acceptance." As I discuss in more detail in Chapter 11 on stress, the preverbal awareness aspect of mindfulness is particularly important. *Preverbal awareness* refers to the sensory experience you have before you can put that experience into words.

Let's try something together: In a moment, put the book down and bring your attention to the fingers of your right hand—just feel your fingers. Next wiggle your fingers gently for a few moments and attend to the sensation in your fingers. Don't try to label or describe the experience with words; just feel the sensations of your fingers wiggling and allow those sensations to be just as they are. Now put the book down and try it. . . . That's mindfulness. Simple, right? It actually is. Being mindful has only a few requirements: being present, accepting, and nonjudgmental of the experience. And yet, something so simple can give rise to a significant improvement in your life, your health, and your performance.

Before I talk about how to practice mindfulness, let me first talk about why you should practice mindfulness. I find that it is a lot easier to find dedicated time for new practices when people buy into the reason they are being asked to do so.

Research on Mindfulness

Mindfulness itself is a tradition dating back thousands of years, first as part of Hindu religious practices, and then as a major part of Buddhist traditions two and half thousand years ago. Mindfulness has remained a major part of many Eastern traditions and practices ever since. The modern concept of mindfulness, the way we know it now, was brought to the West and popularized by Jon Kabat-Zinn, a scientist at the University of Massachusetts Medical School, in the 1970s. Initially, there was a lot of resistance to the integration of mindfulness into our medical system and into ordinary people's lives. Many people considered it to be too touchy-feely, too new-agey, too passive, and so on. You might have some of those doubts yourself. I discuss and try to alleviate some of those doubts in the section on myths and concerns later in this chapter. Kabat-Zinn set up the first research program investigating the effects of mindfulness of people's health. Since then, research on mindfulness has blossomed, and we now know a lot more about the effects of mindfulness on people's brains, bodies, health, and performance. This means that mindfulness is no longer mainly a religious practice but is also a scientifically based intervention.

Some of the most remarkable research on mindfulness has looked at the effects of mindfulness on the brain. For example, Sara Lazar, Britta Hölzel, and their team at the Massachusetts General Hospital have conducted several brain imaging studies looking at the changes in people's brains after mindfulness meditation training.[27] For many of these studies, the researchers invited people to participate in mindfulness-based stress reduction (MBSR) training, a program pioneered and initially studied by Jon Kabat-Zinn. MBSR program is an 8-week course consisting of weekly 2.5-hour meetings and one day-long retreat, along with daily home practice. During the program, participants learn various kinds of meditation techniques, such as the body scan, mindful movement, and sitting meditation. Extensive research has documented efficacy of MBSR in reducing pain, anxiety, and depression.[28]

In Sara Lazar's lab, people who had never done any kind of meditation and were interested in taking part in the MBSR program had their brains scanned with functional magnetic resonance imaging (fMRI). This technique shows structure and functional activity of the brain, providing detailed images of different parts of the brain and showing how active each part of the brain is at the time of the scan. After the brain scans, half of the participants went on to take part in the MBSR program for 8 weeks, and half were placed on a waiting list, to take part in the program after the study was over. The MBSR group was the experimental group, and the wait-listed group was the control group. Both groups returned to have their brains scanned after 8 weeks, to track any brain changes that may have occurred.

Results of multiple studies showed that after 8 weeks, brains of people who took part in the MBSR program and practiced mindfulness showed both structural and functional changes. Some parts of the brain became larger—they actually increased the amount of gray matter! Other parts of the brain became smaller, and others became more active. Here is a summary of the brain changes in participants' brains showed after 8 weeks of mindfulness meditation training, reported in several published studies:

- Increased gray matter concentration and higher activation in
  - Hippocampus, part of the brain responsible for learning, memory, and emotion regulation
  - Right insula, responsible for body awareness, empathy, and perspective taking
  - Temporoparietal junction, responsible for conscious experience of the self, social cognition, and compassion
  - Posterior cingulate cortex, responsible for integration of self-referential stimuli
  - Lateral cerebellum and cerebellar vermis, responsible for emotional and cognitive regulation: speed, capacity, consistency, and appropriateness of cognitive and emotional processes
- Increased activation in the anterior cingulate cortex, responsible for regulation of attention and behavioral control
- Decreased gray matter in the right amygdala, responsible for fear and anxiety

Here's an interesting twist: the right amygdala is responsible for the immediate, automatic, often overly intense response to potential danger. This is the part of the brain that gives you the most trouble when you are worried or anxious. The left amygdala is responsible for a more measured response to potential danger. It is only the right amygdala that decreases in size with mindfulness meditation training. The left amygdala stays the same. This explains in part why mindfulness meditation is associated with an increased ability to think through the most helpful response to stress, rather than going with the automatic, unhelpful one.

Since these original studies, many more have been conducted examining the effects of mindfulness meditation on the brain. In 2016, Rinske Gotink and her team at Erasmus University Medical Center in the Netherlands conducted a meta-analysis of brain imaging studies investigating the effect of mindfulness practice on the brain.[29] Meta-analytic studies are designed to review data from all existing studies on a particular intervention and determine whether collectively the data shows the intervention to be effective. While not all research findings are consistent, and some methodological issues need to be addressed in future studies, some of the findings were consistent and robust. This meta-analysis confirmed increased activation of the insula, hippocampus, and anterior cingulate cortex, along with decreased activation of the amygdala, after 8 weeks of mindfulness training. The authors also reported increased activation of the prefrontal cortex and increased connectivity between the prefrontal cortex and the amygdala, an important part of emotion regulation.

In summary, these studies show that mindfulness meditation training changes your brain in ways that are conducive to positive changes in your life. After as little as 8 weeks of consistent practice (participants in the MBSR studies meditated an average of 27 minutes a day), your brain will likely become better at being able to pay attention, making decisions, learning and remembering, regulating emotion, recognizing how other people feel, experiencing compassion, and responding to stress in more helpful ways. Of course, the more you practice, the more changes you experience. And you need to continue practicing to retain the benefits. If you stop meditation, the positive effects will eventually disappear.

Other studies have also shown that long-term meditation practice is likely to help our brains age better. For example, Sara Lazar looked at the images of brains of people of different ages who had practiced meditation regularly for several years and compared them to brain images of similarly aged people who had not meditated at all.[30] She found, that with age, people with no meditation practice were more likely to experience a decrease in the thickness of the brain cortex, the area where a lot of our cognitive function takes place. This finding was not new—other research has shown that our cortical thickness tends to decrease with age. What was new, though, was the finding that long-term meditators experienced no such decrease—the thickness of their cortex remained the same. While this study is correlational, and therefore cannot prove that meditation produced these changes, it does point to the possibility that regular meditation practice protects against the effects of aging on our brains. Since then, other studies have contributed further evidence for the protective effect of meditation against aging related declines in functioning.[31]

In addition to MBSR, many more mindfulness-based interventions have been created and tested in the last 40 years. These interventions include Acceptance and Commitment therapy (ACT), Mindfulness-Based Cognitive

Therapy (MBCT), Dialectical Behavioral Therapy (DBT), among many others. A large body of research has examined the effectiveness of the various mindfulness-based interventions on people's physical and mental health and overall well-being.

In order to be able to conclude that an intervention is effective for a particular issue or disorder, multiple studies need to show similar effects. Meta-analytic studies have shown that mindfulness-based interventions are effective in improving overall quality of life, as well as decreasing pain, depression, and anxiety and positively affecting sleep and weight loss.[32] In addition, mindfulness-based interventions have a positive impact on physiological markers of well-being, such as reduced cortisol (a stress hormone), C-reactive protein (an indicator of inflammation in the body), blood pressure, heart rate, triglycerides (a type of lipid that stores unused calories in your body, which in excess contributes to heart disease), and increased immune response.[33]

Keep in mind that, when an intervention has been shown to be effective, it does not mean that it is a cure. It only means that the intervention produces a helpful change. Some of the changes reported are fairly large (such as reduction in anxiety and depression), and some of the changes are small or medium (such as for pain). This is important to keep in mind in order to manage your expectations about the utility of mindfulness in your own life.

Myths and Concerns About Mindfulness Meditation

The popularity of mindfulness is based on a solid body of research that supports the use of mindfulness to improve health and performance and enrich lives. At the same time, many myths perpetuate in our society about mindfulness, including myths that overstate effectiveness of mindfulness as a treatment. Many people have concerns about mindfulness practices as too touchy-feely or new agey. This section addresses these myths and concerns about mindfulness and mindfulness meditation.

Mindfulness Is Not a Cure for Everything

As any popular and effective treatment, mindfulness has been misused, and its effectiveness has been overstated. It is not a cure for everything, and, in fact, it is not a cure at all. Mindfulness is a practice that is often effective in improving people's health, performance, and quality of life.

Several investigations have focused on identifying areas of intervention where the research supporting the use of mindfulness is solid. These investigations support mindfulness as an effective intervention for a limited number of disorders, including anxiety, depression, and pain. Research is also convincing on the underlying neurological mechanisms of mindfulness. These mechanisms provide a solid foundation for ways in which mindfulness helps improve general health, well-being, and performance. (See previous section on research for a more detailed review.)

In summary, mindfulness is a powerful and effective intervention in many areas of human life, but it is not a cure for all ailments, and it does not replace other medical or psychological interventions.

Some People Fear It Is Too Hard

This is one of the most common concerns people have about mindfulness, much like George did in the earlier example. I often hear from my clients that they have tried mindfulness meditation but that it was too hard. When we talk about what they mean by *too hard*, it usually turns out that they mean their mind wanders off a lot and that it feels difficult to keep their mind still and focused for long periods of time. The good news is that mind wandering is a completely normal and expected experience. Novice meditators often find that their minds wander off within the first minute of their meditation, and they may not even realize that this has happened until the bell sounds to end the meditation.

Human minds are not built for staying still. Meditation teachers often compare the human mind to a monkey that jumps from tree to tree and does not spend much time sitting still. When you begin your mindfulness practice, expect that your mind will wander off, more than once. The only thing you need to do is to gently return your attention back to your anchor (discussed in more detail in the next chapter). It does not matter whether your mind wanders off 5 times, or 20 times, or 100 times. As soon as you notice that your mind has wandered off, gently bring it back, and repeat as many times as necessary.

With practice, your mind will wander less, you will notice sooner when your mind wanders off, and it will become easier to bring it back. If you have a particularly had time with staying focused, it may be easier to start with

WALKING MEDITATION

Walking meditation is particularly well-suited for being outside in nature, but you can practice it anywhere, including indoors. Choose your walking path, allow yourself to settle into your body before moving, take a few low and slow breaths at your resonance frequency or 6 breaths per minute. Observe your surroundings: what do you see, what do you hear, what do you smell? Observe your feet, feel them firmly planted on the ground, safe and secure. Allow your arms and hands to rest comfortably by your sides or clasp your hands in front or behind your back. Now slowly lift one of your feet off the ground, attend to the sensations of the foot and leg moving through space and coming back down, the foot planting on the ground firmly and securely. Feel your weight shifting as you get ready to lift the other foot. Feel the other foot and leg moving through space, and coming back down, with the foot planting on the group firmly and securely. Continue taking small comfortable steps, going slowly, attending to all the sensations of walking, and allowing these sensations to stay as they are. Notice the temptation to hurry or take large steps, and let it go. When your mind wanders away from the movement of your body, notice where the mind has been, and gently bring it back to the sensations of walking, with kindness. Once you've reached the end of your chosen path, pause for a few moments, take a few low and slow breaths, take note of your surroundings. Then bring your attention back to your feet and legs, and walk back in the same mindful way, fully present and grounded.

meditation practices that involve movement, such as walking meditation (see sidebar), or a yoga meditation described in Chapter 4 or mindful progressive muscle relaxation exercise included in Appendix A.

When you decide on how to start your meditation practice, using the guide in the next chapter, keep this in mind.

What If I Can't Empty My Mind?

Many people believe that meditation requires emptying your mind of thought. Most people find that they can't do that. The good news is that you don't have to. Mindfulness is about developing a different way of relating and responding to your thoughts, not about getting rid of them. Instead, you practice noticing your thoughts and letting them come and go without engaging with them during your meditation.

Mindfulness Isn't the Same as Relaxation Exercises

Many stress reduction books and websites list meditation among relaxation techniques. However, relaxation is not the goal of meditation, although it is a frequent side effect. The goal of meditation is to be in the moment. Being present is often, but certainly not always, relaxing. Meditation produces different effects on your mind and body than relaxation exercises and is therefore not the same thing. This does not mean that you should not practice relaxation. Relaxation exercises play an important role in your health and well-being. They are just not the same as meditation. In fact, a study by Gunes Sevinc, Sara Lazar, and their team revealed that both meditation and relaxation practices have beneficial effects but influence the brain in different ways.[34]

What If I Am Not Religious Enough?

There are many ways to practice mindfulness. Some people choose to practice as part of their religious tradition, and others choose to practice in completely secular ways. I describe mindfulness practice from a secular standpoint. There is no requirement to believe in God or to be religious.

It's Not Just for Weaklings

Mindfulness practice encourages looking at some of your most difficult and unpleasant emotions, including fear, sadness, guilt, and shame. It requires courage and willingness to face those tough experiences and is therefore far from a pastime for "weaklings."

The Default Mode Network: Why the Mind Wanders

Think about the last time you listened to a radio show, a podcast, or a lecture, or just a friend telling a story. Were you focused the whole time, or did your mind wander off sometimes? If you said yes to mind wandering, you are among the great majority of people. Our human minds wander a lot. Harvard psychologists Matthew Killingsworth and Daniel Gilbert set out to find out exactly how much minds wander and whether it affects how happy we feel.[35] The researchers developed an iPhone app that pinged over 2,000 participants at random times of day to ask them the following questions:

1. "How are you feeling right now?" Participants rated their level of happiness on the scale from 0 (most unhappy) to 100 (most happy).
2. "What are you doing right now?" Participants selected an activity from a list of possible choices.
3. "Are you thinking about something other than what you are currently doing?" Possible answers were no, I am thinking about what I am currently doing; yes, thinking about something pleasant; yes, thinking about something neutral; and yes, thinking about something unpleasant.

The results of the study showed that people are distracted 47 percent of the time—almost half the time! This may not be terribly surprising to you—you know your mind wanders quite a bit. The good news is that it is the same for other people, too. It may not even be very surprising that people feel happier when they are focused on what they are doing than when they are not. What may be surprising, though, is that participants were happier focusing even on unpleasant activities than thinking about something pleasant while engaging in those unpleasant activities. So, it is likely that, if you dislike washing dishes, for example, you are still better off mindfully washing those dishes than you are washing dishes while daydreaming about a beach vacation (assuming you like the idea of a beach vacation).

The researchers concluded from this study that the particular activities people engaged in throughout the day did not matter very much to their happiness, but whether or not people were mindful and present while doing them mattered a lot. The more present they were, they happier they felt. The more their minds wandered, the more unhappy they felt. And their data analyses suggested that mind wandering was generally the cause, not the result, of unhappiness.

The reason for mind wandering and the consequential decrease in happiness is a particular mode of operation our minds get into when not actively engaged in a task. As soon as our minds begin to wander, the so-called default mode network (DMN) kicks in. Marcus Raichle, a neurologist at Washington University, discovered the DMN by chance in 2001 while investigating brain activity during active problem solving.[36] Raichle and his team scanned participants' brains while they were engaged in a focused task. In between tasks, when participants rested quietly with eyes closed, the researchers expected to see a general decrease in their brains' activity, but that is not what happened: once the participants' minds were no longer focused on the task, their brain activity did not decrease, but it did change. While the participants were engaged in the problem-solving activity, the prefrontal cortex in the front of the brain was most active. Once participants were no longer actively engaged on a task, a series of structures along the midline of the brain from front to back came online. These structures are what Raichle came to call the default mode network.

In the years that followed this discovery, we have learned a lot about the origins and function of the DMN, although a lot still remains to be discovered. The DMN is active when the mind it at rest and when the mind wanders. The DMN is inactive when the mind is focused and engaged in a task, such as solving a problem, interacting with other people, playing at instrument, reading, or meditating.

At rest, as the DMN is activated, our minds tend to drift to one of three places:

- Reviewing autobiographical memories, often remembering and replaying events or problems from the past
- Envisioning the future, often anticipating problems that may occur
- Exploring the self for problems that need to be fixed, and comparing self to others

You might notice that all of the places where our minds wander have to do with ourselves. The DMN is *self-referential*, meaning that it tends to bring our attention to thoughts somehow related to ourselves. Most of the time these thoughts point us to various problems, whether it is regretting our actions in the past, worrying about making mistakes in the future, or figuring out various ways in which we are not as good as someone else we know in the present. These are also the thoughts that we often struggle with in periods of heightened depression or anxiety. In fact, increased activation of the DMN is correlated with clinical diagnoses of depression and anxiety disorders.

The natural question that arises is why we would have a whole area of the brain devoted to making us depressed and anxious. Scientists believe that this is not the purpose of the DMN but, rather, its side effect. There are two hypotheses about the intended function of the DMN. The first is the *sentinel hypothesis*, which proposes the DMN to be an evolutionarily adaptive protective mechanism that supports low-level global focus of attention. In other words, the DMN continuously monitors the external world for unexpected events and alerts us to potential dangers. The second is the *internal mentation hypothesis*, which describes multiple internal processes of our brains that involve the DMN:

- Ability to successfully retrieve memories
- Ability to interpret our own and other people's thoughts and emotions, understanding that other people's experiences are different from ours—what we call *theory of mind*.
- Creativity—the daydreaming quality of the unfocused attention common to DMN activity, is necessary for creativity in any field, whether in art, music, writing, or science
- Moral decision making, involved in our ability to make decisions based on our core beliefs and values

Therefore, the DMN does not exist in order to torture you. Its activation is vital to other important areas of your functioning. Sometimes, activation of the DMN is necessary and adaptive, and other times it leads to unhelpful consequences. You can learn to recognize when your experience may be due to the unhelpful activation of the DMN and reduce its activation.

You would know that your DMN is activated if you find yourself stuck in one of the unhelpful modes of its activity:

- Reviewing events or problems from the past or regretting past action or inaction

- Anticipating or worrying about problems that may occur in the future
- Thinking about ways in which you may not be good enough, particularly in comparison to other people, in the present

Once you identify activation of the DMN, the way to reduce its activity, and therefore the unhelpful consequences of its activation, is to bring your mind to a focused state. You could do that by bringing your attention to whatever activity you were doing before your mind wandered off, or by directing your attention to an activity that requires focused attention, such as solving a puzzle or reading. Mindfulness practices, discussed in more detailed in Chapter 8, particularly concentration practices, are helpful in refocusing your attention and decreasing activation of the DMN.

Mindfulness Meditation

Jason is a thirty-one-year-old software engineer who has always described himself as a "little on edge." He has a hard time settling down after a long day, sometimes has trouble sleeping, and does not always know how to relax. Jason's therapist suggested that he try mindfulness meditation to help him settle his mind. Jason downloaded a meditation app and sat down to meditate. He practiced focusing on his breathing, but for some reason that left him feeling more on edge. He switched to an emotion-based practice, which brought up memories of being in a car accident and having difficulty breathing. That didn't feel good. Jason didn't know what he was doing wrong. The idea of meditation seemed great; he just could not figure out how to get it to work for him.

There are different ways to practice mindfulness. You can practice mindfulness meditation, and you can practice mindfulness-based skills. These are two different kinds of practices. If you feel that the practice of meditation is just not for you, you don't have to meditate—you could still derive the benefit of mindfulness-based skills described in the Chapter 9. Or, you can practice meditation and forgo mindfulness-based skills. You can also choose to practice both and derive maximum benefit. In this chapter and the next I discuss meditation and mindfulness-based skills—you choose what works best for you. This chapter focuses on the practice of mindfulness meditation. I discuss different types of mindfulness meditation and different ways to practice it. I also provide suggestions for starting and deepening your meditation practice and for fitting meditation into your everyday life. I address challenges that might come up during meditation practice and ways to combine meditation and biofeedback.

Ways to Practice

Mindfulness meditation is an intentional practice of being in the present moment, observing nonjudgmentally, maintaining relaxed attention. Mindfulness meditation may be practiced in three ways:

MINDFUL SHOWER

Mindful shower is a great way to start or end your day and a great way to build mindfulness practice into it. You probably take a shower most days, and typically you are doing nothing else while in the shower—both of these criteria make showering a great candidate for informal meditation practice.

When you get into the shower, give yourself a few moments to feel the sensation of warm water on your skin, noticing the temperature of the water and the sensations of the stream of water hitting the skin.

Allow your mind to return to the sensation of the water whenever it wanders off.

Then bring your attention to the sound of the water. Just listen.

Bring your attention to the smell of the soap or shampoo. Stay with it, gently retuning your mind back whenever it wanders off.

Mindfully attend to the rest of the shower experience in the same way.

- *Informal practice.* Informal practice does not require setting aside specific time for meditation. Instead, it involves mindfully doing something you are already doing. Informal practice is a great way to start your mindfulness habit and often solves the problem of being too busy. Your schedule may be packed on most days, but you probably have some activities that you habitually engage in most days of the week. Your informal practice would involve doing those activities mindfully. For example, you might take a mindful shower, brush your teeth mindfully, drink your morning cup of coffee mindfully, eat a piece of chocolate mindfully, or take a mindful walk to work. The exact activity is not very important, as long as it is not something excessively challenging—you probably don't want to begin your mindfulness practice when you are in the middle of a stressful situation. Once you have some practice under your belt, bringing mindful attention to stressful situations will be much easier to do. Take a moment now and think about which informal practice or practices you might want to start with.

- *Formal practice.* Formal meditation practice means that you have set aside some time to meditate, doing nothing else at the same time. How much time depends on you. If you are first starting out, you might dedicate 5 or 10 minutes for a meditation. As you have more experience, you might sit for 20 minutes, maybe even 30, 40 minutes, or more. Formal meditation practice typically consists of one or more of the components outlined in the next section.

- *Intensive retreat practice.* Meditation retreats are a great way to deepen your practice but may not be a good choice for beginners, unless the retreat is specifically geared for beginners. Retreats are often multiday, silent, intense meditation practices, where the whole day is spent in meditation—you take mindful walks, you eat mindfully, and you sit in formal meditation.

Types of Mindfulness Meditation

Mindfulness meditation consists of three components, each of which can be practiced independently or can be combined as part of one practice: concentration or focused attention practice, open monitoring or open awareness practice, and compassion or self-compassion practice.

HERE-AND-NOW STONE

One of my favorite concentration practices is the here-and-now stone, which I learned from Christopher Germer.[37] I have a bowl full of colorful stones in my office that I often give to my clients to practice with. You may use any stone you wish—a pebble you picked up from the ground, a small gardening stone, a mineral gemstone you can buy at a souvenir shop or online. Once you have your stone (or two, if you like, one for each hand), let yourself settle in comfortably in your seat, or stand in an upright but relaxed posture. Close your eyes, and allow yourself to explore the stone with your fingers. Examine its texture—notice the smooth portions, and the rough ones. Notice temperature changing from cool to warm as the stone picks up the warmth of your hands. Notice the way the stone's shape feels in your fingers. Just let yourself stay with the sensations of the stone in your hands, allowing the sensations to be just as they are, gently bringing your mind back whenever it wanders off.

Concentration or Focused Attention Practice

In this type of meditation, you find an anchor for your attention and allow your attention to gently focus on that anchor. The anchor may be a single object or experience—your cup of coffee, your breath, sounds around you, or the sensations in your body as you walk. See Appendix A for meditation scripts, or for recordings go to www.innakhazan.com/meditation_recordings.html.

The choice of object of attention matters. External objects, like sounds around you, your cup of coffee, or a smooth stone, are often easier for novice meditators because they provide a bit of distance and psychological safety. Focusing on an external object allows you to practice a new skill of mindful concentration without immediately diving into difficult experiences. As your practice develops and you become more comfortable with the skill itself, you may feel ready to move on to internally focused objects, such as your breath.

The practice itself is simple. Here are the steps :

1. Choose an object or sensation of focus or anchor for your attention, such as your cup of coffee, a piece of chocolate, a smooth stone, or your breath.
2. Allow your attention to gently settle on that object or sensation.
3. Notice when you mind wanders off (and it will do so, often!).
4. Gently bring your mind back to your anchor.

5. Let go of judgment you might have experienced when you noticed
    your mind wandering.

Concentration practices often bring down the intensity of difficult emotions and bring calm to a charged situation. Therefore, these practices are excellent when you are feeling overwhelmed, when emotional activation seems to be getting in the way of clear thinking, when it is hard to make a decision in the middle of emotional chaos.

Concentration practices also train stability and flexibility of attention, making them ideal to start your meditation journey, before moving on to open awareness practices, where the skill of stable yet flexible attention will be quite helpful. In addition, more stable and flexible attention is also useful in everyday life, when working, studying, having a conversation, or listening to a lecture.

Concentration practices train your ability to recognize and accept distracting events as fleeting and momentary. This skill is useful both in future meditation practice and in everyday life. As you strengthen your ability to recognize the frequent extraneous activity of your brain as momentary and fleeting, you will become better able to disengage from these distractions without getting stuck and without beating up on yourself for being distracted. Distractions are inevitable; getting stuck in them is not.

Open Monitoring or Open Awareness Practice

Open monitoring or open awareness means that you are attending to whatever predominates in your awareness, moment to moment—sights, sounds, thoughts, feelings, physical sensations, and so forth.

Open awareness practices help cultivate insight and equanimity. You get to know yourself and your inner workings better through meditation. You also train the ability to stay calm and focused in stressful and chaotic situations. This ability strengthens through meditation because you learn to experience current cognitive, emotional, or sensory events without evaluating or interpreting these events. This means that you are less likely to get caught up in the meaning of your thoughts or the potential consequences of the physical sensations you experience.

Moreover, through open awareness meditation you learn to allow your thoughts, feelings, and sensations to be the way they are at that moment, as you make mindful changes to the way you respond to those sensations. That is, instead of getting caught up in your experience, you take a step back and decide how to respond. This choice of response is key to a better outcome.

Here are the steps to open awareness practice:

1. Find an anchor for your attention, such as your breath or a smooth stone. Allow your attention to gently settle on the anchoring object or sensation.
2. When you are ready, open up your awareness from the anchor to whatever arises.
3. Let thoughts, feelings, physical sensations, sounds, fragrances, and other experiences come and go.
4. Bring your mind back to your anchor when you notice it has wandered off.
5. Let go of whatever judgment may have arisen when your mind wandered off.
6. Remember that the goal is just to be, nothing else.

Open awareness practices that call for attention to thoughts and feelings may be initially challenging because thoughts and feelings are intangible, and the idea of observing them and letting them go may seem too abstract. If that is your experience, I suggest the field of vision exercise as a great primer to an open awareness practice:

1. Find a place to sit comfortably either inside or outside, someplace where you have a good view of activity in front of you. There may be people walking by, cars driving, birds flying, and so on. A park bench on a nice day or a window overlooking a busy street are great options.
2. Once you pick your spot, sit quietly and observe activity in front of you, looking straight ahead only.
3. Allow your attention to fall on a moving object, and follow the movement of that object with your eyes only, up until the edge of your field of vision.

4. Once the object is out of your field of vision, allow it to go; do not follow the object by turning your head.

5. Bring your attention to another moving object within your field of vision, repeating steps 3 and 4 as long as you feel comfortable.

This is similar to observing your thoughts, feelings, and physical sensations without engaging with them. You will notice yourself turning your head to follow moving objects quite frequently, especially when you first begin your practice. This is akin to your mind latching on to a thought and following it during a meditation practice. When this happens, just notice that you've turned your head to follow the object, and then gently bring it back to face forward and attend to a new object, just to the edge of your field of vision. This is just like what you would do when your mind wanders off during meditation—you notice where your mind has been, and gently bring it back to your anchor.

Here are some other examples of open awareness meditations:

- Mindfulness of body sensations (body awareness or "body scan")
- Mindfulness of thoughts, feelings, and physiological sensations
- Mindfulness of emotion in the body
- Thoughts on leaves

See Appendix A for scripts of these practices, or for recordings go to www.innakhazan.com/meditation_recordings.html. Keep in mind that guided open awareness practices using recordings are not, strictly speaking, open awareness because your awareness is being guided by the recording. This is something to be aware of, and it is still OK to use the recordings. When you are new to meditation practice, having a recording to guide you is often quite helpful and may make the difference between practicing and not. As you get more practice and feel more comfortable, you may do at least some of your practices without a recording, paying attention to whatever predominates in your awareness in the moment.

Compassion or Self-Compassion Practice

There is a lot to be said about compassion and self-compassion. I devote Chapter 10 to this very important practice. This section briefly describes the way in which compassion and self-compassion fit into a regular meditation practice. Please refer to Chapter 10 for a more detailed discussion.

There are two ways to practice compassion or self-compassion in meditation. One is to do a compassion-focused meditation such as the Mettā (loving kindness; Chapter 10), difficult emotion practice (Appendix A), or tonglen (Appendix A; recordings for all at www.innakhazan.com/meditation_recordings.html). The other is to incorporate elements of self-compassion into your concentration and open awareness practices, such as kindness in response to your mind wandering off and in response to judgments that often come during the practice, and a gentle tone of the self-talk that inevitably occurs during your practice. Both of these elements of self-compassion mean bringing curiosity, kindness, and acceptance to the inevitable thoughts, judgments, and other wanderings of your mind during meditation—it is normal for your human mind to wander. A kind response to mind wandering may look something like this: notice that your mind has wandered, gently acknowledge where it's been, and kindly guide it back to your anchor.

The goal of compassion and self-compassion practices is to bring good will, kindness, and comfort to yourself and your relationship to other people. These practices do not make problems or pain go away but, rather, bring comfort when you are feeling bad. This is similar to when someone brings you chicken soup when you have the flu—the soup will not cure the flu, but you will feel comforted.

Where Do You Start?

If you are new to meditation, follow the steps in this section to begin and deepen your practice. If you already have an established meditation practice, you can use the guidance in this section to see how you might deepen your practice.

When you are new to meditation, I recommend starting with a concentration practice, then moving to an open awareness practice, and then incorporating compassion practice. In addition to deciding whether to practice formally or informally, and whether to choose a concentration, open awareness, or compassion practice, you have more choices to make regarding posture and object of attention. Below I discuss each of these choices.

Posture

There are two issues to consider when choosing a posture: comfort and open-ness. Meditating in an uncomfortable posture may turn into a frustrating experience. At the same time, meditating in a scrunched up or crossed position may leave you closed off from the full experience of the moment. You may begin your meditation practice lying down or reclining, with your arms and legs uncrossed. You may also choose to do a movement-oriented practice, such as walking meditation (Chapter 7) or yoga meditation (Chapter 4), particularly if it is hard for you to lie or sit still. The more traditional meditation posture consists of the following elements:

1. Choose a sitting position—you may sit cross-legged on the floor or meditation cushion, or you may sit on a chair with a straight back, possibly with a small pillow to support your lower back, legs uncrossed and planted on the floor.

2. Elongate your spine and drop your shoulders—you might imagine a string attached to the top of your head. As the string is pulled, your head and spine straighten and elongate, while your shoulders gently drop down, without pulling back.

3. Allow your hands to rest on your lap or at your sides.

4. Tuck your chin in toward your chest, and release the jaw, allowing the mouth to stay closed, with the top and bottom teeth not touch-ing each other. You may place your tongue to the roof of the mouth, behind, but not touching, the top teeth to facilitate a more relaxed position.

5. Allow your eyes to close fully or partially. Closing your eyes may ini-tially feel unsettling. If that happens, allow your gaze to turn down-ward and gently focus on a spot a few feet in front of you. A soft focus will minimize distraction.

Object of Attention

When choosing an anchor for your attention in meditation, whether as a main focus of the concentration practice or as an anchor to return to in an open awareness or compassion practice, you can choose an external or an internal object. External objects are those outside of yourself, such as sights and sounds of nature, taste of food, or sound of a bell. Internal objects are, as you might have already guessed, those inside of you. Internal object of attention may be your thoughts or emotions, or physiological and body sensations, such as your breath, your heartbeat, or the sensations in the soles of your feet. Among body sensations, you might choose sensations in distal body parts, such as your hands and feet, or more centrally located sensations, such as your breath, your heartbeat, or sensations in your chest or belly.

As you begin your practice, it is often easiest to start with an external focus for your attention—such as a stone (see the here-and-now stone meditation earlier in this chapter), a cup of coffee, a piece of your favorite food, observing nature, or listening to sounds around you. External objects are easier to focus on and are less likely to produce discomfort. If you tend to feel anxious when focusing on internal sensations, if you've experienced panic attacks or have trauma in your background, it is definitely a good idea to start with an externally focused concentration practice. See Appendix A for externally focused concentration practices, or for recordings go to www.innakhazan.com/meditation_recordings.html.

Once you are comfortable with an externally anchored practice, move on to an internally focused concentration practice, starting with distal body parts (such as soles of your feet) as an anchor, and then moving on to more centrally located sensations, such as mindfulness of the breath (see Appendix A for a script, or for recordings go to www.innakhazan.com/meditation_recordings .html).

Focus on "safe" objects—those that are comfortable for you—before you focus on objects that make you uncomfortable, or "sharp" objects. Safe objects are a good way to cultivate stability of attention, improve emotion regulation, and pave the way for attending to more difficult internal processes. Safe objects may be external (smooth stone, sounds, etc.) or internal (walking meditation, for example, if it is not associated with pain or emotional distress). Sharp objects are often internal, associated with difficult thoughts and emotions. For Jason, in the example at the beginning of the chapter, the breath and memories of being trapped in a car having difficulty breathing are sharp objects. He needed to establish a safe meditation practice without focusing on his breath before being able to gradually bring his attention to the sensations of the breath.

Take a moment now to think about your safe objects and your sharp objects. Which focus would feel safe and comfortable to you? Which focus may come with distress or discomfort? Moving from safe to sharp objects should be done gradually, and in some circumstances (such as with experiences of severe anxiety and/or trauma) is best done with the help of a psychotherapist.

In summary, if you are new to meditation, begin with:

- Sitting, reclining, or lying down comfortably
- Concentration practice
- External object of attention
- Focusing on safe objects

As you become more familiar and comfortable with meditation, move on to:

- More traditional sitting meditation posture
- Open awareness and compassion practices
- Internal object of attention
- Gradually bringing attention to sharp objects

As with any skill, meditators experience challenges during their practice. I briefly review a few most common ones you are likely to encounter:

- Your mind will wander off during any meditation practice—that's a guarantee. It is natural for your mind to wander. The point of your meditation practice is not to keep your mind 100 percent still but, rather, to notice when it wanders off and gently bring it back to your anchor. Once you become aware of your mind wandering, make a conscious decision to gently bring your mind back to your anchor, with kindness.
- It is easy to get caught up in a particular goal for your meditation, whether it is to decrease anxiety or pain, get really good at meditation, keep your focus on your anchor, or any of the other numerous goals. Getting caught up in a particular goal takes you out of the moment and turns your meditation experience into chasing a particular experience. If you notice yourself doing this, first of all, rest

assured, it is normal! Most meditators have had this experience. Give yourself a break, be kind and gentle with yourself. Second, refocus your attention on the present moment and the process of your meditation, allowing yourself to let go of the goal.

- Meditation may not feel relaxing. Contrary to popular belief, meditation is not a relaxation exercise. Relaxation is often a side effect of meditation, but it is not the goal and not a requirement. Meditation is a way of being in the moment, not an exercise in achieving a particular outcome.

Fitting Meditation Into Your Life

I hope that at this point you are convinced that mindfulness meditation is a useful and healthy addition to your everyday life. At the same time, you may feel overwhelmed at the thought of fitting yet another thing into your day. You may have heard that you are supposed to meditate for 40–60 minutes each day. But how are you supposed to fit that into your life?

The most important part of bringing meditation into your life is to make your goals realistic. If 40 minutes a day is not something you can realistically fit into your day, then it is not a helpful goal to have. Start with 5 or 10 minutes a day. If your days are extremely packed, start with an informal practice, bringing mindfulness to something you already do every day—a shower, brushing your teeth, your morning cup of coffee, or a walk to work (even if the walk is from the parking lot to your office). This is a great place to start. Once informal mindfulness practice becomes familiar and perhaps even habitual (give it a couple of weeks), move on to setting aside 5 or 10 minutes for formal meditation, starting with a concentration practice. Once you are able to do 10 minutes, extend that time to 15 minutes for another week or two, and then extend to 20 minutes. You could remain at 20 minutes of practice most days of the week. If you feel that you have a bit more time in your day, extend to 30 or 40 minutes.

In addition to these formal and informal practices, you can incorporate moments of mindfulness into your life. The famous Buddhist monk, author, and mindfulness teacher Thich Nhat Kahn suggests small ways of being mindful:

- *E-mail meditation.* Take a few mindful breaths before hitting the send button, and/or pay attention to the movement of your arm as you hit the send button.
- *Traffic jam meditation.* Being stuck in traffic is often a frustrating experience. Yet getting stuck in that frustration will not change traffic patterns and will make your experience all that much more difficult. A mini-meditation break will give you an opportunity to practice and will allow you to not make the experience any more difficult. To practice traffic jam meditation, bring your awareness to your breath, then to the sensations of your hands on the steering wheel, your back against the back of the seat, your foot on the pedal. You could just stay there, or expand to what you see and hear around you—the taillights of cars in front of you, the sea of cars all around, sound of car horns and other people's frustration. Allow your experience to be just as it is.
- *Telephone meditation.* Even though we don't communicate through phone calls nearly as much as we used to, on the occasion that your phone rings, let yourself listen mindfully to the ring tone for a few moments before picking up the call. If you are the one making the call, mindfully listen to the sound on the other end before the person picks up.
- *Waiting in line meditation.* Similarly to traffic jam when you are waiting in line, you don't have control over how fast or slowly the line moves, or how long each person takes to do whatever is needed. Allow yourself to attend, with kindness and acceptance, to your internal sensations, such as your breath or sensations of your body standing upright, and/or to the people around you, just observing, letting go of judgment and evaluation.
- *Washing hands meditation.* Given that this is something you do several times a day, mindful hand washing is a wonderful way to bring mindful moments into your day. Each time you wash your hands, bring your attention to the sound of the running water, the smell of the soap, the sensation of water on your hands, and the feel of the towel or hand dryer.
- *Smiling meditation.* Thich Nhat Kahn calls this "yoga for the mouth." Allow yourself to put a half smile on your face. Do not force a big fake clown smile, just allow the corners of your mouth to rise gently. Notice

the physical sensations of your face smiling, and then notice the emotional components of the smile—how does your mind feel?

Combining Meditation and Biofeedback

There are several ways to bring biofeedback and mindfulness together. I discuss mindfulness elements in biofeedback practice in Chapter 9 on mindfulness-based skills. Here I describe ways to include biofeedback into your mindfulness meditation practice. This may be done with using biofeedback devices or simply by following psychophysiological principles underlying biofeedback.

- The most effective way to bring biofeedback skills into your meditation practice is to use both at the same time. Practice biofeedback skills first, incorporating mindfulness-based skills as described in Chapter 9. Then bring these biofeedback skills into your mindfulness meditation.
  - To incorporate breathing training (Chapter 2), begin your meditation practice with mindful low-and-slow breathing, and use the breath as your anchor throughout the practice.
  - To incorporate HRV training (Chapter 3), begin your meditation with mindful low-and-slow breathing at your resonance frequency or at 6 breaths per minute, and use the breath as your anchor throughout the practice.
  - To incorporate muscle health practices (Chapter 4), review your posture and body position before the meditation practice, returning your attention to your muscles throughout the practice.
  - To incorporate finger temperature practice (Chapter 5), bring your image or sound of warmth into your meditation practice.
  - To incorporate skin conductance practices (Chapter 6), since mindful breathing is the most effective way to reduce skin conductance, incorporate a mindful low-and-slow breathing component into your meditation practice.
- If you use a biofeedback device, use it together with meditation to give yourself a real-time reflection of the physiological changes taking place while you meditate. Psychophysiological monitoring with a bio-

feedback device, whether it measures HRV, muscle tension, breathing, finger temperature, or skin conductance, will allow you to assess effectiveness of your practice. For example, an increase in HRV as a result of your meditation practice (both during each sitting and as an overall trend longer term) lets you know that your ability to self-regulate is increasing. If your muscle tension decreases during meditation, you know that you are learning to give your muscles a break and are producing less unnecessary effort during your meditation practice. If your temperature increases and/or your skin conductance decreases during your meditation practice, you know that are you learning to decrease unnecessary activation and reduce effort.

- If you are having trouble with meditation, psychophysiological monitoring with a biofeedback device may let you know what is interfering with your meditation practice. Low or nonincreasing HRV may indicate that you would benefit from priming your meditation practice with resonance frequency breathing (see Chapter 2) to improve self-regulation. An increasing breathing rate may signal potential over-breathing and overactivation. Revisit Chapter 2 on breathing for tips on reducing or eliminating overbreathing. An increase in muscle tension and/or skin conductance and/or a decrease in finger temperature may indicate bracing, unnecessary effort, and overactivation. Use your device in combination with tips on regulating these physiological parameters in Chapters 4, 5, and 6 to reduce effort and activation.

- If you do not use a biofeedback device, you could simply incorporate psychophysiological principles discussed in Chapters 1–6 of this book to augment and enhance your meditation practice. Here are some ways of doing this:
  — Begin your meditation practice with mindful low-and-slow breathing, and use this breathing as your anchor throughout the practice. You could bring your breathing rate to 6 breaths per minute in order to include elements of HRV training.
  — Review your posture and body position before the meditation practice and release your muscles before and throughout the practice.
  — Incorporate your image or sound of warmth into your imagery-based meditation practice.

Safety in Meditation and Possible Side Effects

While generally quite safe, mindfulness meditation can come with unintended side effects. Most of them are mild and can be corrected with a few changes, which I discuss in this section. However, in rare cases it is possible to experience more serious side effects that will likely require professional intervention. I discuss what those effects may be and how to recognize and address them.

Breathing Changes

It is natural for your breathing to change when you meditate. Just the process of bringing awareness to your breath will likely slow down the rate of your breathing. In addition, many people believe that they are supposed to breathe deeply during meditation. Purposefully deepening your breath increases the volume of air you take in. Recall from the discussion in Chapter 2 on breathing that deep breaths that are not slow enough, particularly without a slow enough exhalation, can easily lead to overbreathing and hypocapnia (lack of carbon dioxide), which interferes with distribution of oxygen. As a result, you may feel lightheaded, dizzy, short of breath, tingly, or nauseous. This was Jason's experience from the earlier example. These symptoms are quite unpleasant, but also quite common.

If you experience symptoms like these during meditation, small changes to your breathing pattern will likely enable you to return to comfortable meditation experience. The goal of these breathing changes is to bring back balance between the rate and size of your breath consistent with a resting physiological state. To do this, practice low-and-slow breathing (see Chapter 2 for details): a normal-size comfortable inhalation, followed by a long, slow, complete exhalation. Breathe in through your nose and out through your nose, or out through pursed lips (as if blowing out a candle), until your lungs feel comfortably empty. It may help to hold a 2- to 3-second pause between the end of the exhalation and the beginning of the next inhalation.

Hidden Emotions

Meditation is all about increased awareness and brings with it increased awareness of your emotional states. Mindfulness helps you form a healthier relationship with your emotions. However, increased awareness may also bring up emotions that you have long stayed away from, such as grief, fear, or shame. For Jason, it was the fear he experienced while being trapped in his car after the crash. If you've worked hard to keep those emotions hidden, sudden awareness of them can feel overwhelming. If that happens, don't just stop the meditation. Rather, bring your attention to your anchor, and stay with a focused awareness practice until the intensity of the emotion decreases. Remember that focused awareness activates the prefrontal cortex of your brain and helps reduce activation of the amygdala, the fight-or-flight center of your brain responsible for the overwhelming emotional state.

Once you feel calmer, take note of the thoughts and emotions that came up during the meditation, allow yourself to return to them later, when you are ready, and then end the meditation. When you are willing to return to the strong emotion, go slowly, and bring kindness and compassion to your practice. Difficult emotion practice in Appendix A could be very helpful here. You may also use other self-compassion practices like Mettā (Chapter 10) to aid your experience. Please be sure to read Chapter 10 on compassion, and refer to Chapters 13 and 18 on anxiety and shame. You may seek the help of a therapist to help you process the strong emotions that come up.

Focused Attention on Painful Sensations

When pain comes up during a meditation experience, you may initially feel an increase in pain, because mindfulness brings greater awareness to your experience. As I discuss in more detail in Chapter 16 on pain, research shows that mindfulness meditation may be associated with *increased* activity in the *sensory* part of the brain responsible for pain but *decreased* activity in the *evaluative* part of the brain, the one that interprets the signals of pain as "terrible." Therefore, longer-term mindfulness practice decreases the suffering caused by pain. However, the initial increase in the experience on pain sensations may be difficult.

If this happens for you, bring your attention to your anchor, reducing activity of the amygdala, and allow the sensations to subside. Be sure to review Chapter 16 on pain and Chapter 10 on compassion, and practice mindful awareness of pain and difficult emotion practice in Appendix A.

Dark Night Phenomenon

Willoughby Britton of Brown University was one of the first to name and study this rare yet difficult side effect of meditation.[38] The dark night phenomenon comes with extreme experiences such as abnormal changes in one's cognitive, perceptual, and sensory experiences, changes in sense of self, and impairment in social relationships. These extreme adverse reactions are not common (but not so rare as to be discounted!) and are more likely to follow prolonged periods of meditation, such as several days or weeks on a silent retreat. If you experience anything that seems extremely disturbing and lasting longer than a few hours, be sure to seek professional help.

CHAPTER 9

Mindfulness-Based Skills

Michelle was on her way to a job interview. She was laid off from her previous job three months ago and has been applying for new jobs tirelessly since then. She finally got an interview for a job that sounded really good. Michelle prepared the best way she could. She got up early that day, gave herself plenty of time to get ready, poured herself a travel mug of coffee, and left the house with more than enough time to get to the interview. She parked, realized that she was 30 minutes early, and decided to stay in the car until time got closer to the interview time. As she was sitting there, Michelle worried about how the interview would go. She worried about how she would explain being laid off, worried that her interviewer would think she wasn't good at her job and got fired. She got more and more anxious, her chest tightened, and her breathing was short and ragged. Realizing that she was getting anxious, Michelle tried to stop thinking about what could go wrong in the interview, tried to stop feeling so anxious. The more she tried to stop thinking about it, the more those thoughts swirled around in her mind, and the more anxious she felt. Michelle tried to breathe deeply to stop the anxiety, but that only made her feel worse. As her mind raced from one scenario to the next, Michelle considered turning around and going home, convinced that she wasn't going to get the job anyway.

Whenever we find ourselves in an unpleasant or difficult situation, feeling scared or sad, uncertain or guilty, we turn to our habitual automatic ways of responding to those experiences. Often, we try to change how we feel, push away unpleasant thoughts, stop feeling difficult feelings, get rid of our pain. And, like Michelle, we often find ourselves firmly stuck in the difficult experience instead. This happens because our habitual go-to ways of responding are not actually helpful and contribute to us getting stuck in the experience rather than helping us get out of it.

This chapter discusses a different way of responding to difficult thoughts, feelings, and experiences, a way that allows you to move on rather than continue getting stuck. Specifically, I describe a collection of mindfulness-based skills designed for moments of high challenge or distress, enabling you to respond to the challenge or distress in the most helpful way. These mindfulness-based skills not only will help you navigate many challenging situations but also may be helpful in developing a more mindful attitude toward life in general.

Mindfulness-based skills can be practiced in the moment of the high challenge or distress, but of course, as with any new skill, when you first learn the skill, it is best to practice in neutral conditions before taking the skill into a challenging environment. Just like when you first learn CPR (cardiopulmonary resuscitation), you want to practice on a dummy before doing CPR on a person having a heart attack in front of you. Or when you first learn a new piano piece, you want to practice on your own before performing in front of an audience.

Mindfulness-Based Skills for Everyday Life

This section offers eight mindfulness-based skills that will help you navigate challenging situations in everyday life and steps to practice and develop these skills. In later sections in this chapter I offer ways to combine these skills for navigating challenging situations and discuss how to apply these skills to your biofeedback practice.

Giving Up Futile Efforts to Control

As human beings, we have a strong need to have a sense of control over our life. That's a very helpful instinct. Research shows that we live better when we have a sense of control over our environment and over what happens to us. People with a stronger sense of control over their lives tend to have better overall physical health, less pain, and quicker recovery from illness.[39] They also tend to have better emotional health, with less anxiety and depression.[40] Our sense of control comes from ability to make choices about what we do on a day-to-day basis—what we eat, what we wear, what movies we watch—and the ability to succeed in our endeavors through conscious effort and to determine the direction of our lives.

At the same time, a lot of things in life are out of our control. For many of us, a sense of control is so important that we will often create an illusion of control over things that we have no control over at all. Ellen Langer, a psychologist at Yale and then Harvard Universities, was the first to discuss and define the term *illusion of control* as expecting a likelihood of personal success that is inappropriately higher than objective probability would indicate. Langer conducted a series of studies showing that people tend to exercise control in situations where they have none. For example, when playing the lottery, people believe that their chances of winning improve if they pick their lottery tickets as opposed to playing a ticket randomly given to them.[41] These findings have been replicated numerous times. Jennifer Whitson from the University of Texas, Austin and Adam Galinsky from Northwestern University showed that when people lack control they tend to try to impose it to uncontrollable situations, such as seeing patterns in situations where none exist.[42]

Given our need for sense of control, when we find ourselves in a situation where the events themselves are out of our control, we attempt to control our thoughts and feelings about it. This is what happened with Michelle, in the earlier example, who tried to control her thoughts about the interview when the outcome of the interview was out of her control.

Unfortunately, our thoughts and emotions are also outside of our control. Try this with me: Give yourself a minute, stay where you are now, and in that minute do your best to not think about a white bear. . . . What happened? If you are like most people, you had a few white bears running around in your mind. Daniel Wegner, a professor of psychology at Harvard University, demonstrated this in the 1980s.[43] He asked one group of undergraduates to spend 5 minutes not thinking about the white bear and another group to spend 5 minutes focusing their thoughts on the white bear. You won't be surprised to hear that the group instructed not to think about the white bear had the most thoughts about the white bear. Similar studies have been done with suppressing thoughts about vehicles and green rabbits.[44] Regardless of what it is you are trying not to think about, the result is the same: the harder you try not to, the more you think about it.

If you think about your experience with unwanted thoughts, these findings make sense, right? You can't just stop thinking about something. And yet folk wisdom tells us that we should be able to do that. How often do you hear the suggestion to just stop thinking about something? It is a mistaken belief that we should be able to have control of our thoughts that perpetuates this well-meaning but unhelpful advice. Most people don't have a lot of luck making unwanted thoughts go away but continue thinking that they should. The result is that they don't accomplish their goal and feel bad about themselves for not being able to do it. A 1993 study by Delia Cioffi and James Holloway of Dartmouth College showed that, after unsuccessful attempts to suppress unwanted thoughts, people have lower feelings of self-efficacy, meaning they don't have much faith in their ability to succeed.[45]

You won't be surprised to hear that attempts to suppress emotional content are just as unsuccessful in the long term. You may be able to distract yourself or suppress your emotions for a short period of time. However, research shows that habitual attempts to suppress emotions actually lead to increased experience of negative emotions over time.

OK, so we cannot banish unwanted thoughts and emotions. But is there any harm in trying? Turns out there is—here's why. Attempts to get rid of certain thoughts and emotions fall under the category of self-control, which is actually a very helpful thing, just like our desire to have control over our environment and what happens to us. Self-control helps us make better decisions, solve problems, focus our attention, prevent us from acting on unhelpful impulses, stay away from committing crime, quit smoking, consume less alcohol, stick with our exercise routines, and make healthy food choices, among many other benefits.[46]

However, exercising self-control uses up resources. If we choose to exercise self-control in one area of functioning, we take some of those resources away from another area. If we exercise self-control in an area where we have no control (thoughts and feelings), we reduce our ability to control what is under our control (actions). Social psychologist Roy Baumeister of Florida State University conducted a study in which he asked four groups of students to watch a movie clip.[47] Two of the groups watched a clip from a comedy with Robin Williams, and the other two groups watched a clip from the movie *Terms of Endearment* showing a young mother, played by Debra Winger, dying of cancer and saying goodbye to her young children. One of the groups watching each of the movie clips was asked to do their best to control and suppress their emotional reaction to the movie, while the other group was instructed to allow their emotions to be as they are. After the movie clips, all participants were asked to solve a difficult anagram. The results of this study showed that participants who tried to control and suppress their emotional experience, regardless of whether they watched the funny or the sad movie clip, performed significantly worse on the anagram task than participants allowed to have their emotional experience as it was. Baumeister hypothesized that these effects were due to depletion of a vital energy source, which is wasted on attempts to control emotional experience.

HEART RATE VARIABILITY AND EMOTION SUPPRESSION

In 2017, Endre Visted and his colleagues at the University of Bergen in Norway showed that difficulty in emotion regulation is associated with lower heart rate variability (HRV). The found that inability to accept negative emotions, exemplified by attempts to suppress or avoid them, showed the strongest association with low HRV.[48]

On the other hand, two studies by Natalie Tuck at the University of Auckland, New Zealand, and her team showed that ability to express emotion is associated with higher baseline HRV.[49]

These studies further illustrate the importance of allowing our emotions to be as they are.

A few years later, Matthew Gailliot and Roy Baumeister, working at Florida State University, investigated the nature of this vital energy source that gets depleted with attempts to control our emotional experience, as well as with other acts of self-control.[50] In one of their studies, once again four groups of participants watched one of two video clips: a video from a slaughter house and a video of the comedian Jay Leno. One of the groups watching each of the movies was asked to control and suppress any emotional reactions they had to the videos. Participants' blood glucose was measured before and after they viewed the video clip. After watching, participants were asked to complete an impossible tracing task, which required them to trace a figure without lifting the pen from the paper. The results of the study showed that "emotional suppression" group had glucose levels significantly lower than their own baseline glucose levels and lower than the group's that did not suppress their emotions during the video—and those with lower blood sugar levels gave up sooner on the impossible tracing task.

Why are these findings important? Glucose is the basic fuel our bodies and brains use to derive energy. If you haven't eaten for a while and your blood sugar levels are low, you are likely to feel tired and sluggish and have trouble focusing on any task. This happens because your body is deprived of the fuel it needs to function properly. Your brain, which takes up about 2 percent of your body mass, consumes about 20 percent of the calories you take in, making it the greatest consumer of glucose. When you deplete your glucose stores by attempting to control your thoughts and emotions, you deplete the limited stores of fuel that could otherwise be directed toward other tasks, such as solving difficult puzzles, performing various tasks at home or at work, making decisions, or choosing a helpful response to difficult thoughts and emotions—futile attempts to control your thoughts and emotions deprive you of the fuel you need to respond to these thoughts and emotions in the most helpful way. You use up glucose on tasks that are not under your control, namely, suppressing your difficult thoughts and emotions, and then you do not have adequate resources left to exercise control over tasks that are otherwise controllable: your actions in response to these difficult thoughts and feelings.

CONTROL AND BIOFEEDBACK

When people think about the goal of biofeedback, very often the very first idea that comes to mind is using biofeedback to control pain, or anxiety, or some other experience. However, biofeedback does not give you any more control over those experiences than attempts to control your thoughts or feelings. When you attempt to use biofeedback to control your anxiety or pain, you become that much more likely to end up in a futile struggle.

In addition, trying to control your physiology through biofeedback leaves you stuck in the same struggle. Take temperature as an example: Biofeedback skills allow your fingers to warm up by dilating blood vessels in your hands and fingers—as more warm blood flows through, your finger temperature rises. Your blood vessel diameter is determined by the nerves of the sympathetic (stress) nervous system only. There are no parasympathetic (relaxation) nerves innervating your blood vessels. When your sympathetic nervous system is activated, blood vessels constrict and finger temperature goes down (for details, see Chapter 5). That means that when you try to control your finger temperature, when you try to make it go up, you activate the sympathetic nervous system, your blood vessels constrict, and your finger temperature goes down—you achieve a result opposite of what you intended.

Similar result happens with effortful breathing: when you exert effort to breathe, you activate the sympathetic nervous system and increase your chances of overbreathing (see Chapter 2 on breathing).

What do you do instead of trying to control your experience through biofeedback?

- Use biofeedback skills as a way to respond to difficult experiences, not as a way to control them or make them go away. For example, practice low-and-slow breathing as a response to anxiety in order to balance your respiratory chemistry, not to control anxiety or make it go away.
- Allow your body to produce the physiological changes you are looking for rather than trying to make them happen. For example, allow your finger temperature to rise as you focus on your image of warmth, instead of trying to make your temperature go up.

You *can* control your actions—you have the ability to choose your actions in response to your thoughts and emotions. And it is this choice that is so incredibly important, because it allows you to direct your resources to what is actually possible. Instead of using up your resources on futile efforts to control the uncontrollable, you can make a choice and direct your resources to efforts that are healthy and meaningful and will bring you closer to your desired goals.

Getting Unstuck

When you attempt to get rid of unwanted thoughts and emotions, you engage in a futile struggle. The more you struggle to do the impossible, the more stuck you get.

One of my favorite metaphors is from acceptance and commitment therapy (ACT): seeing the futile struggle with our thoughts and emotions as quicksand. You are probably familiar with quicksand—it is sand so saturated with water that it forms a thick liquid, with little friction between sand particles, and is unable to support much weight. When you step into quicksand, it becomes more liquid and gives in, and you sink in. Of course, your first instinct when you sink into quicksand is to struggle, to try to pull your legs out, perhaps thrash and flail. As you thrash and flail, the sand and water mixture becomes even more liquid, and you sink in farther. When you pull one of your legs out, you reduce the surface area of your body in contact with quicksand, thereby increasing the pressure on the quicksand, and sinking farther. The struggle keeps you stuck. The only way to get out of quicksand is not to struggle but, rather, to slowly lie down on the quicksand. Slow, gentle movements do not disturb and liquefy quicksand as much, and lying down increases the surface area of your body in contact with the quicksand, distributing your body weight more evenly and decreasing the pressure. This prevents you from sinking. Quicksand is denser than water—once you are lying down on it, it is easy to float, just like it is easier to float in saltwater than in freshwater, since saltwater is denser than freshwater. Once you are floating, you can slowly paddle or be pulled to safety.

Until I came across this metaphor and did some research, I always thought that quicksand was very dangerous and that people drown in quicksand all the time—at least that is how the books and movies that feature quicksand have portrayed it. Just think about the scene in *The Princess Bride* when the princess is sucked under by quicksand, or the scene in *Lawrence of Arabia* when a young man is sucked under by quicksand in the desert. Scary as those scenes may be, it turns out that the dangers of quicksand are quite exaggerated. Quicksand is rarely more than a couple of feet deep, so most people would not drown in it. The real danger of quicksand is not drowning but, rather, getting stuck and not being able to get out. Being stuck in quicksand leaves you vulnerable to lack of food and water, exposure to heat or cold, and hungry white bears. Most people think like I used to, that quicksand is dangerous. If you are like most, if you were to stumble into quicksand, you would struggle to get out. And of course, the more you struggle to get out, the more stuck you get. Allowing yourself to open up to the quicksand, no matter how unpleasant it may be, is the only way to get out and move on.

The situation is very similar when it comes to difficult and painful thoughts, emotions, and physiological sensations. When you experience them, your habitual automatic reaction is to try to get out, get rid of them, make them go away. And the more you try to make them go away, the more persistent they become and the more stuck you get. Many people also believe that difficult emotions, usually called "negative" emotions, are somehow bad for us and our health. This is very much a myth. The so-called negative emotions do not endanger your health, nor are they actually negative. As you read more in chapters devoted to such emotions (anxiety, stress, sadness), you'll learn just how important, normal, and human these emotions are. These emotions are indeed difficult to have, but it is not bad for you to experience them. Getting stuck in these emotions is what is actually bad for you, just like quicksand. Getting stuck in difficult emotions prevents you from being present in other experiences, prevents you from being able to see the full picture of your life and from being able to fully participate in it, and makes the suffering created by the difficult emotions a lot worse.

In addition, getting stuck in difficult emotions may lead them to become chronic. You've probably heard or read about research linking things like chronic anxiety, depression, or anger to poor physical health, heart disease, and early death. The key word here is *chronic*. Research does indeed link chronic stress, anxiety, depression, and anger to negative health outcomes. When difficult emotions first present themselves in your awareness, they are not dangerous. But if you see them as bad for you, if you struggle to get rid or get away from them, you are likely to get stuck. The more you struggle, the more stuck you get, and the more likely these emotions are to become chronic and affect your health.

The solution, then, just like with quicksand, is to open up to the difficult experience in the moment, be fully present with it, let go of the struggle, "float" through it, and be able to move on. Mindfulness practice allows you to open up to the difficult experiences of your life in a way that also allows you to move on with your life.

Change of Intention

You might be wondering what you need to do to give up the futile struggle to control the uncontrollable and get unstuck. The purpose of this book is to give you plentiful skills to allow you to choose helpful responses to difficult experiences without futile efforts to control and unnecessary struggles. The intention for using those skills is as important as the skills themselves. If your intention is to get rid of certain thoughts or emotions, or to change the way you feel right at that moment, you are likely to continue getting stuck. Any skill you employ has to be used with the intention of choosing a healthy and helpful response to the difficult experience, with the focus on what is most important in that moment and which response is in your best interest.

For instance, if you are using your breathing skills to make anxiety go away before a big exam, you are likely going to get caught up in the anxiety—your focus will be not on the breath but on the futile effort to make the anxiety go away. As a result, your breathing skills may actually turn into overbreathing, exacerbating the anxiety, making it that much more difficult to focus on the exam, and leading to even more distress. This is what happened to Michelle when she tried to use deep breathing to stop anxiety.

If, on the other hand, you change your intention from making the anxiety go away to allowing anxiety to simply be, while you focus on what's most important in that moment, and use your breathing skills as a way of bringing balance to your physiology, your experience of anxiety will change, and you will be able to move on. With a focus on your breath, without struggling with anxiety, you will enable yourself to turn your attention to the exam and use all your resources for the exam, rather than wasting them on futile efforts to control anxiety.

A change of intention could turn a totally unhelpful skill into a very helpful one. For example, an attempt to make yourself feel less sad by watching a funny show may not work, but a choice to watch a funny show as a way of treating yourself with kindness when you feel sad (while allowing the sadness to be) could help you feel comforted.

When it comes to biofeedback, your intention in using biofeedback skills will likely influence the result of your practice. If you are attempting to use biofeedback to control your thoughts or feelings, to make anxiety, anger, or pain go away, you are likely to fail and get stuck in a struggle. If you use your biofeedback skills as a way of responding to the anxiety, anger, pain, or any other difficult experience, you are much more likely to succeed.

As you use the skills from this book, or other skills that you believe may be helpful, pay attention to the intention of the skill—are you using it to make unwanted experience go away, or are you using it as a helpful response to the difficult experience?

Here are some examples of helpful intentions for whatever skills you may choose to use:

- Take care of yourself at the time of distress or suffering
- Restore balance to blood chemistry
- Restore balance to the nervous system
- Improve self-regulation
- Allow your mind to refocus on the present moment
- Bring comfort when you feel bad

Mindful Language

Along with change of intention, mindful language is key to facilitating a helpful response to a difficult experience. The way you talk yourself through choosing a response can make the difference between calming the amygdala and overactivating the fight-or-flight response. Your mind and body form strong associations with certain words and learn to respond to these words in very specific ways.

Words like *try*, *must*, *make*, *should*, and *work* are associated with effort. So, when effort is what you are looking for, these words are exactly what you need. When, on the other hand, you want to take time to release effort and recover, these words are not helpful, even when used in conjunction with words like *relax*.

TRYING TO RELAX IS AN OXYMORON

"Try to relax" is a very common phrase—you've probably used it yourself many times. Most of us have had the experience of trying to relax. Let's look at what happens physiologically when you try to relax. Trying involves activity of the sympathetic nervous system, the branch of your autonomic nervous system associated with physiological activation.

Relaxation involves activation of the parasympathetic nervous system, the branch of your autonomic nervous system associated with relaxation and recovery. Your mind and body have learned that when you say *try*, the appropriate response is *effort*: physiological or mental activation. But then, you follow the instruction to "try" with an instruction to "relax." You are instructing your body to do something that is physiologically impossible, namely, to activate sympathetic and parasympathetic branches of your nervous system at the same time. In a healthy nervous system, these two branches cannot be dominant at the same time, which is what would be required according to the instruction "try to relax." If you want to let your body and mind recover, then words like *allow*, *permit*, *let*, and *guide* are much more consistent with your goal. Give yourself *permission* to relax.

Mindful language in your biofeedback practice is equally important. Using biofeedback skills as a way to "make" your finger temperature go up, or "try to relax," or "control" anxiety, or "rid" yourself of pain is likely to be a futile struggle and limit the effectiveness of these skills. On the other hand, using your biofeedback skills to "allow" your body to recover or to "guide" a healthy physiological response to anxiety and pain will maximize the effectiveness of your skills.

Similarly, words like *weak*, *stupid*, *fat*, *lazy*, and many other choice words that are a common part of our self-talk vocabulary are incompatible with a helpful, kind, compassionate response to a difficult experience. Refer to Chapter 10 on compassion for more on this.

What I'd like you to take away from this section is the importance of paying attention to how you talk yourself through difficult situations. Word choice is not just semantics—it is an important part of choosing the most helpful response.

Observation

Mindful, nonjudgmental observation is necessary in differentiating between what we can and cannot control. Mindful observation allows us to take a step back and observe the initial preverbal experience, before evaluations of and automatic reactions to that experience kick in.

Try this—read the following instructions, and then put the book down for a few minutes: Bring your attention to your breath (you may choose to close your eyes), and observe the sensations of your breath, as you breathe in and as you breathe out. Do this for a couple of minutes.

What did you notice? Did you notice the physical sensations of your breath coming in and out of your nose, and the gentle rising and falling of your chest and abdomen? Or did you notice your mind thinking "breathe in, breathe out . . . breathe in, breathe out." Or perhaps you noticed both? There is a difference between simply observing the sensations themselves, without words, labels, or judgments, and your mind's commentary, its interpretation of the experience.

Belgian artist René Magritte makes this distinction beautifully with his painting titled *Ceci n'est pas une pipe* (*This Is Not a Pipe*). Look at Figure 9.1—if that is not a pipe, what is it? . . . If you said that it is a picture of a pipe, not the pipe itself, you are correct. It is the artist's interpretation of the actual pipe he may have had in front of him when he painted this.

FIGURE 9.1: René Magritte, *Ceci n'est pas une pipe*   *Credit: © 2019 Herscovici/Artists Rights Society (ARS), New York*

Our minds are so quick to name, interpret, and judge our experience that it is difficult to tell the difference between the experience itself and our interpretation of it. And yet it is crucial to learn to recognize and observe the experience for what it is, rather than what our minds say it is.

Let's return to breathing again. Chapter 2 on breathing discusses the experience of overbreathing, which results in very unpleasant physiological sensations that are identical to severe anxiety. When you notice these sensations, your mind may habitually jump to the interpretation, "This is anxiety" or "This is panic," and then race on to "Oh no, this is bad" or "Why is this happening?" or "Am I going to have a heart attack?" Fear and anxiety escalate, intensifying unpleasant physiological sensations, in a cycle of distress and suffering. If, on the other hand, you are able to just experience the sensations of overbreathing, pause and identify them for what they are, and practice breathing skills as a helpful response to overbreathing, you won't get into the spiral of fear.

The skill of mindful observation gives you the ability to move away from habitual automatic and often unhelpful interpretations and judgments of the present moment. You can then direct your resources to choosing and implementing a more helpful response.

Labeling

Disengaging from unhelpful automatic reactions by observing your experience mindfully allows you to then give a name to your thoughts and emotional experiences. This skill accomplishes two very important goals. First, naming your unpleasant experience gives you some emotional distance from the experience—you and your experience are not the same. You are a person who is having an unpleasant experience, not unpleasantness itself. This means that you may have the experience of anxiety, but there is a lot more to you than the anxiety. Or you might have the experience of pain, but there is a lot more to you than the pain.

Second, giving a name to your emotional experience actually changes the neurological pathways within your brain at work at that moment. Typically, strong emotions are associated with activation of the amygdala, the fight-or-flight center of the brain, triggering a cascade of physiological and emotional reactions, which often lead you to feel overwhelmed and unable to respond in a helpful way. Imaging studies have shown that giving a name to your emotional experience, a skill called *affect labeling*, significantly reduces activation of the amygdala and increases activation of the areas of the brain that are important in choosing most helpful response to difficult emotions.

HEART RATE VARIABILITY AIDS IN EMOTION RECOGNITION

A study by Daniel Quintana and his team at the University of Sydney asked a group of healthy college students to identify emotions portrayed by images of eyes from different faces.[51] Participants with higher HRV were better at recognizing emotions than participants with lower HRV. This means that training your HRV may make it easier to recognize other people's emotions, and may help in labeling and recognizing your own emotions.

Matthew Lieberman and his colleagues at UCLA invited volunteers to come into the lab and look at a series of emotion evoking images (faces with various emotional expressions) while their brains were being scanned with functional magnetic resonance imaging (fMRI),[52] a technique that identifies activity levels in various parts of the brain at any given moment. These volunteers were asked to engage in a series of six tasks:

1. Just watch the faces the way they usually do.
2. Choose the correct name for the emotion expressed on the face (80 percent of faces portrayed "negative" emotions, such as anger, fear, or sadness).
3. Name the gender of the face.
4. Choose a face that expressed the same emotion as the face they were looking at.
5. Choose a face of the same gender as the face they were looking at.
6. Choose a shape that matched a shape they saw on the screen.

The results of this study showed that activity of the amygdala, the fight-or-flight center of the brain, was reduced only when the volunteers were asked to give a name to the emotion expressed on the face they saw. This means that giving a name to your emotional experience reduces activation of the fight-or-flight response. The study controlled for a variety of cognitive processes—comparing amygdala activation during emotion labeling to passive viewing of images as well as to tasks involving other kinds of cognitive processing: naming and matching gender, and matching affect. Therefore, the authors could safely conclude that the reduction in amygdala activation was due specifically to the action of emotion labeling of the image and not just cognitive processing of the image in general.

In addition to the reduced amygdala activation, the study found increased activation in two areas of the prefrontal cortex, part of the brain responsible for executive function, such as decision making and problem solving. Specifically, one of those areas, the right ventrolateral prefrontal cortex, is responsible for helping you choose an action most appropriate for the situation. The other area, the medial prefrontal cortex, is directly involved in regulation of fear. This means that giving a name to your emotional experience increases your brain's ability to regulate fear and choose a helpful response.

Findings of this study are consistent with a number of other imaging studies examining the effect of emotion labeling on brain activity. Further research has also shown that these changes in brain activation correspond to people's subjective experience. Another study by Matthew Lieberman and his colleagues showed that labeling emotional experience produced the same kind of changes in brain activation, as well as an alleviation in distress people felt as they viewed pictures with intense emotional content.[53] Interestingly, participants expected to feel worse after naming their experience, but they actually felt better. So, if you are reading this thinking that bringing more attention to unpleasant emotional experience is not going to help or will make things worse, please give it a try. There is a good chance you'll be pleasantly surprised.

Another study by the same group—Matthew Lieberman, with his colleagues Katharina Kircanski and Michelle Craske at UCLA—showed that labeling our emotions (anxiety in this case) has an effect on our physiological responses.[54] When participants labeled their own emotional states in a fearful situation and later experienced a similar situation, they showed reduced activation of the sympathetic nervous system, measured by skin conductance, compared to participants who had not previously labeled their emotions. You may recall from Chapter 6 that skin conductance is an excellent indicator of stress activation and is very responsive to intense physiological activation that comes with anxiety.

These findings tell us that naming our emotional experience produces three very important changes in our brain functioning:

1. Reduced automatic fight-or-flight response
2. Increased ability to choose the most helpful way to respond to challenges
3. Decreased intensity of emotional distress and physiological overactivation accompanying a difficult emotional state

You may be wondering what all of this has to do with mindfulness. It turns out that mindfulness enhances the effect of affect labeling on helpful changes in brain activation. David Creswell and his colleagues (including Matthew Lieberman) measured volunteers' ability to be mindful in everyday life and then scanned their brains with functional magnetic resonance imaging while they labeled emotional states.[55] The study showed that volunteers who were more mindful in daily life experienced a greater degree of change in brain activity—their amygdala was less active and their prefrontal cortex was more active. This means that regular mindfulness practice is likely to allow you to reap an even greater benefit from the simple act of labeling your difficult emotional experiences.

What does this mean, from a practical standpoint? The exercise of affect labeling itself is pretty simple: when you experience a difficult or unpleasant feeling, pause for a moment and give a name to the feeling. Use the following as a guide to labeling your feeling:

1. The label should be short—there is no need for lengthy and time-consuming descriptions.
2. It should be nonjudgmental and descriptive. This isn't an exercise in mentally beating up on yourself or figuring out your faults. For example, "Here's me being an idiot again" is not a great label for a difficult experience. A general guideline you can use here is to ask yourself, If you were to tell another person your chosen label, would that person have a pretty good idea of what you mean? "Being an

FIGURE 9.2 LABELING YOUR EMOTIONS

Intensity of Feelings	Happy	Sad	Angry	Afraid	Ashamed
High	Elated	Depressed	Furious	Terrified	Sorrowful
	Excited	Agonized	Enraged	Horrified	Remorseful
	Overjoyed	Alone	Outraged	Scared stiff	Defamed
	Thrilled	Hurt	Boling	Petrified	Worthless
	Exuberant	Dejected	Irate	Fearful	Disgraced
	Ecstatic	Hopeless	Seething	Panicking	Dishonored
	Fired up	Sorrowful	Loathsome	Frantic	Mortified
	Passionate	Miserable	Betrayed	Shocked	Shameful
Medium	Cheerful	Heartbroken	Upset	Apprehensive	Apologetic
	Gratified	Somber	Mad	Frightened	Unworthy
	Good	Lost	Defended	Threatened	Sneaky
	Relieved	Distressed	Frustrated	Insecure	Guilty
	Satisfied	Let down	Agitated	Anxious	Embarrassed
	Glowing	Melancholy	Disgusted	Intimidated	Secretive
Low	Glad	Unhappy	Perturbed	Cautious	Bashful
	Contented	Moody	Annoyed	Nervous	Ridiculous
	Pleasant	Blue	Uptight	Worried	Regretful
	Tender	Upset	Resistant	Timid	Uncomfortable
	Pleased	Disappointed	Irritated	Unsure	Pitied
	Mellow	Dissatisfied	Touchy	Uneasy	Silly

FIGURE 9.2: Labeling your emotions.   *Adapted with permission from Emotional Intelligence 2.0, by Travis Bradberry and Jean Greaves*

idiot" is not a clear description of a feeling. Feeling "defeated" and feeling "overwhelmed" are descriptive nonjudgmental labels that will be understood by others.

3. The label should be accurate enough, but not too accurate. There is no need to spend a lot of time and effort in figuring out whether you are feeling "scared" or "afraid" or "nervous." Any of these labels will likely be good enough. If you find it difficult to come up with simple words to label your feelings, Figure 9.2 provides a handy chart that breaks down five major feelings categories into levels of intensity, to help you identify what you may be feeling.

4. Use a gentle internal tone of voice for your labels. You will notice a big difference between labeling "anger" in a gentle or neutral tone and labeling "ANGER" in an exasperated and harsh tone.

As with all new skills, I strongly encourage you to practice labeling your feelings in neutral circumstances first, and then use the skill in mildly difficult situations, before bringing the skill into most challenging or difficult circumstances. To begin, pause for a moment several times a day (you may want to set up a reminder on your phone for a few days), and label whatever feelings you may be experiencing in those moments. It is helpful to write down your labels so that you may be able to go back and review them at another time. If you are keeping a notebook for enhanced practice, as I suggest in the introduction to this book, this is a great exercise to keep in that notebook.

Let's do the first practice now—read these instructions and then put the book aside for a moment: Pause, perhaps close your eyes, and bring your attention to your current emotional experience. What feelings do you notice? Give them a short, nonjudgmental label, using a gentle tone of voice. Take a moment to write them down.

Willingness

Most of the skills described so far in this chapter have one thing in common: accepting your difficult experience as it is and allowing it to stay, giving yourself permission to stop trying to make it go away. But these are unpleasant, difficult, painful experiences, and I would bet that at least at some point you've thought to yourself, "But I don't want to do this," "I don't want to feel the pain," "I don't want to feel the fear," and so on. What will help you implement skills that involve experiencing all those difficult feelings and sensations you've worked so hard to avoid or fight off? The answer is willingness.

Wanting is a feeling, and whether or not you want or don't want something is not under your control. There is nothing I can say to you to make you want to have your anxiety, sadness, or pain. The good news is, you don't have to want any of it. You just have to be willing.

Willingness is a choice and a decision to take action, a commitment to follow through with the most helpful response. Willingness is not a feeling; it is a commitment to action, and it is therefore under your control. Think about a food that you really don't like—not something you are allergic to or something that would otherwise be dangerous to you, just a food that you really dislike. Now ask yourself, Do you want to eat some of that food right now? I am guessing your answer is no. But can you imagine a situation in which you would be willing to have that food? Perhaps if you were really hungry and there wasn't anything else available to eat? Or if your favorite aunt worked really hard to make it for you, not realizing you don't like it? Or if your child cooked it for you as a birthday present? You get the point—despite a strong dislike for this food, most of us can imagine circumstances under which we would be willing to eat it.

I once had a conversation with a friend about willingness. I asked him about his least favorite food. It turns out that my friend is a very adventurous eater, and he had trouble coming up with a food he didn't like (I was getting worried that my analogy was going to fail miserably as I waited for him to come up with something). Finally, he said, "Sea urchin. I really don't like sea urchin." He gave me an emphatic "No" to the question of whether he would like some sea urchin at that moment. Then I asked him: "OK, can you think of a situation under which you would be willing to have some?" His said: "Yes, and in fact I have." He turned to his wife: "Do you remember one of our first dates when I ate that sea urchin?" "Yes," his wife responded, "why did you do that?" "I was trying to impress you." His wife wasn't impressed. But what a great way to demonstrate willingness rather than wanting!

The same applies to difficult or unpleasant internal experiences. Of course, you don't want to feel scared or ashamed or sad—it would be strange if you did. But can you imagine a circumstance under which you would be willing to feel your feelings? What if allowing yourself to feel how you feel meant that you could go and make new friends? What if it meant being able to go on an interview for your dream job? What if it meant you could feel free to engage in your life the way you'd like it to be? Would you be willing to experience your fear, shame, or pain then? The answer to such questions is entirely your choice—sometimes you are willing, and other times you are not. *No* is an acceptable answer. The point is to make this be a *choice* rather than automatically defaulting to *no*.

When deciding whether or not you are willing to experience your thoughts and feelings as they are, or whether avoiding/escaping them is a better choice, ask yourself two questions:

1. *Is experiencing the pain or discomfort worth it?* Is it worth having your experience if it means that you get to do something you value? For example, Arthur, a father of three, has had a lifelong fear of being in crowded places. Anytime he found himself in a place with a lot of people, he felt like the walls were closing in on him, had trouble breathing, and just wanted to get out. Arthur avoided being in crowded places as much as possible, always worrying whether a place he is going to may be too crowded. His oldest son played basketball. It was important for Arthur to go to his games. Most of the time the gyms where the games took place were not too crowded. But then came the championship game. Arthur's son was so excited to play in it. All Arthur could think about was how many people were going to crowd into the gym for the big game. He considered skipping the game. But then he thought about how disappointed his son would be if he weren't there. He asked himself whether being there for his son was worth experiencing the anxiety. He decided the answer was yes, he was willing to have his anxiety and be there to watch his son play.

2. *Which discomfort would I rather have, the one that comes right now with experiencing my thoughts and feelings, or the one that may happen if I avoid experiencing them?* Often, the current unpleasant experience, what acceptance and commitment therapy (ACT) founder Steven Hayes calls the "pain of presence," is temporary and short-lived. The "pain of absence," the one that happens when you avoid your experience,

often lasts longer and follows you around for indeterminate length of time. For Arthur, the choice was between the temporary pain of being anxious during his son's game and the much longer pain of knowing that he wasn't there for his son during an important moment of his life. Realizing that avoiding the pain of presence would just be exchanging it for the pain of absence, Arthur decided to go to the game.

Another way to increase willingness to experience your difficult thoughts and feelings is through connecting with your values and acting according to those values, called *value-based action.*

Value-Based Action

Victor Frankl, a renowned psychiatrist, author, and Holocaust survivor, once said: "What man actually needs is not a tensionless state but rather the striving and struggling for some goal worthy of him. What he needs is not the discharge of tension at any cost, but the call of a potential meaning waiting to be fulfilled by him."[56]

Knowing our values helps us figure what gives meaning to our lives. You can think of values as a beacon, a guiding light that points you in the right direction. Values are what is important to you in life, what you stand for, your chosen life directions.

You need a reason to engage in most actions, especially those that come with difficult emotions or pain. You have a choice between immediate relief from difficult feelings through avoidance, escape, or struggle, and opening to the experience of difficult emotions and pain. Given how much you may not want to experience those feelings, you need a good reason to be willing to have them. Knowing your values will help you make the choice between an immediately relieving, but ultimately unhelpful, action and the potentially difficult action that leads to a healthier outcome.

When you think about your values, make sure to think about what is important to *you* regardless of what other people think you should do. Values are not what is important to other people; they are not what other people think should be important to you; they are not what you think *should* be important to you, and not what society at large says should be important to you. Knowing what truly *is* important to you requires a very personal look inside. You are the only person who knows what truly matters to you, and there are no right or wrong answers except those that are true to your own values.

Keep in mind that values are different from feelings. Feelings come and go, and you have little control over them. Values, on the other hand, are chosen by you and are stable. Certainly your values change over time, and the importance you place on each of your values changes in different stages of life. The value of parenting when you are in your early twenties, just starting a career, may not be the same as it will be when you are ready to start a family. While values change over longer periods of time, they don't change moment to moment the way feelings do.

It's also important to distinguish between values and goals—they are not the same thing. Goals are concrete actions that you can take and then check off your list as done. Values are not something you can ever check off your list. They always remain something that you are working on. Goals may help you act in accordance with your values. For example, Arthur's value is to be an involved and supportive parent. This is not something he can ever check off his list and be done with, right? He may also have a goal of making it to all of his son's basketball games for the season. That goal is consistent with his value of being an involved and supportive parent and is something that he can say has been achieved.

How do you figure out your values? This takes some time and reflection. Below, I outline areas that have been used in ACT values questionnaires (such as Kelly Wilson's Valued Living Questionnaire and Russ Harris' Values Worksheet). Rank order these areas in order of importance to you now, and then spend some time thinking through each one, starting with the most important, and write down your thoughts. There is no need to go through all the areas at once—do as many as is realistic at one time. I provide you with some questions to prompt your thinking about each of these values. Notice that the questions listed all have to do with *your* values and actions, which are under your control. I don't ask about other people's thoughts, feelings, perceptions, or actions, which are not under your control. For example, on the topic of parenting, I ask you to think about what kind of parent you want to be and what you would like to teach your children, not what you would like them to learn or how you want them to see you. If you are keeping a notebook to enhance your practice, use it for this exercise.

IDENTIFYING YOUR VALUES

- *Romantic/intimate relationships.* What is most important to you in an intimate relationship? What kind of partner do you want to be? What kind of partner do you want to have? How would you like to interact with your partner?

- *Parenting.* What is most important to you as a parent? What kind of parent do you want to be? What would you like to teach your children? How do you want to act toward your children? What kind of interaction is most important between you and your child?

- *Family-of-origin relationships.* What is most important in your relationship with your family of origin? What kind of son/daughter/sister/brother/grandchild do you want to be?

- *Friendships.* What characteristics are most important in a friendship? What kind of friend do you want to be? How do you want to act toward your friends? How do you want to spend your time with friends?

- *Education and personal growth.* What personal characteristics are most important to you? Which strengths and virtues would you like to grow and nurture? What educational goals would you like to pursue?

- *Career.* What is most important to you about your job and workplace environment? What kind of worker/leader/professional do you want to be? What personal qualities do you want to bring to your work? What kind of work brings meaning to your life?

- *Self-care/health.* What do you value most about your health and self-care? How would you like to take care of yourself and your health?

- *Leisure time and recreation.* What kind of activities do you enjoy? What are your hobbies and interests? How would you like to fit them into your life? How do you relax and rejuvenate?

- *Spirituality/religion.* How does spirituality fit into your life? What kinds of activities nurture your spirituality? (Remember there is no right or wrong answer; whatever spirituality means to you is just fine.)

- *Community.* How do you find your place in a community? What do you value about being part of a community? How would you like to contribute to your community?

- *Environment.* What is important to you about taking care of your environment (whatever kind of environment it is, whether it is your room, your house, your neighborhood, or the planet). What kind of environment would you like to spend time in? What do you value about your environment?

- *Anything else?* If there is any set of values that have not been covered in this list, please list them and think through how each value is important and how it fits into your life.

Once you've determined your values, use them as a guiding light in choosing the most helpful way to respond to difficult thoughts, feelings, and situations. When thinking about a response, identify the value that is most applicable to the situation at hand and ask yourself, "Which action is most consistent with my value of . . ." For Arthur, the most relevant value was that of being an engaged and involved parent. Going to his son's basketball game was the action most consistent with that value.

Checking in with your values in a difficult situation gives you a reminder of what's important, allowing you to choose the most helpful response. In addition, a study by Brandon Schmeichel from Texas A&M University and Kathleen Vohs from the University of Minnesota showed that knowing your values allows you to use your emotional and physical resources in more efficient ways, reducing resource depletion that otherwise comes with acts of self-control, such as choosing a nonhabitual response to a difficult situation.[57] Knowing your values makes it easier to then follow through on your chosen response, because you have access to greater resources in doing so.

Step-by-Step Mindfulness Skill: FLARE

The seven mindfulness-based skills described so far in this chapter are ones that you can use in everyday life. You may find use for some of these skills in some situations, and other skills in other situations. In most challenging situations, it is helpful to have an aggregate of multiple skills to help you move through the challenge. This way you won't have to figure out which skills you should be using (this can be hard to do in the middle of a difficult situation); rather, you will have a concrete combination of skills to fall back on. This section introduces a step-by-step technique that combines the skills described earlier in this chapter and will help you navigate challenging situations. I've chosen the acronym *FLARE* to describe this technique:

Feel

Label

Allow

Respond

Expand awareness

To illustrate FLARE, let's return to the example of Michelle, described at the beginning of the chapter, and see how she might use it.

Feel

This is a sensory, nonverbal step, becoming aware of difficult feelings, thoughts, or sensations. The goal here is just to be aware of these sensations as they are, without automatic evaluations or judgments (think back to the pipe that's not a pipe in Figure 9.1). This step uses the power of mindful observation.

As Michelle is sitting in the car, she would bring her awareness to the physical sensations she is experiencing (rapid heartbeat, faster breathing, sweaty hands, butterflies in her stomach), thoughts going through her mind ("I am not going to get this job," "I can't sit here and be scared, I should just go home"), and emotions she was feeling.

Label

This step involves giving a name to your experience at the moment—a short, nonjudgmental label, said in a kind and gentle internal tone of voice. Labeling reduces activation of the fight-or-flight response and increases activation of the prefrontal cortex and the ability to choose a helpful response. This step gives you the ability to decrease intensity of emotional activation and follow through with the remaining steps. Michelle would label her experience as "uncertainty" or "insecurity."

Allow

In this step, you allow your thoughts, feelings, and physiological sensations to be as they are. You give up futile efforts to control your thoughts and emotions, preserving your resources to control what is under your control— your actions and your response to these thoughts, feelings, and physiological sensations. You give up the struggle to make these thoughts and emotions go away, and you open yourself up to them, allowing yourself to experience them and move on without getting stuck.

LITTLE ALBERT AND THE WHITE RAT

Back in the 1920s, when the field of psychology did not have the strict regulations over acceptable research practices that we have now, psychologist John Watson wanted to see how people came to be afraid of things. He used a nine-month-old child he called Albert B., who became known as Little Albert. Little Albert enjoyed furry animals and liked playing with a white rat. One day, as Little Albert was playing with the rat, Watson produced a loud clanging noise behind Little Albert, scaring him and making him cry. Watson repeated this several times, until eventually Little Albert came to associate the white rat with fear. From then on, Little Albert would get scared, start crying, and try to get away every time he saw the white rat, even without the presence of noise. With a little time, the fear generalized, as fear often does. Little Albert became afraid of all fluffy white things, including white bunnies, stuffed animals, and fur coats.

This story demonstrates the difference between the existence of a fear and the validity of the content of the thought behind it. Let me ask you: Are white fluffy things dangerous? Usually not, right? But given what you know about Little Albert, does it make sense to you that he was terrified of white fluffy things? It does, right? He was afraid not because there is danger but because of his previous experience. And while we often don't know the reason that we feel the way we do, we can allow and validate the existence of our experience, without believing that thoughts that come with the feelings are true.

It does not matter whether the presence of your thoughts and emotions makes sense to you, or whether you know the reason for how you feel. Thoughts and feelings are out of your control, so you don't have a choice but to allow them. Keep in mind that you are allowing the presence of your thoughts, emotions, and physiological sensations, not necessarily the literal content of the thoughts (so if you are afraid that the plane you are on will crash, you allow the experience of fear and the presence of fear-related thoughts, but you do not agree with the thought that the plane is going to crash). The story of Little Albert and the white rat illustrates this principle.

In allowing her thoughts and feelings to be as they are, Michelle would say to herself: "It is OK to feel this way . . . it is OK to be uncertain of what's going to happen."

Respond

In this step, you choose the most helpful way to respond to your difficult experience. By allowing your experience to be as it is, in the previous step, you preserve the resources you need to control what *is* under your control: your response to the experience, rather than the experience itself.

Base your choice of response on the value that it would serve the most. Michelle would ask herself, "Which action would be most consistent with my career value of pursuing a job that would bring meaning to my life?" She might also ask herself, "Which action is in my best interest right now." When choosing your response, here are a few points to consider:

- *Is there something you need to do to remedy a problem?* For example, if you have an exam coming up the next day, and you are worrying about it because you have not studied enough, then the most helpful response is to study.
- *Are your feelings related to a specific action you need to take?* For example, Michelle is worried about her job interview. Her mind was telling her that she should skip the interview in an effort to reduce anxiety. However, that action would not be in her best interest. The most helpful response is one that allows her to follow through with the job interview.
- If nothing concrete needs to be done, your only choice is to focus on having your experience the way it is, responding with kindness and curiosity. For example, if someone cuts you off in traffic, it is not wise to "do" anything about it. Your only choice is to allow yourself to feel annoyed and frustrated and choose the most helpful response to those feelings.

Here are some options that would allow you to choose and follow through with a helpful response:

- *Call up your value.* Which value is most relevant in the current situation? Which action is most consistent with this value? For Michelle, going to the job interview is the action most consistent with her value of having a job that brings meaning to her life.
- *Check in on willingness.* Are you willing to experience your thoughts, feelings, and physiological sensations in order to act in accordance with your values? In other words, is the temporary unpleasant experience worth having at that moment, to give yourself a chance to reap the long-term benefits of having that experience, such as going to the job interview? For Michelle, the answer is yes. She is willing to experience discomfort of uncertainty and insecurity right now in order to give herself the chance to get the job.
- *Balance your physiology.* Use your biofeedback or psychophysiologically based skills to help your body self-regulate in the moment of challenge. These skills may involve mindful low-and-slow breathing at your resonance frequency, releasing your muscles, or bringing to mind your image of warmth. Michelle chose to practice mindful low-and-slow breathing to conserve her carbon dioxide and remind her body to self-regulate as she focused on the job interview.
- *Practice mini-meditation.* Bring your awareness to your here-and-now stone (see Chapter 8) or listen to the sounds around you. Notice your thoughts, feelings, and physiological sensations and allow them to come and go.
- *Practice self-compassion or compassion for others.* Michelle noticed her harsh self-talk—"There is no point in going, I am not good enough to get the job anyway"—and responded with kindness: "It is hard to feel uncertain and insecure. I don't know what's going to happen, but it's worth a shot to see what will happen."
- *Place the intention of your response on what is under your control.* Aim for a healthy response to difficult feelings, rather than trying to change the feelings or make them go away. Michelle's intention was to help her body and mind regulate themselves while she focused on what she needed to do for the interview.

Expand Awareness

The goal of this step is to help you follow through with your chosen response to difficult thoughts, emotions, or physiological sensations. Expanding awareness allows you to see the problem you are experiencing as only a part of your overall experience, instead of as all of your experience. It allows your focus to soften and for you to see that there is more to your experience than this one problem. This is another concept from ACT.

Let's try an ACT-based exercise to help explain this skill. You may want to read the full directions first and then do the exercise.

1. Take a piece of paper with something written on it. It can be this book opened to the page you are currently on, or something else nearby.
2. Hold the paper or the book very close to your face, almost touching your nose and forehead. Take a few moments to look around and notice what you see.
3. Now put the paper or the book down on your lap or on the desk in front of you. Take a few moments to look around and notice what you see now.

KEEPING A GRATITUDE JOURNAL

To expand awareness, keep an appreciation or gratitude journal to help you focus on the positive things in your life. When you feel stuck in difficult emotions or difficult situations, your distress may take up so much of your awareness that it may be hard to see anything but the "bad stuff."

Your brain is built to be on the lookout for danger—that's how human beings survived as a species. Your brain is excellent at finding problems and thinking about things that are not going well. Looking out for the things that are going well is much less important, evolutionarily speaking, so your brain is not primed to look for them. As a result, you may find yourself seeing only the negatives and not paying much attention to the positive experiences in your life. This keeps you even more stuck in the difficult emotions.

While being on the lookout for the negative is entirely normal, it is not very helpful. You can, however, retrain your brain to become aware of and process the positive experiences in your daily life. Keeping an appreciation or gratitude journal on a daily basis will help you expand your awareness and see the positives in your life.

Here's how you can do it: At the end of each day, write down three things you've appreciated or been grateful for. You can pick anything you want. If it is hard to come up with ideas, try writing down one thing you appreciated about yourself, one thing you appreciated about other people, and one thing you appreciated about the world around you.

Writing down small things is even better than large things. While it is important to appreciate the big things, like your family or your health, it is equally important to notice small things throughout the day that you would otherwise not notice at all. Some examples are your friend calling just when you were feeling lonely, a train engineer waiting a few extra seconds before closing the train doors to let you get on, hearing a bird sing outside your window, an extra hug from your child, feeling successful in using a skill from this book, or making time for meditation or biofeedback practice today.

Knowing that you have to write down at least three things at the end of the day will help your brain notice the positive experiences, expand your awareness, and take in things that would have gone unnoticed. A broader outlook that includes the positive sides of life as well as the difficult ones will help improve your mood and reduce suffering.

When you were holding the paper very close to your nose, did you see blurry spots, vague shapes and colors, and not much else? Once you put the paper on your lap or on a desk, could you see the words more clearly? Could you read what was written? Could you also see your feet, and the chair you are sitting in, the floor and the walls around you? Perhaps you could also see people in front of you, what's going on outside your window, and the books on your bookshelf.

Notice the difference between the two experiences. When you held the paper very close to your face, you could barely see what was there and could not make any sense of it. This is what happens when you are super focused on one problem—you are stuck in it and cannot see the full picture, make sense of the situation, or figure out a solution to the problem. When you moved the paper away from your face, when you put some distance between yourself and the paper, you could see it much more clearly; you could read and make sense of it. You could also see everything else going on around you. The paper did not disappear or go away, but it became a lot easier to see in the context of the rest of your environment.

The same thing happens with your problems or difficult experiences. Once you are no longer stuck in the middle of them, once you soften your focus and expand your awareness to the rest of your environment, you become able to see the problem much more clearly and find a solution. The problem does not go away, nor does it change in any way. What changes is your perception of it—the problem is now a part of your experience, not all of your experience.

To practice expanding awareness, take a few moments to bring mindful attention to your external environment—the chair you are setting in, the floor under your feet, the person sitting next to you, the sky outside, and so on. Then, bring mindful attention to your internal environment—your breath, your heartbeat, your itchy nose. . . . Finally, notice your feelings, from positive, to neutral, to difficult—the whole spectrum.

Exactly when you expand awareness, when practicing FLARE, can vary— sometimes you'll take this step after you've completed your chosen response, sometimes after choosing but before implementing the response, and sometimes as part of your response. Michelle expanded her awareness after she decided that going to the interview was in her best interest, after she practiced mindful low-and-slow breathing, and before getting out of the car.

The purpose of FLARE is to provide with you a concrete set of skills you can have at your fingertips in difficult situations without having to think too much about them. In order for FLARE to be the most useful to you in difficult times, it has be well-practiced. I encourage you to first use each of the 7 skills described earlier in the chapter one by one in mildly difficult situations, perhaps the kinds of situations where you would typically not need any particular skill to be able to handle them well. For example, you may pause for a few moments to label your emotions as you are going through your day, or you may attend to the internal language you use with yourself in mildly difficult situations, and rephrase your internal self-talk to a more mindful one. You may also notice temptation to control your thoughts and emotions and allow yourself to have them just as they are instead. Once you have a good grasp of the skills, practice them in more difficult or challenging situations. Do the same thing with FLARE—first practice in mildly difficult situations, just to get the hang of the steps, and then gradually increase the difficulty of the situations in which you use it. The beauty of FLARE is that with practice you'll be able to use it to help navigate any challenging situation.

CHAPTER 10

Compassion and Self-Compassion

Claire had a hard day at work, her commute home took longer than usual, and she felt completely drained when she arrived home. Her sixteen-year-old son, Tim, was waiting for her in the kitchen. He seemed upset. Claire wasn't sure she was up for a discussion of another problem. Before she could even say a proper hello, Tim blurted out: "Mom, I failed my math midterm." This was the midterm that Claire had asked Tim about a few days ago. This test was important. She'd asked him how studying was going and whether he needed help. Tim had assured her that everything was under control. Now this. . . . Claire took a breath and considered her options for response—she could yell at him (that idea seemed quite satisfying at the moment), remind him of the conversation they had, and accuse him of being lazy and unmotivated. Or she could say something like: "I can see how upset you are about failing this test. It must have been really hard to see that F. How can I help you?"

Which response do you think would leave Claire feeling better after the conversation? Which response would help Tim be more likely to study more and get the help he needs for the next exam? I suspect you know the answer; it may even seem obvious to you: the second option would be the more helpful one.

But why? The answer to that may not be as clear. The first response may feel satisfying to Claire for a moment (admit it, it sometimes feels really good to yell and say something mean to someone when you are not feeling so great yourself). And after a few moments of letting off steam, Claire would likely be filled with guilt and regret over what she had said to Tim. She may then beat up on herself with harsh words about her parenting and feel even worse. The next time Tim has a math test, Claire may not know how to talk to him about it. For fear of repeating the same unpleasant interaction, she may avoid asking Tim whether he needs help. And she would miss the opportunity to connect with and help her son.

To Tim, that first response would also feel pretty terrible—he would feel ashamed and defeated. When another math test comes up in the future, the feelings of shame and defeat would return, and Tim would likely try to avoid thinking about the test for as long as possible in an attempt to stave off the shame and defeat. As a result, the next test will likely go the same way as the first, perpetuating the cycle.

The second response is filled with both compassion for Tim and self-compassion for Claire. For Tim, a compassionate response from his mother would help him feel connected and supported, stop beating up on himself for failing the test, and address the problem for the future and would allow him to ask her for help. For Claire, a compassionate response to Tim is also a way of being compassionate toward herself—she would feel connected with her son, feel validated in her parenting, and be available to help him in the future. A compassionate response would prevent a cycle of shame, helplessness, and guilt for both Tim and Claire.

This chapter discusses the science of compassion and self-compassion, ways in which you can use both of these powerful skills in improving your life, and mindfulness- and biofeedback-based skills for nurturing these qualities within yourself.

What is Compassion and Self-Compassion

Compassion can be defined in many different ways. The Dalai Lama sees it as a wish for oneself or another person to be free from suffering. Paul Gilbert, a British clinical psychologist and the founder of compassion-focused therapy, defines compassion as "sensitivity to suffering in self and others, with a commitment to alleviate and prevent it."[58]

You would not be surprised to learn that compassion is good for those at whom it is directed. People do better when someone is there for them in a kind and supportive way when they suffer. At the same time, compassion is also good for those who exhibit it. Research shows that people who are more compassionate tend to have less pain, less anxiety, less depression, and less inflammation.[59] They also recover more quickly from illness and have better overall physical health.[60]

Research also shows that compassion training helps us improve many parameters of our health and well-being. A 2017 meta-analysis by James Kirby and his colleagues at the University of Queensland examined results from 21 randomized controlled trials of compassion-based interventions from the last 12 years, with data from 1,285 participants.[61] Results showed that people who take part in compassion training show significant improvements in self-report measures of compassion, self-compassion, mindfulness, depression, anxiety, overall psychological distress, and well-being. Good news, right? When we are compassionate toward others, both sides benefit.

Just like there is a need to treat others with compassion, we need to treat ourselves with the same compassion we give others. Self-compassion offers this. Self-compassion is a way of treating ourselves with kindness in times of distress and suffering. Christopher Germer of Harvard Medical School, the codeveloper of mindful self-compassion training, defines *self-compassion* as "a way of holding ourselves when things go wrong." He defines *mindful self-compassion* as "bearing witness to one's own pain (that's mindfulness) and responding with kindness and understanding (that's compassion)."[62] The goal of self-compassion, as with all other skills described in this book, is not make the pain, anxiety, grief, or any other difficult experience go away or even get better. Instead, the goal of self-compassion is to bring comfort when you feel bad.

Kristin Neff, professor of psychology at the University of Texas and codeveloper of mindful self-compassion training, describes self-compassion as having three components:

- *Self-kindness versus self-criticism.* Self-compassion means being warm and understanding toward yourself when you suffer, fail, or feel inadequate. It is often easier to treat other with kindness than it is to be kind to yourself. Self-kindness is about treating yourself the way you are likely to treat people you love. One way to do this is by making your internal conversation gentle and encouraging instead of harsh and critical.

• *Common humanity versus self-isolation.* Self-compassion encourages recognition that you are a human being, and as all human beings, you are not perfect. All human beings suffer, and you are not alone in your suffering. Suffering and imperfection go hand and hand as entirely normal, though difficult, human experiences.

• *Mindfulness versus emotional entanglement.* Self-compassion encourages you to turn toward your painful thoughts, emotions, or physical sensations, allowing yourself to see them just as they are, without suppression or turning away. Being mindful means becoming aware and open to painful thoughts, emotions, and physical sensations without getting caught up in them.

As Christopher Germer says, people who practice self-compassion do not lead easier lives, but they respond to stress differently when it occurs. Instead of wishing it weren't so, they respond with acceptance to the present moment and with kindness toward themselves because that moment is a moment of suffering.[63]

Concerns About Self-Compassion

Whenever I speak with people about self-compassion, they often respond with skepticism. Our society does not encourage self-compassion, and it is often very difficult for people to allow themselves to feel it. Here are some of the concerns and doubts people may have about self-compassion:

"It's only for the weak." I once I had a conversation about what it means to practice self-compassion with a group of Army Rangers I had worked with. They are undeniably some of the bravest people out there. They are also extremely compassionate toward others. Not surprisingly, their initial reaction to the idea of self-compassion was skeptical. It did not seem strong; it did not seem brave. We talked about one of the goals of self-compassion—allowing ourselves to face and feel our darkest, scariest, most difficult emotions. Does that sound like something weak people

do? What kind of person does it take to stand up in front of a room full of people and give a speech while feeling terrified of public speaking? What kind of person does it take to sit with and tell someone about the shame they feel about having been sexually assaulted? What kind of person does it take to talk about being on the battlefield seeing their comrades be killed or injured? Hardly a weak and cowardly one. It takes enormous courage and enormous strength to allow ourselves to feel the dark, difficult feelings we all experience from time to time. Self-compassion allows you to do exactly that. Just ask the Army Rangers.

"Self-compassion is selfish." People worry that they should be placing more emphasis on taking care of other people and not themselves. OK, taking care of others is certainly important. But can you be an effective caretaker for others if you don't take good enough care of yourself? If you've ever been on an airplane, you've probably heard the flight attendant tell you that, if in case of emergency an oxygen mask comes down, to put one on yourself first and only then help people around you. Is that selfish? Can you be of any use to others if you can't breathe yourself? Self-compassion gives you the same breathing room that enables you to help others. It is not about always putting yourself first. It is about taking care of yourself so that you may be able to lead the life you want *and* be able to help others. Research supports this stance; for example, those who exhibit more self-compassion tend to experience less burnout and more satisfaction with their role for caregivers, as well as greater ability to be supportive to their romantic partners and experience compassion, empathy, and forgiveness for others.[64]

"Self-compassion is self-indulgent." This is another common belief. Does facing your fears or allowing yourself to feel sadness or shame sound self-indulgent? Does that sound like a fun thing to do? Self-compassion is about opening to your most difficult feelings, not about indulging yourself. Self-criticism, a common habit of those of us who would not want to be self-indulgent, can be paralyzing, preventing us from being able to change any of those things we criticize ourselves for. Self-compassion, on the other hand enables us to move forward.

"Self-compassion means allowing myself to be lazy and to slack off." Self-compassion is not at all about letting yourself off the hook and allowing

yourself to take the easy way out. Again, self-compassion allows you to face the things that you have long been putting off and avoiding because of the discomfort they create. Self-compassion can help you apply for a job and go on a job interview when the idea scares you to death. Self-compassion can help you eat a healthier meal when it is so much easier to stop at a fast food joint. Self-compassion allows you to play with your child when you have chronic pain. Self-compassion is the opposite of letting yourself be lazy and slack off. It allows you to do the most difficult things that may not have been possible otherwise.

Again, research findings support this argument. Studies show that people who practice self-compassion are more likely to be motivated to change and improve their lives. For example, a study by Anna Friis and her team at the University of Auckland in New Zealand showed that patients with diabetes who practice self-compassion exhibit less depression and better blood sugar levels.[65] In another study, Kristin Homan from Grove City College and Fuschia Sirois from the University of Sheffield in the United Kingdom found that people who are more self-compassionate engage in more, not fewer, health-promoting behaviors.[66] With self-compassion, we are not stuck in indulgence and laziness, but are more likely to make the difficult changes to improve our lives.

"Self-compassion is just a way to sugarcoat the truth and pretend that things are OK when they are really not." In fact, self-compassion is all about exposing the truth about how you feel and allowing yourself to fully experience that truth.

"Self-compassion is just wallowing in self-pity." The opposite is actually true. Self-compassion is what allows you to disentangle from your suffering and move on to live in accordance with your values and achieve your goals. Rather than wallowing in self-pity, self-compassion allows you to look at feelings and experiences that have been so difficult you've avoided looking at them at all costs. Consider Tim, from the example at the beginning of this chapter. If he is in the habit of beating up on himself when he does not achieve his academic goals, his mind forms the association between studying and feeling bad. And when something feels bad, he naturally would not want to look at it and deal with it. So, when the next math test comes around, Tim will be more likely to try to avoid studying

as much as possible in order to avoid feeling bad. This often happens with kids who have learning challenges, and as a result they don't do as well as they actually could. If, on the other hand, Tim (and his mom) responds with compassion at times when he does not do as well as he'd like to, the association between studying and feeling bad is less likely to form. And as the next test comes around, far from wallowing in self-pity, Tim will be more motivated to study and more willing to ask for help.

As Christopher Germer and other mindfulness and self-compassion experts often say, "What you resist persists; what you can feel you can heal." Chapter 9 on mindfulness-based skills talks about counterproductive attempts to control your thoughts and emotions—the more you try, the more stuck you get. When you are under a lot of stress or feeling a lot of difficult emotions, you may try to get a handle on the stress or difficult feelings by pushing yourself harder. The harder you push, the more stuck you get, the more stuck you get, the more you beat up on yourself for failing to feel better. Of course, this makes the whole thing even worse. Learning to respond to difficult situations with kindness and compassion will change the way you experience stress and help you turn it from a threat into a challenge.

Research on self-compassion is very consistent. Numerous studies have shown that self-compassion protects us from various kinds of psychopathology, including anxiety, depression, self-criticism, and body shame.[67] Self-compassion is also associated with greater overall happiness, optimism, life satisfaction, and perceived competence.[68] Research has shown that higher self-compassion is associated with better overall physical health, lower perceived stress, reduced inflammatory response, and better ability to practice health promoting behaviors like healthy eating and exercise.[69] There is also a strong association between higher self-compassion and higher heart rate variability (HRV). I say more about this later in the chapter.

It seems clear to me, and I hope you agree, that developing compassion and self-compassion is the way to go—it is good for everyone involved. But when you stop and think about how to do it, the answer may not be as clear. Sometimes it is easy to feel compassion—when we see images or hear stories of children hurt in a civil war, or a dog mistreated by its owner, or an elderly person kicked out of her home. But there are also times when we have a hard time feeling compassion—like when your child fails a test you specifically asked him about and offered help, or when your spouse promises to pick up your dry cleaning that you need the next day and then gets stuck at work, leaving you without the clothes you need. In those moments compassion may not come naturally. And it is moments like this when we need compassion the most.

Self-compassion can often be even harder to experience. When you yell at your child unnecessarily or when you fail to meet your goal, your habitual automatic response is often self-criticism, self-judgment, and emotional "beating up" on yourself.

Fortunately, we have three excellent ways to cultivate compassion and self-compassion, and I discuss how to use all three of them together. One way to cultivate compassion and self-compassion is through the practice of compassion- and self-compassion-focused meditation. A second way is through learning to pause in moments of difficulty and choose the most helpful compassionate response. Third, as research has shown us, heart rate variability (HRV) biofeedback is an important medium to cultivate compassion. HRV biofeedback supports the physiological aspects of compassion and self-compassion. Because HRV provides a stronger foundation for developing compassion, I will begin with HRV.

HRV Biofeedback and Compassion

There is a physiological, emotional, cognitive, and behavioral component to compassion. James Kirby of Stanford University and his colleagues have described ways in which HRV underlies compassion.[70] On a physiological level, compassion requires the following elements:

- *Ability to orient and bring attention toward the person in need of compassion.* This part is as simple as it sounds—for us to experience compassion, we need to orient and focus our attention on the presence of the other person and that person's needs.
- *Ability to engage socially with others in times of stress.* Compassion is impossible without social engagement, a way of connecting with the person in distress.
- *Ability to feel safe while engaging with others.* Engaging with other

people in a compassionate way is difficult when we don't feel safe ourselves. If we don't feel safe, our evolutionarily developed self-protective instincts are quite strong and would take precedence in attempts to protect ourselves over others.

* *Ability to regulate our own physiology.* At times when we feel dysregulated, our physiological and emotional chaos may prevent us from being able to experience compassion toward someone else.

The physiological connections between compassion and HRV are quite remarkable—HRV relates to each of these four physiological components of compassion:

> *Ability to orient and bring attention toward the person in need of compassion.* The ability to pause, orient, and direct your attention to the person in distress is driven by your parasympathetic nervous system), which also happens to underlie HRV (Chapter 3). High HRV indicates greater ability to orient and focus your attention on the person in distress.
>
> *Ability to engage socially with others in times of stress.* Social engagement at times of stress is mediated by the parasympathetic nervous system. Stephen Porges's polyvagal theory very eloquently describes the way in which the parasympathetic nervous system is responsible for this process. As mentioned in Chapter 3 on HRV, our parasympathetic nervous system comprises primarily the vagal nerve, which has two branches, the myelinated and the unmyelinated (meaning that one branch is covered in a protective sheath that speeds conduction of electrical impulses along the nerve, while the other branch is not). Stephen Porges describes different evolutionary development and function for the two branches of the vagal nerve. The unmyelinated vagus is older, evolutionarily speaking, meaning that it developed earlier and can be found in nonhuman mammals. The myelinated vagus is newer, in evolutionary terms, and responsible for cuing us to social engagement as a way of responding to stress.
>
> According to Porges, the process by which our body chooses the pathway through which it responds to stress is hierarchical, from newest mechanisms to oldest. This means that our first line of response to stress is to reach out for social engagement and support, a process mediated by the myelin-

ated vagus, the newest mechanism for responding to stress. Reaching out for social engagement and support lies at the heart of compassion. A strong vagal reflex is necessary for your ability to express compassion, as described by polyvagal theory. A strong vagal reflex happens when your HRV is high. Studies show that people with high HRV are more likely to act with compassion in response to someone else's suffering.[71] HRV biofeedback strengthens vagal reflexes, increases HRV, and may be used as foundational training in increasing our capacity to express and act with compassion.

In addition, in the times of stress our bodies release stress hormones. One of those stress hormones is oxytocin, a hormone that has been dubbed the "love hormone" because it helps us reach out and make connections with other people. A study by Andrew Kemp and his colleagues at the University of Sydney showed that release of oxytocin in humans is associated with an increase in HRV.[72] This connection further illustrates the importance of HRV in developing compassion.

Ability to feel safe while engaging with others. One challenge that may get in the way of our expressing or acting with compassion is when you don't feel safe yourself. Your evolutionarily developed self-protective instincts take over and direct you toward actions aimed at protecting yourself. However, often you don't feel safe because of your emotional reaction to a situation, and not the presence of actual danger. For example, you might feel scared when a loved one is diagnosed with a life-threatening illness. For human beings, fear is associated with not feeling safe. So, while you are not actually in physical danger, the fear you feel when you hear the scary diagnosis may provoke the feeling of not being safe. Not feeling safe triggers the fight-or-flight response, which in turn may get in the way of you acting with compassion toward the person you care so much about.

Polyvagal theory supports this idea. Stephen Porges suggests that the second-tier response to stress is fight-or-flight response. The fight-or-flight response occurs when we don't feel safe in interpersonal situations, either because we are threatened or because our ability to regulate our response to stress has been compromised. HRV biofeedback will, once again, help train our ability to feel safe even in the presence of difficult emotional experience and to be able to express and act with compassion.

Ability to regulate our own physiology. When we witness someone else's suffering, we may sometimes feel dysregulated ourselves. We may feel over-whelmed and unable to respond in a compassionate way, not because we don't feel compassion but because we are unable to regulate our own phys-iology and emotions in response to someone else's suffering. For exam-ple, witnessing victims of a bad earthquake searching for survivors and mourning their losses may be overwhelming to many of us. Porges would say that it may be so overwhelming that we may respond with fight-or-flight response, as described in the previous paragraph, or with a freeze response, one that's mediated by the unmyelinated branch of the vagus nerve that gets activated when no higher-level options are available. Our HRV decreases in both of these situations, impacting our ability to self-regulate. As a result of our own difficulty regulating our physiological and emotional reactions, we may be unable to respond compassionately. The best way to train our ability to self-regulate is through HRV biofeedback.

Connections between HRV, our ability to connect with others, and our ability to regulate our own physiology are also illustrated in brain imaging studies such as that conducted by Catie Chang of the National Institutes of Health and her team at Stanford University and Otto-von-Guericke University in Germany.[73] These scientists examined the way in which different parts of our brains connect with each other and how those connections relate to HRV. Generally, a better-connected brain is a better functioning one. Previous research has shown that strong connec-tions between the prefrontal cortex and amygdala enable the prefrontal cortex to regulate activation of the amygdala and therefore the intensity of the fight-or-flight response. This connection is also improved with strong HRV. I say more about this in Chapter 13 on anxiety and fear. The study by Chang and her team looked at the way in which the connectivity between the anterior cingulate cortex (ACC) and other parts of the brain changes in response to changes in HRV. They found that high HRV is associated with a stronger connection between the ACC and parts of the brain responsible for our ability to connect with others and regulate our own emotions. For example, an increase in HRV was associated with an increase in connectivity between the ACC and the insula, a part of the brain responsible for empathy and the ability to understand other people's emotions, feel gratitude and connection with others, and make sense of our own physiological states, as well as bring our nervous system back to state of balance. As your HRV increases, your brain's ability to connect with others and to regulate your own emotions may increase as well.

Finally, we have evidence that self-compassion at the time of our own distress and suffering is also associated with HRV. A study by Xi Luo from China West Normal University and his colleagues examined the relationship between HRV and self-compassion.[74] They found a strong relationship between higher HRV and stronger vagal tone, and greater self-compassion at baseline. More self-compassionate individuals also exhibited stronger vagal tone and HRV when exposed to a social stressor. A similar study by Julie Svendsen at the University of Bergen and her colleagues in Norway confirmed these findings.[75]

What all four of these points tell us is that HRV is central to the physiological foundations of compassion and self-compassion. HRV training improves your ability to pay attention, engage socially, feel safe, and regulate your own physiology and emotions in the presence of your own or others' suffering. Does this mean that you cannot nurture compassion and self-compassion without HRV biofeedback? Of course not. But doing the structured, straightforward, and easily accessible HRV training will help you in developing and nurturing your ability to express and act with compassion toward others and self-compassion for yourself.

The steps to training HRV are detailed in Chapter 3. Follow those instructions to increase your HRV. Once you are comfortable with HRV breathing practice, bring in compassion-focused meditation practice, described in the following section.

Compassion- and Self-Compassion-Focused Meditation Practice

Compassion and self-compassion meditation is a kind of mindfulness practice. Before you practice compassion and self-compassion meditation, spend some time practicing basic mindfulness techniques, as outlined in Chapters 8 and 9. I also encourage you to practice HRV breathing at your resonance frequency

(RF) breathing rate, or at 6 breaths per minute, as described in Chapter 3. This practice will prime your mind and body to nurture and cultivate compassion and self-compassion.

The foundation for compassion meditation is the intention to bring comfort and good will to the present moment. The goal of compassion practice is not to make the pain, anxiety, grief, or any other difficult experience go away or even get better. Instead, the goal of compassion practice is to bring comfort as a helpful response to feeling bad, whether for yourself or for someone else.

Mettā

One of my favorite practices combines both self-compassion and compassion for others. This practice is called *Mettā*, or loving kindness. There are many ways to practice loving kindness, and Sharon Salzberg wrote an excellent book by this title.[76] Loving kindness is a foundational practice in mindful self-compassion training developed by Christopher Germer and Kristin Neff. The version I present here is the one I learned from Chris Germer.

1. Find a quiet comfortable place to sit or recline, gently close your eyes, fully or partially. Start your practice with mindful RF breathing, gently allowing your body to fall into the RF breathing rhythm, breathing in and out . . . in and out. Feel your body settling into a place of balance and comfort. Take a few minutes to just breathe.
2. Now bring to mind a person or another living being for whom you feel love, kindness, and compassion. It can be a child, a grandparent, or a pet—anyone for whom you feel warmth and affection. Allow yourself a few moments to just feel the warmth, kindness, love, and affection you have for your loved one. Allow those feelings to stay in the moment with you.
3. Keeping the warmth, kindness, love, and compassion you have for your loved one close to your heart, repeat to yourself, silently or out loud, slowly, softly and gently, feeling the importance of your words:

MAY YOU BE SAFE AND FREE FROM HARM.
MAY YOU BE HEALTHY AND FREE FROM SUFFERING.

MAY YOU HAVE CONTENTMENT AND PEACE OF MIND.

MAY YOU CARE FOR YOURSELF WITH EASE AND WELL-BEING.

When you notice that your mind has wandered, gently return your attention to the words and the image of the loved one you have in mind. Return to the feelings of warmth, kindness, love, and compassion.

4.   Repeat one more time:

MAY YOU BE SAFE AND FREE FROM HARM.

MAY YOU BE HEALTHY AND FREE FROM SUFFERING.

MAY YOU HAVE CONTENTMENT AND PEACE OF MIND.

MAY YOU CARE FOR YOURSELF WITH EASE AND WELL-BEING.

5.   Now add yourself to your circle of warmth, compassion, and good will. If it feels comfortable, put your hand over your heart, feel the warmth and comfort of your hand, and say, slowly and gently:

MAY YOU AND I BE SAFE AND FREE FROM HARM.

MAY YOU AND I BE HEALTHY AND FREE FROM SUFFERING.

MAY YOU AND I HAVE CONTENTMENT AND PEACE OF MIND.

MAY YOU AND I CARE FOR OURSELVES WITH EASE AND WELL-BEING.

6.   Now let go of the image of your loved one, but let the feelings of warmth, kindness, and compassion linger in the moment. Scan your body in your mind's eye; notice any tension, discomfort, stress, or uneasiness that may be lingering within you, and offer warmth, comfort, and kindness to yourself:

MAY I BE SAFE AND FREE FROM HARM.

MAY I BE HEALTHY AND FREE FROM SUFFERING.

MAY I HAVE CONTENTMENT AND PEACE OF MIND.

MAY I CARE FOR MYSELF WITH EASE AND WELL-BEING.

7.   Now bring your attention to your breath. You may return to the HRV breathing one more time. Take a few easy comfortable breaths, and

just rest quietly in your own body, savoring the good will and compassion that flows naturally from your own heart. Know that you can return to the Mettā phrases and the feeling that comes with them anytime you wish. Whenever you are ready, gently open your eyes.

There are many variations of the Mettā phrases. If you wish for simpler phrases, you may use these:

MAY YOU (I) BE SAFE.

MAY YOU (I) BE PEACEFUL.

MAY YOU(I) BE HEALTHY.

MAY YOU (I) LIVE WITH EASE.

You could also design your own phrases, ones that are uniquely suited to your needs for self-compassion. Take a few moments now and think about what those phrases might be. If you are keeping a companion notebook, these phrases would make a great addition to your notes. Think about your needs at this moment and for your life in general. What do you need most? Is it comfort or peace or love or contentment or connection? *May I have peace. May I have comfort. May I feel connected. May I be loved.* Design your phrases around your own needs. You can mix and match your own phrases with the ones suggested in the meditation practice.

I recommend practicing Mettā on a regular basis so that you remember the words and create a strong association between those words and the feelings of warmth, kindness, love, and comfort. This association will be helpful when you use Mettā phrases as a way to respond to difficult moments. Many people find it helpful to practice Mettā either right when they first wake up in the morning or before going to sleep at night.

In addition to Mettā, you may practice any other compassion and self-compassion meditations that appeal to you. Included in Appendix A (with recordings available at www.innakhazan.com/meditation_recordings.html.) are the following:

Tonglen, the giving and receiving practice
Difficult emotion practice (soften, soothe, and allow)
Light meditation

Backdraft

When you first start practicing self-compassion, it is possible to experience initial feeling of discomfort that Christopher Germer in his book *The Mindful Path to Self-Compassion* refers to as "backdraft."[77] *Backdraft* is a term firefighters use to describe a situation when a fire suddenly intensifies as more oxygen becomes available through an open door or window. When your heart and mind become more open to your experience with self-compassion, the difficult feelings you've suppressed and kept at bay for years may suddenly resurface and intensify. These feelings are not created by the practice of self-compassion, but the practice may let the difficult feelings that have been hiding inside you to come out into the open. The initial experience of these feelings is likely to be uncomfortable. When that happens, please remember that backdraft is a common and normal experience and will help you learn to respond to difficult thoughts and emotions in more helpful ways.

When you experience backdraft, respond to it as you would to any difficult feeling using FLARE:

Feel it, noticing where in your body the feeling resides as tension, or an ache, or a soreness.

Label it, by giving it a name—you can call it backdraft, or you can name the feelings that come up with it: fear, sadness, shame, and so on.

Allow the feelings to stay, reminding yourself that this is a normal part of the healing process.

Respond by bringing your attention to an anchor, such as your here-and-now stone, sounds around you, or your breath. You could mindfully practice low-and-slow breathing, at your RF, or at 6 breaths per minute, allowing your body to regulate itself in a difficult time. Any of these concentration practices will reduce the intensity of the difficult feelings, making it easier to have them.

Expand your awareness to other aspects of your external environment (the floor under your feet, the chair you are sitting in, the walls around you, the sky overhead, sound of birds outside) and internal environment (your breath, your heartbeat, anticipation of a delicious dinner).

COMPASSION WITH EQUANIMITY

In their Mindful Self-Compassion Workbook, Kristin Neff and Christopher Germer offer a beautiful meditation for caregivers, adapted here with permission. If you are a caregiver, please try this. Find a comfortable position and take a few low-and-slow breaths, at your RF or at 6 breaths per minute. Settle into your body and into the present moment. If it feels comfortable, put your hand on your heart, as a way of bringing comfort and reminding yourself to bring warmth and kindness into the moment.

Bring to mind someone you are caring for and someone you care about, someone who may sometimes frustrate, exasperate, or exhaust you. In your mind's eye, visualize the person and the caregiving situation. Feel the struggle of being in that situation in your own body.

Slowly say the following words, letting them roll through your mind:

EVERYONE IS ON HIS OR HER OWN LIFE JOURNEY.

I AM NOT THE CAUSE OF THIS PERSON'S SUFFERING,

NOR IS IT ENTIRELY WITHIN MY POWER TO MAKE IT GO AWAY,

EVEN IF I WISH I COULD.

MOMENTS LIKE THIS ARE DIFFICULT TO BEAR,

YET I MAY STILL TRY TO HELP IF I CAN.

Compassion and Empathy

People often talk about compassion fatigue, a kind of burnout people in caregiving roles experience. It may be people who work in caregiving professions, such as doctors, nurses, teachers, psychologists, and other mental health professionals. It may also be people who are caring for their family members—children, spouses, or elderly parents or grandparents. One of the most difficult parts of being a caregiver is personal experience of the other person's distress and suffering. Many caregivers take on the feelings of the person they are caring for, and they end up feeling burnt out and depleted. This is what is often called *compassion fatigue*. However, what people describe is actually not compassion fatigue but, rather, empathy fatigue or empathic distress. The difference lies in our experience of the other person's suffering. Empathy means "I feel what you feel," sharing the feeling that the person you are caring for feels. When the other person is in pain, distress, or suffering, the shared experience becomes draining and depleting for the caregiver. Compassion offers us a different way to relate to other people's suffering. Compassion means, "I am here for you when you suffer." Instead of sharing others' feelings, we bear witness to their suffering, with warmth, care, acceptance, support, and nonjudgment. As Tania Singer, a neuroscientist at the Max Planck Institute in Germany, puts it, "Compassion is feeling *for* and not feeling *with* the other."[78]

I am certainly not saying that you should stop feeling empathy—not at all. Empathy is very important for maintaining connection with others. Empathy makes it possible to understand and resonate with the other person's experience and is therefore necessary to be able to experience compassion.

Empathy is difficult to experience all the time, because of the heavy weight of other people's suffering. In a 2014 paper, Tanya Singer and Olga Klimecki describe empathic distress in response to other people's suffering as a strong negative reaction that creates a feeling of personal suffering and a desire to withdraw from the situation in order to protect oneself.[79] Research shows that empathic distress or empathy fatigue is associated with poor health outcomes and burnout for the caregivers.[80] Compassion, on the other hand, creates other-oriented emotions, such as concern, love and care, with motivation to approach and help the person who is suffering. Research also shows that compassion is associated with good health outcomes and less burn out for the caregivers.[81]

Singer and her colleagues have conducted a number of studies examining brain activation when people experience compassion and empathy. In one of these studies, the researchers first trained a group of participants in empathy and then scanned their brains while they viewed movie clips of other people in distress.[82] These scans revealed increased activation of the insula (responsible for self-awareness, empathy, and perspective taking) and the ACC (involved in processing of emotion and pain). Participants also reported increased levels of personal distress. The same participants were then trained in compassion, and their brains were once again scanned. They reported a decrease in emotional distress and an increase in positive emotions while watching the movie clips. Brain scans revealed activation of completely different brain structures—medial orbitofrontal cortex (involved in emotion regulation and decision making) and ventral striatum (part of the reward system in the brain).

These findings show the importance of differentiating between empathy and compassion. Both are extremely important for our ability to connect and relate to other people. The findings also point us to the importance of cultivating compassion and self-compassion when we find ourselves taking care of others.

Compassion-Based Skills for Responding to Difficult Moments

As with mindfulness meditation and mindfulness-based skills, there is a difference between compassion and self-compassion meditation practices and skills you can use in moments of distress and suffering. This section describes six ways to use compassion- and self-compassion-based skills as part of a healthy response to difficult situations, thoughts, and emotions. You may use these skills in the same way and together with mindfulness-based skills described in Chapter 9.

- *Check in with your values.* You may recall the values exercise from Chapter 9. One of the reasons knowing your values is so helpful is that they can guide your action in a difficult moment. Compassion is a feeling, but it is also a way of acting—you may choose to act compassionately regardless of how you feel. In the moment of challenge, check in with what value may be most relevant and choose a compassionate response most in line with that value.
- *Compassionate language.* Think about what you might say to a friend who is having a hard time. Which words might you use? What would be the tone of your words? You might say something like, "I am here for you. I care," in a gentle and kind tone. This may come easily to you most of the time. Now think about the words you might use for yourself when you are having a hard time. It is often a lot harder to be compassionate toward yourself. You might find yourself saying things like, "Come on, just get over yourself," "What's wrong with you? Be strong!," or "You always do this. Why can't you just do better?" Think about the effect of those words. Do they make you feel better? Do they help you make a change? Do they provide comfort? Probably not. Instead, talk to yourself the way you would to a friend or a loved one.

As strange as it may sound to you, talking to yourself in the second person is actually more effective than in first person. So, I want you to literally talk to yourself the way you would to a friend or a loved one: "I know it's really hard to feel this way," "You are doing your best," "You could really use a break right about now," "I am here for you. I care."

- *Permission not to do anything.* When you are having a particularly difficult time, when you feel overwhelmed by difficult thoughts and emotions, you may feel an intense urge to just get away from these feelings, and you may not feel like you are able to "do" anything useful in that moment. However, these moments often happen when you are faced with a need to make a decision or take some sort of action. Moments like these are not a good time to be making decisions or attempting to make big changes—your judgment is clouded by the intense emotions. In your brain, amygdala is taking over and the prefrontal cortex is not strong enough to put the brakes on amygdala activation. In these moments, the action dictated by the amygdala is aimed at reducing the discomfort you are in, not the long-term benefit of your decisions or actions. When this happens, all you can do is pause and give yourself permission not to do anything until you are able to reregulate and return control of your brain to the prefrontal cortex. Often, what seems like an urgent decision or change in the moment ("I have to talk to my boss about having too much on my plate!" or "I have to decide how to solve this problem!") can actually wait a few hours or overnight, until you are able to make a sound decision not driven by desire to get rid of the discomfort you are feeling. Even in situations when the need to act is urgent (such as deciding how to respond to your opponent in a difficult negotiation as its happening), you can still allow yourself a few moments to pause, "do nothing," and use the time to reregulate using HRV breathing and the skills described in this section. The pause will give you a better chance of choosing a helpful response to the challenge.
- *Compassionate anchor.* In moments of intense distress, what you need the most is the ability to regulate the activation of your brain and your body, allowing amygdala activation to decrease and prefrontal cortex activation to increase, reducing the intensity of overall

activation. As discussed in Chapter 8 on mindfulness, a concentration practice can reduce activation of the amygdala, increase activation of the prefrontal cortex, and strengthen the connection between the two areas of the brain (allowing the prefrontal cortex to put the brakes on amygdala activation). Bringing your attention to your anchor will achieve this purpose without effort. Your anchor may be your here-and-now stone or anything else you can touch or hold in your hand; it may be sounds and sights around you; it may be your breath; or it may be other sensations in your body. Practicing low-and-slow breathing at your RF or at 6 breaths per minute allows you to both anchor your attention and remind your body to regulate itself in a difficult moment.

- *Self-compassion break.* Kristin Neff suggests using this short compassion practice in moments of difficulty to reduce suffering. The self-compassion break combines the three foundational principles of self-compassion described earlier in this chapter: recognizing that this is a moment of suffering (mindfulness) and that suffering is a part of life (common humanity), and asking yourself to be kind to yourself (self-kindness). The practice is simple: take a breath, exhale slowly, and say these words to yourself, feeling the importance of what you are saying:

THIS IS A MOMENT OF SUFFERING.

SUFFERING IS A PART OF LIFE.

MAY I BE KIND TO MYSELF.

- *Self-compassion mantra.* If you've been practicing Mettā or the difficult emotion practice (soften, soothe, and allow; see Appendix A), your mind has learned to associate the words you use in those practices with feelings of comfort and compassion. In moments of difficulty when you don't have a lot of time, you may use the phrases from those practices to just roll around in your mind, as a way to anchor attention, reduce activation, and provide comfort and compassion. You could use the phrases you typically use with Mettā, or you could ask for what you need in that specific moment: "May I have comfort," "May I be at ease," "May I be kinder to myself," "May I have peace," or "May I be free from suffering."

FLARE for Compassion and Self-Compassion

Let's return to the example of Claire, from the beginning of this chapter, to practice an example of FLARE as it applies to compassion and self-compassion:

Feel. As Claire hears Tim tell her that he failed the test, she might feel her heart racing, her face flushing, her breathing quickening. She might notice a tightness in her chest and a thought of "I can't believe this."

Label. Claire would label her experience as "frustration" and "surprise."

Allow. She would allow herself to feel how she feels. The feeling is not under her control, and it is OK to have it.

Respond. In figuring out her response, Claire would call on her value of parenting. She would remind herself of the importance of being supportive and kind to her son. She would also recognize her need for self-compassion toward the difficult feelings she has for her son in that moment. She would take a few mindful low-and-slow breaths to regulate her physiology, silently say a Mettā phrase for what she needs in the moment ("May I have peace"), and respond to Tim with, "Thank you for telling me. You must feel pretty sad about failing this test. How can I help you?"

Expand awareness. Claire would expand her awareness to the love she feels for Tim, allowing the frustration of the moment to become just a part of all of her feelings for him, the strongest of which is love.

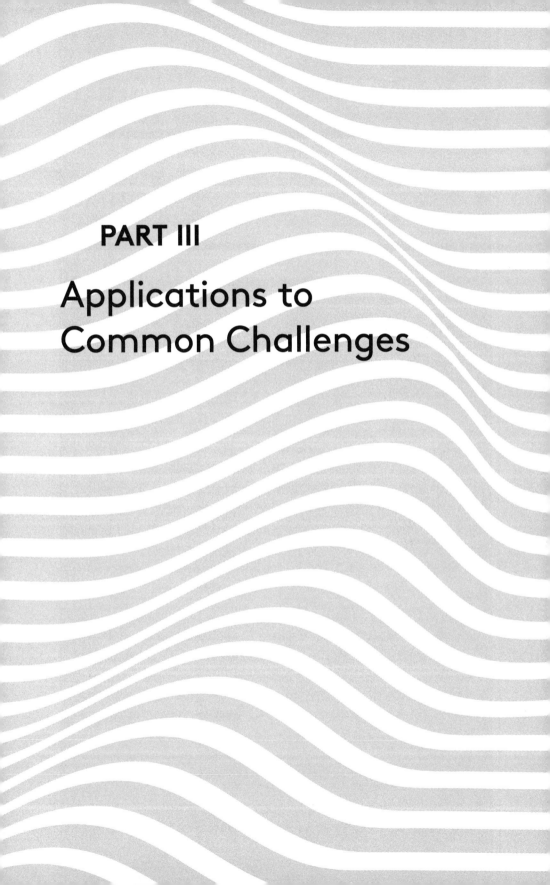

PART III

Applications to Common Challenges

CHAPTER 11

Sleep

Kaitlyn suddenly finds herself awake. It's dark in the room around her, and it must still be dark outside. Kaitlyn wonders what time it is. Then she worries that it might be close to the time her alarm is set to go off and that she does not have much time left to sleep. She wonders what would happen if she does not get back to sleep. She worries if she'll be able to function the next day. Her mind feels more and more awake as it races from one thought to another.

Sleep is as foundational to our well-being as food and water. And in our modern society it is one of the most frequent elements of well-being that we lack. People don't get enough sleep for a variety of reasons, which can be divided into two categories: not allowing ourselves enough time for sleep, and not being able to sleep enough. This chapter discusses the importance of sleep and reasons that people do not get enough, and presents behavioral, biofeedback, and mindfulness-based skills for improving the quality and quantity of your sleep.

Importance of Sleep

I am sure you've heard about the need for 8 hours of sleep. If you suffer from insomnia, you've probably spent a lot of time tossing and turning, worrying about all the terrible things that might happen if you don't get enough sleep. The paradox with sleep is that, while it is indeed necessary for our health and well-being, worrying about not getting enough sleep will not help you sleep better. I briefly discuss the reasons we need sleep and the consequences of not getting enough. As you read these descriptions, keep in mind that this is *not* to give you more reasons to worry about your sleep (that won't help), but to motivate you to do something to improve your sleep, whether you struggle with insomnia or don't allow yourself enough time to sleep.

Many of the consequences of not getting enough sleep are short term. This is good news for those who suffer from insomnia, since these consequences will improve once your sleep improves. There is also good news for those who are inclined to sacrifice sleep in order to work, study, or get other things done during the day: if you allow yourself more time to sleep, you will likely be more productive, function better, and accomplish more.

The immediate short-term consequences of not getting enough sleep include difficulty regulating your mood, feelings of fatigue, difficulty learning and retaining information, and significantly degraded performance in making judgments and decisions. Moreover, lack of sleep makes you more prone to making errors and impacts your ability to perform daily tasks, such as driving safely.

In the long term, chronic sleep deprivation affects your immune system and your ability to regulate hunger and satiety and puts you at higher risk for certain illnesses. Again, the good news is that, once you make changes in your sleep, you also decrease the risk of these negative consequences happening to you.

Effect of Sleep on Productivity and Quality of Life

If you suffer from insomnia and worry about the effect of sleep deprivation on your health and well-being, you might want to simply skip this section. You already know how sleep deprivation affects you, and there is no need to amplify your anxiety. Most of the research I discuss in this section applies to sleep deprivation that results from not allowing yourself enough time to sleep, not to insomnia-related sleep deprivation. Yes, there is a difference between effects of insomnia and effects of not allowing yourself enough time for sleep. If you suffer from insomnia you may want to stop here and proceed to the next section on improving your sleep.

If you tend to sacrifice sleep for the sake getting more done, I have only two words for you: stop it! It may seem logical that if you sleep less you will have time to do more. Research shows that in productivity terms this is simply not true. People who consistently sacrifice sleep in order to have more time to do things actually accomplish less. Lack of sleep affects your executive function: learning, memory, and ability to make decisions, pay attention, and solve problems.[83] Lack of sleep also slows down your cognitive processing and reaction time, meaning that it takes you more time to process information and respond to it. As a result, lack of sleep makes you less efficient, less productive, less capable of solving problems. You end up accomplishing less than you would have had you gotten enough sleep. Slower reaction times may put you in danger of not being able to respond appropriately in situations when a quick response is essential, such as driving.

What's more, research shows that in the sleep-deprived state you are not aware of the deficits in functioning that result from lack of sleep. So, if you are thinking that this is not true for you, that you are able to handle lack of sleep just fine, think again. Studies have consistently shown that, when people who have been deprived of sleep are assessed for their executive function abilities, these abilities are decreased, while the same people may report that they are functioning just fine. Lack of sleep significantly impacts your ability to function effectively, and it does so often outside of your awareness. Even if you do realize that your performance is reduced by the lack of sleep, you may still be underestimating the overall impact.

Lack of sleep also significantly affects your ability to make good decisions. Have you ever been to Las Vegas? Have you noticed that none of the casinos have windows or clocks? They are also very noisy, with very bright lights. This design works very well to trick you into not noticing the passage of time. You cannot see what's going on outside, so you don't notice the change in time of day, and the bright lights will keep you believing it's daytime. This lack of awareness prevents you from realizing that you need to sleep. This is very good news for the casinos, because sleep-deprived gamblers tend to make much poorer decisions that well-rested ones.

Vinod Venkatraman and his colleagues at Duke University compared risk-related decision making for sleep deprived and well-rested participants.[84] You may not be surprised to learn that those who were sleep deprived tended to shift into a decision-making process that focused on gains rather than trying to diminish losses. Brain imaging for these individuals showed an increased activation of the areas of the brain associated with reward anticipation and emotion processing, meaning that their decisions were guided by emotional rather than rational reasoning. Additionally, parts of the brain that would normally alert us to unacceptable losses were less activated for the sleep-deprived participants, meaning that they did not view the consequences of their poor decisions as negatively as they would have had they been well rested. This might explain why we sometimes make decisions that seem perfectly reasonable when we are tired, only to slap ourselves on the forehead the next day with, "What was I thinking?" This is the case for important life decisions, but it is also the case for small, everyday decisions. One poor decision can lead to other poor decisions, and this chain of events can lead to noticeable undesired effects.

In addition, lack of sleep affects your mood and makes you feel tired, which affects your general well-being. It is hard to be content and satisfied with your life when you are walking around grumpy and tired from lack of sleep. This is OK when it happens every once in a while in exceptional circumstances, such as because you went to hear your favorite band play, or you stayed up catching up with friends you haven't seen in a long time, or even in order to finish up a project at work. You may sometimes consciously choose to sacrifice sleep and feel that the consequences the next day are worth it. However, when you are consistently sacrificing sleep, the consequences affect your overall quality of life and are contrary to the goals you are trying to accomplish.

If you picked up this book in the hopes of learning better emotion regulation strategies, or better stress management techniques, or better ways to function at work, at school, or at home, and you are not getting enough sleep on a regular basis, no amount of skill learning will counteract the effect of sleep deprivation on your brain. Jared Minkel and his colleagues at the University of Pennsylvania compared emotion regulation for sleep-deprived individuals and those who are well rested.[85] They found that the sleep-deprived participants had much greater negative reactivity to mild stressors compared to their own baseline before sleep deprivation and compared to well-rested participants. Specifically, they exhibited greater anger, stress, and anxiety responses to what would normally be perceived as mild stressors.

This heightened emotional reactivity and difficulty with emotion regulation are linked to activation of the amygdala, the part of the brain responsible for the fight-or-flight response. Seung-Schik Yoo at Harvard Medical School and his colleagues at UC Berkeley scanned brains of sleep-deprived and well-rested participants while they viewed pictures with intense negative emotional content.[86] They found that the amplitude of amygdala activation was as much as 60 percent higher for sleep-deprived participants than for well-rested participants. They also found that sleep-deprived participants had a three-fold increase in the number of neurons participating in amygdala activation. Finally, for sleep-deprived individuals, the prefrontal cortex showed a weaker connection to the amygdala than for the well-rested individuals. This means that when participants were sleep deprived the prefrontal cortex was much less able to put the brakes on the fight-or-flight response triggered by the amygdala.

Chapter 13 on anxiety and fear describes brain imaging studies showing higher amygdala activation and weaker connectivity between prefrontal cortex and amygdala for anxiety-prone individuals. Amygdala activation in those prone to anger is also higher than typical. The effect of sleep deprivation on the brain is almost identical, making those people more prone to anger and anxiety reactions disproportionate for the situation. This further demonstrates the importance of adequate sleep on emotion regulation.

You may feel that you don't have a choice but to sacrifice sleep—"there are not enough hours in the day." You may have a lot of work or studying to do, you may have children or elderly parents to take care of, you may have housework to take care of, or other important responsibilities. You may think, "Easy for you to say, just get enough sleep. I can't!" It's true, I don't know your unique life circumstances, and I know from firsthand experience just how difficult it can be to make a choice between sleep and everything else that has to get done. All I can say is do your best. If you decide to devote more time to sleep, you will likely notice that you become more efficient at everything else you have to do. As your mood and energy levels improve, you will be able to get more done during the day. I devote the next section to ways you may be able to allow yourself more time for sleep.

How to Give Yourself Permission to Get More Sleep

For those of you that have too much on your plate and have a hard time allowing yourself sufficient time for sleep, I hope that I have convinced you of the importance of prioritizing sleep and getting more. You might be wondering how much sleep you actually need. The answer to that question is not completely straightforward. The general guideline is 7–8 hours. However, everyone has different needs—some people need less sleep, and others need more. To determine how much sleep you need, you can experiment by adding small amounts of sleep to the time you have already allotted for sleep. This will achieve two goals: help you figure out how much sleep you need and make it easier to make a change by doing it gradually. In your experiment, go to bed 15 minutes earlier for a week. Go to bed another 15 minutes earlier the second week. Continue extending your sleep time this way until you are waking up in the morning without an alarm feeling refreshed—then you'll know you've found your ideal sleep time.

I know that is it not nearly as easy to make a change as it sounds. The following are some strategies you can use in allowing yourself more time to sleep:

- *Check in with your values.* You may recall the values discussion from Chapter 9. This is a good time to review your values and think about how sleep fits into them. If your work or career is important to you, getting adequate sleep will help you be more productive and effective. If your family and friends are important, getting adequate sleep will help you be more patient and engaged with them. If self-care is important to you, getting adequate sleep will help you improve your health and generally feel better.
- *Willingness.* Ask yourself whether you are willing to make changes in order to act in accordance with your values. Is acting in accordance with your values worth the effort of prioritizing your sleep? If it is difficult to think about making long-term changes, see if you are willing to make a change for 2 weeks and then evaluate whether the results are worth continuing to make changes.
- *What keeps you from going to sleep?* Take a little time now to think about what keeps you staying up too late at night. I am not talking about things that happen occasionally, like a sick a child or a work project due the next day. I am talking about things that happen on a consistent basis. The following are some possibilities:
  — Having to work at home in the evening
  — Studying late at night
  — Housework
  — Needing time for yourself or with your partner after the kids go to bed at night

- — Desire to do more fun things, like watching TV, playing video games, or reading
- — Belief that sleep is a waste of time—I hope I've convinced you otherwise!

- *What kinds of changes can you make to prioritize sleep?* Of course, to devote more time for sleep, that time has to come from somewhere. This may be difficult at first, before you notice becoming more efficient during the day because of getting more sleep at night. Take some time to think about where that time could come from. The following are some suggestions:
  - — Delegate some of your tasks at work.
  - — Say no to extra responsibilities at work.
  - — Perhaps some things can wait until the next day or maybe do not need to get done at all.
  - — Think about whether you spend too much time on perfecting tasks that would be OK with less time spent on them.
  - — Discuss division of responsibilities with your spouse. Perhaps there is something that he or she can take over.
  - — Have the kids take over some of the chores: folding laundry, loading/unloading the dishwasher, making their own lunches, tidying up the living areas.
  - — Adjust your daily routine so that your day finishes earlier (gradually, 15 minutes at a time).
  - — Balance the time for fun things and sleep.
  - — If you need time for yourself in the evening after the kids go to bed, think about adjusting the kids' bedtime to an earlier time (gradually, 15 minutes at a time). This way everyone will get more sleep.

- Read the section below on improving your sleep for more tips about ways to improve the quality of your sleep as you allow yourself more time to sleep.

Insomnia

Insomnia is quite different from not allowing yourself enough time to sleep. If you've ever experienced insomnia, you don't need a definition—you know what it is. Clinically, *insomnia* is defined as difficulty getting to sleep, staying asleep, or waking up too early, at least 3 nights a week over 3 months or more, despite adequate time allotted for sleep, where this difficulty impacts daytime functioning. Insomnia often starts out as acute, in response to a significant stressor, such as increased stress at work or school, birth of a child or another change in the family circumstances, financial troubles, significant health problems, being a witness or a victim in a life-threatening situation, or loss of a loved one. The tricky part about insomnia is that it often persists even after the initial stressor is gone. You may have found peace with losing someone you love, stress at work may have decreased, or your child may now be sleeping through the night, but the insomnia may have taken on a life of its own. This often happens because, when insomnia first presents itself, it leads to the development of unhelpful habits that enable rather than diminish insomnia.

Some of the unhelpful habits arise out of the mental associations you form with your bed and sleep. If you toss and turn for hours trying to fall asleep while thinking about work, listening for your baby, or trying to figure out a solution to a problem, your body and mind start associating being in bed with tossing and turning instead of sleeping. You might start becoming anxious about going to bed as bedtime approaches, because of the distress you are anticipating from a poor night's sleep. These factors can maintain the insomnia long after the initial trigger is gone, transforming acute insomnia into chronic insomnia. The most important part of breaking the insomnia cycle is changing these unhelpful associations and creating new, helpful ones. If you suffer from insomnia, you may consider seeking out a sleep specialist who is trained in cognitive behavioral therapy for insomnia (CBT-I) to help you through the process of improving your sleep. Improving your sleep may in turn also help you with symptoms of depression, anxiety, and chronic pain.

Medical Conditions and Sleep

A number of medical conditions can affect your sleep in negative ways. Sleep apnea, a potentially serious sleep disorder, is the most common one. People who have sleep apnea periodically stop breathing during the night. Sleep apnea can be initially confused for insomnia, because people who have it do not sleep well at night and feel tired during the day. However, while reasons for insomnia are typically behavioral, sleep apnea is a physiological condition that requires medical treatment, along with behavioral modifications. Common signs of sleep apnea are snoring at night, the sound of gasping or cessation of breathing at night as witnessed by the bed partner, and excessive daytime sleepiness. If you suspect that you may have sleep apnea, be sure to speak with your doctor.

A variety of other sleep disorders exist, such as hypersomnias, parasomnias, sleep movement disorders, and circadian rhythm disorders. These require different treatment than is covered by this book. Be sure to consult with your doctor if you experience any of these.

Improving Your Sleep

As described by Donn Posner of Stanford Medical School in a workshop he taught on CBTi, there are three important components to good sleep. First is a strong *sleep drive*—the need for your body to sleep. Sleep drive increases throughout the day, as more time goes by after you wake up. Adenosine is a neurotransmitter that regulates your sleep drive. It accumulates in your brain throughout the day, gradually increasing sleep drive and making you feel sleepy. Throughout the night, adenosine stored in your brain diminishes, gradually decreasing your sleep drive, and eventually causing you to feel alert and awake.

> The reason caffeine helps you feel less sleepy is because it binds to the adenosine receptors in your brain. Adenosine is a neurotransmitter that regulates your sleep drive. When caffeine binds to those receptors, it blocks adenosine from having its effect. With adenosine action decreased, caffeine helps you maintain alertness.

Second is your *circadian clock*, located in the suprachiasmatic nuclei of your hypothalamus, which regulates your sleep and wake time by sending alerting signals of various strengths to your mind and body across the 24-hour day. Circadian rhythm is biologically predetermined and universal for all people, regardless of culture and lifestyle (although it can be disrupted by irregular schedules and complicated lifestyles common in Western cultures). The central circadian clock coordinates the time-sensitive activity of other biological functions, such as temperature, hormone secretion, metabolism, and heart rate variability (HRV). Body temperature and sleep clocks fluctuate in synchrony, such that you feel sleepiest when your body temperature is lowest, and you feel most awake when your body temperature is highest.

Alerting signals of the circadian clock are stronger during the day and weaker at night. Alerting signals are lowest in the 2–4 a.m. time range, and so is your body temperature. This is the time when you are most likely to sleep. Your alerting signals begin to strengthen around 7 a.m., but they don't stay steady through the day. There is another dip in the strength of the alerting signals in the 1–3 p.m. time frame. This is what we call the "after-lunch slump," except that it has little to do with food and a lot to do with your circadian rhythm. Your body temperature decreases during the 1–3 p.m. time range, and so does your alertness level. Scientist think that the drop in the body temperature contributes to the "slump" far more than a full stomach. The sleepiness you experience during the afternoon slump will be more intense if you are sleep deprived and less intense if you are well rested. There is also an increase in the strength of the alerting signal around 7 or 8 p.m., and your body temperature rises. This is a time when you may experience "second wind"—a sudden increase in energy after a tiring day. Alerting signals begin declining again after 9 p.m. and reach their lowest point by 2–4 a.m.

The third component of good sleep is *low physiological activation*. Your parasympathetic nervous system—the part of your autonomic nervous system responsible for relaxation—needs to be dominant to allow you to fall asleep. Mindfulness and biofeedback skills are particularly helpful in regulating levels of activation and allowing activation to decrease enough to sleep.

The skills helpful in improving your sleep are based on three approaches that address the three components of good sleep described above:

1. Behavioral skills that increase your sleep drive at night, strengthen your circadian signals for sleep, and strengthen the association between bed and sleep
2. Mindfulness skills that decrease cognitive activation
3. Biofeedback skills that regulate physiological activation

I discuss these skills in detail in the sections below. If you have insomnia, whether occasional or chronic, all three sections will be helpful to you. If you don't have insomnia but have difficulty allowing yourself sufficient time for sleep, you should skip the description of sleep restriction in the section on stimulus-control skills for sleep. Read the sections on sleep hygiene and on mindfulness- and biofeedback-based skills. My descriptions of the behavioral skills of sleep hygiene and stimulus control are based on CBT-I, an empirically validated treatment for insomnia.

Behavioral Skills
SLEEP HYGIENE SKILLS

Sleep hygiene has nothing to do with cleanliness but a lot to do with setting up an environment most conducive to sleep. If you tend to not give yourself enough time to sleep, these skills may be particularly important for you. If you have insomnia, these skills are necessary, but not sufficient, to improve your sleep.

- *Watching the clock.* Once you get in bed, put away the clock. If you need to wake up with an alarm, be sure to set it and then place the clock or the phone out of sight, but within earshot. Of course, it is OK to look at the clock during the day and in the evening before bed-time. Once you are in bed, however, seeing the clock will only lead to more sleep disruption. Watching the clock before falling asleep or seeing it when you wake up during the night produces unnecessary worry. Have you ever woken up in the middle of the night, looked at the clock, and felt horrified at how little time you have left to sleep? Or if you've had trouble falling asleep, have you looked at the clock seeing the time go by, each time calculating in your head how much time you have left to sleep, feeling that time slip away? Was knowing the time helpful to you? It rarely is. Watching the clock produces anxiety and activates your mind, making you stay awake longer. So, put away or cover all clocks, including the cell phone. Even when you keep a sleep diary (Table 11.1), do not look at the clock to see what time you've woken up; estimate the best you can, that's all you need.
- *Sleeping environment.* Create a safe and comfortable sleep environment. Feeling safe is paramount to being able to fall and stay asleep. If you've experienced trauma and don't feel safe at night, consider working with a therapist to address trauma and feelings of safety.

Your room at night should be dark and quiet, temperature cool but not cold, your mattress comfortable. Having a TV or radio on at night is likely to wake you up since the noise from TV and radio is often irregular, causing you to wake up to see what's going on. If it's helpful to have some sort of sound on, make sure it is steady and regular, like a sound machine or a fan. If it is hard to control the amount of light in your room at night, consider wearing a sleep mask to keep the light out. Light perception stimulates the alerting mechanisms in your brain, so it is important to keep the light out of your room in order to allow your brain to rest.

- *Food.* Do not eat heavy meals within 4 hours of bedtime. This is particularly important if you tend to wake up with heartburn. Your digestive system slows down at night, and having food that has not been digested at night might disturb your sleep. If you are hungry in the evening, a light snack may be OK. If you tend to wake up to use the bathroom, try to limit your liquids 2 hours before bedtime.

- *Body temperature.* Avoid raising your body temperature close to bedtime. Your body temperature follows a circadian rhythm that is very similar to your sleep rhythm. You feel sleepiest when your body temperature is lowest (at night and around the 1–3 p.m. slump), and you feel most awake when your body temperature is highest (in the morning and around the 7–8 p.m. second wind). If you like to take a bath or a shower in the evening, don't make the water very hot. Make sure the clothing you wear to bed is not making you hot, and the temperature in the room itself is as comfortable as possible.

- *Exercise.* Exercise is excellent for your overall health and will help your sleep. However, exercise close to bedtime may have a negative impact on your sleep, in part because it raises your body temperature and in part because it is activating. Exercise earlier in the day is likely to help you sleep better at night; just make sure that at least 4 hours pass between the end of your exercise routine and sleep time. A relaxed walk, yoga, or gentle stretching before bedtime may be helpful.

- *Wind-down time.* Taking some time to relax before bedtime is helpful in giving your body time to gradually reduce activation. If you come home from a stressful day, your body is likely experiencing strong sympathetic activation that was necessary to meet the challenges of the day. It takes some time for the activation to come down, and attempting to go to sleep before winding down is likely to backfire. Give yourself at least an hour to wind down before bed. You can use that time for perform your bedtime routine, read, or do some other relaxing activity.

- *Blue light*. Avoid blue light, such as that produced by LCD screens on your phone, computer, tablet, and TV, which has been shown to disrupt your body's melatonin production and shift your circadian rhythm.[87] Melatonin is a sleep-regulating hormone that acts in concert with your circadian clock to prepare your body for sleep. Melatonin production in your body increases in the evening. Blue light exposure after 9 p.m. disrupts melatonin production by the pineal gland in your brain and shifts your circadian rhythm, making it harder to fall asleep and stay asleep. Stay away from blue screens at least an hour before bed, and preferably after 9 p.m.

- *Naps*. Naps during the day decrease your sleep drive at night. Your body needs only a certain amount of sleep each day. If you fulfill some that need with a nap, you will experience less need for sleep at night. In his workshop on CBTi, Donn Posner, a sleep researcher at Stanford Medical School, compares napping to snacking—if you eat before dinner, you will be less hungry at dinner. If you nap before bedtime, you will be less sleepy at bedtime. Your best bet is to stay away from naps.

- *Substances*. Certain substances like alcohol and nicotine affect your ability to fall asleep and stay asleep.
  - *Alcohol*. Do not consume alcohol at least 3 hours before bedtime. While alcohol may help you fall asleep faster, it disrupts your sleep cycle and increases the chances of waking up and having trouble getting back to sleep. This does not mean that you can never have a drink with dinner, but if you are actively working on improving your sleep, forgo alcohol until your sleep is consistently better. Once your sleep improves, having an occasional drink in the evening should be fine.

IS COFFEE BAD FOR YOUR HEALTH?

In the past, a lot of health advice included the suggestion to stop drinking coffee—it can raise your blood pressure, cause heart disease, make you anxious, interfere with sleep, and even cause cancer. However, research has now shown the opposite—caffeine is actually good for your health. Older studies reporting associations with cancer and heart disease have been refuted for various reasons. The World Health Organization has taken caffeine off its carcinogen list. In 2015, Ming Ding at Harvard School of Public Health and her colleagues published an extensive long-term study of over 200,000 people, examining associations between coffee consumption and health outcomes.[88] They reported an 8–15 percent *decrease* in risk of death among caffeinated coffee drinkers, with greater benefit for those who drank more coffee. The authors noted a decreased risk of death from heart disease, neurological diseases, and suicide among coffee drinkers. There was no association between coffee drinking and risk of death from cancer. Other studies have found that coffee drinkers may have a lower risk of developing heart disease (such as heart attack, heart failure, and stroke), type 2 diabetes, Parkinson's disease, uterine and liver cancer, cirrhosis of the liver, and gout.[89]

— *Caffeine.* Caffeine exerts its alerting effect for about 5 hours, and more slowly in older adults and pregnant women, as well as in conjunction with certain medications, such as some antidepressants and oral contraceptives. Research has rehabilitated coffee as quite healthy for us (see box). However, coffee may still interfere with your sleep. Limit your coffee intake to 3 cups a day, and have your last cup of the day at lunch or shortly after. Keep in mind that some teas and sodas also contain caffeine.

— *Nicotine.* Nicotine in tobacco and in e-cigarettes is a stimulant that leaves your body fairly quickly, in about 2 hours. This means that you may wake up craving nicotine in the middle of the night. Quitting smoking or using other products containing nicotine is a good idea for a variety of reasons, including improving your sleep.

— *Medications*. Prescription sleep medications may offer a solution in cases of acute insomnia, when taken for a limited amount of time. Keep in mind that sleep medications have limited effect on sleep and come with side effects. Sleep studies have found that sleep medications help people fall asleep only about 8 to 20 minutes faster, add less than 35 minutes of sleep each night, and tend to lose their effect after 3 months of use.[90] Sleep medications may not be additive physiologically (although some are), but all of them can be quite addictive psychologically. If you are used to taking a pill to fall asleep, when you don't have that pill you will naturally worry that you won't sleep well, and you probably won't, simply because of that belief, not because of any physical effect the medication might have. If you are taking sleep medications, you may want to consider asking your physician for a slow taper off of it. If you choose to remain on it, you will still benefit from the skills described in this chapter. Just keep in mind that if you were to go off the sleep medications at some point, your sleep is likely to get worse temporarily and you will need to retrain your sleep strategies.

Taking over-the-counter sleep aids, Benadryl and other antihistamines, and cold medications for sleep is not likely to improve your sleep long term. You might feel drowsy initially, but your quality of sleep will not be good, since many of them disrupt your sleep cycle. For some people, antihistamines and cold medications have an activating rather than calming effect. These medications also come with a high likelihood of psychological addiction that makes it hard to stop using them.

— *Supplements*. Many people believe that melatonin can be a useful sleep aid. It carries the same potential downsides of psychological dependence, while having little effect on your ability to fall asleep. Melatonin is a chronobiotic, not a hypnotic. This means that it can help regulate your circadian clock, making it quite useful for adjusting to jet lag, resuming regular schedule if your sleep-wake cycle has been disturbed by an irregular schedule, and treating circadian rhythm disorders.

Chamomile tea, valerian root, Kava, and other herbal supplements are believed to help you sleep. These supplements may have a calming effect on your nervous system, but they are unlikely to help you fall asleep, while still carrying the high likelihood of psychological dependence, preventing you from sleeping without them. Does this mean you should not have a cup of chamomile tea in the evening? No! If you enjoy it, go ahead. It can be a nice part of your wind-down time. Just don't treat it as a sleep aid.

— *Cannabis.* Marijuana has often been suggested as a helpful sleep aid. It can indeed help people fall asleep faster, but people develop tolerance to it and end up waking up more frequently at night as that happens. The problem with using marijuana as a sleep aid is the same as using any substance to help you fall asleep—you are likely to become psychologically addicted to it and have trouble sleeping without it, even when it no longer has an effect.

STIMULUS-CONTROL SKILLS FOR SLEEP

Stimulus-control skills have to do with those associations that our minds and bodies form with sleep and bed. You want your body and mind to associate your bed with sleep (and sex) and not with anything else. When it comes to insomnia, research shows that stimulus-control skills are the most important ingredients for improving sleep. If you do not have insomnia but wish to improve your overall quality of sleep, you may implement all of the skills in this section except the sleep restriction protocol.

This section describes stimulus-control techniques that will help you improve your sleep. Some of those changes may seem difficult to make. When thinking about making these changes, refer back to the concepts of willingness and values in Chapter 9, and ask yourself whether the discomfort of making these changes is worth the improvement in sleep you are likely to experience.

- *Regular wake-up time.* Waking up at the same time every day will strengthen your circadian clock and your drive to sleep. Sleeping in reduces your sleep drive at night and confuses your circadian clock.

Pick a regular wake-up time and stick to getting up within 30 minutes of it, even on weekends.

- *Do not go to bed until you are sleepy.* Even if it is your bedtime, if you are not sleepy when the clock says it's time to go to bed, you will likely toss and turn rather than go to sleep. This will perpetuate the association between your bed and tossing and turning rather than sleeping. If you are not sleepy at bedtime, do something low key and relaxing (such as reading, listening to music, practicing breathing or meditation) until you feel sleepy. Can you tell the difference between sleepy and tired? It is possible to feel tired physically without feeling sleepy. Think about what the difference is for you. Feeling tired is something you feel in your body. Sleepy is more of a feeling in your mind.

  If you do not have insomnia and tend to stay up too late to get things done, you may be in the habit of pushing past the time when you are sleepy. For you, the recommendation is to retrain yourself to listen to your body and go to bed when you feel sleepy.

- *Do not stay in bed longer than 15 minutes if not sleeping.* If you get in bed feeling sleepy but then find yourself mostly alert after about 15 minutes (without looking at the clock—approximate!), get out of bed, go to a different room, and do something low key and relaxing. Low-and-slow breathing at your resonance frequency and/or meditation are always good choices. Do the same thing if you wake up at night and have trouble falling back asleep. Do not linger in bed not sleeping in the morning, either. It is OK to give yourself a few minutes to wake up, but then get out of bed and start your day, even if it's earlier than you'd like it to be. Staying in bed not sleeping also perpetuates the unhealthy association between your bed and not sleeping. Getting out of bed when not asleep trains your body and brain to once again associate your bed with sleep.

  When you first start using this skill, you may find that when you get out of bed, go somewhere else, and then head back when feeling sleepy, you suddenly feel wide awake once you get back to your own bed. It is tempting to attribute this to the idea that walking back to bed reactivated you and you should have just stayed where you were. In fact, the reason that you suddenly don't feel sleepy is the association your mind has formed between your bed and not sleep-ing. If this happens, get out of bed again so as not to perpetuate the unhelpful association, stay out of bed until sleepy, and then get back again. Don't fall asleep in the other place, since you want your mind to relearn to associate your bed (not your couch or another bed in the house) with sleep. This will likely feel frustrating the first few times, but it will be difficult to improve your sleep without it.

- *Sleep restriction.* This is the most effective method in improving your sleep. It is also the most difficult to implement. Below, I provide sim-plified instructions that may make it easier for you to implement. You may consider seeing a trained sleep specialist to assist you.

  With sleep restriction, you may feel worse before you feel bet-ter. You may want to implement the other changes described in this chapter first to make the process of sleep restriction less difficult. The goal of sleep restriction is to increase your sleep efficiency—the amount of time you spend in bed sleeping—in order to strengthen the association between your bed and sleep. You do not have control over the amount of time you sleep, but you do have control over the amount of time you spend in bed. Therefore, you will initially cut down the amount of time you spend in bed, increase your sleep efficiency, and strengthen the association between your bed and sleep. As that association gets stronger, you will be able to gradually extend the amount of time you spend in bed until you get to your ideal number of hours of sleep.

  The first couple of weeks of sleep restriction will be hard, and you may feel even more tired than usual. Choose a time to start sleep restriction when you don't have to drive while feeling tired or perform any other potentially dangerous activities. If you are willing to experience the extra fatigue for a couple of weeks and stick with the protocol, you will likely experience improvement in your sleep by the second or third week. Getting to full number of hours you need may take 6–8 weeks.

  — Keep a sleep diary for a week or two before making any changes. This will help you figure out the kind of changes you need to make. (Table 11.1 is a simplified version of the CBT-I sleep diary.) The sleep diary will help you determine the amount of time you

TABLE 11.1 SLEEP DIARY

Fill in this information each morning when you wake up. The first column is filled in as an example.

Today's date	12/15						
1. What time did you get into bed?	10 p.m.						
2. What time did you turn off the lights and decide to go to sleep?	10:30 p.m.						
3. Approximately what time did you fall asleep?	11:15 p.m.						
4. How many times did you wake up at night, not counting the final time you woke up for the day?	3						
5. Approximately how long did those awakenings last altogether?	45 min						
6. What time was your final awakening for the day?	6:30 a.m.						
7. What time did you get out of bed for the day?	7:30 a.m.						
8. Rate your quality of sleep on the scale from 1 (poor) to 5 (great)	3						
9. In total, how long did you sleep? (time from row 3 to row 6, minus time in row 5)	6.5 hours						
10. In total, how many hours did you spend in bed? (time from row 1 to row 7)	9.5 hours						
11. Calculate your sleep efficiency for the night (row 9 divided by row 10, multiplied by 100)	68%						
12. Did you take sleep medication (prescription or over-the-counter)?	No						

Source: adapted with permission from Carney et al. (2012), Oxford University Press currently spend in bed and the amount of time you are sleeping. The formula for calculating sleep efficiency is

$$\text{Sleep efficiency} = \frac{\text{Time spent asleep}}{\text{Time spent in bed}} \times 100$$

Ideal sleep efficiency is over 90 percent. As you fill out the sleep diary, do not watch the clock after you get into bed. Approximate times are just fine.

— Once you are ready to restrict your sleep and increase your sleep efficiency, set a wake-up time you would like to stick with long term—perhaps a time you need to get up for work or school. This will be your wake-up time for the duration of sleep retraining, even on weekends.

— Determine the total number of hours you can spend in bed by taking the average number of hours you've spent sleeping for the week or two you were keeping your diary, and add to it 25 percent of the time you spent in bed awake. If that number is less than 5 hours, set a minimum of 5—do not go lower than that. So, if you slept for 6.5 hours a night on average for a week, and you spent an average of 3 hours not sleeping each night, then you would add 45 minutes (one-quarter of 3 hours) to your 6.5 hours and set the time in bed at 7.25 hours. Now subtract your time allotted in bed from the time you've set as your wake-up time, and that's your bedtime. So, if you've selected 7 a.m. as your ideal wake up time, subtract 7.25 hours and you get 11:45 p.m. as your bedtime.

— Stick with your sleep schedule, even though it may be really hard to do. Do your best not to dose off on the couch or in front of the TV at night. If you feel sleepy before it's time to get in bed, stand up, walk around, do the dishes, or any other low-key activity that does not involve sitting or lying down until it's your bedtime.

— If your bedtime comes around and you don't feel sleepy yet, don't get into bed—wait until you feel sleepy. Get up at the predetermined time—do not extend your sleep time if you went to bed later than planned.

— If you wake up at night and find yourself awake for approximately

15 minutes (without looking at the clock), get out of bed and do something low key in a different room until you feel sleepy again.

— Continue keeping your sleep diary. If your sleep efficiency at the end of the week is at least 85 percent, push your bedtime to 15 minutes earlier and stick with the predetermined wake-up time. If your sleep efficiency at the end of the week is less than 80 percent, push your bedtime 15 minutes later (but do not make your total time in bed less than 5 hours; if you are at 5 hours, continue utilizing the sleep skills in this chapter until your sleep efficiency improves). If your sleep efficiency is between 80 and 85 percent, stay with the same schedule for another week.

— Each week that your sleep efficiency is at 85 percent or above, you can extend your bedtime by 15 minutes. Sometimes you will spend a couple of weeks with the same bedtime until your sleep efficiency goes up to 85 percent.

— Once you hit the point when you are getting a good number of hours of sleep, getting good-quality sleep, and waking up refreshed, with your sleep efficiency at 90 percent or above, you can stop extending your bedtime—you have determined the ideal number of hours of sleep you need. Stick with the sleep schedule as much as possible.

— If your sleep gets disrupted again, return to the skills you've used here, and do a mini-sleep restriction again. It won't take as long or be as hard if you start it as soon as you've noticed a sleep disruption lasting longer than 2 weeks.

Mindfulness-Based Skills for Sleep

Mindfulness-based skills for sleep are aimed at helping you disengage from the chatter of your mind that happens when you get into bed. That chatter may be upsetting and activating. Mindfulness-based skills will help you experience your thoughts without getting stuck in them or the feelings that they might produce.

- *Giving up futile attempt to control sleep.* As Donn Posner of Stanford Medical School asks, What do you do to go to sleep? A good sleeper will answer, "I don't know . . . nothing." A person suffering from insomnia might say, "Breathe or clear my head or reduce anxiety." Our perception that we can somehow induce sleep leads to sleep effort. Sleep effort is a major factor maintaining chronic insomnia—the more you try to sleep, the less sleep you get. The more you try to sleep, the more activated and anxious you get. This is similar to the trying to relax oxymoron I described in Chapter 9. Sleep effort is just as much of an oxymoron: attempts to make yourself go to sleep will activate your sympathetic nervous system, when what you need is a strong parasympathetic nervous system activity to allow you to go to sleep. All you can do is set up an environment most conducive to sleep (see the section on sleep hygiene skills above) and then allow your body and mind to sleep. They will do so on their own.

- *Mindful language.* Many of the words we use when talking about going to sleep are associated with sleep effort: "I am *trying* to sleep," or "I *have* to go to sleep now," or "I *must* try to sleep." These kinds of words produce effort and unhelpful activation. Instead, allow your mind and body to sleep. Trust that your mind and body will sleep, and they will—your body and mind cannot go without sleep for long, and they will get sleep. All you need to do is allow your mind and body to do what they know how to do—sleep.

- *Sleep-related thoughts and emotions.* When sleep is a chronic problem, you might find yourself thinking about sleep during your waking hours and more and more as bedtime approaches. You might worry whether you will get enough sleep (anticipatory anxiety). You might worry about how the night is going to go when you are in bed (intrusive thoughts). You might think of all the terrible things that might happen if you don't get enough sleep (catastrophizing). You might find yourself feeling scared of what will happen if you don't get a certain number of hours of sleep. You might find yourself feeling frustrated or sad or angry about not being able to sleep.

    These difficult thoughts and emotions are likely a result of default mode network activity (DMN). You may recall the discussion of the DMN in Chapter 7 on mindfulness. The DMN comes online when your brain is at rest and not focused on anything in particular. This is exactly what happens when you get in bed—your mind is at rest and the DMN comes online as a result. The DMN typically directs your thoughts to reviewing problems from the past, anticipating problems in the future, and comparing yourself to other people in the present, usually in unfavorable ways. This is why it sometimes feels like you can't sleep because your mind is so busy. In reality, the DMN activates when you are lying in bed not sleeping, so your mind is busy because you are not sleeping. Learning to deactivate the DMN will help to disengage from the busy mind.

You can't control whether thoughts and emotions come into your mind. You can, however, control how you respond to them. Use FLARE, described in Chapter 9, as a foundation for a helpful response to difficult thoughts and emotions related to sleep. I provide an example of FLARE for sleep at the end of this chapter.

Be sure to review Chapter 9 on mindfulness-based skills for general approach to difficult thoughts and emotions. Mindfulness skills that are particularly helpful as part of responding to sleep-related thoughts and emotions are as follows:

- *Reminder that you've done this before.* If you've struggled with insomnia for a while, there have been plenty of days when you have not gotten enough sleep, and you've been able to function. This day is no different.
- *Here-and-now stone* (see Chapter 8 for full instructions). This practice will help you reduce the intensity of difficult feelings and the likelihood of DMN activity.
- *Thoughts-on-leaves meditation practice.* This is a nice way to respond to unhelpful thoughts because it gives you a way to respond without engaging with them. You learn to notice your thoughts and let them come and go. See the full description of the exercise in Appendix A, or you can download the recording at www.innakhazan.com/meditation_recordings.html.
- *"Don't know" mantra.* This is a great way to respond to all those *what ifs* that go through your mind: "What if I don't sleep tonight?" "What

if I can't function tomorrow?" "What if I am really groggy in the morning?" The truth is that you don't know the answer to any of these questions. The best way to answer them is with "I don't know . . . let's see what happens." This allows you to respond to unhelpful thoughts (instead of trying to ignore them) without getting stuck in them (by attempting to come up with answers and solutions).

- *Mindfulness of thoughts, feelings, physiological sensations.* This practice will allow you to disengage from difficult thoughts and emotions and reduce intensity of activation. See instructions in Appendix A, or download the recording at www.innakhazan.com/meditation_recordings.html.

- *Difficult emotion practice.* This practice allows you to attend to difficult emotions with kindness and compassion, gently disengaging and allowing your mind and body to quiet down. See instructions in Appendix A, or download the recording at www.innakhazan.com/meditation_recordings.html.

- *Mettā practice.* This is a great practice to do whenever you are feeling distressed. The time when you can't sleep is also a great opportunity to practice Mettā for yourself and your loved ones. See instructions in Chapter 10, or download the recording at www.innakhazan.com/meditation_recordings.html.

Whichever skills you choose to practice, notice the intention behind your practices. If your intention is to get to sleep, consider reframing that intention to choosing a helpful response to a time when you are not sleeping. The change of intention will allow you to create an internal environment most conducive to sleep, rather than struggling and failing to sleep.

Biofeedback-Based Skills for Sleep

Research has shown that HRV may be impaired in people suffering from chronic insomnia, with the sympathetic nervous system being overactivated and parasympathetic nervous system not being able to effectively put on the brakes. For example, a study by Benedetto Farina at Universita Europea and his colleagues in Italy showed that people suffering from insomnia have higher sympathetic activation before sleep and during early stages of sleep, but not during deep or dream sleep or upon waking.[91] These findings explain why it is harder for those who suffer from insomnia to get to sleep and why they are much more likely to awaken when it seems like they are drifting off to sleep—the increased sympathetic activation before sleep and in the early stages of sleep may be responsible for these difficulties.

Studies have also shown the effectiveness of HRV biofeedback in management of insomnia.[92] HRV biofeedback trains your body's ability to regulate itself and strengthens the ability of the parasympathetic nervous system to put the brakes on sympathetic activation. This is exactly what is needed to allow your mind and body to reduce activation in preparation for sleep.

Review Chapter 3 on HRV, and follow instructions in that chapter to determine your resonance frequency breathing rate and train your HRV at that rate, or practice at 6 breaths per minute. Regular practice of HRV skills will gradually strengthen your ability to regulate activation for sleep, as well as at other times during the day. You may choose bedtime as your regular practice time for HRV skills in order to both get your training time in and prepare yourself for sleep. Ideally, do your practice close to bedtime, but not in bed, in order to reduce the temptation to use HRV breathing as a tool to make yourself sleep. This intention will create sleep effort and be counterproductive to your goals. Instead, use your HRV practice time with the intention of improving your ability to self-regulate and to prepare your body for sleep.

HRV breathing practice may also be a part of a healthy response to not being able to sleep. Getting out of bed after not being able to sleep may create a wonderful opportunity for HRV practice.

FLARE for Sleep

Let's go through an example of the FLARE technique as it applies to sleep, using the example of Kaitlyn from the beginning of the chapter.

> *Feel.* In this step Kaitlyn would notice the tension, rapid heartbeat, a lump in her throat, and a tightness in her chest as she finds herself awake in the middle of the night. She would notice thoughts of "I wonder what time it is," "I hope I can get back to sleep," and "I won't be able to function tomorrow if I don't sleep." She would notice her thoughts racing from one worry to another.

Label. Kaitlyn would label her experience as "worry" or "anticipation." She might also label her racing mind as default mode network activity.

Allow. Kaitlyn would say to herself, "It is OK to feel this way. It is OK to have these thoughts. Everyone has a default mode network. It is OK to have this experience,"

Respond. Kaitlyn would check in with her willingness to get out of her warm cozy bed and go into the living room because she has been awake for a while. She would ask herself, "Am I willing to experience the discomfort of getting out of bed in order to improve my sleep in the long term?" She would answer, "Yes, I am willing," and go to the couch. Once on the couch, Kaitlyn might choose to practice her mindful HRV breathing in order to remind her body to regulate itself and in order to reduce the intensity of the activation she is experiencing. She might also add a Mettā practice for herself and her family members sleeping in the house, simply because that is a nice thing to do when one cannot sleep.

Expand awareness. As she allows her experience to be as it is and decides on the most helpful way to respond to it, Kaitlyn would expand her awareness to the feeling of the sheets on her bed, and the sound of her wife breathing next to her, and the shadows on the wall. She would also notice her breathing and her heartbeat and the thought about what she might have for breakfast that crosses her mind. The intensity of focus on the fact that she is not sleeping would diminish, she would be able to see this experience as a part of her larger experience, and it will be easier for Kaitlyn to get out of bed and implement the rest of her chosen response.

CHAPTER 12

Stress and Performance

Imagine one of your best friends, a talented pianist, calls you to tell you about his big break—a chance to perform with the Boston Symphony. He tells you what a big deal this performance is and how important it is for him to do well. His future career depends on this one performance. He is feeling very nervous about it. What would be the one piece of advice you'd give him? Take a moment now and think about it, before reading on.

What kind of advice did you give? Did it contain some version of *try to relax and calm down*? If so, you are in great company—about 90 percent of people out there would give the same advice. Harvard business school psychologist Alison Brooks asked 300 people this question: What would you advise a coworker who is preparing for a big speech in front of the whole company, including the CEO, and is feeling nervous about it?[93] Over 90 percent of responses contained the idea that calming down or relaxing is the answer to doing one's best. This idea makes sense, right? Being nervous before an important performance could not possibly be good for us, could it? We have to calm down in order to do our best, don't we?

Turns out we don't. Brooks's research showed that attempts to calm down before a stressful performance are not only ineffective but also not necessary.[94] She examined the effects of different perceptions of the signs of stress on people's performance in three separate studies. She asked participants, all university students with no prior training on any of the tasks, to sing karaoke in front of a group of strangers, while being evaluated on the accuracy of the singing; give a persuasive 2-minute speech about why they are a good work partner; or complete a difficult math task under time pressure, while being judged for accuracy. Before the performance, the participants were asked to repeat self-statements designed to induce one of three mind-sets: being excited, being anxious, or being calm. There was also a control group with no self-statements. Slightly different self-statements were used for different types of performance, and included statemements such as "I am excited," "I am anxious," "I am calm," "Try to get excited," "Try to remain calm."

Brooks found that all the participants had equal physiological activation, meaning that those who were instructed to calm down did not succeed in doing so. Across all three studies, participants in the "excited" condition performed the best in their tasks—sang more accurately, delivered the best speeches (as evaluated by judges blind to the participants' mind-set condition), and did the best on the math task. The excited participants also felt the best about their performance—they felt the most confident and comfortable with the challenge.

These findings tell us that we do not need to purposefully change our physiological response to stress—we do not need to calm down—in order to do our best. All we need to do is to interpret the sensations of activation in a more helpful way. Self-statements of "I am excited" instead of "I am anxious" or "I need to calm down" will go a long way toward helping you feel more comfortable and confident and actually do better during your challenge.

> We do not need to purposefully change our physiological response to stress. We do not need to calm down in order to do our best. All we need to do is interpret the sensations of activation in a more helpful way.

This is great news if you have ever tried to calm down before an important challenge—a meeting, a presentation, a test, a competition, or anything else. You can now give yourself permission to stop using up your resources on something that is not possible and not necessary—attempts to relax—and direct them toward something that you actually have control over: the task or challenge itself. If you are about to give a presentation, you can focus on the material you are presenting, delivering a clear and meaningful message, and engaging with your audience, instead of trying to relax. If you are about to play a piano concerto, you can focus on being in the moment with the music, on expressing the emotion of the piece, and on captivating the audience's attention, instead of trying to relax.

Calming down before a performance is hard work—it requires trying to get your mind to do something completely different from what your body is doing. Your body is preparing for action—increasing heart rate, speeding up your breathing, making you sweat—while your mind is attempting to bring all of that down. If this sounds familiar, take a moment to think about how this worked for you. I will hazard a guess that it didn't. At best, you could not actually relax before the challenge, and at worst, you became even more anxious, and the physiological symptoms of anxiety interfered with your ability to perform. This effort to calm down in the face of a challenge is what I call "futile effort to control the uncontrollable" (see Chapter 9 for a detailed discussion).

> You can now give yourself permission to stop using up your resources on something that is not possible and not necessary—attempts to relax—and direct them toward something that you actually have control over: the task or challenge itself.

Even though most of us believe that relaxation or calming down is necessary for us to do our best, scientific evidence to the contrary has actually been around for a while. As early as the beginning of the twentieth century, psychologists Robert Yerkes and John Dodson demonstrated the importance of an optimal level of physiological activation in peak performance. They formulated what is now known as the *Yerkes-Dodson law*, which states that when physiological activation is too low, so is our performance. If our physiological activation is too high, our performance suffers as well. There is a sweet spot of activation that allows us to perform at our best. See Figure 12.1 for an illustration of the Yerkes-Dodson curve.

The specific level of physiological activation we need do our best varies from task to task—the level of activation necessary for running a 100-meter dash is quite different from the level of activation needed to deliver a great presentation. The trick is for your body to be able to achieve this optimal level of activation. How does your body know how much of a boost to give you, and how does it get there? Self-regulation lies at the heart of your body's ability

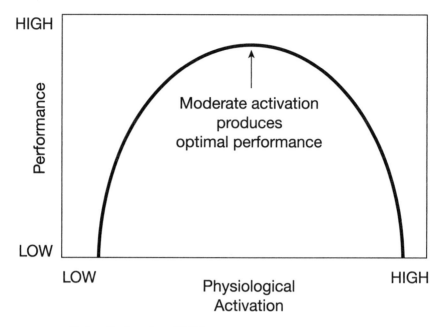

FIGURE 12.1: Yerkes-Dodson law (1908)

to settle into the sweet spot of activation for each task. This is where heart rate variability (HRV) comes in again. You may recall from Chapter 3 that HRV is an indicator of the ability of your body to regulate itself. And training to increase your HRV increases your ability to self-regulate. I return to HRV training later in this chapter.

Right now, let's focus on the kind of physiological arousal that happens when you are not excited about the challenge that lies ahead and you cannot see yourself getting excited. Imagine that you are working on an important time-sensitive project at work, and you realize that you've made a mistake and will not make the deadline. You have to go talk to your boss about the problem. Your heart is beating fast, your breathing is shallow, your hands are sweaty, and the butterflies in your stomach are dancing a jig. You are not at all excited about this conversation. So, how can you respond to the physiological signs of stress in a helpful way and perform at your best? I have good news for you. Research has shown that simply recognizing sensations of stress as being helpful and adaptive is just as effective in improving performance in challenging situations.

One specific way to allow stress to be helpful is to move away from seeing stress as a threat and move toward seeing stress as a challenge. Psychologist James Blascovich at University of California, Santa Barbara and his colleagues were first to discuss our interpretation of stress in terms of challenge and threat. When you interpret a stressful situation as one that you can handle, a situation where you have the resources to meet the demands of the situation, the situation becomes a challenge. If, on the other hand, you perceive your resources as inadequate in meeting the demands of the situation, meaning that you don't feel you can handle it, the situation becomes a threat.

Studies conducted by Blascovich and his team showed that human body responds to challenges differently than it does to threats.[95] When you interpret the situation as a challenge, your heart functions more efficiently and your coronary blood vessels dilate. When you interpret the situation as a threat, your heart has to work harder to pump the blood out to your body, and your coronary blood vessels constrict, which may raise blood pressure and make less blood and oxygen available to the rest of your body. Repeated activation of the threat response may lead to cardiovascular disease and faster brain aging in the long term.

So, how do you turn a threat into a challenge? The answer is actually simpler than you might think. Turns out, the choice of which of those physiological changes (challenge or threat) your body goes through in response to stress is very much up to you. It all has to do with the way you interpret the presence and experience of stress—your interpretation of the experience is what makes the difference. How do I know that? There is research to back this up.

Jeremy Jamieson, a psychologist at Harvard University, and his colleagues conducted a study examining the effects of interpretation of stress on participants' cardiovascular response and ability to perform in a difficult situation.[96] In this study, fifty participants came into the lab, where their cardiovascular function was assessed and recorded. After the initial assessment, participants were divided into three groups. One group read an article on the beneficial effects of stress, a second group read an article advocating for ignoring stressful stimuli, and the third group participated in an unrelated task. Then, all the participants delivered a 5-minute video-recorded speech in front of two evaluators. Unbeknownst to the participants, the evaluators were trained to give negative nonverbal feedback—frowning, furrowing the brow, crossing arms, and other discouraging body language—while the participants were speaking. You might imagine what that experience felt like! Researchers also assessed participants' perceptions of whether they had sufficient resources to meet the demands of the situation (threat vs. challenge mentality) and whether they were more likely to pay attention to threatening stimuli than neutral ones.

The results of the study were fascinating. The group that was trained to interpret stress as helpful and adaptive exhibited the healthiest cardiovascular response to stress—with increased cardiac efficiency and lower vascular resistance—compared to the other two groups. These participants also reported having access to greater internal resources and showed less attention to potential threats. At the same time, there was no difference in arousal levels among participants, meaning that those who interpreted stress as helpful and adaptive were no less physiologically activated than all the others. Overall, this study showed that interpreting stress as helpful and adaptive leads to healthier heart function and to a greater likelihood of responding to stress as a challenge, rather than a threat. Interpreting stress as helpful does not decrease physiological activation, but it reshapes the way we respond to it, both emotionally and physiologically.

In another study, Jamieson and his colleagues examined the effects of interpreting physiological arousal as a challenge response on GRE scores.[97] In this study, sixty students preparing to take the GRE came to the lab, where all of them were told that it is normal to experience anxiety before a test. Then half of the students were also told that the physiological arousal not only does not hurt performance, but actually helps it. Both groups then went on to practice and eventually take the GREs. Guess what the study found? You may not be surprised to hear that those who learned to interpret their physiological arousal as helpful did better on both practice GREs and the actual exam.

In addition to a healthier cardiovascular response, there is another important physiological measure of a challenge response. This one has to do with the stress hormones your body produces during the stressful event. One such stress hormone is cortisol, which is necessary to give your body the energy it needs to meet a challenge—it helps increase your blood sugar levels to give your body more energy, and then helps your body use that energy more efficiently. However, cortisol also suppresses your immune system and prevents wounds from healing. In the long term, too much cortisol is associated with chronic health conditions such as diabetes and heart disease.

The other stress hormone is called dehydroepiandrosterone (DHEA), which counteracts some of the negative effects of cortisol, including boosting immune response and wound healing. DHEA is released by the adrenal glands, just like cortisol, but it is also produced in the brain, therefore increasing its action on the central nervous system. Higher levels of DHEA are associated with improvements in memory, attention, and decision making, as well as reduction in interference of negative emotional cues on your ability to focus on the task at hand, and improvements in performance under stressful conditions.

For example, a 2009 study by Charles Morgan at Yale University and his colleagues examined the levels of DHEA in soldiers tasked with extremely stressful and dangerous underwater navigation at night.[98] This task demanded a high level of performance both cognitively (ability to focus and stay on course) and physically (swimming fast with limited supply of oxygen). Soldiers with higher levels of DHEA at baseline performed the best during underwater navigation and exhibited the fewest negative symptoms of threat, such as anxiety and underwater dissociation.

Both DHEA and cortisol are important for human functioning in different ways. A ratio of cortisol to DHEA is what determines whether your response to stress is that of a challenge or that of a threat. Higher levels of DHEA and lower levels of cortisol are associated with a challenge response, while higher levels of cortisol and lower levels of DHEA are associated with a threat response. Not surprisingly, research has also shown that interpreting stress-related physiological activation as helpful and adaptive is associated with higher levels of DHEA and lower levels of cortisol, consistent with a challenge response.

Sometimes, when I speak with others about ways of interpreting our physiological sensations in challenging situations as helpful and adaptive rather than damaging and dangerous, people wonder whether I am just telling them to trick themselves into thinking that stress isn't actually so bad and perhaps not stressful at all, when in reality what they are experiencing is bad and dangerous. Let me tell you why I am not asking you to trick yourself but, rather, to come to a more accurate conclusion about your experience.

What do you feel physiologically when you are excited? Perhaps your heart beats faster, your breathing quickens a bit, the palms of your hands get a little sweaty, and you feel butterflies in your stomach? What do you feel when you are anxious? Perhaps your heart beats a little fast, your breathing quickens a bit, the palms of your hands gets sweaty, and you feel butterflies in your stomach? What happens when you are preparing for a run? Perhaps your heart beats a little fast, your breathing quickens a bit, the palms of your hands gets sweaty, and you feel butterflies in your stomach? Can you tell the difference between the physiological sensations of excitement, anxiety, and the physiological activation of your body in preparation for a physical challenge? All those experiences are pretty similar to us subjectively—so similar, in fact, that you probably could not tell the difference between them. So, how do you know what you are experiencing? The context of your experience plays a big role.

In the 1960s social psychologists Stanley Schachter and Jerome Singer conducted an experiment showing how our environment influences the way we interpret our physiological sensations.[99] They invited a group of participants into their lab and told them that they are testing a vitamin to improve vision, which will be given by injection. In reality, the injection contained epinephrine, also known as adrenaline, a neurotransmitter responsible for the fight-or-flight response and all of its accompanying physical sensations, such as rapid heartbeat, faster breathing, sweating, muscle tension, and so on. Participants were divided into four groups. The first group was told that the "side effects" of the vitamin shot are faster heartbeat and breathing, sweatiness, shaky hands, flushed face, muscle tension, and such, describing the effects of epinephrine. This was the "epinephrine-informed" condition. The second group was told that the side effects of the shot may include the feeling of numbness in the feet, an itchy sensation in their body, and a slight headache, none of which were expected to actually happen. This was the "epinephrine-misinformed" condition. The third group was not told what to expect at all. This was the "epinephrine-ignorant" condition. The fourth group was given a saline shot instead of the adrenaline shot. This was the control group. Everyone's heart rates were measured, and everyone was asked to fill out a questionnaire about how they felt before the shot.

After the shots were administered, each participant was placed into a room and asked to wait for the next part of the study. In reality, this *was* the next part of the study. Unbeknownst to the participants, also in the room was a confederate researcher, a person who was part of the study. This confederate acted in one of two ways. For some of the participants, the confederate acted in a very happy, excited way, showing in all sorts of ways just how happy he was to be part of the study. For other participants, the confederate acted in an angry way, showing just how miserable he thought taking part in the study was. Participants were then asked to once again fill out a questionnaire about how they felt, while they "waited." Participants were also video-recorded and later assessed for body language expressions of happiness or anger by judges blind to the confederate's behavior.

The results the study were as follows:

- All the participants' heart rates were about the same, except for those who received the saline shot. This shows that the epinephrine achieved its effects.
- The epinephrine-misinformed group did not experience the numbness, itching, and headache that they were told to expect. This means that the participants' experience was not due to the power of suggestion.
- The epinephrine-informed participants, who expected to feel their hearts racing, breathing quickening, sweatiness, and other effects of epinephrine, did not experience any change in their emotions after being in the room with the confederate.
- Epinephrine-ignorant participants, who were not expecting to feel their physiological symptoms, became either more happy or more angry, depending on the confederate they interacted with.

These results indicate that when we experience an otherwise unexplained physiological change, we tend to explain this change by assigning an emotional label based on the context of our experience. So, when we expect to feel stressed or anxious before a challenge, as dictated by the social norms of what we are supposed to feel in that situation, we tend to interpret the normal sensations of our bodies activating and gearing up for challenge ahead as somehow not normal, bad for us, or something to be changed.

However, as clearly shown by the Yerkes-Dodson law, and the research describing what happens in our bodies before a challenge, the activation that we experience is healthy, normal, and necessary in order for us to perform at our best. Misinterpretation of this activation as abnormal leads to an automatic reaction of threat. Reminding ourselves that this activation is normal, adaptive, and healthy is not in any way lying to ourselves or trying to change how we feel. This reminder simply serves as a way of allowing our body to do what it knows how to do.

Stress and Meaning

STRESS LEADS TO GROWTH: THE STORY OF A LOBSTER

Rabbi Abraham Twerski, professor of psychiatry at the University of Pittsburg and an ordained rabbi, tells the story of a lobster. Do you know how lobsters grow? I had never thought about it until I heard Rabbi Twerski talk about it.

Lobsters are soft, squishy animals. They live in a hard shell that protects them. Lobsters themselves grow, but their shells do not. As the lobster grows, it starts feeling compressed and uncomfortable in it shell—it feels stressed. The lobster then hides under a rock, sheds its old shell, and grows a new one. The lobster continues growing, and eventually becomes stressed and uncomfortable again in the new shell, hides under the rock, sheds the shell, and grows a new one. This process repeats itself until the lobster is fully grown.

For the lobster, stress literally leads to growth—if the lobster did not feel stressed in the small shell, it would not know to get a bigger one and be able to continue growing. Stress provides you with the same opportunity to grow. If you don't experience stress, you don't move forward, you don't challenge yourself, and you don't get the opportunity to live a fulfilling, meaningful life.

In addition to the physiological and performance-related benefits of seeing stress as helpful and adaptive, we also need to recognize the importance of stress for our emotional well-being. I know you've heard many times that stress is bad for you. You've heard that too much stress can give you heart disease, stroke, and high blood pressure and can lead to premature death. You hear about stress reduction efforts at work, from your friends and family, on TV, and on social media. In fact, most people in the United States believe that they experience too much stress and that it is bad for them. But is it possible to live your life without stress? Let me rephrase that—is it possible to live a full, meaningful, enjoyable life without stress?

Take a moment now to think about one of the most important parts of your life . . . what is it? It may be your work, or your family, or your friendships, or your hobbies, or a cause you care about. Now think about whether it is possible to have that important part of your life and not have stress associated with it. Is it possible to have relationships you care about and never stress or worry about them? It is possible to have a meaningful job and not feel stressed by the demands of that job at least some of the time? Probably not, right? Anything you care about, anything that brings meaning and fulfillment into your life comes with stress and worry. They are two sides of the same coin. Research by Jina Park and Roy Baumeister at Florida State University showed that greater sense of meaning in people's lives is strongly associated with greater level of stress when what's important to them in life is threatened.[100]

At the same time, lack of meaning and fulfillment in life is even more stressful for people than when there are too many important things going on. Victor Frankl, a Holocaust survivor, psychiatrist, and author, once said, "Life is never made unbearable by circumstances, but only by lack of meaning and purpose." Research also shows that, while people expect to feel happier when they are less busy and less stressed, that is not the case in reality. People are happier when they are busier, even if they are busier than they would like to be.[101] People who are often bored are more than twice as likely to die of a heart-related issue than those who do not experience frequent boredom.[102] And many studies have shown that people who have a greater sense of purpose in their lives tend to live longer, healthier lives.[103] This discussion links back to the discussion of values in Chapter 9. This may be a good opportunity for you to reflect on the values in your life and the way stress allows you to live in accordance with your values.

As with other emotional experiences discussed in this book, the answer is not trying to get rid of stress or fighting with stress—this will likely turn stress into a threat and make your experience that much more difficult. Instead, you need to find different ways to respond to stress—through regulating your physiology, finding meaning, recognizing the value of stress and its physiological manifestations, and responding with acceptance, kindness, and compassion. I address each of these steps in the sections that follow.

Biofeedback and Psychophysiological Training for Stress and Performance

The main role of biofeedback and psychophysiological training is in helping your body find the sweet spot of activation needed for any activity. Recall the Yerkes-Dodson curve mentioned earlier in this chapter (Figure 12.1). Any activity you engage in requires a certain amount of activation, whether it is getting ready for the day while having a conversation with your family members in the morning or preparing to lead a meeting, perform surgery, or play in NFL playoffs. Your body has a built-in mechanism to finding that sweet spot of activation: the sympathetic branch of your autonomic nervous system produces activation and the parasympathetic branch puts on the brakes once that activation has reached optimal levels. Sometimes, the ability of your nervous system to find optimal activation becomes dysregulated and needs some help regaining its edge. Other times, you just want to fine-tune this mechanism to work even better and allow you to perform at your very best.

There is no better way to retrain or fine-tune the ability of your body to reach optimal activation than biofeedback, which trains self-regulation. Any modality of biofeedback will help you train self-regulation. HRV biofeedback is particularly well suited for the task, as it strengthens the ability of your parasympathetic nervous system to put the brakes on sympathetic activation once it has reached an optimal level.

In addition, HRV biofeedback helps us change the threat response into a challenge response. Recall the discussion of DHEA and its strong role in a healthy stress response. Interestingly enough, one way in which DHEA produces its positive physiological effects is through its action on the parasympathetic nervous system. DHEA levels are related to HRV, which is a major indicator of the strength of the parasympathetic nervous system. People with higher HRV have higher DHEA levels.[104] Moreover, as shown by Rollin McCraty and his colleagues in 1998, activities that raise HRV also increase DHEA.[105] Therefore, it stands to reason that HRV biofeedback training would facilitate higher levels of DHEA and a more helpful response to stress.

Refer back to Chapter 3 on HRV for a step-by-step guide to HRV training. At the same time, I encourage you to include breathing training into your HRV training. Since HRV training is done through breathing, developing healthy breathing skills is crucial to an effective HRV practice. Refer to Chapter 2 on breathing for a detailed discussion of breathing training.

Mindfulness Training for Stress and Performance

With biofeedback training, you train your body's ability to reach optimal activation. The next step is to allow it to stay there. It is our frequent habit to try to decrease the level of our physiological activation once we notice it rising (remember the advice to relax and calm down to someone about to perform?). If our bodies learn to achieve optimal activation, but our minds continue trying to beat it down, we end up stuck in a futile struggle of attempting to prevent our body from doing what it needs to be doing at that moment. Habitual automatic labeling of the sensations of activation as "bad" precipitates this struggle.

Mindfulness training can help in two ways. First, mindfulness can help you become aware of the sensations of activation before your mind automatically labels them in an unhelpful way. Recall the pipe that is not a pipe— Figure 9.1 in Chapter 9? Mindfulness can help you distinguish between the physiological sensations you experience and the interpretation your mind assigns to them. Becoming aware of the sensations without automatic interpretations allows you to assign a more helpful label to your experience, such as "I am excited" or "My body is doing what it needs to do to help me do my best."

Second, mindfulness can help you let the physiological sensations of activation be as they are, accepting these sensations just the way they are, thus allowing your mind and body to function at their best.

Biofeedback and Mindfulness Approaches for Stress and Performance

In this section, I provide a summary of steps to biofeedback- and mindfulness-based approaches to stress:

1. Establish a mindfulness-based biofeedback and meditation practice.
   - Mindful low-and-slow breathing (Chapter 2)
   - HRV training (Chapter 3)
   - Meditation training (Chapter 8)

2. Determine and write down your values (Chapter 9).
3. With each challenge, practice FLARE for stress:
    — Feel the sensations of stress-related activation.
    — Label the sensations as helpful and adaptive.
    — Allow the sensations to be as they are.
    — Respond:
        ▪ Use mindful low-and-slow breathing at your resonance frequency to remind your body to regulate itself in moments of challenge.
        ▪ Remind yourself of the value this challenge brings to your life.
        ▪ Decide on helpful actions for that specific challenge in accordance with your values.
    — Expand awareness to other external and internal sensations to take in the full spectrum of your experience.

Let's go through an example of FLARE for stress, using the example of pianist from the beginning of the chapter—let's call him Adam. He is preparing for a performance with the Boston Symphony. He is pacing backstage, waiting to go on and play. Adam feels the pressure—he knows just how important this performance could be for his future.

Feel. Adam feels his heart beating faster, his breathing quickening, the palms of his hands feelings clammy.

Label. He names this experience: "I feel excited! My body is preparing to help me do my best."

Allow. Adam allows his experience to be as it is, by saying to himself, "It is OK to feel this way. My body is doing exactly what I need it to do."

Respond. Adam takes 10 mindful low-and-slow breaths at his resonance frequency of 6 breaths per minute, with the intention of balancing his respiratory physiology and reminding his body to regulate itself. He reminds himself of the tremendous meaning his piano playing has brought to his life. He connects with his value of performing for his audience, being in the moment with his music, expressing the emotion of the piece to the best of his ability. This is what his body is preparing him to do!

Expand awareness. Adam expands his awareness to the members of the orchestra he'll be playing with, the curtain in front of him, the sound of voices coming from the concert hall. He moves on to the anticipation he feels in preparing to step out onto the stage, his goal of connecting with his audience, and the feeling of readiness in his fingers.

He steps out onto the stage. . . .

CHAPTER 13

Anxiety and Fear

Annie came into work this morning feeling happy and content, looking forward to a quiet productive day. She checked her e-mail as soon as she sat down at her desk, as was her habit. The first message she saw made her heart skip a beat—her manager requesting that she come in for a meeting with him later that day. The e-mail was uncharacteristically terse and provided no explanation for the meeting. Annie could not figure out what may have happened. After a few minutes of playing through different scenarios, Annie decided that she must be getting laid off. There was no other explanation that she could come up with. As she sat at her desk thinking about the meeting, she became more and more convinced that she is about to lose her job. Annie called her boyfriend, Mark, crying. He listened patiently, asked for her reasons for coming to this conclusion, thought for a moment, and then said, "Annie, you really have no reason to think you are getting fired. It must be something else. Don't worry about it. Just go do something else and don't think about this." Annie took another minute to think—yes, Mark must be right, he usually is about these things. Annie did her best not to think about the upcoming meeting, but she could not get rid of the sinking feeling in her stomach or the racing thoughts in her head. She tried telling herself not to worry. She did her best to fight off the anxiety. With every effort she felt only more dread and fear and a strong sense of failure for not being able to "get a hold of herself."

Have you experienced situations like Annie's when you've felt intense anxiety, worry, or fear and could not shake it off? Have you tried distracting yourself, fighting off the anxiety, reassuring yourself that the thoughts running through your head cannot possibly be correct? Have those attempts left you feeling even more anxious and, on top of that, like a failure for not being able to fight off the anxiety?

One of the most common misconceptions about anxiety is that it is the enemy. This is a myth that we hear and internalize from an early age. We are taught that anxiety is not an OK feeling to have. Imagine three-year-old Katie, who is scared of monsters under her bed. When she tells her parents about the monsters, her well-meaning and loving parents might say, "Don't be afraid, there aren't any monsters." And yet she feels afraid. So now, Katie is still feeling scared, but she has also learned that she shouldn't feel that way. Throughout her childhood, Katie might hear other well-meaning advice, like "Don't be scared of the flu shot, it won't hurt," or "Don't feel nervous, you are going to do just fine on that test." She won't know how to turn off the fear or anxiety in any of these situations, and she will continue learning that feeling anxious or scared is not OK. Katie will also learn that there is something wrong with her, because she cannot turn off that feeling, which everyone else seems to be able to control.

Even our idea of courage and bravery is maintaining this myth of fear being the enemy. "Don't be afraid, be brave"—I hear some version of this all the time from the people I interact with, on social media, on TV, and in movies. And every time, I think, "Hmm, how do you do that? How is it possible to be brave without being afraid?" In fact, the very definition of the word *brave* involves the experience of fear. Merriam Webster dictionary defines *brave* as "having or showing mental or moral strength to face danger, fear, or difficulty." It is impossible to be brave without experiencing fear. And yet, so many of us believe that fear gets in the way of being brave and that experiencing fear is a sign of weakness. We appear to be digging ourselves into a hole we can't get out of—we value bravery and condemn fear, and yet one cannot exist without the other.

To solve this conundrum, we need to look at the value of fear. What purpose does it serve? Why do we feel it? Fear is a response developed through evolution to enable animals to survive as a species. Imagine one of our ancestors, an early human, hanging out in his cave when he hears a noise outside.

The noise may be nothing, or it may be a hungry tiger or another human coming to take his food. If this human has a strong fear response, he runs away or prepares to defend himself and his food supply quickly, and he has a higher chance of surviving and passing on his genes to future humans. If he does not have a strong fear response, he may not run away or prepare to defend himself in time and is therefore less likely to survive and pass on his genes. Our ancestors with the strongest fear responses were the most likely to survive and pass on their genes. This is why fear is such a well-established response for most of us. Fear produces the fight-or-flight response that enables us to run away or fight to protect ourselves from danger.

WHERE DOES FEAR COME FROM?

Fear is generated by a part of your brain called the amygdala, part of the so-called lizard brain, also called the "reptilian brain." The scientific name for this part of the brain is the limbic system. We call it the reptilian brain because it is the part of the brain we share with all sorts of other animals, including reptiles. When a snake is sunning itself on a rock and observes a shadow overhead, its amygdala will spring into action and get the snake to hide under the rock, in case the shadow is a hawk looking for prey. It is the same mechanism that warns you, a human being, about potential danger. The amygdala is nonverbal and irrational. It has no ability to "think" through the reasonableness of running or fighting in any situation. Its job is to get you to safety fast. If the amygdala allowed you to think about the appropriateness of running when you see a tiger, you may not live long enough to pass on your genes.

Of course, there are not a lot of tigers running around these days, at least not in places where most of us live. So, does the fear response still have value? The short answer is yes. How else might your five-year-old know not to jump down from a tall tree she climbed? How would you know to jump out of the way from a car coming too fast around the corner? Fear continues to keep us safe.

However, it often happens that fear and anxiety come up when there is no actual danger around. You may feel afraid or anxious when you are about to get on a plane or before going on a first date. Your first instinct is to figure out a way to avoid the experience all together—maybe the trip to Disney World you are taking is not all that important and you could just not go, or maybe you could come up with a good excuse to reschedule the date. This instinctual temptation to avoid an anxiety-provoking situation is driven by the amygdala, whose job is to keep you safe. And yet, in these situations, the reaction it is dictating is not very helpful—the vacation to Disney World that the family has been looking forward to for months is not something that is a good idea to cancel, and making up an excuse to postpone a date may mean that you miss out on a meaningful relationship.

In situations like these you are the most likely to view fear and anxiety as the enemy—"I can't go on a date, anxiety always gets in the way," or "Anxiety is ruining my life, I can't do anything that's important to me." And of course, when confronted with the enemy, your automatic response is to run or fight. Attempts to escape or fight off your thoughts and feelings are doomed to failure and to perpetuate and intensify suffering (for more on this, see the discussion on control and being stuck in Chapter 9).

The tricky part here is that the anxiety you feel when being chased by a tiger and the anxiety you feel before going on a first date are generated by the same part of the brain: the amygdala, which is nonverbal and nonrational—it does not have the ability to tell the difference between the threat posed by a tiger and the threat posed by a plane ride or a date. As far as the amygdala is concerned, when it perceives signs of danger, its job is to keep you safe first and let you think about it later.

The purpose of the amygdala is to keep you safe, not to make your life miserable and keep you from doing what's important in your life. The amygdala does its job by sending out danger signals, and it is your job as a human being to decide the most helpful response to those danger signals, which take the form of anxiety or fear. Making this choice is key to living well with anxiety. Let me emphasize that *your task is not to make anxiety stop or go away*. That is biologically impossible and, as just discussed, not actually helpful. As much as it may sometimes feel that anxiety is not normal and you should work hard to banish it forever, please remember that the difference between someone who has an anxiety disorder and someone who does not is not whether or not they have anxiety—all people have anxiety. The difference is how they respond to that anxiety. A person for whom anxiety is a problem is likely to get stuck in it, while the person for whom anxiety is just part of life experiences it, responds in a helpful way, and moves on. If you feel that your response to anxiety is not always a helpful one, there are changes you may be able to make.

The first step to choosing a helpful response to anxiety is to change your view of anxiety. Remember that having anxiety is a normal human experience. Every "normal" human being experiences anxiety. You may be used to thinking that anxiety is not normal and that you are therefore somehow broken or defective for having it, but this is just an unfortunate outcome of your internalized fight with anxiety. Once you see anxiety as a friend rather than an enemy, a protector rather than a nemesis intent on ruining your life, your response to anxiety will change as well—away from fight-or-flight and toward acceptance and compassion. Once you change your response to anxiety, you will be able to experience it and move on rather than continue getting stuck.

One particularly helpful way of rethinking anxiety is seeing it as an overprotective caregiver. Imagine yourself as a child at a playground with your mom, dad, grandparent, or another caregiver. You are super excited to climb a cool rock wall or do some tricks on the monkey bars. But as soon as you are about to climb, your caregiver runs up to you saying: "No, no, don't climb up there, it's too high, you'll fall and hurt yourself." At this point, you have several options for a response: you might listen to the caregiver and climb down disappointed, you might yell at the caregiver to leave you alone and not get in the way of having fun, or you might turn to your caregiver and say: "I've got it, I'll be careful, thanks for the warning," and then keep climbing.

In the first scenario, you don't get to do the fun things at the playground because your caregiver signaled potential danger, which you avoided, but you've also forgone the chance for fun. In the second scenario, you get in a fight with your caregiver and potentially have to leave the playground for being disrespectful, and again, you miss out on having fun. In the third scenario, you climb with care and have fun (although admittedly also expose yourself to the risk of falling).

In this situation, what do you think the intention of the caregiver telling you to get off the monkey bars would be? Would it be to ruin your day and not let you have fun? Probably not, right? The caregiver's only intention is to keep you safe. Preventing you from having fun is an unintended consequence. In the third, most helpful scenario, you recognize the positive intention of the caregiver, acknowledge the existence of potential risks, and make a choice about the best way to act—still climb on to the structure, have fun, but exercise caution.

Anxiety acts just like that overprotective caregiver. It sends danger signals whenever any kind of threat to your well-being presents itself, such as the discomfort of meeting a new person and the possibility of having your feelings hurt on a first date. An automatic reaction to the danger signal, interpreting that signal literally as a need to escape danger, may lead you to cancel or reschedule the date. Alternatively, getting mad at the anxiety and trying to make it go away will likely get you more anxious and stuck in the anxiety, still leading you to cancel the date.

A more helpful response to the danger signal is to recognize anxiety as well intentioned and protective. Seeing anxiety as a friend rather than the enemy will allow you to observe the situation mindfully, acknowledge the possibility of an awkward meeting and the vulnerability to hurt feelings, and then decide whether or not to keep the date based on what is in your best interest.

In summary, once you are able to see anxiety as a friend rather than an enemy, you let go of the struggle with anxiety and open up a whole host of other possible responses that would not have been possible during a struggle. Without the struggle with anxiety, you allow yourself to live life to the fullest—having fun, pursuing great opportunities, and meeting new people.

A big part of making friends with your anxiety is recognizing the value of what it is telling you. How can you do that without getting stuck in the signal of danger? There are three types of anxiety messages, each requiring a different response:

- *A signal of real physical danger.* Even though there is not nearly as much physical danger around you now as there was thousands of years ago, you should not lose sight of the fact that danger still exists, and anxiety and fear are there to warn you about it. If you find yourself in real danger, listening to the anxiety and getting yourself to safety is a priority and the most helpful response.
- *Requirement for a change in behavior.* Sometimes anxiety points you to a situation that would have dire consequences unless you make

changes in your actions. For instance, if you haven't done any work in a class and feel anxious about an exam coming up the next day, the only helpful response to that anxiety is to sit down and study. Anxiety in these situations points you to a concrete action that needs to be taken in order to resolve the situation (not merely resolve the anxiety). The most helpful response to this kind of anxiety is accepting its presence and deciding how to accomplish the action it is pointing you toward.

- *Seemingly unreasonable and baseless anxiety.* In these cases, following the action dictated by the content of anxious thoughts would lead you to unhelpful results. This is the overprotective caregiver type of anxiety. Trying to make this anxiety go away will achieve the opposite result and lead you to being more stuck. The same will happen with attempts to ignore it. The most helpful response to this kind of anxiety is to accept its presence without fighting and decide on an action that is in your best interest.

The nature of anxiety is such that figuring out the most helpful response is not always easy. The way your body and your brain function in the moment of anxiety may sometimes get in the way of choosing a helpful response. Fortunately, biofeedback and mindfulness-based skills can help you train your mind and body to facilitate rather than hinder choosing a helpful response to anxiety. The next two sections discuss some of the unhelpful patterns of activation that happen with anxiety, together with biofeedback and mindfulness skills that will train optimal activation.

Biofeedback-Based Skills for Anxiety and Fear

If you've ever struggled with anxiety, you know that heightened anxiety often comes with a host of unpleasant physiological and cognitive sensations: rapid heart rate, fast and shallow breathing, sweatiness, difficulty focusing, muscle tension, gastrointestinal discomfort, and overall feeling of agitation. Sometimes, anxiety also comes with feelings of lightheadedness or dizziness, "brain fog," tingly hands or feet, nausea, and feelings of unreality. These sensations are a result of overactivation of the fight-or-flight response, which happens when your autonomic nervous system is having trouble regulating itself, and may also result from breathing dysregulation.

Heart Rate Variability

Research has consistently implicated low HRV, an indicator of difficulty with self-regulation, in symptoms of anxiety. John A. Chalmers and his colleagues at the University of Sydney conducted a meta-analysis of 36 studies with 2,068 total participants examining HRV in people struggling with anxiety.[106] They concluded that people who struggle with panic disorder, posttraumatic stress disorder, generalized anxiety disorder, and social anxiety disorder exhibit reductions in HRV, indicative of difficulty in regulating physiological activation. Moreover, the same research team conducted a study examining the relationship between worry and HRV.[107] They found a robust difference in HRV between high worriers and low worriers, regardless of whether or not they were diagnosed with any anxiety disorder. These findings indicate that decreased HRV is associated with higher propensity for worry. Studies have also shown that use of antidepressant medication, often prescribed for managing anxiety, reduces HRV. Andrew Kemp of the University of Sydney and his colleagues have conducted several studies demonstrating this effect.[108]

The good news is that HRV biofeedback is an effective way to both alleviate symptoms of anxiety and increase HRV. Vera Goessl and her colleagues at Boston University conducted a meta-analysis of twenty-four studies of HRV biofeedback as an intervention for anxiety.[109] They reported large reductions in self-reported symptoms of anxiety as a result of HRV biofeedback.

Combined, this evidence strongly suggests that HRV biofeedback is an effective way to train your body's ability to regulate its activation and reduce symptoms of anxiety. Please refer to Chapter 3 on HRV for a detailed explanation of what HRV is and a step-by-step guide for training your HRV.

Breathing

Breathing dysregulation and overbreathing in particular have been implicated in several anxiety disorders. Panic disorder is most commonly associated with overbreathing, which is sometimes referred to as hyperventilation. Massimiliano Grassi at the Villa San Benedetto Hospital in Italy and his colleagues conducted a meta-analysis showing that people struggling with panic disorder overbreathe at baseline.[110] A study by Carolyn Davies and Michelle Craske at University of California, Los Angeles showed that overbreathing and the resulting low levels of carbon dioxide are associated with higher anxiety symptoms regardless of the specific type of anxiety.[111] They also reported that overbreathing is associated with lower quality of life at 6- and 12-month follow-ups, above and beyond severity of baseline anxiety symptoms. Moreover, the authors reported that overbreathing and low levels of carbon dioxide are associated with worse outcomes from therapy for anxiety. These findings are similar to those reported by David Tolin and his team at Yale University, who found that lower levels of carbon dioxide are associated with a greater likelihood of dropping out of cognitive-behavioral therapy for various anxiety disorders.[112]

Alicia Meuret at Southern Methodist University and her team have conducted several studies showing that biofeedback breathing training to reduce overbreathing is an effective treatment for panic disorder and for fear of injections and the sight of blood.[113] A recent multi-sight study by David Tolin and his colleagues showed significant improvement in symptoms of panic disorder with biofeedback breathing training.[114]

While we need more research on the effectiveness of breathing retraining on other kinds of anxiety disorders, these findings strongly suggest that overbreathing may interfere with success of other treatments for anxiety, while breathing training and elimination of overbreathing are likely to lead to improvement in symptoms. See Chapter 2 on breathing for a detailed discussion of breathing and overbreathing, as well as a detailed guide to breathing training.

Neurobiology of Anxiety and Foundations for Mindfulness Training

Imaging studies have examined the function of the amygdala, the fight-or-flight center of the brain, and areas of the prefrontal cortex (PFC), including the anterior cingulate cortex (ACC) and the ventrolateral PFC, which are involved in emotion regulation and ability to choose which actions we might take in response to various stimuli. Many studies have found increased activation of the amygdala and decreased activation of the PFC in people who suffer from anxiety disorders. Marina Mochcovitch and her colleagues at Federal University of Rio de Janeiro in Brazil conducted a meta-analysis of multiple brain imaging studies of anxiety.[115] They concluded that people who struggle with anxiety show low activation of the PFC in general and the ACC in particular. Low activation of these brain regions makes it more difficult to both regulate difficult emotions themselves and choose helpful ways to respond to them.

A study by Jack Nitschke and his colleagues at Dartmouth College showed that people who suffer from anxiety show increases in amygdala activation during anticipation of stimulus presentation.[116] Interestingly, the amygdala was overactivated regardless of whether the anticipated cue was neutral or negative in nature. This explains why people who struggle with anxiety have a hard time not only during stressful events but also while expecting future events to occur, whether or not they turn out to actually be stressful.

Other studies have examined connectivity between the PFC and the amygdala. The PFC is involved in emotion regulation, and one way it regulates emotion is through the connective fibers that run between it and the amygdala. These fibers allow signals from the PFC to regulate activation of the amygdala. People who struggle with anxiety exhibit decreased connectivity between the PFC and the amygdala, meaning that the PFC is less able to communicate with the amygdala and put the brakes on its activation. For example, Amit Etkin and his team at Stanford University first demonstrated that the ACC regulates emotional conflict by dampening activity in the amygdala.[117] In a subsequent study, they showed that for people who suffer from anxiety, the ACC-amygdala connectivity is impaired, leading to difficulty in regulating emotional conflict.[118]

DEFAULT MODE NETWORK AND ANXIETY

You may recall the default mode network (DMN) first discussed in Chapter 7 It is the part of your brain that comes online when your mind is not focused on anything in particular. It is also the part of your brain that is responsible for much of the unpleasant thinking that comes with anxiety—reviewing and regretting your actions from the past, anticipating unpleasant events and feelings in the future, and comparing yourself to other people in unfavorable ways.

Neuroimaging studies have implicated DMN activity in anxiety. For example, a 2018 study conducted by Francesca Zidda and her team at Heidelberg University in Germany found increased connectivity between the DMN and the amygdala in people who experience anxiety and fear.[119] This means that increased communication between the DMN and the amygdala may be involved in the experience of anxiety. Reducing activation of both the DMN and the amygdala is also likely to reduce anxiety symptoms.

Britta Hölzel at Harvard Medical School and her team examined the effects of mindfulness-based intervention for anxiety on the brain.[120] They recruited participants diagnosed with generalized anxiety disorder and those who were free from any anxiety diagnoses and scanned their brains at the beginning of the study. Then half the participants who suffered from anxiety took a mindfulness-based stress reduction (MBSR) course, and the other half took part in traditional stress management education (control condition). Everyone's brains were scanned again after the intervention was complete.

This study confirmed previous findings that people struggling with anxiety show higher activation of the amygdala, particularly in response to neutral images. This means that people who suffer from anxiety tend to experience an anxiety reaction in situations that other people perceive as nonthreatening. The study also confirmed the previous findings of reduced activation of ventrolateral PFC, as well as reduced connectivity between the amygdala and PFC, indicating that the PFC is not active enough and is not able to put on the brakes to the fight-of-flight activation of the amygdala as necessary.

The good news is that 8 weeks of mindfulness meditation training brought about a reduction in symptoms of anxiety and produced helpful brain changes. Brain imaging showed that after taking the MBSR course, participants exhibited higher ventrolateral PFC activation and greater connectivity between the PFC and the amygdala, compared to their own baseline and compared to those who suffered from anxiety but did not take the MBSR course. These changes corresponded with symptom improvement, meaning that those with greater brain changes also experienced less anxiety after the study.

Other studies have confirmed the effectiveness of mindfulness-based interventions in reducing symptoms of anxiety. A meta-analysis conducted by Stefan Hofmann and his team at Boston University examined thirty-nine studies of mindfulness-based interventions for anxiety and other mood disorders.[121] The authors concluded that mindfulness-based interventions are effective in reducing symptoms of anxiety and depression. Jon Vøllestad and his team at the University of Bergen in Norway conducted a similar meta-analysis and came to the same conclusion.[122]

Taken together, these research findings point to the fact that mindfulness training alleviates symptoms of anxiety, reduces activation of the fight-or-flight response, and increases activation of your ability to regulate emotion and make helpful decisions at times of stress. The next sections describe mindfulness-based skills particularly useful in anxiety. Please review Chapter 8 on mindfulness meditation and Chapter 9 on mindfulness-based skills, which present a more general guide to mindfulness meditation and mindfulness-based skills.

Mindfulness Meditation for Anxiety and Fear

Because of the overactivation of the amygdala and the fight-or-flight response in anxiety, learning concentration meditation practices is a particularly great place to start. Concentration practices reduce activation of the amygdala and increase activation of the PFC, thereby reducing intensity of difficult sensations. Moreover, concentration practices reduce activation of the default mode network, which also appears to be involved in anxiety and worry. Try these concentration practices:

- Here-and-now stone (Chapter 8
- Mindfulness of sound (Appendix A)
- Mindfulness of nature (see sidebar)
- Mindful low-and-slow breathing at your resonance frequency, or at 6 breaths per minute (Chapter 3)

MINDFULNESS OF NATURE

Find a comfortable spot outside or next to a window. Bring your attention to the nature around you. Notice and observe trees, grass, flowers, the sky, the clouds, birds, and other animals. Just notice. Whenever your mind wanders off, gently bring it back to observing the nature around you.

If you are ready to move on to open awareness practices, these are my favorite ones for anxiety (you can find scripts for all of them in Appendix A or download recordings at www.innakhazan.com/meditation_recordings.html).

- Mindfulness of thoughts, feelings, physiological sensations
- Mountain meditation
- Anchor meditation
- Mindfulness of anxiety in the body
- Thoughts on leaves meditation

Now add self-compassion practices:

- Mettā (Chapter 10 and www.innakhazan.com/meditation_recordings .html)
- Difficult emotion practice (soften, soothe, and allow; see Appendix A and www.innakhazan.com/meditation_recordings.html)

Mindfulness-Based Skills for Anxiety and Fear

In this section I present a collection of skills to help you attend to anxiety and choose a helpful response, in the context of choosing a response that's different from a habitual, unhelpful one.

Instead of arguing with your anxious thoughts, look beneath the surface of the anxiety message and check in with your values. Let's come back to the example of Annie at the start of the chapter. Annie is worried about the meeting with her boss because she thinks she'll be fired. As she is thinking that the terse e-mail from her boss requesting a meeting might mean that she is going to get fired, Annie's conversation with the anxious voice in her mind might go something like this:

ANNIE: "No way, I've been a great employee, I've done a great job, there is no way I am going to get fired."

ANXIOUS VOICE: "Are you sure? What about that time you were late for work? And what about the mistake you made in your presentation a month ago?"

ANNIE: "Well, those are not reasons to fire someone. Everyone makes mistakes, right?"

ANXIOUS VOICE: "Yeah sure, everyone does, but maybe you make more than others. And besides, maybe he just doesn't like you."

ANNIE: "No, he is usually pretty nice to me, and I don't make all that many mistakes."

ANXIOUS VOICE: "But how can you be sure? He may just be waiting for an excuse to fire you."

And on and on this may go. If you think this conversation is totally irrational, you are right. Anxiety is often like that. Arguing with your anxiety is like arguing with a toddler. Rational reasoning will not get you very far. There is no way for you to convince yourself and the anxious voice in your head that your fear will not come true. Even in the face of evidence that anxiety is wrong, that voice can always come back with "but this might still happen." And that's true. The reason arguing with your anxious thoughts is not helpful is because there is no way to provide 100 percent guarantee that your fears won't come through. There is always a chance, however small.

Instead of arguing with your anxiety and trying to prove it wrong, try looking beneath the surface content of the anxiety. Rather than getting stuck in the literal meaning of the anxious thoughts ("I am going to get fired"), try looking at the meaning behind those thoughts. Why is your mind coming up with such scary thoughts? What is the value the overprotective part of your brain is trying to point you toward?

The underlying reason you worry is the importance of whatever it is you worry about. Whenever you care about someone or something, whenever someone or something is important to you, it leaves you vulnerable to anxiety. If it wasn't important, you wouldn't worry about it. And because it is important, you worry about losing it. So, anxiety is a natural consequence of caring and valuing something. This is also the reason you can't talk yourself out of the anxiety—caring and worrying go hand in hand. You can think of it as two sides of the same coin: you cannot care without experiencing some degree of anxiety.

Recognizing the importance of what you are worrying about will help direct your attention toward the value most relevant to the situation and help you make the most helpful choice in responding. See Chapter 9 for a discussion of value-based action—I encourage you to review your values, as described in that chapter, when practicing this skill. If you haven't already identified your values with the help of the list in Chapter 9, now may be a great time to do it (you may consider writing about your values in the notebook for ideas and exercises I suggested in the introduction).

In Annie's case, her anxiety is pointing her to the importance of her work and her value of doing a good job. Worry about being fired is running through her mind not because she is actually likely to get fired but because her job is important. In employing the skill of looking beneath the surface, Annie would recognize that the worry is a result of caring about her job and point her toward her value of doing her best. Once Annie is able to disengage from the argument with her anxiety and see the value anxious thoughts are pointing her toward, she will be able to move on to a helpful response. A response consistent with the value of doing her best at her job may be turning to the task she is supposed to be working on.

Instead of reassuring yourself that your fears will not come true, look beneath the surface and check in with your values. When we worry, we often try to reassure ourselves or seek reassurance from others that the thing we worry about happening won't actually happen. Annie sought reassurance from her boyfriend, who did his best to tell her that she won't get fired. But the voice in her head continued insisting that she still might. Just like in the case of arguing with anxiety, reassurance does not work because there is never 100 percent guarantee that the bad thing you worry about won't happen, no matter how unlikely it may seem.

For example, Ray worries about getting sick with some terrible life-threatening disease. Every time he experiences a strange symptom or sensation, his mind jumps to the terrible thing it could be. If he has a headache, it might be a brain tumor. If he has a cough, it may be lung cancer. If his leg feels numb, it may be multiple sclerosis. Each time this happens, Ray goes to see his doctor, gets checked out, and gets a clean bill of health. After each visit, Ray feels reassured that he really is OK . . . until the next strange symptom he experiences. And even though he had recently gotten a clean bill of health, the anxious voice says, "But it may be something bad this time," and the cycle starts over again: Ray worries about his health until he goes to see his doctor, gets temporary relief from reassurance that he is OK, and on and on it goes. As a result, Ray continues to suffer.

What can we do instead of look for reassurance? Looking beneath the surface exercise applies here as well. For Ray, seeing his anxiety as a signal that his health is important rather than that he is about to die helps him disengage from those thoughts without fighting, ignoring, or getting stuck. Connecting with the value of health and self-care helps Ray choose a response consistent with that value. If anxiety about his health is a signal to take good care of himself, a helpful response may be to nourish himself in some way—perhaps get a drink of water, eat a healthy meal, go for a walk, or connect with a friend.

Instead of answering all the questions and all the what ifs, practice the "I don't know" mantra. Along with anxiety often come a million questions that seemingly require an answer: Have you thought about this? And what if this happens? And what if that happens? Your mind doesn't like not knowing what's going to happen in the future, and it tends to generate all sorts of questions that you may feel compelled to answer. Of course, you don't actually have the answers. You don't know what's going to happen in the future. The appearance of safety that comes with thinking through every possible scenario robs you of valuable time and energy and rarely actually helps you come up with useful solutions. And no matter how many answers you come with, the questions don't stop. Instead of spending so much time and effort answering the unending questions and what ifs, respond to them with, "I don't know what's going to happen—let's see." This allows you to disengage from anxiety and keep an open mind about the future.

Instead of escape and avoidance, allow your anxiety to be, and be willing to experience it. Anxiety is often so unpleasant that your natural response is to try to get away from it, avoid it all together or escape when you are in the midst of it. How do you do that? By avoiding or escaping situations that produce it. If you are afraid of dying in a car crash, you might avoid getting into a car. If you are afraid of embarrassing yourself in front of people, you might avoid being around people you don't know very well or leave social situations when you start feeling uncomfortable.

What happens when you avoid or escape anxiety? Initially you just feel relieved, right? When you decide that you are not going to get in the car and just walk instead, you feel relief. When you leave the dinner party, you feel relief. But then the next time you have to get in the car and the next time you are in a social situation, your mind tells you that the only way to feel better is not to go, so you don't, and again you feel relief. But then you need to get to a meeting at a place where you can't walk to. You decide to take the bus, but then you worry about the bus crashing, so you don't go. Or you are invited to a get-together with old college friends you haven't seen in a long time, but you worry that you might say something to embarrass yourself, so you don't go. And soon enough, your world starts getting smaller and smaller, as there are more and more things you cannot do and places you cannot go. And as your world gets smaller, you just feel bad for not being able to do all those things you want to do. By using avoidance and escape from anxiety, you trade one kind of suffering for another, and you don't actually feel any better. You are just stuck in a world that's getting smaller, feeling anxious.

What can you do instead? You get unstuck by opening up to the anxiety, to all the difficult thoughts and feelings, allowing yourself to feel them. You practice feeling them, little bit at a time. And then you choose which action is in your best interest. You ask yourself whether it is worth it to experience anxiety in order to be able to get in the car to go on a hike with your family. Ask yourself whether you are willing to experience anxiety in order to be able to meet new friends and catch up with old friends. You ask yourself which action is most consistent with your values of family and friendships. Refer back to Chapter 9 on mindfulness skills for a reminder of these skills.

Keep in mind that if you've been stuck in the escape and avoidance pattern for a while it will take a while to get unstuck. It is important to do it in small steps so that you don't get overwhelmed. And you may want to consult a therapist trained in mindfulness-based exposure techniques to help you.

Instead of trying to control and fight against anxiety, allow anxiety to be, and see it as overprotective caregiver. Attempts to control or fight are another unhelpful automatic reaction you might engage in when you feel anxiety and fear—if only you could get control of the anxiety, if only you could make it go away. But is that possible? You may recall the white bear and the blood sugar studies from Chapter 9. Trying to control what you are thinking or feeling in the moment does not work, and it depletes the fuel that you would otherwise have for actions under your control.

Instead of trying to control anxiety, allow yourself to feel it, and practice mindful observation and acceptance of your experience. Practice meditation skills mentioned in the previous section as particularly helpful in allowing and accepting anxiety.

Instead of fighting with your anxiety, transition to seeing it as a friend or an overprotective caregiver who really means well and is not intent on ruining your life. This will allow you to disengage from a fight that gets you stuck and will give you the space you need to find a helpful response.

Instead of distraction, change your intention. Distraction can sometimes be an effective way to give yourself a break from difficult thoughts and feelings. If you decide to watch a movie to distract yourself from anxiety, it may work. Or you may find yourself not being able to fully pay attention to the movie, with anxiety intruding into your movie experience.

Instead of attempts at distraction, you may consider changing the intention of the activity that would otherwise be a distraction. You may decide to give yourself a break and take good care of yourself when you are anxious by engaging in a pleasant activity, such as watching a movie. The intention of the pleasant activity is not to make anxiety go away but to take care of yourself when you feel anxious. Use this one in moderation, so that you don't end up avoiding difficult feelings through "taking care of yourself."

Instead of self-blame, practice self-compassion. When something goes wrong, your habitual response may be to blame yourself and spend time figuring out how the situation is all your fault. This appears to be an attempt to gain control over uncertainly that is so difficult to bear: If you can figure out how this bad situation is your fault, then maybe you can gain control over it. If you can figure out how you made it happen, then maybe you can also figure out how to prevent it from happening again. The reality is that we don't have control over the future, and there is no guarantee what will happen. No amount of blaming or emotionally beating up on yourself will change that. But it will certainly make you feel even worse. Uncertainly is difficult to bear. All you can do when faced with uncertainty is be kind and practice self-compassion. A modified version of Kristin Neff's self-compassion break may be particularly relevant:

THIS IS A MOMENT OF UNCERTAINTY.

UNCERTAINLY IS DIFFICULT TO BEAR.

AND YET IT IS A PART OF LIFE.

MAY I BE KIND TO MYSELF.

FLARE for Anxiety and Fear

Let's explore now how you might be able to use all of the skills outlined in this chapter as part of FLARE:

> *Feel* the physiological sensations in your body, such as faster heart rate, shortness of breath, and sweatiness. Notice the questions, doubts, and arguments that come through your mind.
>
> *Label* your experience with a short, descriptive, nonjudgmental label, such as "uncertainty," "worry," "fear," "questions," or "default mode network activity."
>
> *Allow* your experience to be as it is: "It is OK to feel this way."
>
> *Respond* with one of the skills described in this chapter:
>> Practice low-and-slow breathing at resonance frequency or at 6 breaths per minute.
>>
>> Check in with your values.
>>
>> Look beneath the surface.
>>
>> Use the "I don't know" mantra.
>>
>> Take a self-compassion break.
>
> *Expand your awareness* to other parts of your external and internal environment. Reflect on what you have appreciated or been grateful for that day (see Chapter 9 for more details).

Let's return to Annie and see how she might use FLARE as a way of responding to her anxiety:

> *Feel.* Annie notices her preverbal experience of anxiety, her heart "skipping a beat" when she first read her boss's e-mail.
>
> *Label.* She brings gentle mindful attention to her experience and in a kind and compassionate tone gives a name to that experience, perhaps calling it "worry." This action increases activation of her PFC while reducing activation of the amygdala, enabling Annie to pause long enough to follow the next three steps of FLARE.
>
> *Allow.* Annie chooses to allow herself to feel the way she does. She recognizes that she cares very much about her job (seeing beneath the surface), so an ambiguous e-mail from her boss would naturally produce

anxiety. Annie allows and validates the existence of anxiety rather than the exact content of anxious thoughts. It makes sense to worry when reading an ambiguous e-mail from your boss, but it does not mean that the content of the anxious thoughts ("I am going to get fired") is actually true.

Respond. Annie chooses the most helpful way to respond to the anxiety. She first thinks about whether there is any action she should take. Other than responding to her boss's e-mail letting him know when she would stop by his office, there is nothing that Annie can do in that moment. So, her response is to take some low-and-slow breaths, to help her body regulate itself in the best way possible, to adopt a "let's see" attitude about what will happen once she actually meets with her boss, and to answer the questions running through her mind ("What's going to happen?" "What does he want to talk about?") with "I don't know."

Expand awareness. Annie brings her attention to her external environment: the desk in front of her, the floor under her feet, the window looking out onto the street. She then brings attention to her internal experience: her breathing, her heartbeat, the sensation of her feet on the floor, the worry thoughts that occasionally enter her mind. As a result, Annie allows anxiety about the upcoming meeting to be just a part of her overall experience, rather than being stuck in the middle of anxiety, not seeing or experiencing anything else.

As a result of this practice, Annie is able to gently bring her mind back to her work (an action consistent with her value of doing a good job), allow anxiety to be without engaging with it ("Let's see" and "I don't know"), and see what her boss wants to talk to her about when the time for their meeting actually comes.

CHAPTER 14

Anger

Nick was having a bad day. He hadn't slept well for a few days, he's had too much on his plate at work, and his projects weren't going according to plan. He came home late, hungry, and tired. His children, Jason and Isabelle, ran up to him, happy to see him and eager to spend time with him. Nick was happy to see them, but all he wanted to do was eat and go to sleep. Jason and Isabelle were persistent—they asked him questions, brought him books to read to them, offered to play games. Nick did his best to keep calm, but he just couldn't do it. He was getting more and more impatient, more curt and agitated. Finally, Nick exploded and yelled at the kids, "Just leave me alone! Why can't you leave me alone?" He then stomped off to his bedroom. He heard the kids crying and his wife attempting to calm them. As he calmed down, Nick felt overwhelming guilt. He didn't want to yell at them. He swore to himself the last time this happened that he would do better next time, that he would learn to control himself. What's wrong with him that he just couldn't do it?

Anger may make you feel out of control. You try your best not to feel anger in order not to act in ways that you later regret, and time and time again you find that it does not work. Chapter 9 on mindfulness-based skills describes how trying not to feel your feelings does not work and is likely to get you stuck in those feelings. When you try not to feel anger, you are fighting a losing battle, with anger getting more intense and your actions feeling more out of control. This chapter distinguishes between the *emotion* of anger and the *actions* that you perform in response to anger. While you do not have control over the emotion, you do have control over the actions. By directing your efforts toward controlling your actions rather than your emotions, you can learn to respond to anger in a more helpful way. These responses can be further aided by recognizing triggers for anger, as well as consistent practice of mindfulness meditation and biofeedback and psychophysiology-based training.

Please note that this chapter is not meant to be a comprehensive guide to anger management—this is, after all, just one chapter. This chapter is meant to guide you in the use of mindfulness and biofeedback skills in responding to anger. If anger is a particularly strong challenge in your life, you may want to engage a therapist in addition to practicing skills described in this book.

Distinguishing Between Feelings and Actions

I imagine that most of the time you can tell the difference between feeling and action quite well. Think about the last time you hugged someone you love—it was probably pretty clear that you felt love and expressed it with a hug. This distinction gets blurry with anger. People often talk about anger as both a feeling and an action. What do you mean when you say, "I get angry"? It is a description of the feeling of anger together with the behavioral expression of it, such as yelling. The same thing happens when people talk about efforts to control anger: "I shouldn't be so angry." A lot of the time people are referring to the regrettable actions they engage in while feeling anger. Nick was regretting the action of yelling at his children that followed the feeling of anger.

There are two reasons this distinction is so important: it is not the feeling that causes you so much trouble but the action that follows the feeling, and you don't have much control over your feelings, but you do have control over your actions. So, when you say, "I should not be so angry," you try to control the feeling. And in attempting to control the uncontrollable, you use up your glucose stores (recall the glucose study described in Chapter 9), depleting the resources you otherwise have available for what is under your control: an action in response to anger.

Your response to anger may be productive or destructive. With a helpful response, anger can lead to positive changes. For example, if you feel angry when you see someone being mistreated because of the color of their skin, religion, sexual orientation, or disability, intervening in helpful ways leads to positive change. Unhelpful reactions to anger, such as chasing after a motorist that has cut you off, can lead you to inadvertently hurt someone and get yourself into trouble. Anger can also be deliberately used in destructive and dangerous ways to manipulate, control, or bully others.

Increasing Awareness of Anger

To find more helpful ways to respond to anger, you have to become aware of anger triggers, as well as first signs of anger experience. One of the more difficult aspects of anger is that once it becomes intense it is hard to get control over your actions. This is why people who experience intense anger often say that anger is out of control. The most effective way for you to gain control over your actions when you feel angry is to recognize triggers and early signs of anger and choose a helpful response before the emotion becomes too intense.

Anger as an emotion is not inherently bad or something to be rid of. Just like any emotion, it serves a purpose. The experience of anger lets you know that something is not right and needs your attention. Anger can point you to an unjust or unfair situation where you need to speak up for yourself or for someone else. Anger can let you know when you are not being treated well and you need to address the situation. Anger can let you know that someone you know is not being treated well and you may need to intervene in some way. Anger may also arise when something gets in the way of achieving your goals or simply getting what you want, letting you know that you need to revise your plan of action or accept some limitations for your desires.

There are also times when anger comes up for a reason other than what is happening in the present moment. Feeling hungry, tired, or sleep deprived can trigger anger in a situation where you would otherwise respond differently. Difficult emotions, such as irritation, shame, or disappointment, left over from a situation that happened earlier in the day may trigger anger in an otherwise neutral situation. Triggers may also come from the past—what's happening in the present may somehow remind you of an unfair or unjust situation from the past and trigger anger.

Every human being experiences the emotion of anger, but different people handle anger in different ways. Some people are able to stay calm and find a helpful solution to the problem at hand, and other people get caught up in the feeling of anger and react in unhelpful or regrettable ways.

These differences have to do with your ability to regulate your emotions and behavior. Heart rate variability (HRV) and brain function have a lot to do with self-regulation and response to anger. I say more about this later in the chapter. In addition to self-regulation, your response to anger is also influenced by learning experience (how did people around you express and handle anger when you were a child?), your problem-solving skills (difficulty in finding solutions to problems often triggers anger), habitual responses (you get used to responding to certain situations in specific ways), and your genetics (some people are predisposed to have a quicker activation of the fight-or-flight response, making it harder to control actions in response to anger).

Regardless of the origin of anger, the goal is to find a way to control your behavior and choose the most helpful way to respond to anger. Whether your anger is justified in the present moment or is due to something else, your goal is to become aware of it and choose a helpful response. For example, you may feel angry when you see your child's friend being mean to your child. Your anger is entirely justified by the situation. Or, like Nick, you come home hungry and tired, and your children just want to spend time with you. Anger in this case is due to your internal state, in the presence of the kids. In both of these situations, you need to become aware of anger rising and choose the most helpful response. Yelling is not a helpful way to respond in either of those situations.

Knowing your triggers is the first step in developing awareness. Triggers for anger may be internal or external. Internal triggers include physiological and emotional states:

- Hunger
- Fatigue
- Lack of sleep
- Lack of down time
- Lack of alone time (particularly for the introverts, who rely on alone time to recharge)
- Feeling rushed
- Feeling frustrated

- Not getting something you want
- Not being able to achieve a goal
- Feeling stressed or overwhelmed
- Being in physical pain
- Misinterpreting another person's intentions (e.g., seeing a threat or insult when one wasn't meant to be)
- Feeling scared, sad, ashamed, or guilty (often anger is easier for people to experience than such emotions as fear, sadness, shame, or guilt; sometimes, anger is a way to cover for the more difficult emotions)
- Memories of suffering, unfairness, or anger from the past

External triggers have to do with your environment and the people around you:

- Having had a fight with another person
- Having an overly busy day
- Having been stuck in traffic or some other delay
- Certain words or behaviors from another person, for example:
  — Your child having a tantrum
  — Your spouse saying something disrespectful
  — Someone cutting you off in traffic
  — Seeing a child being mean to another child
  — Someone being mean to you or another person in your presence
  — Coworkers not doing their jobs
  — Your boss being overly harsh

Take a few moments now to think about your triggers. What are the times when you are most likely to experience the kind of anger that leads to a regrettable outcome? If acting in anger is something you are working on changing, it may help to keep a notepad (on paper or on your phone) and note triggers as you encounter them. If you are already keeping a notebook, as I suggest in the introduction, to help you follow through on your goals, that is a good place to keep track of your triggers.

As you get to know your triggers, the next step is to learn to recognize early signs of anger. How can you tell that you are getting angry? Physical sensations are often a good warning sign:

- Increase in breathing rate, breathing becoming faster and deeper
- Your body, particularly face and back of the neck, feeling warm or hot
- Hands and fingers getting cold
- Your heart beating faster
- Feeling sweaty
- Tightening or clenching of the jaw
- Tightening of the fists
- Body feeling shaky

Certain thought patterns are another way to recognize anger. For example:

- What's wrong with these people?
- Why do they always have to do this?
- How dare they?!
- I can't stand this!

Take a moment now to think about the physical and cognitive warning signs of anger. Note them in your notebook. The next time you experience anger, take some time to think about the early warning signs you noticed as soon as you feel calm enough to do so. Write down what you noticed.

Physiology of Anger

The experience of anger, as with any emotion, is a combination of activation of the body and the brain. Anger first arises in the brain, as the amygdala receives a signal of threat or danger, activating the fight-or-flight response. At times when behavioral reaction to anger gets out of control, the amygdala is hyperactivated and the prefrontal cortex, responsible for behavioral control, in underactive and unable to put the brakes on amygdala activation.

In the body, the sympathetic branch of the autonomic nervous system activates physiological correlates of the fight-or-flight response, such as rising blood pressure, increased heart rate, faster and deeper breathing, and increased sweating and muscle tension.

When anger and hostility become chronic, your health is affected in significant and negative ways, including increased risk of high blood pressure, heart attack, and early death. While anger is a normal human emotion that is OK to experience as it arises, it is in your best interest to learn to respond to anger in ways that keep you from getting stuck, making anger chronic and damaging your health.

Mindfulness and biofeedback training are aimed at helping you choose helpful responses to anger and preventing you from getting stuck or engaging in undesirable actions.

Mindfulness Training for Anger

Mindfulness practice is beneficial in two ways in helping you manage anger. First, by meditating at neutral times, 10–20 minutes a day, you retrain your brain to produce a more helpful response in triggering situations. Second, mindfulness-based skills are helpful in the moment of rising anger, giving you greater flexibility in responding.

Meditation Practice for Anger

If you've already started some sort of mindfulness practice, as described in Chapter 8 on mindfulness meditation and Chapter 9 on mindfulness-based skills, then you've already begun to rewire your brain to help you produce a more helpful response to anger. If you have not yet started a mindfulness practice, now is a good time to do so.

You may recall from Chapter 7 on mindfulness that regular meditation practice has the following results:

- A smaller, less active amygdala, which is typically overactivated in times of anger
- A more active prefrontal cortex, responsible for problem solving, decision making, and emotion regulation—all helpful skills in responding to anger
- Greater connectivity between the prefrontal cortex and the amygdala, allowing the prefrontal cortex to regulate activation of the amygdala and the fight-or-flight response

- A larger and more active insula, responsible for the ability to understand other people's perspectives, be aware of your own body, and empathy.

In one study, David DeSteno at Northeastern University and his colleagues examined the effects of 3 weeks of daily meditation on behavioral expressions of anger.[123] Half the participants in their study took part in daily mindfulness meditation for 3 weeks, while the other half solved puzzles for the same amount of time. In the lab, all the participants were asked to give a presentation on their future goals in front of judges. The judges were trained to give harsh critical feedback, no matter how good the presentation actually was. Then all the participants were asked about how angry they felt and were given a chance to prepare a culinary treat for the judges with a choice of ingredients, which included a super spicy hot sauce. By looking at the amount of hot sauce added to the treat, the researchers assessed people's aggression and willingness to be vengeful and inflict harm on another person.

They found that, while all the participants reported similar levels of anger in response to unfairly harsh criticism, the meditators added much less hot sauce to the treat they prepared. In other words, the meditators were much less vengeful in their actions in response to anger. This study beautifully demonstrates the main point of this chapter: anger is a natural emotion that may arise in various situations, such as when you are being treated unfairly. Mindfulness training allows you to choose the most helpful response to anger, reducing the chance of regrettable actions.

Greater awareness of your body helps you recognize early signs of anger and gives you a chance to respond in a helpful way. The ability to understand another person's perspective and to empathize can help you reduce your chances of misinterpreting the other person's intention, see the situation differently, and deescalate your response. Combined with better problem solving, decision making, and emotion regulation, these benefits help you respond better to anger.

I recommend starting with a concentration practice, in order to learn to deescalate the strong fight-or-flight reaction in anger. The here-and-now stone (Chapter 8) and mindful breathing (Chapter 2 and Appendix A) are a good place to start. Mindful movement, such as the walking meditation described in Chapter 7 may also be very helpful in deescalting fight or flight reaction.

When you are ready, move on to open awareness practices. This may include any or all of the following (you will find scripts for all of these practices in Appendix A and recordinds for download at www.innakhazan.com/meditation_recordings.html).

- Mindfulness of thoughts, feelings, physiological sensations
- Body awareness (body scan)
- Mountain meditation
- Anchor meditation

Now add compassion practices:

- Mettā (loving kindness)
- Tonglen
- Difficult emotion practice
- Compassion with equanimity (Chapter 10)

Mindfulness-Based Skills for Anger

Mindfulness-based skills are helpful in the moment of rising anger, giving you greater flexibility in responding. Be sure to review Chapter 9 on mindfulness-based skills, as most of them apply to anger. Here I specifically highlight a few skills you can use in the moment of difficulty:

- *Check in with your values.* Your values are your guiding light when it comes to choosing a response. Knowing what's important will help you choose between the immediately gratifying reaction that anger sometimes dictates and a more helpful response that may be more difficult in the moment. For example, keeping in mind your value of being a compassionate leader, you may be able to disengage from the desire to yell at someone who works for you and address the problem in a more constructive way.

- *Think about what outcomes you are hoping to achieve.* When you experience a difficult situation, you may automatically respond to it first and then see what the outcome turns out to be. Often the outcome it not what you were hoping for. This is particularly true for anger. For example, throwing your phone at the wall may feel satisfying in the moment of anger or frustration, but the outcome of a broken phone is not one you were hoping to achieve. Instead of reacting automatically, allow yourself a moment to think about the outcome you would like to achieve and then respond in a way that is most likely to achieve that outcome. Instead of situation → reaction → outcome, give yourself space to think situation → desired outcome → response.

- *Willingness.* Is following through with the more helpful response, albeit difficult in the moment, worth it to you? Are you willing to act in accordance with your values in order to achieve the desired outcomes?

- *Mindful communication.* Since anger often involves another person, discussing the situation in productive ways is a helpful response. Refer to Chapter 15 on interpersonal communication for a more detailed guide.

- *Compassion.* Compassion is one of the most powerful antidotes to anger. When you experience anger at another person, this anger may feel justified and valid. The other person may have behaved in a way that hurt your feelings or was disrespectful towards you. This may be a family member who frequently behaves in ways that are not acceptable to you. You may feel at the end of your rope with this person. And yet, you may still find that you wish to change the habitual unhelpful response to the anger you justifiably feel. Choosing to experience compassion is a powerful way to make this change. You can decide to experience compassion for the person who may be having difficulties in their own life that leads them to behave in unacceptable ways. Let me be clear, I am not suggesting that the other person should be excused, coddled, or not held responsible for their actions. Not at all. This is not about the other person at all. He or she may not even be aware of your response. When you choose to experience compassion for the person who has wronged you, *your* experience changes and enables you to navigate the difficult relationship in a healthier way. One of the most powerful examples of this that I have seen came from a Tibetan monk who visited Boston with the Dalai Lama in 2009. I was fortunate enough to attend the Meditation and Psychotherapy conference where the Dalai Lama spoke. This monk spoke of the horrors of torture he experienced at the hands of Chinese soldiers. To the great amazement of the audience, he also spoke of the compassion he felt for his torturers. When asked about how he could possibly experience compassion for the people who have hurt him so badly, he answered that it was the only way for him to be able to live his life in peace. Next time you experience anger at someone, see if you can bring up compassion for that person, and then see how it changes your response. Might you find yourself being more willing to talk with the person in more productive ways, or perhaps move on with your day in peace if there is nothing that you can do to actually improve the situation?

- The FLARE technique, described in detail in Chapter 9 on mindfulness-based skills, is a great model for responding to the feeling of anger in the moment. I review FLARE as it applies to anger at the end of this chapter.

Biofeedback Training for Anger

Just like mindfulness, biofeedback is helpful as a preventive practice done at neutral times and as a set of skills to be used at the moment of rising anger. Biofeedback training develops your ability to self-regulate, which in turn helps you change your response to anger triggers. Part of the reason actions in response to anger can be difficult to manage is because of the quick over-activation of the fight-or-flight response and difficulty of the parasympathetic nervous system in putting the brakes to it, as well as breathing dysregulation and high muscle tension. Biofeedback training can help you reduce activation of the fight-or-flight response, regulate your breathing physiology, and reduce muscle tension.

Specifically, biofeedback training may help you with responding to anger in the following ways:

- *Breathing practice regulates your respiratory chemistry.* Overbreathing is a common contributor to feeling out of control when angry. As described in detail in Chapter 2 on breathing, overbreathing results in insufficient oxygen being delivered to the brain, making it difficult to think through your decisions and control your actions. Recognizing and correcting overbreathing early on in the experience of anger will help you make better decisions and regulate your words and actions.
- *HRV trains your body's ability to self-regulate.* People for whom anger is a problem tend to have lower HRV and a less strong parasympathetic nervous system, the brake that regulates our levels of activation. HRV training increases your body's ability to regulate activation in moments of anger, reducing the intensity of the fight-or-flight response and giving you an opportunity to choose a more helpful response. See Chapter 3 for detailed guidance in training HRV.
- *Muscle tension biofeedback allows you to recognize one of the early warning signs of anger.* When you get angry, your muscles get tense. As you become aware of this effect, you can learn to release them. This gives you a helpful way to respond to anger, breaking the typical unhelpful cycle of anger and unhelpful action early on. See Chapter 4 for a detailed guide to muscle training.
- *Temperature biofeedback allows you to recognize early signs of anger-related stress response.* Sometimes when you get angry your hands get cold even as your core gets hot. Practicing temperature skills as a response to those early signs of anger is another good way to respond and break the unhelpful cycle of anger and action. See Chapter 5 for more.
- *Skin conductance biofeedback is a great way to learn more about your triggers.* While hooked up to a skin conductance sensor, you can practice the word association exercise described in Chapter 6 on skin conductance. Come up with a list of words that includes some neu-

tral words, like chair and pencil, and some words related to potential anger triggers, such as frustration and argument. Ask your partner or a friend to read those words to you in random order at 30-second intervals. As you hear each word, respond with the first word that comes to mind. After the exercise, take a look at your skin conductance response—which words produced the highest elevation, and did your skin conductance return to baseline after the elevation? If not, you know that those triggers affect you more than others. Skills you use to reduce skin conductance in Chapter 6 can also be used as a healthy response to anger.

Preventative and Rescue Skills for Anger

One of the hardest things about anger is how hard it is to respond in a helpful way once anger has gotten intense. People often experience being out of control of their actions when anger is intense. Therefore, the earlier you intervene, the more likely you are to succeed in responding to anger in a helpful way. This is why regular meditation and biofeedback practice at neutral times is so important—this preventive training provides you with a foundation for better physiological and emotional self-regulation and helps you recognize triggers and first signs of anger as early as possible. The more you practice the preventative skills, the easier it will be for you to become aware of the triggers and early warning signs.

Your response to anger may come at one of three time points: when you first recognize a trigger, when you notice rising anger, or when you find yourself feeling quite angry and responding in unhelpful ways.

Triggers

In response to triggers, your best course of action is to take care of the trigger itself. Some responses are very trigger specific. If you feel hunger, get something to eat. If you are tired, take a 20-minute catnap, take a short break, go for a brisk walk, or do a few minutes of exercise. If you are in pain, take medication or practice mindfulness and biofeedback-based pain management skills. Take a few moments now to think about your common triggers and ways you could address them when you notice them. It is helpful to think this through at a neutral time (such as while you are reading this chapter) and have options available for use when you notice the presence of a trigger, rather than trying to figure out what to do when you are already feeling bad. If you are keeping a notebook with ideas as you read this book, a reflection on your triggers and helpful responses is helpful to write down.

Early Signs of Rising Anger

More general mindfulness and biofeedback-based responses apply to many triggers that involve difficult feelings that are likely to spill over into anger later. These skills are also helpful in responding to early signs of rising anger. The goal of these skills is to regulate your brain and autonomic nervous system, enabling you to respond to your rising anger in the most helpful way. If you notice that triggers such as having had a stressful interaction at work, frustration over not having met a goal, or having too much on your plate are leading to rising anger, take 10–15 minutes to practice your mindfulness meditation and biofeedback skills. These skills will help your body and mind regulate themselves in the moment, as well as reduce the chance of difficult emotions spilling over into the rest of the day. The following are some skills particularly helpful in response to emotional triggers and early signs of rising anger:

- Mindful low-and-slow breathing (at resonance frequency breathing rate or at 6 breaths per minute; see Chapter 3)
- Mindful concentration meditation practice with an external focus, such as the here-and-now stone (Chapter 8)
- Difficult emotion practice (Appendix A)
- Body awareness (Appendix A)
- Mindful yoga practice for muscle release (Chapter 4)

Once you've taken a few moments to practice your mindfulness or biofeedback skills and feel in better control of your decisions and actions, check in with your values. You may ask yourself the following questions, to help you choose the most helpful response to the specific situation you are facing:

- What kind of response is in my best interest right now?
- Which value is most relevant to this situation?
- Which action is most consistent with this value?

In addition, if the interaction involves another person and you find yourself angry at what you perceive is the intention of his or her actions or words, ask yourself:

- What may his or her intention be? Could it be something other than what I think it is?
- Could I give this person the benefit of the doubt (allowing for the possibility of a more benign intention)?
- How can I communicate with this person about my feelings?

Rescue Skills for Intense Anger

When you find yourself in the middle of intense anger and unhelpful action, the following are some rescue skills you can use at that moment:

- Whenever you notice the anger and unhelpful action, just pause. Remember, it is not too late to change your response.
- Say to yourself or out loud, "This is not helpful. I am going to take a break to calm down. I'll be back."
- Leave the situation where the anger is expressing itself (go outside, to the next room, into the bathroom, whatever works).
- Practice a skill that will help further decrease the intensity of activation you are experiencing:
  — Go for a brisk walk, do jumping jacks, or engage in some other physical activity.
  — Practice low-and-slow breathing (at resonance frequency or at 6 breaths per minute) to remind your body to regulate itself.
  — Do a concentration mindfulness practice, such as the here-and-now stone, which gives you a concrete anchor that's easy to focus on, allowing your mind and body to reduce the intensity of reaction.

FLARE for Anger

The FLARE technique is a great way to practice and implement a helpful response to anger. This section describes each step as it applies to anger, and using the example of Nick from the beginning of this chapter.

Feel

In this step you become aware of the early signs of anger—recognizing a trigger, noticing cognitive, emotional, or physiological signs of anger rising. Nick may notice the hunger, fatigue, and irritation from the day, even before coming through the door at home. If he missed those triggers, he might notice the thoughts of "I just want to be left alone," along with increasing heart rate, quickening breathing, and tightening jaw and shoulders, as his children run up to him with requests for attention.

Label

In this step, you give yourself some distance from the triggers and the rising anger by giving a name to your experience, such as "anger," "frustration," "irritation," or "unhelpful thinking." See the emotion naming chart in Chapter 9 (Figure 9.2) to help with naming your experience. Labeling also helps decrease the activation of the amygdala and the fight-or-flight response and increase activation of the prefrontal cortex, giving you greater flexibility and choice in responding to rising anger. If Nick notices the experience of hunger, fatigue, and irritation, he might label that experience just like that: "I am noticing hunger, tiredness, and irritation." If he does not tune in to his experience until he comes in the door, he might label it as "irritation, fight-or-flight response, rising anger."

Allow

In this step, you give yourself permission to have your experience as it is, letting go of the struggle with your thoughts, emotions, and physiological sensations: "It is OK to feel this way." And yes, it is OK to feel irritated and angry. Remember that trying not to feel what you feel will only get you stuck in those feelings and prevent you from choosing a helpful response. As Nick notices his experience, whether before he comes home or after, once anger has shown itself all he can do is give himself permission to feel the way he does. The phrase "It is OK to feel this way" applies to any experience you may have.

Respond

In this step, you choose the most helpful response. Your response may come when you first recognize a trigger, when you notice rising anger, or when you find yourself feeling quite angry and responding in unhelpful ways. Of course, the earlier you become aware, the easier it will be to choose a helpful response.

If Nick notices his triggers of hunger, fatigue, and irritation before heading home, he will grab a snack and practice a calming meditation practice, such as the mindful low-and-slow breathing at his RF rate. He then heads home once he feels less irritated, and he may take a few more low-and-slow breaths before coming in.

If he notices his anger rising as he walks in and his children rush to him, he can take 10 low-and-slow breaths before he does anything else, and then give his children a mindful hug (just noticing what the hug itself feels like) and say: "Kids, I love you very much. I am feeling very hungry and tired, so let me get something to eat, and then I'd love to hear about your day." Kids being kids, they may not actually give him more than a few seconds of breathing room, but using those few seconds to take a few more breaths will help Nick repeat the same request again.

If Nick does not notice his anger until he is already yelling at his kids, he can stop and say: "I know I am yelling, this is not helpful. I will go outside for a bit to calm down." Nick would practice his rescue breathing skills until the intensity of the emotion passes and he is able to choose the most helpful response to the situation, such as apologizing for yelling and going to get some food before continuing interaction with his kids.

Expand Awareness

In this step, your goal is to take the sharp focus off the problem in front of you, allowing yourself to see the full spectrum of the external and internal environment. This allows you to see the problem as one of the many happenings in your environment—neutral, positive, and negative—rather than the only one big negative experience that overwhelms everything else.

To expand awareness, start with identifying what you are aware of in your external environment—the floor underneath your feet, the sky or the ceiling above you, the trees outside your window. Then move on to what you are aware of in your internal environment—your breath, your heartbeat, your rumbling stomach, tension in your jaw, thoughts about dinner, as well as the sensations of anger—the sensations of anger become just a part of your experience rather than all of your experience. The softer focus on the problem as only one part of the experience increases your willingness to follow through with the decision you made regarding the most helpful way to respond to anger.

If Nick expands his awareness when he first becomes aware of the triggers of being hungry, tired, and irritated, he might notice the chair he is sitting in, the desk with his computer in front of him, the walls of his office, and sounds of his colleagues' voices outside his office door, as well as his breath and heartbeat, his rumbling stomach, the sensation of fatigue, thoughts about the conversation with a coworker that irritated him to no end, and anticipation of a tasty dinner at home and listening to his favorite podcast on the way home. His willingness to eat and then practice mindfulness and biofeedback skills to increase self-regulation at that moment would increase as a result of no longer being focused only on how terrible he feels.

CHAPTER 15

Interpersonal Communication

Maggie woke up on a Saturday morning feeling tired and over-whelmed even before she set foot out of bed. She'd had a tough week at work, the house was a mess, they had guests coming in that after-noon, and she had no idea what she was going to feed them. Her hus-band, Kevin, was waking up too. Maggie knew that he'd had a busy week, too, plus he hadn't been sleeping well and had a cold last week. She hated to pile stuff on for him to do, but she needed a break badly. Plus, she'd been feeling a bit resentful for everything she'd had to do by herself. As Kevin was getting out of bed, Maggie asked, "Could you please take the kids out for breakfast, so I can get a bit more time to sleep? And then do some grocery shopping after? We don't have any food for dinner with the Masons tonight. And I'll clean up when I get up—the house is such a mess." In response, Kevin snaps at Maggie: "Fine, I'll do it. Why do you have to make such a big deal about this? Why are you acting like I don't do anything around here? Do you have to pile on the guilt?"

Human beings are social creatures. We don't do well without connection to others. Our connection with others is often a source of great comfort and strength. It can also be a source of stress and frustration. Knowing how to communicate with others may reduce many sources of interpersonal stress, such as misunderstandings, misjudgments, and unhelpful emotional and physiological reactions that derail communication. This chapter discusses the concept of mindful listening, a way of focusing on what the other person is saying while disengaging from your own reactions and interpretations, thereby enabling you to respond in the most helpful way. I also discuss a common source of misunderstandings and conflict between people: the mistaken beliefs that the way in which you interpret what the other person says is what that person actually said, and that your interpretations of other people's intentions and feelings are entirely accurate. I also discuss mindfulness, biofeedback, and psychophysiology-based skills for healthy communication.

Mindful Listening

Communication starts with listening. Without listening we have no ability to understand where the other person is coming from and what his or her needs are. Without listening, we have no way of responding to the other person in a helpful way. Listening can often be difficult because of the human propensity for mind wandering, judgment, and evaluation, and because of our tendency to try to figure out a response to the speaker while she or he is speaking, instead of fully listening to them. As a result, we do not fully attend to what the person says and are more likely to misjudge or misunderstand what the person is saying.

Mindful listening means anchoring your attention on the speaker and what he or she is saying and committing to listening only, letting go of evaluations, judgments, interpretations, reactions, temptations to interrupt, and concerns about how you might respond. Of course, mindful listening also means not being distracted by your smartphone, tablet, TV, radio, or background noise. Mindful listening means only listening, bringing your mind back to the speaker as soon as you've noticed that it has wandered off.

Try it with someone you trust—a friend or a family member. Find a quiet place to talk where you won't be distracted by the external environment. Ask your conversation partner to tell you about something important that has happened or something he or she has been thinking about recently (choose a noncontroversial topic to start with). You could set a timer for 5 minutes. Let your partner speak while you listen. Anchor your attention on what your partner is saying, and return to the speaker any time your mind wanders off. Notice judgments, evaluations, automatic reactions, and anticipation of your own response rising in you, and let them go, returning your attention back to the speaker. Once the speaker is done, reflect on your own experience: What was it like to just listen? What was different from how you usually listen? What did you hear? Now switch places, and ask your conversation partner to listen mindfully while you tell him or her about something important you've done or thought about. After you are done, reflect on what it was like to be listened to mindfully. Share your experiences with each other.

Like any skill, mindful listening requires practice. It is helpful to do your initial practices in low-stress conversations and then use your skills in more intense or difficult conversations. Take a few moments now to think about situations in which you may be able to use your mindful listening skills and the relationships that would benefit the most. It could be your spouse, your child, your parent, a friend, coworker, teacher, doctor, or any other important person. What you say may not be what the other person hears, and what you hear may not be what the other person intended.

What is a mental filter? When you choose your words, you have multiple possibilities of saying the same thing. All those possibilities pass through the filter of how you'd like to say things. Most of these words get filtered out, and only one choice of words gets spoken. As you say those words, they pass through a similar filter of the other person. There are numerous ways to interpret what you said, and all but one interpretation gets filtered out, with only one passing through to the listener's mind.

These filters consist of your previous learning experiences, including your experience interacting with the person you are speaking with, and your current internal state, such as hunger, tiredness, and presence of difficult feelings, like frustration, guilt, shame, or fear. The filter also contains your opinions and values, habits and automatic reactions. These filters are never the same for different people, so two people's experience of the same situation may be very different.

Let's talk about one of the most common sources for misunderstandings between people: what you say may not be what the other person hears, and what you hear may not be what the other person intended. When you have something to say, your choice of words passes through your mental and emotional filters. When other people hear what you say, they use filters to interpret what they heard. Your filters often do not line up. You know what you are trying to say but may not stop to think or have no way to predict how it may come across to other people. When others interpret what you said through their filters, they also don't stop to consider that their interpretation may not be what you intended. Once they make their interpretations, they respond to you based on those interpretations. You, in turn, interpret what they said through your filter, not knowing which filter the information passed through for them. Your filters, once again, are not the same. Your interpretations of what each of you has said are even further apart, triggering more unhelpful reactions, and the conversation turns into one big misunderstanding.

Let's take the example of Maggie and Kevin from the beginning of this chapter. When making her request for time to herself, Maggie did not provide any context—she did not explain how she was feeling. After all, she knew perfectly well how she felt and why she needed a break. Kevin, on the other hand, had no way of knowing how she was feeling or why she was asking for him to take the kids and do grocery shopping. Maggie made her request through her filter of having had a hard week and needing a break. Unbeknownst to Maggie, Kevin has been feeling guilty for not doing as much around the house as he usually does since he's been sick. Kevin heard what Maggie said through his filter of guilt. As a result, Kevin felt defensive and, having interpreted Maggie's words through the filters of guilt and defensiveness, concluded that she was attacking him.

Let's play that part of their conversation out again, this time highlighting Maggie's and Kevin's filters through which the conversation passed through.

MAGGIE (THROUGH THE FILTER OF "I AM SO TIRED, WHAT'S WRONG WITH ME? I JUST FEEL OVERWHELMED, SO MUCH TO DO!): "Could you please take the kids out for breakfast, so I can get a bit more time to sleep? And then do some grocery shopping after? We don't have any food for dinner with the Masons tonight. And I'll clean up when I get up—the house is such a mess."

KEVIN (THROUGH THE FILTER OF, "UGH, I HAVEN'T BEEN DOING MUCH AROUND THE HOUSE AND SHE'S NOTICING. I'M NOT

PULLING MY WEIGHT AND I'M LETTING HER DOWN JUST
BECAUSE OF A STUPID COLD, AND FEELING DEFENSIVE AS A
RESULT"): "Fine, I'll do it. Why do you have to make such a big
deal about this? Why are you acting like I don't do anything
around here? Do you have to pile on the guilt?"

Her request is perfectly reasonable, knowing where it came from. Kevin's reaction is also understandable, knowing the filter that Maggie's request passed through in his mind. Neither of them knew each other's filters, and a big misunderstanding happened as a result.

Misunderstandings like this happen not because anyone has done anything wrong but simply because we do not have access to other people's internal workings. While such situations are normal and no one's fault, they create a lot of conflict. Such conflict may be minimized with mindfulness and biofeedback-based skills. These skills serve two purposes: regular biofeedback and mindfulness training at neutral times train your physiological and emotional self-regulation, which supports healthier communication; and biofeedback and mindfulness-based skills used in the moment of difficult communication allow you to respond to the challenge in more helpful ways.

Biofeedback Skills for Healthy Communication

Regular biofeedback practice trains your body's ability to self-regulate. Better self-regulation means that during a difficult conversation your body and your mind are better able to achieve optimal activation, reducing the chances of overreacting, snapping, storming out, and other unhelpful automatic reactions.

The most helpful modalities for regular biofeedback training in supporting healthy communication are breathing and heart rate variability (HRV) training. Difficult or heated conversations are a frequent trigger for overbreathing, which reduces the amount of oxygen available to your brain, making it more difficult to regulate emotions, make quick decisions, pay attention, and decide a helpful response to the challenging conversation. Breathing training reduces the probability of overbreathing in the moment, and teaches you to recognize overbreathing when it happens and to take steps to correct it. See Chapter 2 on breathing for a detailed training plan.

HRV biofeedback trains your body and mind to produce most optimal levels of activation needed in the moment of challenge. With HRV training, your parasympathetic (relaxation) nervous system gets stronger and better able to put the brakes on sympathetic (stress) activation as needed, not letting your physiological activation to get out of hand and interfere with ability to respond in a healthy way. See Chapter 3 on HRV for a detailed training plan.

For romantic partners or parent-child or sibling dyads, it is often helpful for both members to practice biofeedback skills together. When difficult conversations arise, both people are likely to get dysregulated. If both people train their baseline ability to self-regulate and acquire biofeedback skills to improve self-regulation in a difficult moment, communication between them will improve as both members of the pair will be able to respond to challenges in communication in a more helpful way.

Mindfulness-Based Skills for Healthy Communication

A consistent meditation practice provides you with an even stronger foundation for helpful brain activation in moments of challenge. You may recall from Chapter 7 on mindfulness that regular mindfulness meditation training leads to helpful changes in brain structure and function. Changes most helpful in communication include increased size and/or greater activation of parts of the brain responsible for emotion regulation (hippocampus), empathy and perspective taking (insula), social cognition and compassion (temporoparietal junction), emotional and cognitive regulation (lateral cerebellum and cerebellar vermis), and regulation of attention and behavioral control (anterior cingulate cortex). In addition, mindfulness meditation training is associated with decreased size and activation of the amygdala, the fight-or-flight center of the brain, which means that a fight-or-flight reaction during the conversation is less likely to happen.

Please see Chapter 8 on more details about starting a meditation practice. Meditations I find to be particularly useful in cultivating skills for healthy communication are the Mettā (Chapter 10), tonglen (Appendix A), difficult emotion practice (Appendix A), and mindfulness of thoughts, feelings, and physiological sensations (Appendix A).

In addition to regular meditation practice, mindfulness-based skills used in the moment can help foster healthy, clear, nonjudgmental communication. Be sure to review Chapter 9 on general mindfulness-based skills that apply to most situations. The following are skills particularly helpful when communicating with others.

Don't assume you know the other person's thoughts, feelings, or intentions. You know only what is overtly observable: words and actions. What you think you know about the other person's thoughts and feelings is an interpretation that has passed through your own filter. Human beings are notoriously bad at being clairvoyant. We think we know what the other person is thinking, feeling, or intending to do, but we are wrong much of the time. We are also often unaware of being wrong.

Let's take the example of Maggie and Kevin. During their difficult conversation, Kevin might say to Maggie, "I know you were trying to make me feel guilty." Maggie will naturally counter with "No, I wasn't," and the argument will continue in the unproductive direction of figuring out whether or not Maggie intended to make Kevin feel guilty. Kevin has no way of proving what Maggie intended or how she felt. She is the only one who knows what her intention was.

Assuming you know what the other person is thinking, feeling, or intending to do always puts you on the "losing" end, because you have no way of proving your belief. The other person can simply say, "No, you are wrong," and that's that, regardless of whether you were actually right or wrong.

Therefore, during interactions with others, comment only on what you can see or hear: words and actions. When feelings, thoughts, and intentions of other people matter, ask! You can, on the other hand, talk about your own thoughts, feelings, and intentions since you typically know what they are. Acknowledging your own feelings will also help your conversation partner better understand where you are coming from.

For example, in the interaction between Kevin and Maggie, Kevin might say, "I felt defensive when I heard you say that our house is a mess. A thought that you were trying to make me feel guilty occurred to me. What did you really intend to do?" Maggie would be much likely to respond to that statement in a calmer way, with something like, "I felt bad about leaving the house so messy last week. I just really wanted to clean it up."

Give the benefit of the doubt when it comes to intentions. When you jump to the conclusion that your conversation partner intended something hurtful or negative, you are going to react accordingly, defending yourself or attacking the other person. If there was, in fact, no ill intent, the conversation will get derailed, and you will not achieve your purpose. Instead, allow the possibility that the person's intention was a positive or a neutral one and respond accordingly. When Kevin assumes that Maggie intended to make him feel guilty, he gets defensive and snaps at Maggie. If Kevin were to take a step back and give her the benefit of the doubt that she did not intend to attack him, his response would more likely be calm and curious: "I wonder what you meant when you said. . . .

Don't take things personally—other people's actions are likely not about you at all. When someone says something you don't like in a conversation, it is very natural to assume that the intention is a personal one, meaning that the other person means to make you feel a certain way. That is true sometimes, but most of the time other people are reacting to something within themselves and are not even thinking about you. We humans tend to think that other people focus their intentions on us way more than they actually do. When Kevin snaps at Maggie she would naturally think that he meant to be dismissive of her needs, whereas he was actually just responding to his own feelings of guilt and defensiveness about not doing more around the house the previous week. Instead of assuming a personal intention for Kevin's words, Maggie might allow for the possibility that his response was not about her but was a result of his own internal experience.

Take responsibility for your own feelings. People frequently say, "You made me feel angry," "He made me feel sad," "She annoyed me," and so on. We attribute control over our feelings to other people all the time. But do other people actually have control over our feelings? Does somebody go into our head and push a button for anger, or sadness, or annoyance? Of course not. Feelings arise as part of our experience, and no one has control over these feelings.

The same words from your partner may trigger completely different reactions at different times, depending on your internal experience. For example, if the interaction between Maggie and Kevin had happened on a different weekend, when Kevin hadn't been sick the week before and had contributed to the household the way he typically does, he would not have felt guilty and defensive in response to Maggie's request. Maggie did not make him feel anything. His feelings of guilt arose in the context of Maggie's request and his worry that he hadn't contributed enough.

Think about it—do you want to turn over control of something as powerful and important as your emotions to someone else? Probably not, right? And yet each time you declare that someone made you feel something, you are effectively stating that the other person has control over how you feel. This frequently leads to unhelpful reactions to these emotions, because you may not feel in control of your response to the feelings as well. But, of course, that is the one aspect of your experience that you have control over: how you respond to your feelings. So, give yourself permission to feel how you feel, and then take control over responding to those emotions in a helpful way.

Don't tell people what to do or how to feel. Do you like it when someone tells you what to do or how to feel? Probably not. Neither does anyone else. Even if you are 100 percent certain that you have the perfect solution to the problem at hand, telling your conversation partner what to do will not help that person be open to hearing you. For example, Maggie might tell Kevin to just stop feeling guilty since he has nothing to feel guilty about. Would that help Kevin feel less guilty? Probably not. But it would make him feel frustrated with Maggie for not getting where he is coming from or with himself for feeling the wrong way. Instead, listen mindfully to your conversation partner and validate that person's experience, as I describe in the next paragraph.

Validate the other's experience, even if you don't get it or agree with it. It is virtually impossible to always truly get the other person's experience and understand why he or she feels that way, simply because you have not been through the same life experiences as the other person. But that never makes the other person's feelings wrong or any less valid. Feelings are not under our control. All we can do is validate the other person's feelings and accept that the other person has them ("I understand that you feel scared," even if you have no idea why or if you do not think you would feel that way in the situation—that does not matter.). Respond based on your acceptance of the other person's experience, not based on what you think that experience *should* be.

When thinking about a difficult conversation, be clear on what you would like to talk about. Don't engage in distractions, and don't go down "rabbit holes" of distraction. If Kevin and Maggie go down the rabbit hole of whether or not she intended to make him feel guilty, the conversation would get derailed and they would not get to a resolution. When you notice a conversation taking a turn for a rabbit hole that will take you off track, respond with something like, "I am not sure that's a helpful direction to go. Could we continue talking about . . . ," or "You know, that's a really important topic. Could we come back to it later, after we figure this out?"

When preparing for a difficult conversation, it is helpful to have an idea of what you would like to achieve as a result. Be sure to set an intention that is within your control—think about what you would like to convey, a decision you'd like to make, and so forth. Do not set an intention of making someone feel a certain way—feelings are not under our control, not for you, and certainly not for other people. You also have no control over what the other person understands, decides, or does as a result of the conversation. You do have control over how and what you would like to say and how you would like to act (but not feel) during the conversation. For example, Maggie would not have control over whether or not Kevin understands that she needs a break, but she does have control over how she asks for it. She might set an intention of conveying her need for a break and say something like, "I am feeling overwhelmed and could really use a break. Could you please take the kids and do some grocery shopping?" This will maximize the chances that Kevin will hear her and respond in a positive way.

Use mindful language. Words and body language that convey contempt (eye rolling and sarcasm), disrespect ("You have no idea what you are talking about!"), judgment and criticism ("Why do you always have to be so mean?"), and lack of consideration for the other person's feelings ("You shouldn't feel that way") are likely to put your conversation partner on the defensive, activate fight-or-flight responses, and derail the conversation. Instead, use words that convey trust ("I know you care about me"), respect ("Can we figure this out together?"), acceptance ("I know you are doing your best"), and validation ("I see how you might feel or think that"). Your conversation partner will be much more likely to be open to what you have to say and to respond positively when she or he feels trusted, respected, and validated.

Adopt an attitude of compassion. A compassionate attitude is one of understanding and accepting where the other person is coming from, with a commitment to respond with kindness. Like mindful language, a compassionate attitude will help your conversation partner be open to what you have to say and be willing to work with you on a solution to the problem. Remember, compassion is associated with the release of oxytocin, a hormone that helps us reach out to other people. A compassionate attitude in a conversation will foster a connection with the person you are interacting with and facilitate healthy communication.

Take responsibility for your actions. Just like no one else is in control of your feelings, no one else is in control over your actions, either. No one "made you do it." We all make mistakes sometimes, hurt someone's feelings, say something we don't mean, act in a thoughtless or inconsiderate way. Blaming other people or some other external event for "making you do it" will not repair the hurt. But taking responsibility for your actions and apologizing may. When an apology is in order, give a real, heartfelt apology that contains the following the elements: words of apology, what you are apologizing for, and what you will do differently next time.

Use FLARE to figure out the most helpful response to a difficult conversation. I will use the example of Kevin to illustrate the skill as it applies to communication:

Feel. When Kevin hears Maggie's request, he might notice a sensation of tightening in his chest, a sensation of warmth rising over the back of his head, the feeling of guilt arising, and the thought of "Why is she trying to make me feel this way?"

Label. Kevin might call this experience "guilt," "regret," and "questioning."

Allow. He would give himself permission to feel the way he does: "It is OK to feel this way. I can allow the feeling to stay."

Respond. Kevin might respond with first taking a few low-and-slow breaths to regulate his physiological response, recognize that he does not actually know what Maggie felt or intended, remind himself that his feelings are his own, and choose to respond with the benefit of the doubt.

Expand awareness. Kevin would expand his awareness to his breath and heartbeat, and then to the sensations of touch or pressure of his mattress, and the feeling of compassion that arises as he thinks about his wife. His response might be, "Sure, I'll take the kids . . . tell me more about how you are feeling."

CHAPTER 16

Pain

*"I just wish I could get out of the house and go play with the kids"—
this thought kept running through Kim's mind as she was lying on
the couch, trying not to move for fear of aggravating her back and
triggering another painful spasm. Kim felt stiff, and tense, and very
unhappy. She saw the beautiful weather outside, and she could hear
her kids laughing as they ran through the sprinklers. She wished that
she could feel well enough to be out there with them. But she knew
better. She first felt back pain after she lifted her toddler up in the
air. She thought it would go away if she rested, but the pain stayed.
Her doctor advised her to avoid lifting heavy things and give her back
some rest. She complied, but the pain stayed. She had a CT scan,
which showed a herniated disk, and the doctor advised gentle movement and physical therapy. Kim tried to move more, but moving hurt.
Every time she even thought about getting to yoga or physical therapy, she felt a twinge in her back—there is no way she was going to be
able to get there or make it through a session. She thought that if she
gave her back a break, she'd feel better, eventually. If only she could
go out and play with her kids. . . .*

Pain is one of the most common causes of human suffering. A survey by the
National Institutes of Health found that 25.3 million US adults (11.2 percent
of adult Americans) experienced chronic pain, nearly 40 million adults (17.6
percent) experienced severe levels of pain, and an estimated 126 million adults
(55.7 percent) reported some type of pain in the 3 months before the survey.[124]
That's a lot of pain and suffering!

Pain can be acute or chronic. Acute pain begins suddenly and is usually sharp, such as pain resulting from broken bones, cuts, and burns. Acute pain typically does not last a long time and disappears when the underlying cause has healed. Some acute pain, however, may develop into chronic pain, which is common with back injuries. Chronic pain may also result from condition that did not start with an acute injury, such as irritable bowel syndrome (IBS), fibromyalgia, and migraine headaches.

This chapter is devoted primarily to chronic pain, including (but not limited to) headaches, IBS, fibromyalgia, and back pain. I briefly touch on the mechanisms of pain, just enough to give you an idea of what happens in your body and your brain when you are hurting. This will then help you understand how mindfulness and biofeedback training can help to alleviate the suffering caused by pain. I discuss mindfulness and biofeedback training as it applies to pain.

The Neurobiology of Pain

THE IMPORTANCE OF UNDERSTANDING PAIN

Research has shown that understanding the physiology of pain and the way our thoughts and feelings affect our pain experience can actually help make pain better.

For example, Ali Oliveira, Richard Gevirtz, and David Hubbard of Alliant International University in San Diego conducted a study of 126 people admitted to an emergency department with whiplash and neck strain after a car accident.[125] All of the participants received standard medical care for whiplash. In addition, half the participants viewed a brief educational video that explained the pain process and the way our thoughts and emotions influence pain.

One month after the emergency visit, the researchers followed up with all the participants by phone and asked them to rate their pain on a scale from 0 to 10. Those who viewed the video rated their pain at an average of 1.5, while those who received only standard care rated their pain at an average of 5. Participants rated their pain similarly at 3 and 6 months follow-ups as well. In addition, at the 6 month follow-up, only 4 percent of those who viewed the video reported using opioid medication to help manage pain, compared to 36 percent of those who received standard care.

Understanding the pain cycle affects the way we respond to it cognitively and emotionally, which in turn reduces pain.

Our experience of pain consists of four distinct components: the sensory experience (perception of pain itself), the cognitive experience (our interpretation of pain, such as "This is going to last forever"), the emotional reaction we have to the sensory experience and its cognitive interpretation, and the behavioral response we have to all of that.

Sensory Perception of Pain

When you experience the sensations of pain, whether it is in your lower back, in your head, or in your stomach, signals travel from the pain receptors at the site of the pain, via nerve fibers in the spinal cord, up to the brain. This pain pathway is called the ascending or "pain-to-brain" pathway, meaning that pain signal travels from the body (including the head, in the case of headaches) to the brain.

Different kinds of pain signals travel to the brain. So-called fast pain is transmitted via quick-conducting nerve fibers. Fast pain pathways produce intense pain, which people often describe as sharp or stabbing. This type of pain is usually the acute pain we feel immediately after an injury occurs. "Slow pain" is transmitted via slower-conducting nerve fibers that are smaller in diameter. People often describe this type of pain as dull and aching. Slow pain is typically involved in long-term, chronic pain, such as low back pain.

Perception of pain in the brain is not controlled by one "pain center" but is processed in a number of brain structures. Interestingly, the slow pain typical of experiences of chronic pain, travels to the hypothalamus, among other places, where it triggers the release of stress hormones, and to the amygdala, responsible for the initiation of the fight-or-flight response. This explains why pain results in the fight-or-flight experience. Your brain treats the slow pain signals as signals of danger. I return to this later in the chapter.

The second pain pathway is the descending, "brain-to-pain" pathway. This is the pathway by which pain-related information is modified within the brain and sent back to the body. This is likely one of the ways in which biofeedback works to alleviate pain.

There is a lot we don't know about pain and how it is transmitted. One theory that gives us some insight into how pain works is the gate control theory of pain, formulated by Ronald Melzack and Patrick Wall in 1965. According to this theory, the nerve fibers of the spinal cord contain "gates" that can narrow or widen to influence how much of the pain impulse reaches the brain.

Moreover, our emotional states can determine whether pain gates open or close. Experiencing "positive" emotions such as contentment, gratitude, and excitement closes the gates, while difficult emotions such as anger, fear, and sadness keep the gates open. I return to this emotional component shortly.

Cognitive Interpretation of Pain

Your interpretation of the physiological pain signal plays a significant role in your experience of pain. The way you interpret pain influences the way you respond to it. If you interpret pain as catastrophic, as something that may ruin your health and your future and keep you from living the kind of life you want to live, your experience of pain becomes more difficult and may prevent you from responding in healthy ways.

Pain catastrophizing, an expectation of an extremely negative outcome of experiencing pain, has long been linked to perception of greater pain intensity and greater disability caused by pain. Catastrophizing may lead to feelings of hopelessness and depression, and may prevent you from taking helpful action in response to pain.

Consider the earlier example of Kim. Her interpretation of her pain is something that keeps her from playing with her kids. She longs to play with them but believes that it will make her pain worse and completely ruin her life. However, research consistently shows that movement, connection with loved ones, and participation in valued activities are vital to recovery.[128] Kim's belief that her pain will get worse if she plays with her kids is keeping her from engaging in activities that will likely help her get better.

For people suffering from IBS, travel may seem off limits, no matter how much they enjoy it, because they may be trapped in a car or an airplane when the pain gets worse. People with chronic migraines might decide not to go for a job interview because they believe that they would not be able to function and perform well if they were to get a migraine during the interview. If you suffer from chronic pain, think about the ways you interpret sensations of pain and how these interpretations influence your actions and decisions.

A concept similar to catastrophizing is the anticipation of pain lasting a long time. Ron Siegel in his book *The Mindfulness Solution* describes a study where two groups of adults were asked to put their hand in ice water.[129] Ice water is a way to induce pain without producing physical damage to the tissues. One group was told that they will keep their hands in the water for 30 seconds, while the other group was told that they will keep their hands in the water for 10 minutes. Ice water was the same temperature for both groups. After 20 seconds of being in ice water, participants were asked to rate their level of distress. The group that was expecting to have to keep their hands in the water for 10 minutes rated their distress level as significantly higher than the group that was expecting only 30 seconds in the water. Anticipation of pain lasting a long time greatly increased people's suffering.

Think about a time when you've had pain. Did a thought like, "This is never going to end" occur to you? If so, the distress you felt probably increased greatly at the thought that pain is not going to end any time soon. Unhelpful interpretations of pain like these are part of the chronic pain cycle that many people have a lot of trouble getting out of.

I'd like to share with you two fascinating stories that demonstrate just how important our interpretation is to the experience of pain.

One is a report published in the *British Medical Journal* in 1995.[126] A twenty-nine-year-old British construction worker came to the emergency department after having jumped onto a 6-inch nail—the nail went all the way through the bottom of his boot. He was in tremendous amount of pain, with the slightest movement of the nail intensifying it. Once the nail and the boot were removed, it turned out that the nail passed between the toes, and there was no injury to the foot at all. He thought that the nail had passed through his foot and experienced very real pain, even though there was no physical damage to the foot.

The other is a story published in *USA Today* in 2005 about an American construction worker who had unknowingly shot himself in the head with a nail gun and did not realize he was injured.[127] Six days later he started getting a toothache and went to the dentist, who discovered the nail embedded in the side of his head. He did not feel any pain for 6 days, and when he finally felt it, he attributed it to a tooth, because that was the only plausible explanation.

These two stories beautifully illustrate the importance of our perceptions and interpretations for our experience of pain. This means that biofeedback and mindfulness training can make a big difference in cases of physical causes of pain that may seem uncorrectable.

Emotional Reactions to Pain

As discussed earlier in this chapter, the amygdala, the fear center of the brain, is part of the brain's pain circuitry. Fear is a common consequence of some of the unhelpful interpretations of pain. Catastrophic beliefs about pain, anticipation of more pain, worry about how the pain will affect the future, regret over having done whatever triggered pain in the first place, blame and harsh self-talk for not being able to control pain, and other difficult thoughts trigger fear. Fear and the fight-or-flight response that comes with it create more pain. Here's how:

- Your muscles tense up, preparing for running or fighting, even though you are not actually planning either of those actions. Your muscles may also tense up in a protective bracing effort. These kinds of unnecessary muscle activation create dysponesis, as discussed in detail in Chapter 4 on muscle health. Dysponesis can trigger or exacerbate muscle-related pain such as back, neck, or shoulder pain, pain related to temporomandibular joint (TMJ) disorder, and tension or migraine headache.
- Your peripheral blood vessels constrict, preparing to divert blood flow to major organs and muscle groups that are directly involved in running and fighting. Your fingers, toes, nose, and even ears may feel cold. The small blood vessels that constrict during the fight-or-flight activation have a large impact on your blood pressure. When these blood vessels are relaxed, more blood can flow freely through them. When they become constricted, the same amount of blood flows

through a narrower space, increasing your blood pressure. In addition, less blood is available to take away metabolic by-products produced by the muscles (such as lactic acid), and their buildup increases muscle pain. Moreover, if you suffer from Raynaud's disease, a condition in which fingers, toes, nose, and/or ears temporarily lose circulation, constriction of the flood vessels in your fingers, hands, feet, nose, and ears can trigger an attack.

- Your gastrointestinal system slows down as part of the fight-or-flight response, to allow more resources to be devoted to running and fighting. With fight-or-flight activation, most systems in your body increase their function (your heart and breathing rates increase, your muscles tense up, your sweat production increases, your brain becomes more alert, etc.), except for the gastrointestinal system, which slows down to make more resources available for running and fighting. As a result, you might experience painful intestinal spasms, bloating, or motility changes (diarrhea or constipation). If you suffer from IBS, you might experience an exacerbation in symptoms.

- You may recall the discussion of muscle spindles in Chapter 4 on muscle health. Muscle spindles are stretch receptors within your muscles that are sensitive to fear and similar difficult emotions. Muscle spindle activity may result in muscle pain even in the absence of muscle tension. If you suffer from chronic muscle-related pain, this may result in a pain flare-up.

- Fear, anxiety, and fight-or-flight activation are among of the most common triggers for migraine headaches. The cortical spreading depression theory, a scientifically supported theory of the causes for migraine, describes a wave of hyperactivation of brain cells followed by long-lasting depression (cessation of activity) in those cells. The spreading of this wave activates the fifth cranial nerve (the trigeminal nerve), which is responsible for sensation in your head and face and for activities such as chewing and smiling. An "irritated" trigeminal nerve releases the hormone called substance P (the P stands for pain). You can surmise what happens as a result. Fear, anxiety, and fight-or-flight response are common triggers for cortical spreading depression and the resulting migraine pain.

- Fear often results in breathing dysregulation, such as overbreathing. See Chapter 2 on breathing for a description of ways in which over-breathing affects your body. Overbreathing may trigger or exacerbate back, neck, and shoulder pain, tension or migraine headache, IBS, and many others sources of chronic pain.

Behavioral Reactions to Pain

Fear and pain are both intensely unpleasant experiences that human beings are strongly motivated to avoid. These behavioral reactions complete the cycle of pain mentioned previously. You may try to avoid pain by avoiding activities that you believe will produce or increase pain and activities that you believe pain may interfere with. For example, Kim avoided playing with her kids because she was afraid her pain will get worse. She was also not going to yoga because she was afraid that pain will prevent her from being able to do the class.

The more you attempt to avoid pain, the more you box yourself in, and the more fear you experience. This triggers other difficult emotions, such as shame, anger, and depression. All of these feelings are likely to make your pain worse, triggering more suffering, more fear, and more avoidance. This is the cycle of pain.

Biofeedback Interventions for Pain

The two main goals of biofeedback training for pain are to increase your body's ability to self-regulate and provide you with helpful skills in responding to pain as it presents itself in the moment. Better self-regulation enables your mind and body to produce the most helpful response to pain. It also raises the threshold for fight-or-flight response rising in the moment of challenge, therefore making it less likely to exacerbate pain. Every modality of biofeedback can be helpful in responding to pain.

Breathing

See Chapter 2 for a detailed review of breathing. In this section, I discuss ways in which breathing practices described in Chapter 2 may be helpful in living better with pain.

- Becoming aware of overbreathing and knowing how to correct it helps you avoid many of the unhelpful consequences of overbreathing that exacerbate pain.
- Shifting your breath from the chest to the belly (the way you do in low-and-slow breathing) helps relieve muscle-tension-related pain in the neck, shoulders, and back.
- Learning mindful low-and-slow breathing provides you with a helpful response to pain. Practicing low-and-slow breathing when you are in pain reduces intensity of fight-or-flight activation, closes some of the pain gates, and redirects attention from the interpretive part of the brain, which may be predicting scary outcomes, to the sensory parts, allowing you to experience the moment without unhelpful interpretations.
- Breathing training is particularly helpful in the following pain disorders:
  - Headaches (migraine and tension)
  - IBS
  - Back, neck, and shoulder pain
  - Repetitive strain injury
  - Noncardiac chest pain

Heart Rate Variability

See Chapter 3 for a more detailed discussion of HRV. In this section, I highlights ways in which HRV practice may be helpful in living better with pain.

- HRV training improves your body's ability to regulate its activation, raising the threshold for pain gates to widen.
- HRV training decreases unhelpful activation of the muscle spindles, which may cause or exacerbate stress-related pain.
- HRV training provides you with a healthy way to respond to pain. Practicing mindful low-and-slow breathing at resonance frequency or at 6 breaths per minute as a response to pain provides you with all the benefit of low-and-slow breathing, as well as a reminder for your body and mind to regulate their activation in the most optimal way.
- Research shows impaired HRV in numerous chronic pain disor-

ders.[130] HRV biofeedback is particularly helpful for the following pain disorders:

- — Fibromyalgia
- — Headaches (migraine and tension)
- — Back pain
- — IBS
- — Arthritis
- — Noncardiac chest pain

Muscle Tension

- See Chapter 4 for a complete review of muscle health. In this section, I discuss muscle related practices particularly relevant to living better with pain. Recognizing unnecessary muscle tension reduces dyspone-sis and allows your muscles to rest and recover. This is crucial in allevi-ating muscle pain, which often results from chronically tense muscles.
- Training proper muscle use prevents your muscles from becoming overtired. Overtired muscles, paradoxically, are more difficult to relax.
- Learning muscle relaxation strategies allows you to avoid bracing and provides you with a helpful response to pain.
- Electromyographic (EMG) biofeedback is particularly helpful for the following pain disorders:
  - — TMJ disorder
  - — Back, neck, and shoulder pain
  - — Repetitive strain injury
  - — Tension and migraine headaches

Finger Temperature

See Chapter 5 for a detailed review of temperature biofeedback practices. In this section, I discuss temperature biofeedback skills particularly relevant to living better with pain.

- Learning to increase your finger temperature helps trains self-regulation and reduce unnecessary fight-or-flight activation.
- Hand-warming skills are helpful in responding to pain, particularly pain caused by

— Raynaud's disease
— IBS
— Migraine headaches

Skin Conductance

See Chapter 6 for a detailed discussion of skin conductance biofeedback. In this section, I discuss ways in which skin conductance skills may be helpful in living better with pain

- Skin conductance training helps you to become aware of the emotional triggers that are associated with the onset of pain. Doing a word association task described on Chapter 6 will help you determine which cues trigger greatest physiological activation.
- Practicing skills in regulating skin conductance provides you with a helpful response to unnecessary activation and pain.
- Research has shown increased skin conductance in response to fearful thoughts about pain.[131] Learning to reduce skin conductance will also help reduce unhelpful fear-driven pain reactions.

How to Practice Biofeedback Skills for Pain

First, determine which biofeedback modalities are likely to be most helpful to you. Choice of biofeedback modalities depends on two criteria: knowing which areas of your own physiology may need training, and research evidence on which modalities have been shown to be helpful for various pain disorders.

In thinking about which areas of your own physiology may need training, consider the following:

- If you know you tend to overbreathe, breathing training is helpful.
- If you tend to feel dysregulated and your HRV is low, HRV training is going to help.
- If you suffer from muscle tension or muscle-related pain, muscle biofeedback will help.
- If your hands, feet, nose, or ears tend to get cold when you feel stressed, temperature biofeedback will help.

- If you would like to learn more about your triggers, skin conductance is very helpful.

Research-based evidence has shown that specific pain disorders can be helped by specific biofeedback modalities:

- Arthritis: HRV biofeedback
- Fibromyalgia: HRV biofeedback
- Tension headache: muscle, breathing, and HRV biofeedback
- Migraine headache: breathing and HRV, temperature, muscle biofeedback
- IBS: breathing and HRV, temperature biofeedback
- Repetitive strain injury: muscle, breathing biofeedback
- Raynaud's disease: breathing and temperature biofeedback
- TMJ disorders: muscle biofeedback
- Noncardiac chest pain: breathing and HRV biofeedback
- Posture-related muscle pain: muscle biofeedback
- Muscle-related chronic back pain: muscle, breathing, and HRV biofeedback
- Phantom limb pain: HRV biofeedback
- Pelvic floor pain: muscle and breathing biofeedback
- Cancer-related pain: breathing and HRV biofeedback

Conditions not on this list, such as complex regional pain syndrome and trigeminal neuralgia, have not been investigated with sufficient rigor to indicate whether or not biofeedback may be helpful. If you have a pain condition that is not listed here, it does not mean that you should not use biofeedback. Biofeedback may still help you with overall self-regulation and well-being, and will provide you with a healthy response to pain.

If you choose more than one biofeedback modality to work with, you'll need to choose where to start. I suggest training in this order: breathing, HRV, muscle, skin conductance, temperature. To begin training, turn to the appropriate chapters focusing on the modalities you are working on and get going.

Mindfulness-Based Skills for Pain

The main goals of mindfulness meditation and mindfulness-based skills for pain are to reduce suffering caused by pain, reduce pain anticipation, and provide you with helpful ways to respond to pain.

Reduce suffering caused by pain. Research shows that mindfulness practice is associated with changes in activation of the parts of the brain responsible for pain.[132] The parts of the brain responsible for interpretation and evaluation of the sensations of pain, the ones that typically come up with thoughts like, "On no, not again, this is going to be awful," and "I can't cope with this pain," become less active. This means that, with mindfulness practice, you are less likely to interpret the pain you feel as a threat. Studies consistently report that people's ratings of pain unpleasantness decrease with mindfulness practice.

Interestingly, some, but not all studies report a corresponding decrease in pain intensity. Studies by Fadel Zeidan and his team at Wake Forest University and Joshua Grant and his team at University of Montreal have reported decreased pain intensity together with decreased pain unpleasantness.[133] On the other hand, studies by Tim Gard and his colleagues at Harvard Medical School and Antoine Lutz and his colleagues at the University of Wisconsin Madison reported no change in pain intensity but a decrease in pain unpleasantness.[134] This means that mindfulness practice may not necessarily reduce the pain you feel, but it can help you suffer less when you feel it.

In addition, another study by Fadel Zeidan showed that people who are generally more mindful exhibit reduced activation of the default mode network (DMN), together with reduced ratings of pain intensity and pain unpleasantness, while experiencing pain.[135] You may recall the DMN from previous chapters. The DMN is a set of brain structures that comes online when the mind wanders, and it is associated with negative thinking about the past, present, and future that creates suffering. This study shows that increasing your everyday mindfulness may help reduce activation of your DMN when you experience pain, thereby reducing suffering.

Reduce pain anticipation. Research also shows that mindfulness meditation practice reduces the distress and suffering caused by anticipation of pain. Thoughts like, "I hope I don't have a headache today," "What if I my pain gets worse," and "I don't know what I would do if this gets any worse" all tend to exacerbate pain and create more suffering. Mindfulness meditation reduces activation of the parts of the brain responsible for pain anticipation. A meta-analysis conducted by Elena Bilevicius and her colleagues at the University of Manitoba showed that mindfulness meditation practice reduces pain anticipation and unpleasantness ratings.[136] These changes are associated with reduced activity in the amygdala and increased activity in anterior cingulate cortex, insula, and dorsolateral prefrontal cortex. These findings are consistent with the idea that mindfulness meditation reduces perception of pain sensations as a threat, while increasing your ability to focus attention on the present moment.

Provide you with helpful ways to respond to pain. In addition to changing the brain mechanisms underlying your experience of pain, mindfulness-based skills give you a way of responding to pain in the moment. The next section reviews these skills, along with meditation practices particularly helpful for pain.

How to Practice Mindfulness Skills for Pain

Start with setting up a regular meditation practice. See Chapter 8 on mindfulness meditation for more details. These practices help train your brain to respond differently to pain.

- I suggest beginning with a concentration practice with an external focus of awareness, such as the here-and-now stone (Chapter 8), mindfulness of nature (Chapter 13), or favorite food, and then moving to an internal focus of awareness (i.e., breath; great to practice along with low-and-slow breathing at resonance frequency or at 6 breaths per minute; see Chapter 3). With these practices, you will train non-judgmental attention as well as reduce overall activation.
- Once concentration practice feels comfortable, move to an open awareness practice, such as body awareness (Appendix A) and mindfulness of thoughts, feelings, and physiological sensations (Apendix A). These practices do not emphasize pain sensations specifically, but

attending to sensations of discomfort is a part of the practice. You will practice awareness of pain sensations without engaging with them or evaluating and interpreting them. Meditations such as the mountain meditation , anchor meditation , and thoughts on leaves meditation (all in Appendix A) are helpful in grounding yourself in difficult times without placing utmost emphasis on the uncomfortable sensations and feelings.

- Practice Mettā for self-compassion (Chapter 10).
- When you are ready, move on to practices that focus on pain and difficult emotions, such as light meditation, difficult emotion practice, and mindfulness of pain sensations (all in Appendix A).

ALTERNATING ATTENTION TO PAIN

Chris Gilbert, pain psychologist at Osher Center for Integrative Medicine at the University of California, San Francisco, teaches his patients a technique he calls alternating attention to pain. This technique may help you change your relationship with pain, reduce unhelpful attempts to avoid it, and learn to experience pain on your terms. I've adapted it here with his permission.

1. Choose a spot of pain in your body, maybe not the worst pain, but a spot that qualifies as hurting.
2. Choose another place in your body that feels comfortable, with no pain, preferably some distance away from the painful spot. That will be your safe spot.
3. Focus all your attention on the painful spot, knowing that in 30 seconds you'll be able to let go of it. But for that half a minute, immerse yourself in it and feel how it stirs you up, tries to pull you in.
4. (30 seconds later) Now let go of the painful spot and quickly bring your attention to the comfortable spot—as if jumping into it, sink deeply into it. Surround yourself with how safe and soothing it feels. The painful spot is no longer a focus of your awareness. Notice how you feel in the safe spot.
5. (30 seconds later) Now get ready to jump back into the pain—get ready—NOW, back to the where it hurts, knowing that you don't

have to stay there. But while you are there, give your full attention to the details: the size of the area, the edges, any pulsations or heat—just allow it to be as it is, knowing that soon you'll let go and be back to your place of comfort and safety.

6. (30 seconds later) Almost ready to jump back to comfort . . . NOW. Leave the pain and immerse yourself in that comfortable place. Maybe it feels like sinking into a warm bath or a hot tub. You left the pain behind, far, far away. You don't need to pay attention to it all the time. In fact, your brain makes it stand out more when you notice it, just in case it's an acute injury that needs your attention.

7. (30 seconds later) Get ready . . . NOW, revisit the pain one more time with your full attention, but this time allow your attention to be more neutral rather than alarmed or worried. You're just check-ing in with it. You don't have to stay there. You can put your atten-tion anywhere you like, like a flashlight in a dark room.

8. (30 seconds later) Get ready . . . you know what to do. Enjoy the safety, the comfort of a place in your body that works just fine, gives you no trouble. You might send some appreciation to the safe and comfortable place in your body. You can stay there in your safe and comfortable place for a while now. You don't have to keep focusing on the pain. You've learned that you can place your atten-tion on pain when necessary, and you've learned to turn that atten-tion from alarmed and worried to neutral. This is good practice for when pain calls your attention in the future. Pain is just part of an alarm system—once you receive the message, it doesn't need to be so loud.

With regular mindfulness practice, you'll be better able to use mindfulness and compassion-based skills in responding to pain arising in the moment—see pain for what it is: an evolutionarily adaptive part of our experience not intended as an instrument of torture. As with all other difficult feelings dis-cussed in this book, pain has a purpose and is a part of the evolutionarily adaptive mechanism that has enabled human beings to survive as a species. Pain alerts you to damage to your body. Imagine if you had no pain. You would continue walking on a broken leg, damaging it beyond repair. You would not be protective of an injury, would not allow it to heal properly.

The following are suggestions for how you can use mindfulness when you experience pain in the moment:

THE STORY OF THE TWO ARROWS

Ron Siegel in his book *The Mindfulness Solution* tells the Buddhist story of the two arrows:

Human experience of pain is akin to two arrows being shot at us: one is the physical sensations of pain itself, and the other is everything we do with that pain—the unhelpful interpretations of pain as never ending and catastrophic, blaming ourselves or others for us being in pain, the emotional reactions of anger or shame, the tense muscles that brace for pain, attempts to avoid pain and make it go away. All of these reactions are the second arrow. The second arrow creates our suffering. Allowing ourselves to experience the first arrow and not engaging in the second arrow allows us to reduce resistance and therefore reduce suffering.

Mindful and compassionate language. You may recall these skills described in detail in Chapters 9 and 10. When applied specifically to pain, mindful and compassionate language means not beating up on yourself for having pain, not beating up on yourself for not being able to control it, and not beating up on yourself for not being strong enough. Is also means using the kind of words and tone that you would with a friend or a loved one. It means using words to provide comfort for yourself at a time of suffering.

The self-compassion break from mindful self-compassion training introduced in Chapter 10 is particularly helpful: "This is a moment of suffering. Suffering is a part of life. May I be kind to myself." You can also use Mettā phrases (Chapter 10) for what you need at that moment: "May I have comfort," "May I be healthy," "May I have ease," "May I have peace of mind."

Give up attempts to control, resist, or suppress pain. Much like trying to control your thoughts and feelings only makes them more persistent and drains your resources in futile efforts to control the uncontrollable, attempts to control, resist, and suppress pain do the same thing. Ana Masedo and Rosa Esteve at the University of Malaga in Spain examined the effects of pain suppression and pain acceptance on the experience of pain.[137] Two hundred and nineteen undergraduate students were asked to place one of their hands into ice water, an experience that produces pain without damaging the tissue. Some were given an instruction to suppress the sensations of pain, and others were given an instruction to accept the sensations as they are. Participants were asked to rate the distress produced by the pain, and researchers noted the length of time they were able to keep their hand in ice water. The authors reported that the suppression group reported higher distress levels caused by the pain and were able to keep their hands in ice water for a shorter time. The acceptance group, in contrast, showed longer tolerance times and reported lower distress ratings.

Shinzen Young, a renowned American meditation teacher, introduced a mathematical formula for pain and suffering: pain × resistance = suffering. This formula describes what happens when you resist pain: the more you try to get away from it, the more you suffer. The reverse is true as well: the more you accept your pain, the less you suffer. You've probably had this experience with mild pain—if you just let it be, it didn't bother you much, but if you focused on it and tried to make it go away, you probably felt worse as a result. I've had this experience multiple times with my kids and vaccines. When they were little, they resisted the shots and what would have been a moment of mild pain turned into a lot of misery for them (and for me). Now my oldest son no longer resists the shots, and his (and mine) experience is no longer miserable.

This is, of course, is much harder to do with more intense pain. But the principle is the same. When you bring mindful attention to the experience of pain, accepting it without fighting, you activate the sensory, but not the interpretive parts of your brain. This allows you to experience pain without as much suffering.

As with any new skills, this one is particularly important to practice in less difficult circumstances first. When your pain is lower than typical, practice mindfully attending to pain without resistance. As the skill becomes more familiar, bring it into more difficult moments when the pain is more intense.

CLOTHESPIN PRACTICE

Chris Gilbert, pain psychologist at the Osher Center for Integrative Medicine, recommends practicing mindful attention to pain sensations with a clothespin.

Attaching a clothespin to your skin produces mild pain sensations, which are different from typical chronic pain and are therefore easier to tolerate. Spend a few minutes just attending to the sensations of pain, allowing them to be as they are, disengaging from temptation to escape.

Live your life in accordance with your values. Chronic pain and attempts to resist or avoid it create suffering not only through the physiological sensations but also by narrowing your life and gradually taking away the things you enjoy doing and the things that bring meaning to your life. For Kim, attempts to resist pain prevented her from playing with her kids, robbing her of the ability to act in accordance with her value of being an attentive and engaged parent. Chronic pain prevents others from getting out of the house, from seeing friends, from going on family trips, from having a job. Not being able to do what's meaningful, important, and enjoyable in your life does not help your pain and makes you feel even worse.

If you haven't already, take a little time now to think through your values using the guidelines in Chapter 9. Think about things you haven't done because of pain. Then pick three that you are willing to bring back into your life, even if not quite in the way you would like it to be. For Kim, her first step would be to take a chair, get outside, and sit with her kids while they play. The next step would to get a gentle yoga video and do just a few of the poses. Eventually, she may be able to throw the ball with her kids and add some more yoga poses or get to the yoga class. Even if she can only stay in class for 15 minutes, that's a win.

Keep an appreciation journal. Chronic pain often takes up so much of your awareness that it is hard to see beyond it. On particularly bad pain days, all you can see and feel is pain. When this happens, you may lose track of the good things that happen in your life, and everything may seem bleak and hopeless. You may not notice or truly pay attention to the good things that happen. Keeping an appreciation journal on a daily basis will help you expand your awareness and see the positives in your life. See Chapter 9 for a guide to keeping an appreciation or gratitude journal.

Practice FLARE for Pain

The FLARE technique can be an effective response to moments of pain:

- *Feel* the sensations of pain and any emotions that may accompany them just as they are.
- *Label* these sensations with a nonjudgmental descriptive label, with a gentle tone of voice, such as "discomfort," "ache," "soreness," "pain." Also name the emotions that you notice. See Figure 9.2 in Chapter 9 for helpful labels.
- *Allow* all of your sensations and emotions to be just as they are: "It is OK to feel this way."
- *Respond* with kindness and compassion:
  — Practice your biofeedback skills, such as mindful low-and-slow breathing at your resonance frequency or at 6 breaths per minute, and release muscle tension (Chapter 2 and 3).
  — Practice Mettā (Chapter 10) or the difficult emotion practice (soften, soothe, and allow; see Appendix A), or take a self-compassion break (Chapter 10).
  — Go for a walk, mindfully attending to the sensations for walking.
  — Take time to practice your favorite meditation.
  — Reflect on your values, decide which one is most relevant in the moment, and choose a response most consistent with your value.

Expand awareness to the world around you:

  — Start with your external environment—the sky overhead, the floor or ground under your feet, trees outside, birds singing, children laughing, dogs barking.

— Continue to your internal environment—your breath, your heart-beat, your grumbling stomach, feeling sleepy, looking forward to a good book and a glass of milk.

— Think of three things you have appreciated that day and something you are appreciative of in that moment.

Now let's think through how Kim might use FLARE when she is in pain:

Feel. Kim feels the physical sensations of pain, the tension in her back. She feels her muscles tightening more in response. She notices the thought, "Oh no, why does this have to happen again?"

Label. Kim labels her experience as "pain" and "fear."

Allow. She allows the feelings to be. She recognizes that it is OK to feel the way she does.

Respond. Kim brings mindful attention to the physical sensations in her back. She softens into them, allows them to stay, and brings comfort to herself because she feels pain (the difficult emotion practice, soften, soothe, and allow). She brings mindful low-and-slow breathing into her practice, allowing her braced muscles to release. She separates the two arrows, allowing herself to feel the initial physical sensations of pain but disengaging from the unhelpful thoughts and feelings that follow the pain. She checks in with her value of being an attentive and engaged parent and her value of self-care. She decides to walk slowly outside and sit on the porch to watch her kids play.

Expand awareness. Kim expands her awareness to the sensations in the rest of her body, the muscles in her arms and legs, her heart beating, the slight soreness of her toe from a shoe that's too tight. She brings her awareness to what she appreciates in that moment—being able to be mindful of her pain, hearing her children laugh, and the beautiful weather outside.

CHAPTER 17

Sadness and Depression

"What's wrong with me? I have so much good stuff in my life—why can't I appreciate it and feel happy? So many people have it worse than me. I have no right to complain." These are the thoughts that kept running through Patrick's mind as he sat at the dinner table picking at his food. The last few weeks had been hard for Pat—his mother was ill, he didn't enjoy his job, and he felt lonely and disconnected from his friends. He wasn't sure where his life was going, and he felt overwhelmed in trying to figure it out. "Stop feeling sorry for yourself" was the next thought in Pat's mind. He could not figure out how to stop it. It didn't seem like anything would cheer him up at that moment.

Much like anxiety, sadness is a feeling that we have been taught to try to chase away since we were kids. We have been taught that it is not OK to feel sad. If three-year-old Janet feels sad because she is missing a friend who had to go home from a play date, her well-intentioned, loving parents might say: "Don't be sad, you'll see Sammy tomorrow." And yet she feels sad. So now Janet has learned that she should not feel sad, but there is nothing she can do about it. Throughout her childhood she might hear other well-meaning advice, like, "Don't be sad, everything is OK," or "Don't feel sad, things are not as bad as they could be," or "Cheer up, it's not so bad." She will hear this and learn that sadness is the wrong feeling to have. She must try to not feel sad, but she continues to feel sad. Her parents' might take her for ice cream, or play a game, or get her a new toy to cheer her up. Janet will learn that whenever she feels sad she must do something to cheer up. She will learn to fight with her sadness in an attempt to make it go away. She will learn that there is something wrong with her for failing to do so.

But is there anything wrong with Janet for not being able to turn off her sadness? If you've read any of the other chapters of this book, I hope you would say no. Sadness is a normal human feeling. It is often difficult for us to experience sadness, but it is not a "negative" feeling, as it is usually called. If the emotion is normal, it must have a purpose, right? So, what is the purpose of sadness? What does sadness do for us?

It turns out that the purpose of sadness is quite diverse. First, sadness allows us to feel joy. If you never feel sad, how would you know what joy or happiness feels like? You get to know much of your experience through contrast: You know what tall is only by also knowing what short is. You know what hard is only by also knowing what soft is. You know what bright is only by also knowing what dark is. Allowing yourself to feel sad also allows you to savor happiness and joy.

Kahlil Gibran in his book *The Prophet* says:

YOUR JOY IS YOUR SORROW UNMASKED.

AND THE SELFSAME WELL FROM WHICH YOUR LAUGHTER RISES

WAS OFTENTIMES FILLED WITH YOUR TEARS.

AND HOW ELSE CAN IT BE?

THE DEEPER THAT SORROW CARVES INTO YOUR BEING,

THE MORE JOY YOU CAN CONTAIN.

Sadness points you to what's important and valued in your life. Sadness brings with it an important message. If you are missing a friend, it is because that friend is important to you. If you feel sad when you've failed at something important to you, the sadness reminds you to think through the changes you need to make in your life. If you feel sad because you've hurt someone's feelings, the sadness reminds you to take responsibility for your actions. Sometimes, sadness just reminds you to slow down and take care of yourself.

Sadness adds value to your everyday functioning in more subtle and perhaps surprising ways as well. Joseph Forgas, professor of psychology at the

University of New South Wales in Sydney, Australia, has conducted extensive research on the purpose and value of sadness. He describes five specific ways in which sadness is important: improving memory, improving judgment, increasing motivation, improving interactions with others, and helping us be more fair and generous.

Sadness Can Improve Your Memory

Research shows that positive mood is likely to contribute to less accurate memories, while sad mood is associated with better attention and memory for small but important details in our environment. For example, Joseph Forgas and his colleagues conducted a study in which they asked shoppers to recall details about the interior of a store they had been in when they experienced negative moods and when they experienced positive moods.[138] Shoppers who experienced more "negative" mood were better able to accurately recall details about the shop than those in a happier mood.

Sadness Can Improve Your Judgment

Research shows that when we are in a happier mood we are more likely to misjudge other people because of common biases, such as the fundamental attribution error, the halo effect, and primacy effect. *Fundamental attribution error* means that we tend to attribute other people's behavior to intentional choices and disregard situational factors, while doing the opposite for ourselves. For example, if you fail a test you are more likely to attribute the failure to the test being too difficult or the teacher being unfair. If someone else fails a test, you are more likely to attribute the failure to the person not being smart enough or not having studied sufficiently. *Halo effect* means that we tend to attribute multiple positive characteristics, such as intelligence and generosity, to people who possess one positive characteristic, such as being good looking. *Primacy effect* means that we tend to place too much importance on information we learn early on and ignore later details, such as what happens with first impressions.

In a series of studies Joseph Forgas showed that people in a more negative mood were much less prone to being influenced by these biases.[139] For example, in one study, he induced happy or sad moods in participants and then asked them to read and evaluate an essay with an attached photo of the supposed writer. Sad participants were much less likely to be influenced by the appearance of the writer in their evaluations of the essay, thereby showing reduced halo effect. A similar study showed that sad participants are much less likely to fall victim to fundamental attribution error in evaluating essays. On the basis of these and other similar studies, the researchers concluded that sad mood can promote a more detailed and attentive thinking style and thereby increase the accuracy of our social judgments.

Sadness Can Increase Your Motivation

Happiness is a sign that everything is going as it should. Therefore, our motivation to make any changes is low. Why would we want to change anything when we are happy? Sadness, on the other hand, is a sign that something needs to change. Joseph Forges calls it a "mild alarm signal" that triggers our willingness to exert effort in improving our situation.

For example, in another study Forges and his team showed participants either happy or sad films and then asked them to answer many difficult questions.[140] The researchers looked at the amount of time participants spent on the questions, how many they answered, and how many were answered correctly. It turned out that happier people were less persistent, spent less time on the questions, answered fewer questions overall, and gave fewer correct answers. Participants in more "negative" mood made more effort and did better overall.

Sadness Can Improve Your Interactions With Other People

As described above in the section on social judgment, people in a more "negative" mood are less likely to rely solely on first impressions of other people and are less likely to make other unhelpful assumptions about them. Their judgments of people are more accurate, which in turn helps them be more accurate in deciding the best way to communicate with people they are interacting with.

You may be thinking that happy people are more likely to have happier, more positive interactions with others. That is true. However, there are times when communication needs to be more cautious and attentive to the needs of the situation, such as when dealing with difficult people. Sad people are more likely to bring increased detail awareness to their interactions with people, read the cues of the situation rather than relying solely on their first impressions, and therefore pick a more effective communication style. Happy people, on the other hand, are more likely to go with the first impression and are less accurate in selecting effective communication strategies.

Sadness Helps You Be More Fair and Generous

Hui Bing Tan and Joseph Forges conducted a study where they asked participants to divide a scarce resource between themselves and others.[141] Study findings showed that happy participants were more selfish, whereas sad participants were more fair and generous in their allocations. These mood effects became stronger with time.

Sadness provides value and is important to our lives. This does not mean that you should seek out sadness or make yourself sad. Rather, the value is in allowing yourself to experience the temporary state of sadness when it appears.

Sadness is often difficult to have. Given our habitual aversion to experiencing sadness, the automatic response is to try to get rid of it. When we attempt to get rid of sadness, we are much more likely to get stuck in it. You may recall the quicksand metaphor in Chapter 9. Difficult feelings themselves are not dangerous, but attempts to get rid of them can be, because they lead to getting stuck. Attempts to get rid of sadness are likely to get us stuck and lead to depression.

Almost every human being has experienced a time when he or she felt sad, tired, defeated, uninterested in engaging in life. For many people, these feelings last a few hours or a few days and then go away. But for some of us these feelings turn into weeks or months of suffering. About 19 million Americans experience some form of depression every year. For some, episodes of depression return again and again. If you believe that you may be suffering from depression, you may consider seeking professional help in addition to reading this book.

Biofeedback Skills in Responding to Sadness and Depression

Heart rate variability (HRV) has been consistently tied to our experience of both sadness and depression. Previous research has indicated the importance of ability to express emotions in health and mental health outcomes. A 2017 study by Natalie Tuck and her colleagues at the University of Auckland in New Zealand examined the relationship between HRV and ability to express sadness.[142] In this study, participants watched a sadness-inducing clip from the movie *Philadelphia* and were then asked to express how they felt. Participants with higher HRV were better able to express their sadness and showed more flexibility in overall regulation of sadness. Jonathan Stange of University of Illinois at Chicago and his colleagues conducted another study in which they also asked participants to view a sadness-inducing movie clip (a scene from *The Champ*, depicting a boy distraught over the death of his father) and measured both their HRV and ability to regulate emotion.[143] The study showed that people with a higher vagal tone component of HRV were better able to adapt to the effects of sadness while they were experiencing it, better able to recover afterward, and make better use of emotion regulation strategies.

Studies such as these demonstrate the importance of high HRV in a healthy experience of sadness and the ability to move on from it. Research also consistently shows that people who experience depression have lower HRV than those who don't. Andrew Kemp from the University of Sydney in Australia and his team conducted an extensive meta-analysis of eighteen studies, which showed an association between depression and lower HRV.[144] This study also showed that, while antidepressant medication may reduce the severity of depressive symptoms for one-third to one-half of those who take them, they do not raise HRV and some may even reduce HRV further.

The good news is that HRV biofeedback can both alleviate the symptoms of depression and raise HRV. Several studies have shown this effect: a 2007 study by Maria Karavidas and her team at Robert Wood Johnson Medical School,[145] a 2008 study by Martin Siepmann and his team at Technical University in Dresden, Germany,[146] and a 2009 study by Terri L. Zucker of Alliant International University and her team.[147] And Yoko Caldwell and Patrick Steffen from Brigham Young University showed that adding HRV biofeedback to traditional psychotherapy improved participants' depression and increased their HRV levels in 6 weeks of treatment.[148]

If sadness and/or depression is a problem in your life, you will likely benefit from regular practice of HRV biofeedback. Please see Chapter 3 for a review of HRV and a detailed guide to HRV biofeedback training.

Mindfulness Skills in Living With Sadness and Working With Depression

Research of the last two decades has shown that mindfulness-based interventions are effective in alleviating symptoms of depression, and several meta-analyses have confirmed these findings. For example, a 2014 meta-analysis by Clara Strauss and her team at the University of Sussex concluded that mindfulness-based interventions are effective for people currently suffering from depression.[149] A 2015 meta-analysis by Rinske Gotink of Erasmus Medical Center in Netherlands and her colleagues showed that mindfulness-based stress reduction and mindfulness-based cognitive therapy alleviate symptoms of anxiety, depression, chronic pain, and cardiovascular disease.[150] A 2018 meta-analysis by Simon Goldberg at the VA Puget Sound Health Care System in Seattle and his colleagues concluded that the most consistent evidence in support of mindfulness exists for depression, pain conditions, smoking, and addictive disorders.[151]

Paul Blanck and his colleagues at the University of Heidelberg in Germany were particularly interested in examining effectiveness of stand-alone mindfulness exercises done outside of structured mindfulness-based interventions in reducing symptoms of anxiety and depression.[152] Their 2018 meta-analysis showed that regular practice of mindfulness even without concurrent psychotherapy or structured mindfulness-based interventions is beneficial in anxiety and depression.

Neurobiological mechanisms underlying the effectiveness of mindfulness-based interventions for depression are not yet entirely clear. We do, however, have some evidence of the kind of brain changes that result from these interventions for people with depression. A 2018 review study by Philippe Vignaud and his colleagues at Université Claude Bernard in France concluded that mindfulness-based interventions for depression are associated with positive changes in the prefrontal cortex, the basal ganglia, the anterior and posterior cingulate cortices, and the parietal cortex.[153] These brain regions are involved in self-awareness, attention and emotion regulation.

Please be sure to review Chapter 8 on mindfulness meditation and Chapter 9 on mindfulness-based skills, as they are all relevant to choosing a helpful response to sadness. The following are suggestions for mindfulness skills particularly helpful in sadness and depression.

Meditation Practice for Sadness and Depression

NOTICING ACTIVITY OF THE DEFAULT MODE NETWORK

This is a simple practice that will help you reduce activation of the default mode network (DMN) and disengage from ruminative thinking:

Find a comfortable posture in a quiet place. Allow your attention to come to your breath. Notice the sensations of the inhalation and sensations of the exhalation. Notice where you feel those sensations most strongly—at your nostrils when you breathe in and out? Your chest or abdomen as they rise and fall with each breath? Pick one location and allow your attention to gently rest there, just observing your breath as you notice it in that location in your body.

Sooner or later your mind will wander off from the breath and go off into reviewing events of the past, anticipating events of the future, or comparing yourself to others in the preset. When you notice your mind wandering, recognize this as activity of the DMN, label it—"here's the default network" or "here's mind wandering"—and then gently bring your attention back to the breath, in the part of your body where you feel it most strongly.

Allow your attention to stay with the breath. Notice the next time your mind wanders off, recognize and label DMN activity, and gently bring your mind back to the breath. Continue your practice for as long as you wish, and when you are ready, return to the rest of your awareness and move on with your day.

If you are first starting your meditation practice, it is helpful to begin with a concentration meditation, such as the here-and-now stone (Chapter 10), sights or sounds around you, or mindful breathing (Chapter 2 and Appendix A). These practices are helpful in reducing intensity of difficult emotions and provide you with a way to ground yourself in the present moment. In addition, concentration practices are helpful in reducing activation of the default mode network (DMN; see Chapter 7), a set of brain structures responsible for unhelpful thinking patters such as rumination. A study by Xueling Zhu from Central South University in China and her colleagues revealed abnormal activity of the DMN for people with depression during rumination.[154]

As you become comfortable with concentration practices, move onto open awareness practices. Choose any that you enjoy. Here are the practices I like the most for allowing sadness (you will find scripts for all of them in Appendix A and recordings at www.innakhazan.com/meditation_recordings.html).

- Mindfulness of thoughts, feelings, physiological sensations
- Thoughts on leaves
- Mountain meditation
- Lotus meditation
- Anchor meditation

Compassion and self-compassion practices are a wonderful way to respond to sadness and depression. Try one of these:

- Mettā (Chapter 10)
- Tonglen (Appendix A)
- Difficult emotion practice (soften, soothe, and allow; see Appendix A)
- Light meditation (Appendix A)

Mindfulness-Based Skills for Sadness and Depression

See Chapter 9 on mindfulness-based skills that are applicable for any situation, including sadness. In this section, I discuss mindfulness-based skills that are particularly helpful in sadness and depression.

Recognize the value that sadness is pointing you toward. Just like with anxiety, the first step in living well with sadness is to stop seeing sadness as the enemy and learn to see its value. If you haven't already, reflect on your life values using the guidelines in Chapter 9. When you feel sad, what value seems most relevant?

- If you feel sad and lonely, perhaps the relevant value is social connection (friends or family).
- If you feel sad and empty, perhaps the value is self-care or growth, family or friendships.

Recognizing the value that sadness is pointing you toward will also help you choose the most helpful response:

- If your value is social connection, think about a way you can reach out to another person—whether it is walking out of your room to go talk to someone, calling a friend, or simply sending a text to people you care about to let them know you are thinking about them.
- If your value in that moment is self-growth, think about a way you can act in accordance with that value—perhaps going to the library to get a book, going to a museum, or signing up for a class.
- If your value in that moment is self-care, action most consistent with that value may be going for a walk or doing some other form of exercise, getting out in nature, doing a meditation practice, or giving yourself more time to sleep.

Decide to do things that are in your best interest even if sadness makes it really hard to move or do things. When you feel sad or depressed, doing even the simplest things like getting out of bed and taking a shower may feel like more than you are capable of doing. You may not feel like getting to work or going to class. You may not feel like going grocery shopping or making a healthy meal when ordering take out is so much easier. You may not feel like going out of the house for any reason. Depression and sadness make what appear to be simple tasks appear impossible. However, when you don't do these important things, you end up feeling worse. The less you do, the worse you feel, the harder it is to do things, and the worse you feel. To get out of this vicious cycle, connect with the value most appropriate to your current experience and think about a few things that you are willing to do that are consistent with that value. Once you do one thing that's been too hard, doing the next one will be a tad easier. The step after that will be a bit easier still. One step at a time and you'll be on your way out of the vicious cycle.

Reach out for connection with others. If you hold the belief that sadness is only something "weak" people feel, you may be tempted to hide your weakness. It may be embarrassing or shameful to tell others about your sadness. And yet sadness is universal, and your mind and body are built for social connection in difficult times. Chapter 10 on compassion and self-compassion discussed the way compassion depends on your built-in physiological mechanism to reach out for connection in difficult times. Your parasympathetic nervous system, which calms you in times of distress, is also designed to help you reach out to others. Oxytocin, the so-called love hormone, is actually a stress hormone released at times of distress to help you reach out for help. It is, of course, OK and sometimes helpful to be sad alone. But that should not be the only way to be sad. Allow yourself to reach out for connection so that you don't get stuck in sadness.

Allow yourself to be sad: "It is OK to feel this way." You may recall from Chapter 9 on mindfulness-based skills that attempts to control sadness or make it go away may lead to getting stuck in it. A meta-analysis by Amelia Aldao of Yale University and her colleagues has shown that attempts to suppress sadness lead to a greater likelihood of developing depression.[155] Author Susan Piver says, "Despair can be the consequence of fighting sadness. Compassion is what happens when you don't."[156]

Practice compassion—self-compassion and compassion for others. The Dalai Lama once said: "If you want to make others happy, practice compassion. If you want to be happy, practice compassion." Often when you are sad there is nothing that needs or can be done about it. The only way to respond to sadness is with compassion. You may practice compassion or self-compassion meditation, or simply roll the Mettā or the difficult emotion (soften, soothe, and allow) phrases through your mind, as a way of bringing comfort.

FLARE for Sadness and Depression

Let's apply the FLARE technique first introduced in Chapter 9 to sadness.

- *Feel* sensations in your body associated with sadness—perhaps tension in your chest or a knot in your belly. Notice thoughts that go through your mind, such as "I don't know how to cope," or "I can't do anything right," or "No one wants to be around me."
- *Label* your experience with a nonjudgmental descriptive label, such as "sadness" or "despair" or "darkness."
- *Allow* yourself to feel the way you do. Your feelings are not under your control: "It is OK to feel this way."
- *Respond* by choosing a response appropriate to your situation:
  — Mindful low-and-slow breathing at your resonance frequency or at 6 breaths per minute
  — Here-and-now stone
  — Mettā or difficult emotion practice
  — Action most consistent with the value sadness is pointing you toward
- *Expand awareness* of your internal and external environment beyond the sadness. You might reflect on three things you have appreciated or been grateful for that day—something about yourself, something about another person, and something about the world around you.

Let's now think through the example of FLARE for Patrick, from the earlier example. You might also think through an example of sadness from your own life using FLARE.

Feel. Patrick notices the lack of energy and the tightness he feels in his chest. He notice the questions "What's wrong with me?" and "Why can't I just be happy?"

Label. He calls this experience "sadness" and "loneliness" and "uncertainty."

Allow. Patrick allows these feelings to stay; he does not control them: "It is OK to feel this way." He allows the presence of the thoughts and feelings, knowing that having them does not mean that the content of his thoughts is true.

Respond. Patrick spends a few minutes doing his mindful low-and-slow breathing at 6 breaths per minute. He brings his attention to the food in front of him and allows himself to focus just on the sensations of eating—the texture, smell, and taste of his food and the sensations of chewing. He reflects on the values his sadness is pointing him toward. Social connection is one of them. Patrick calls a friend he has not spoken with in a while and sets up a time to have dinner together. He also gives himself permission not to figure out the direction of his life right at that moment. He will return to this question once he feels more grounded.

Expand awareness. Patrick expands his awareness to the larger environment around him—his food, his cat that is patiently waiting for attention nearby, and the plant on his window sill that could use some water. Patrick also notices his appreciation for the nice conversation he had with his friend and the fact that he was able to complete an important project at work that week.

CHAPTER 18

Shame and Guilt

Michael has been out of work for two years. When he first lost his job he remained hopeful and optimistic, but after unsuccessfully applying for numerous job openings he began to lose hope. Every time he got a rejection letter or an e-mail that he did not get the job, he heard his father's voice in the back of his mind saying, "I told you, you are no good. No one wants to hire you. Why would they? You are stupid and useless." Michael's wife and children were supportive and loving. Anna, his wife, often reassured him that they will be OK and he will eventually find a job. At first that was helpful, but over time Michael started feeling dejected and ashamed. The voice in the back of his head kept saying things like, "You are weak, you will never get through it. Anna will leave you and take the kids. She is better off without you." Michael tried to silence the voice by distracting himself with mindless TV watching for hours at a time. The more he tried to avoid the voice, he more prominent it seemed to become. Michael started snapping at Anna and the kids whenever they attempted to reassure him. He felt ashamed and overwhelmed and didn't know how to stop feeling that way.

Shame lies at the core of much of human suffering. When you feel shame, you may experience yourself as fundamentally damaged, broken, not good enough, undesirable to others, and ultimately unlovable. When you feel shame, the thoughts that go through your mind may sound something like this: "I am stupid," "I am useless," "I am a failure," "I will never be good enough," "I am bad." These thoughts and feelings typically come with a tremendous amount of emotional and physical distress and a strong desire to run away from them or somehow get rid of them. Attempts to avoid or get rid of shame lead to getting more and more stuck in it. The more you fight with shame, the more stuck you get, the more ashamed you feel, the more you lash out at yourself or others around you. Shame has a way of eating away at you. You may be reluctant to seek help because that means looking at what makes you feel shame and admitting it to others. Shame can make you feel alone and isolated in its secrecy. This chapter discusses the origins of shame, how you may get stuck in the cycle of shame, and ways to use mindfulness, compassion, and biofeedback skills to change the way you relate and respond to shame.

Origins of Shame

As any difficult emotion, shame serves a function other than to torture us and make our lives difficult. The evolutionary function of shame is to alert us to a problem that could alienate us from our social group. Humans survived as a species because of our strong social connections and belonging to a group. As part of a strong social group, we are strong and able to defeat enemies and keep ourselves and our children safe. By ourselves we are more likely to fall prey to larger animals or unfriendly humans. Our brains needed a way of letting us know when we are in danger of being thrown out of our social group. Shame is our brains' way of letting us know that our actions are somehow unacceptable and may result in the loss of our social group. Making changes to our behavior in response to shame to conform to the social norms of our group allows us to return to a sense of belonging.

SHAME VERSUS GUILT

Shame and guilt have similar origins but are very different emotions. *Guilt* points you to mistakes you've made, actions you've taken that may have harmed or hurt someone else. Guilt is adaptive because it points you to unhelpful actions you have taken and changes you can make now to take responsibility and make amends. *Shame*, on the other hand, points to parts of you that are fundamentally unacceptable and can eat away at you because you cannot change who you are at the core. Brene Brown, a research professor at University of Houston who studies shame, says that guilt is "I *made* a mistake," while shame is "I *am* a mistake." Brown also points out that shame is associated with increased risk of anxiety, addiction, depression, suicidal ideation, and violence. Guilt, on the other hand, is associated with a decreased risk of these issues, likely because guilt points you to actions under your control, while shame creates a feeling of being stuck.

Evolutionarily, shame has enabled human beings to survive as a species. And shame still continues to serve a similar function: it helps us follow social norms of speech and behavior. Even though there are many fewer physical dangers around us nowadays, being cast out of our social group continues to be a threat to our existence. If we are rejected by our group, we don't do so well, physically or emotionally. People who are alone without strong social connections experience more physical and emotional problems than those with strong social ties. Shame continues to be a strong motivator for appropriate social behavior.

Often, however, shame develops with no clear sense of what's wrong with our actions and over time becomes toxic, developing into a pervasive sense of being bad, defective, broken, and unlovable. This kind of toxic shame can come from several sources:

- Genetics makes some people much more vulnerable to shame than others. Just like genetics predisposes some of us to developing heart disease or depression, it predisposes some of us to developing toxic shame in response to adverse circumstances, such as those described below.
- Abuse or neglect in childhood leaves the child feeling rejected, alone, and unlovable.
- Sexual trauma often comes with a stigma that the traumatized person is somehow responsible for being assaulted, asked for it, or deserved it, all with the implication that the victim is "bad."
- Cultural influences can devalue, disrespect, and make invisible members of certain groups, such as racial, ethnic, and religious minorities, people of different sexual orientations, women, or people who somehow look different from others. Growing up in an environment where you are continuously rejected and devalued because of some

attribute about you that you have no control over and cannot change often leads to global feelings of shame about yourself.

Once shame becomes a part of your life, two factors maintain it: attempts to avoid or escape it, and silence and secrecy about it.

Attempts to Avoid or Escape Shame

Shame feels terrible. Think about something about which you feel ashamed or embarrassed (a lesser intensity of shame). How does that memory feel in your body? Does a chill and a shudder go through you? Perhaps a pit in your stomach or tightness in your chest? And a strong desire to make it stop? Like most of us, you'd want to just stop feeling shame and stop thinking about the event that caused it. You might go to great lengths to avoid the feeling of shame or at least escape it once it appears. You might avoid places, events, activities, and people that remind you of or provoke the feeling of shame. You may find ways to escape the experience of shame through distraction (e.g., watching TV), use of alcohol or other substances, and attempts to suppress it. You might unconsciously substitute feelings of shame for other feelings, such as anger. Anger is easier to experience than shame, so you might act in anger when you feel shame.

What all of these ways of dealing with shame have in common is that they don't work. As discussed throughout this book, attempts to control or suppress emotions backfire and get you stuck in the difficult experience. Attempts to avoid shame prevent you from experiencing life to the fullest, because many activities that produce the feelings of shame seem off limits. Your world narrows as you avoid more and more places and activities in an effort to avoid shame. Attempts to escape shame can have destructive consequences, such as drug and alcohol abuse, lashing out and hurting people you love, getting fired from a job, not being able to achieve your goals, and getting stuck in beating up on yourself for being weak and unable to control your emotions. The more you try to avoid or escape shame, the more shame you feel, spiraling into a cycle of shame.

Silence and Secrecy About Shame

Because shame is so painful to experience, you may do your very best to not only not feel it yourself but also avoid telling other people about it. If you can't even think about what makes you feel ashamed, the idea of telling others is probably even more terrifying. If you tell someone, they will judge you, they will not like you, they will not want to be around you—or so goes the voice in your head. So, you keep your shameful past to yourself, do your best not to think about it, never share with others, and suffer in silence.

As awful as it is to feel shame and be stuck in it, shame is what Christopher Germer, co-developer of the mindful self compassion (MSC) program, calls an "innocent" emotion, because its presence stems from a universal need to belong and to be loved. When you feel shame, you fear that you will get rejected and that you are not worthy of love. Connection with others is what people long for the most. In your longing to connect, you may keep your shame secret in an effort to protect yourself from rejection. Protecting a shameful secret prevents you from truly connecting with others and leads to isolation and loneliness. In an effort to protect yourself from rejection, you doom yourself to loneliness. As Christopher Germer says: "You are only as unlovable as your secrets."

Self-Compassion as an Antidote to Shame

Thankfully, there is something you can do to get out of the cycle of shame. Self-compassion offers an antidote to shame and the suffering it creates. Self-compassion offers you a way to respond differently to shame, turning toward it rather than turning away, and reversing the unhelpful cycle of shame, avoidance, loneliness, and more shame.

Chapter 10 on self-compassion discusses the three components of self-compassion described by Kristen Neff. Each of these components applies directly to shame:

- *Mindfulness versus emotional entanglement.* Self-compassion offers you a way of observing and accepting shame without getting stuck in it. Mindfulness allows you to accept your need to be loved and the fear of being unloved. Mindfulness allows you to observe your thoughts and feelings as passing events without buying into and getting stuck in them. Mindfulness also reduces activity of the default mode network (see Chapter 7), which often gives rise to shame-related thoughts and feelings by leading you to review difficult events of the past, anticipate unpleasant events in the future, and compare yourself to others in unfavorable ways in the present.

- *Self-kindness versus self-criticism.* Self-compassion offers you a way of turning toward the fear of being rejected and unloved rather than getting stuck in self-blame, self-criticism, and beating up on yourself. Expectation of feeling unbearably bad if you were to face your shame keeps you in the loop of shame avoidance. When you gradually turn to the shameful parts of yourself with kindness, you gradually change the expectation of feeling unbearably bad to being able to tolerate and eventually accept the difficult feelings. Self-kindness gradually allows you to feel worthy of love.
- *Common humanity versus self-isolation.* Self-compassion offers you a way of connecting with others around your feelings of shame, rather than keeping them secret and silent. Suffering is universal and something you have in common with all people. Self-compassion gives you the freedom from keeping painful secrets and the courage to reveal these secrets to people you love, with the trust that you are worthy of love no matter how people in your life react to learning your shameful secrets.

Heart Rate Variability and Shame

Heart rate variability (HRV) offers an additional benefit in improving your ability to self-regulate in response to shame. The physiological experience of shame often feels dysregulating, as if your body is not able to cope with the suffering. That feeling is quite accurate. Research shows that feelings of shame correspond to reduction in HRV, which means that your body has more trouble regulating itself when you feel shame. A study by Steven Freed and Wendy D'Andrea from the New School for Social Research showed that for survivors of interpersonal trauma shame, fear, and anxiety were strongly associated with reduced HRV at baseline and while viewing pictures with trauma related images.[157] These findings confirm previous findings that people with posttraumatic stress disorder have difficulty regulating their physiological activation. Moreover, Freed and D'Andrea's study revealed a unique association between shame and low HRV during periods of recovery from exposure to trauma reminders. This means that shame may prevent you from regulating your physiological activation after being exposed to reminders of trauma significantly more than fear and anxiety would.

HRV biofeedback, as discussed in detail in Chapter 10 on self-compassion, also helps nurture a sense of personal and interpersonal safety, both of which are crucial in allowing you to open up to the experience of shame and respond to it with kindness.

In developing a healthier relationship and response to shame, start with HRV biofeedback training to develop a foundation of better self-regulation and a stronger sense of personal and interpersonal safety. After a few weeks of consistent HRV training, once your ability to self-regulate becomes stronger, gradually add elements of self-compassion as a way of responding to shame, as a reminder that you want to be loved, and as a way of comforting yourself when you feel unloved. With HRV and self-compassion training, you'll be able to turn toward shame with curiosity and kindness. As Christopher Germer says, you'll learn to hold yourself and all your imperfections with tenderness and compassion.

COMPASSIONATE FRIEND MEDITATION

This is a wonderful practice for healing yourself from shame. It allows you to disclose whatever you are ashamed of in a kind and gentle way. It is adapted from Kristin Neff and Christopher Germer's compassionate friend meditation (*The Mindful Self-Compassion Workbook*), with permission.

1. Find a comfortable position, either sitting or lying down. Gently close your eyes. Take a few low-and-slow breaths at your resonance frequency or at 6 breaths per minute. Allow yourself to settle into the body. Put one or both hands over your heart to remind yourself to give yourself loving attention.

2. *Safe place.* Now imagine yourself in a place that is safe and comfortable. It might be a cozy chair in front of a fireplace, or peaceful sandy beach with warm sun and cool breeze, or a beautiful mountain lake with blue sky overhead. It can be a place you've been to before or an imaginary one—any place that feels safe and comfortable to you.

3. *Compassionate friend.* Soon you'll receive a visitor, a warm and compassionate presence, a compassionate friend, who embodies

the qualities of wisdom, strength, acceptance, and unconditional love. This being may be a spiritual figure, a wise, compassionate teacher, or a loving relative. It may also simply be a warm presence, not a specific person. Your compassionate friend cares deeply about you and would like you to be happy and free from unnecessary struggle.

4. *Arrival*. You can choose to invite your compassionate friend to come into your safe place, or you can go out to meet your friend outside of it. Take a moment to decide which you prefer.

5. *Meeting*. Your compassionate friend is wise and all-knowing, and knows exactly where you are in your life's journey. Your friend might want to tell you something, something that is just what you need to hear right now. Please take a moment and listen carefully to what your compassionate friend might have to say. . . . If no words come, that's OK too—just continue to experience your friend's kind company. Enjoy it.

6. Perhaps you would like to say something to your compassionate friend. Your friend listens deeply, nonjudgmentally, and completely understands you. Is there anything you'd like to tell your friend?

7. Take a few more moments to enjoy your friend's presence. . . . Continue breathing low-and-slow. As you continue to enjoy your friend's company, allow yourself to realize that your friend is actually a part of yourself. . . . All the compassionate feelings, images, and words that you are experiencing flow from your own inner wisdom and compassion.

8. *Reflection*. When you are ready, allow the images to gradually dissolve in your mind's eye, remembering that compassion and wisdom is always within you, especially when you need them the most. You can call on your compassionate friend anytime you wish.

9. Settle back into your body and let yourself savor your experience, perhaps reflecting on the words you may have heard or shared.

10. Finally, let go of the meditation and allow yourself to feel whatever you feel and to be exactly as you are. Gently open your eyes.

Below are some guidelines you can follow in learning to hold your shame. If you have unresolved trauma in your background, consider seeing a trauma-trained therapist to work with in addition to implementing strategies from this book. These steps are based on the foundations of HRV (Chapter 3), mindfulness meditation (Chapter 8), mindfulness-based skills (Chapter 9), and self-compassion (Chapter 10). Be sure to read these chapters before implementing this training. Move through these steps without rushing—take as much time at each one as you need. I recommend not skipping steps before approaching the emotion of shame itself in step 8, in order to hone your skills in more neutral circumstances before approaching a very difficult and painful emotion.

1. Start with mindful low-and-slow breathing practice (Chapter 2) to regulate your respiratory physiology and reduce activation in the moment of difficulty. If paying attention to your breath produces distress or discomfort, start with learning a concentration mindfulness practice, such as the here-and-now stone (Chapter 8). Then, bring in mindful low-and-slow breathing practice, just a few breaths at a time, going as slow as you need, returning to the here-and-now stone as needed if feeling discomfort. Gradually extend your practice time.

2. Determine and begin training at your resonance frequency breathing rate or at 6 breaths per minute (Chapter 3) for HRV training.

3. Incorporate meditation practice, starting with concentration practice with external awareness, such as the here-and-now stone or sights and sounds around you. When ready, transition to concentration practice with external awareness.

4. Next, move on to open awareness practices with a neutral focus, such as the body scan, or mindfulness of thoughts, feelings, and physiological sensations, or thoughts on leaves meditation (all in Appendix A).

5. Incorporate self-compassion training. Mettā (Chapter 10) is often a great place to start as a way to develop a kinder and more compassionate attitude toward yourself.

6. Compassionate friend practice described earlier in this chapter is very helpful in responding to shame in particular, because it helps you open to the shameful secret you are carrying.

7. Practice labeling your emotions, as described in Chapter 9.

8. Turn to the difficult emotion practice (soften, soothe, and allow; see Appendix A) and gently bring attention to the emotion of shame specifically.

9. Practice FLARE when you experience shame to help you decide on the most helpful response:

   — *Feel* the physical sensations in your body and observe the thoughts that come into your mind.

   — *Label* the experience with a gentle, nonjudgmental name, such as "suffering," or "shame," or "difficult emotions."

   — *Allow* your feelings to be just as they are: it is OK to feel this way.

   — *Respond* by choosing a response that is in your best interest:

      ▪ Get in touch with your values and consider what kind of response is most consistent with your values.

      ▪ Practice mindful low-and-slow breathing at your resonance frequency or at 6 breaths per minute to activate the safety signals of the parasympathetic nervous system.

      ▪ Use the here-and-now stone to reduce intensity of suffering.

      ▪ Recall your compassionate friend and see what he or she might have to say.

      ▪ Practice Mettā or the difficult emotion practice.

   — *Expand awareness* to your internal and external environment. Reflect on three things you appreciate or are grateful for.

Let's walk through FLARE using the earlier example of Michael, when he is having a hard time:

Feel. Michael feels the knot in his stomach and the flush of his cheeks. He notices thoughts of "You are weak and you are no good."

Label. He calls this experience "embarrassment" and "unhelpful thinking."

Allow. He reminds himself that he does not have control over how he feels in this moment: "It is OK to feel this way."

Respond. Michael reflects on his values of self-care and relationship with his immediate family:

He takes 10 low-and-slow breaths at his resonance frequency of 5 breaths per minute.

As he begins to feel more regulated, he practices Mettā for what he needs in this moment: "May I be kind" and "May I have peace."

As Michael opens to his experience, he decides that he will continue looking for a job. He sends an e-mail to a friend who has a connection at a company he'd like to work at.

Expand awareness. Michael expands his awareness to the room he is in, sounds of his children's voices, and the sensations of touch where his body is in contact with the chair he is sitting in. He reflects on his appreciation for his friend who offered to help, and his family who do their best to be there for him, and for himself for sending that e-mail.

Meditation Scripts

Anchor Meditation

(adapted with permission from Sitting Together *by*
Susan Pollack, Thomas Pedulla, and Ronald Siegel)

Settle into a comfortable position in your chair, close your eyes, release your muscles, and spend a few moments observing your breath, perhaps allowing your breath to fall into your resonance frequency breathing rate, a gentle rhythm of comfortable inhalations and long, slow exhalations.

Now bring to mind an image of a boat. Give yourself a moment to solidify that image. What does your boat look like? What is it made from? Does it have sails? What color is it?

Picture your boat in an ocean harbor, gently rocked by the waves. Notice the gentle rhythm of the ocean waves, perhaps in synchrony with your own breath—in and out, in and out. . . . Notice that your boat is firmly anchored in the ocean floor. . . . Feel the weight and solidity of the anchor, firmly planted in the ocean floor. Nothing can dislodge it. . . .

The waves are getting stronger now, the wind is picking up, and yet the anchor is keeping the boat from drifting away, firmly and solidly planted in the ocean floor. . . . Now a full-blown storm arises, with high crashing waves, rain, and strong winds. . . . Observe the anchor keeping the boat from being swept away into the open ocean, strong and firm. . . . No matter what might be going on around the boat, the anchor will always keep it safe, prevent it from being swept away.

Now imagine you can dive down below the surface of the water, below the storm, encased in a safe, protective bubble that will keep you safe under water. Bring yourself down to the anchor of the boat, the solid, reliable anchor that keeps the boat safe. Allow yourself to rest by the anchor, safe from the storm above you. Even as the storm rages above you, allow yourself to feel safe, calm, and protected. Let yourself be still in the storm.

Now take a few moments to reflect on what anchors you in your own life. Reflect on your ability to remain safe and anchored amidst the storms of life. Whenever you are ready, open your eyes and return to the rest of your awareness.

Autogenic Training

(adapted with permission from The Clinical Handbook of Biofeedback *by Inna Khazan).*

For this practice, you are going to get in contact with parts of your body and repeat certain phrases, silently to yourself. Begin with silently saying, "I am at peace. I give myself permission to relax. I am at peace. . . ."

Now get in contact with your right arm: see or feel the right arm in your mind's eye, saying silently to yourself, "My right arm is heavy. My right arm is heavy. My right arm is heavy and warm. My right arm is heavy and warm. . . ."

Now get in contact with your left arm, saying silently to yourself, "My left arm is heavy. My left arm is heavy and warm. My left arm is heavy and warm. My left arm is heavy, warm, comfortable, and relaxed. . . ."

Now get in contact with both arms, saying silently to yourself, "Both arms are heavy. Both arms are heavy and warm. Both arms are warm, comfortable, and relaxed. Both arms are warm, comfortable, and relaxed. . . ."

Make inner contact with both legs now, saying silently to yourself, "My legs are comfortably heavy. My legs are heavy and warm, Both legs are warm, comfortable and relaxed, Both legs are warm, comfortable and relaxed. My arms and legs are warm, comfortable and relaxed. My arms, and legs are warm, comfortable and relaxed. . . ."

Make contact now with your neck and shoulders, saying silently to yourself, "My neck and shoulders are warm and relaxed. My neck and shoulders are warm and relaxed. My neck, shoulders, arms, and legs are warm, comfortable, and relaxed. My neck, shoulders, arms and legs are warm, comfortable and relaxed. . . ."

Make inner contact with your heart now, saying silently to yourself, "My heartbeat is calm. My heartbeat is calm and regular. My heartbeat is calm and regular. My heartbeat is calm, regular, and relaxed. . . ." Make contact with the breath now, saying, "My breath is calm, and regular, and relaxed. My breath is calm, regular, and relaxed. My abdomen is warm. My abdomen is warm and relaxed. My abdomen is warm and relaxed. My heartbeat is calm and regular. My breath is calm, regular, and relaxed. My abdomen is warm and relaxed. . . ."

Now make inner contact with the forehead and say to yourself, "My forehead is cool. My forehead is cool and comfortable. My forehead is smooth, cool, and comfortable. . . ."

Now once again make inner contact with the neck, shoulders, arms, and legs, saying silently to yourself, "My neck, shoulders, arms and legs are heavy, warm, comfortable, and relaxed. . . ." Make contact with your heart again and repeat silently to yourself, "My heartbeat is calm and regular. My heartbeat is calm and regular. My heartbeat is calm and regular. . . ." Make contact again with your breath and say to yourself, "My breath is calm, regular, and relaxed. My breath is calm, regular, and relaxed. . . ." Make contact with the abdomen again and repeat silently to yourself, "My abdomen is warm. My abdomen is warm. My abdomen is warm and comfortable. . . ."

Now make contact with the forehead and repeat silently to yourself, "My forehead is cool. My forehead is cool. My forehead is cool, smooth, and comfortable. . . ." Now follow this with, "My body is warm, calm, comfortable, and relaxed. My body is heavy, warm, calm, comfortable, and relaxed. . . ."

Beach Meditation

(adapted with permission from The Clinical Handbook of Biofeedback *by Inna Khazan).*

Imagine that you are on a wonderful vacation, with no cares, no worries, no one to be responsible to, completely free from the daily hassles and expectations. . . . You are walking on the beach, feeling safe and protected, seeing the beauty of the colors, hearing the sounds, smelling the fragrances, feeling each step you take. . . .

It is a beautiful day, the perfect beach day for you. The sky is blue, a deep beautiful blue, filled with fluffy white clouds. You watch the clouds, slowly moving, gradually changing shape, transforming. You feel enveloped by a feeling of peace and tranquility. The sun is just right, warm and comfortable, not too hot. There is plenty of shade when you want it. . . .

Notice the gentle sea breeze on your face, the healing smell of sea air—you can almost taste the salt in the spray. Notice the sparkle of the water, the colors of the sand, pretty rocks, colors that dance and shift, patterns of reflection in the sea. Notice the horizon where sky touches the water. Right on the edge of the horizon you see a sailboat, white sails billowing in the wind, moving away from the shore. Watch it for a moment as it disappears over the horizon on its way to faraway lands. . . .

Continue walking, and as you walk, listen to the sound of the waves as they roll into the shore and back down into the sea. Listen to the sounds, hear the birds overhead. Perhaps you notice a place to sit now. You feel invited to touch the sand, notice the sensations as you sift the sand your fingers, see and feel the seashells and the pebbles at your fingertips. Now as you look back toward the sea, the sun is beginning to set, a brilliant sunset with rich colors, oranges, reds, and yellows, glowing, so beautiful. As you take in the beauty of the beach, allow yourself to feel centered, and calm, and tranquil. . . .

Body Awareness

(adapted with permission from The Mindful Self-Compassion Workbook *by Kristin Neff and Christopher Germer)*

Lie down flat on your back or sit up comfortably. Leave arms and legs uncrossed, hands resting on your lap or at your sides, whichever is most comfortable for you. Allow your eyes to close.

Begin with bringing attention to the feet, noticing the physical sensations in your feet. What you are noticing? Perhaps the sensations of warmth or coolness, dryness or moisture. Notice the sensations, whatever they are, and let them be. Bring gentle curiosity to the experience of your feet. Explore every part of your right foot—the sides, the arch, the ball of the foot, the top of the foot, the bottom of the foot, and each toe, one at a time. Notice the sensations and make space for them. Let them stay just the way they are. Now the left foot—the sides, the arch, the ball of the foot, the top of the foot, the bottom of the foot, and each toe, one at a time. Notice the sensations, and allow them to stay.

Now move your attention up to your ankles, noticing all the sensations in the right ankle and the left ankle. Whatever sensations you notice, explore them and allow them to be there just as they are. Now move your attention up to your calves, the right calf and the left calf, observing the sensations and letting them be just as they are. There is no need to change anything about your experience right now. Simply allow yourself to attend to your experience just as it is.

Your mind will wander from time to time. That is what human minds do. Notice the thoughts that come into your mind, and then gently bring your attention back to your body. Allow yourself not to struggle with the wanderings of your mind. Simply bring your mind back each time you become aware of its wandering. If any judgments enter your mind, acknowledge them and let them go. Bring kindness and compassion to the wanderings of your mind and to all of your experience.

Now, bring your attention to your knees and make space for whatever sensations you notice in your knees—the right knee and the left knee. If you notice any discomfort or more intense sensations, attend to them with kindness and compassion—you may want to place your hand on the knee and gently rub it, as a way of expressing compassion.

Now move your attention up to your thighs, noticing all the sensations in the thighs, the right thigh and the left thigh. Let the sensations be just as they are, exploring them, making space for all the sensations, whatever they might be.

Bring your attention now to your backside, paying attention to the sensations of touch or pressure where your backside comes in contact with the chair or floor. Explore the sensations with kindness and curiosity. Again, remember there is no need to change anything, no need to fix anything about your experience. Just allow yourself to attend to the experience as it is.

Now guide your attention to your abdomen, exploring the sensations in your abdomen and letting them be. Notice the sensations of your breath as your abdomen gently moves up and down, with each inhalation and exhalation.

If you notice any discomfort or more intense sensations, attend to them with kindness and compassion—you may want to place your hand on your abdomen, allowing the warmth of your hand to provide comfort.

If you notice your mind wandering, acknowledge where the mind has been and then gently escort it back to the sensations in your body, letting go of any thoughts or judgments that come along the way.

Now bring your attention to your lower back, noticing all the sensations in the lower back, allowing them to be, bringing gentle curiosity to the sensations in your lower back. If you notice any discomfort, attend to it with kindness and compassion. Stay with the sensations, allowing them to be just as they are, guiding your breath toward the area of discomfort.

Gently bring your attention to your chest now. Notice the sensations of your heartbeat, allowing them to be just as they are. Observe all the sensations in your chest with curiosity and make space for the sensations, letting them be. There is no need to change anything right now, nothing that needs to be fixed. Make room for all the sensations in your chest, attend to them with kindness.

Now bring your attention to your upper back, observing and exploring all the sensations in your upper back. Notice the sensations of touch or pressure where your back comes in contact with the chair or floor. Make space for all the sensations. If you notice any discomfort, attend to it with kindness and compassion. Stay with the sensations, allowing them to be just as they are, guiding your breath toward the area of discomfort.

Move your attention now to your right arm and hands: the upper arm, the lower arm, the hand and each finger, the thumb, the index finger, the middle finger, the ring finger, and the little finger. Attend to the sensations in the right arm, allowing them to stay. Now the left arm: the upper arm, the lower arm, the hand and each finger, the thumb, the index finger, the middle finger, the ring finger, and the little finger. Explore sensations in your left arm and hand with curiosity and kindness.

When you notice your mind wandering, acknowledge where the mind has been and gently bring it back to the sensations in your body. Notice and let go of any judgments and thoughts that come along the way.

Now bring your attention to the shoulders—the left shoulder, and the right shoulder. Observe the sensations, acknowledging them and letting them be. If you notice any discomfort, make space for it and attend to it with kindness and compassion. You may want to gently rub your shoulders in the area of discomfort, as a way of showing compassion. Stay with the sensations of discomfort, exploring them, noticing what they are really like, and allowing them to be.

Gently move your attention to the neck, bringing gentle curiosity to your experience of the sensations in the neck, allowing them to be just as they are. If you notice any discomfort, or more intense sensations, attend to them with curiously and compassion. Make space for the sensations and allow them to stay. You might place your hand over the area of discomfort, allowing the warmth of your hand to bring soothing and comfort.

Now move your attention to the head, starting with the chin, mouth, and lips. Notice all the sensations in your chin, mouth, and lips, allowing them to stay. Then move on to the cheeks, the nose, the eyes, making room for all the sensations in the cheeks, the nose, and the eyes, exploring them with gently curiosity. Move to the ears, the forehead, and the top of the head, allowing all the sensations in the ears, the forehead, and the top of the head to stay, attending to them with kindness and compassion.

Finally, give yourself a moment to reflect on the hard work your body does every day. Bring some gratitude and appreciation to each part of the body, to each organ, each muscle for the work they do every single day. Bring some kindness to your body, bring some compassion, and appreciation. Whenever you are ready, slowly open your eyes and return to the rest of your experience.

Difficult Emotion Practice

(adapted with permission from The Mindful Self-Compassion Workbook *by Kristin Neff and Christopher Germer)*

Find a comfortable position, sitting up or lying down. Allow your eyes to close, either fully or partially. Bring your awareness to your breath for a few moments, noticing the sensations of your breath as it comes in and as it goes out. Allow your breath to fall into your resonance frequency breathing rate, with comfortable inhalations and long, slow exhalations. Notice the sensations of air entering your nostrils, your chest and belly gently rising with each inhalation and falling with each exhalation, as the air flows back out of the nostrils. Notice the sensations in your body, especially the sensations of touch or pressure where it comes in contact with the chair (or floor)—your back against the back of the chair, your arms on the armrests, your feet on the floor. Notice the external sensations of the position of your body in the chair or the floor, and the internal sensations within your body—your breath, your heartbeat, the pulsation and vibration of your body.

Now let yourself remember a mildly difficult situation. Recall what happened, what you were thinking, and especially what you were feeling. Now expand your awareness to your body as a whole. While you recall the emotion, notice where you feel the emotion in your body. In your mind's eye, sweep your body from head to toe, stopping where you can sense a little tension or discomfort.

Now choose a single location in your body where the feeling expresses itself most strongly, perhaps as a point of muscle tension or an achy feeling. In your mind, incline gently toward that spot. Continue to breathe naturally, allowing the sensation to be there, just as it is. If you wish, place your hand over your heart as you continue to breathe. Allow the gentle, rhythmic motion of the breath to soothe your body.

If you feel overwhelmed by an emotion at any point, bring your attention to your breath and stay with it until you feel better, and then return to the emotion.

Allow yourself to soften into the location in your body where you feel the emotion most strongly. Let the muscles be softer without a requirement that they become soft or that they relax. Just let the muscles soften like they do when you apply heat to sore muscles. You can say silently to yourself, "soft . . . soft . . . soft . . ." as you allow your muscles to soften around the area of discomfort. Remember that you are not trying to make the sensation go away. You are simply allowing your body to soften while letting the sensations of discomfort stay.

Now soothe yourself for struggling in this way. If it feels comfortable, place your hand over your heart and feel your body breathe. Or you might direct some kindness to the part of your body where you feel the difficult emotion by placing your hand over that place. Feel the warmth of your hand, soothing and bringing comfort. You might send your breath to the part of the body where you feel the difficult emotion, soothing and comforting. Silently say to yourself, "soothe . . . soothe . . . soothe."

Finally, allow the discomfort to be there. Abandon the wish for the feeling to disappear. Let the discomfort come and go, make space for it, and allow it to be just as it is. Repeat silently to yourself, "allow . . . allow . . . allow."

Now put it all together, letting your body soften, soothing yourself for struggling, and allowing the difficult feelings to stay, saying silently to yourself, "Soften, soothe, and allow . . . soften, soothe, and allow." You can use these three words like a mantra, rolling them around in your mind.

Stay with your feelings and with the mantra for as long as you wish, and whenever you are ready, slowly open your eyes and return to the rest of your experience.

Experiencing Anxiety

Get into a comfortable position in your chair, and allow your eyes to close, either fully or partially. Begin with bringing your attention to your breath, observing your breath, allowing your breath to fall into your resonance frequency rate, with gentle, comfortable inhalations and long, slow exhalations. Stay with your breath for a few moments, observing all the sensations and letting them be.

Now bring your attention to your body and gently scan your body. Where do you feel your anxiety? Feel your heart rate, your breathing, your muscles, your abdomen. Notice any perspiration, shaky or tingly feelings in your hands or feet, feelings of restlessness or tightness, or any other sensations. Observe all the sensations with kindness and curiosity. As you notice each sensation, label it with a descriptive, nonjudgmental word or short phrase, such as "here's my heartbeat" or "here's tightness."

As you observe the physical sensations of anxiety, you might notice thoughts about those sensations, such as interpretations or evaluations of the physical sensations, or predictions what might happen next. Label those thoughts as "interpretation" or "evaluation" or "prediction," and let them go, bringing your attention back to the sensations in your body, observing how the body feels at that moment.

When you mind wanders away from the sensations in your body, notice and acknowledge where your mind has been and then gently bring it back to your body and the sensations of anxiety.

Notice how the sensations change from moment to moment, sometimes becoming more intense, sometimes staying the same, and sometimes becoming less noticeable and weaker. Allow all the sensations to be just as they are. There is nothing that needs to change right now. Notice any temptation to make the sensations stop or go away, and let it go. Bring your awareness to the sensations of anxiety with kindness, compassion, and curiosity. Notice any temptation to get up from your chair, move, or walk away, and then let it go.

Again, allow all the sensations to be just as they are, no matter how intense they may be. Watch the sensations change from moment to moment, sometimes growing stronger, sometimes staying the same, and sometimes growing weaker. Observe those sensations with kindness and compassion. Label them nonjudgmentally and allow them to stay.

Whenever you are ready, open your eyes, stretch, and return to the rest of your awareness.

Giving and Taking Meditation (Tonglen)
(adapted with permission from The Mindful Path to Self-Compassion *by Christopher Germer)*

Settle into your chair, allow your eyes to close, and take a few slow, regular breaths. Allow your breath to fall into your resonance frequency rate, with gentle, comfortable inhalations and long, slow exhalations. Observe each breath, experience all the sensations of the inhalation and the exhalation. Feel your breath fully as you inhale and as you exhale. Notice the gentle rise and fall of your abdomen with each inhalation and each exhalation.

Now bring your attention to the physical sensations in your body at this moment. Locate any tension or discomfort. Where do you feel it? Your head, your neck, your shoulders, your back or abdomen, your arms or legs . . . ?

Now focus on your heart, and see if you are carrying any emotional distress. If so, how does it feel to you? Does it feel harsh, or heavy, tough, or turbulent? How does it look in your mind's eye? Does it appear dark, or gray, or murky? Get a feel for the discomfort, and label it with a short, nonjudgmental label. You can call it "discomfort" or "pain" or "fear."

Now bring your attention to your breath again. With every breath in, take in all of your distress and discomfort. Inhale the discomfort from where ever it is located in your body. Notice the slight pause between your inhalation and your exhalation, and imagine that the light and warmth of your heart are transforming each breath from distress and suffering into relief and light.

Remember how your distress felt and looked to you in the beginning of this practice. Now let your exhalation be the opposite of your inhalation. If you were breathing in darkness, breathe out light. If you were breathing in harshness, breath out softness. If you were breathing in turbulence, breathe out peace.

Now bring to mind an image of another person who might be suffering right now—perhaps with hopelessness, sadness, or anxiety, or pain or anger. With every breath in, breathe in the suffering of that person, and with every breath out, send the person peace, contentment, calmness, and comfort, inhaling distress and suffering, exhaling peace and comfort, inhaling hopelessness and pain, exhaling contentment and well-being, inhaling sadness and anger, exhaling kindness and compassion.

Continue breathing, in and out, slowly and calmly, until your breath settles back into a regular rhythm, perhaps the rhythm of your resonance frequency breathing, breathing in distress, your own and the other person's, and breathing out kindness and compassion for yourself and others. Stay with the rhythm of this breath for as long as you wish, and whenever you are ready, open your eyes and return to the room.

Light Meditation

Find a comfortable spot for you to sit or lie down, gently supported. Allow your breathing to fall into your resonance frequency rate, with gentle, comfortable inhalations and long, slow exhalations. Allow your breath to become smooth and regular. Bring your attention into the present moment and to the sensations of your breath and the sensations of your body, particularly where it is making contact with the chair or floor. Continue breathing.

Now gently scan your body for the difficult feeling of pain, anxiety, depression, sadness, or hopelessness. Notice where in your body you feel the difficult feeling most strongly. Once you've located the feeling, notice how its texture feels to you. Does it feel harsh, or heavy, or rough? How does it look in your mind's eye? Does it appear dark, or gray, or murky? Get a feel for the discomfort, and label it with a short, nonjudgmental label. You can call it "sadness" or "pain" or "worry" or "fear" or "discouragement."

Continue to breathe at your resonance frequency, and as you breathe, imagine that you sitting in front of a spectacular sunrise. See the spectrum of soft colors—pink, purple, red, orange. . . . As the sun rises, feel its light gradually illuminating your body—first your head, then your neck, shoulders, chest, arms, abdomen, your legs and feet. If it feels comfortable, allow the light to envelop your body, filling it with golden light. Feel every organ, every muscle, every bone, every cell in your body touched by the warm and gentle light. Imagine every cell in your body sparkling with light.

Now allow the light to illuminate those places in your body where you feel the difficult feelings, the sadness, depression, anxiety, hopelessness, or pain, most strongly. Allow the light to linger there. Feel the gentle warmth of the light soothing, bringing comfort. Feel the texture of the difficult feelings change as the gentle light illuminates it—from harsh to soft, from heavy to light, from rough to smooth. See the color of the feelings change as they sparkle with light. See the dark, gray, murky colors lighten and lift, transforming into the iridescent colors of the sunrise.

Now let the light expand outside yourself to include others in the room, your house, your city, your country, the entire world. In your mind's eye see yourself and your surroundings enveloped in warm, gentle, comforting light.

Allow yourself to stay with this light for as long as you wish, and whenever you are ready open your eyes, bringing the light and its gentle warmth into the present moment and the rest of your day.

Lotus Meditation

Get into a comfortable position in your chair, with your back gently supported. Allow your eyes to close, either fully or partially. Now bring your awareness to the physical sensations in your body, beginning with the sensations of touch or pressure where your body makes contact with the chair or floor—your back against the back of the chair, your arms on the armrests, your feet on the floor. Take a few moments to get in touch with the movement of your breath in your chest and abdomen. Allow your breath to fall into your resonance frequency rate, with gentle, comfortable inhalations and long, slow exhalations. Feel the rhythm of your breath in the body, breathing in and breathing out. Focus on each inhalation and exhalation, breathing in and out. Notice the changing patterns of sensation in your chest and abdomen as you breathe in and out.

As you breathe, in your mind's eye imagine a beautiful white lotus flower floating on a pond. The water in the pond is dark and murky. The whiteness of the lotus petals starkly contrasts with the dark waters on the pond. Observe the pristine flower for a few moments—the shape of its petals, the pink or yellow center, the green leaves around it, the long stem disappearing into the murky waters. Observe that stem, which leads to the root system of the lotus, anchored deeply in the mud and muck at the bottom of the pond. The lotus derives its life and its beauty from the dark muddy waters, which support and nourish it.

Now look within yourself, noticing any dark, murky, sad, and painful places within you. Allow yourself to see beyond the darkness, sadness, and pain to see if you can find value in your experience. See the spots of light gleaming through the darkness, being supported and nourished, just like the lotus flower. Just like the lotus flower is born from the darkness and muck, allow your light to emerge from the pain.

Give yourself as much time as you'd like to reflect on your own ability to bring light from darkness, the strength you might derive from the pain, and the beauty that may be born out of it.

Mindfulness of Pain Meditation

Find a comfortable position, sitting up or lying down, gently supported. Allow your eyes to close, either fully or partially. Notice the sensations in your body, especially the sensations of touch or pressure where it comes in contact with the chair (or floor)—your back against the back of the chair, your arms on the armrests, your feet on the floor.

Allow your breath to fall into your resonance frequency rate, with gentle, comfortable inhalations and long, slow exhalations. Bring your awareness to the sensations of your breath as it comes in and as it goes out. Notice the sensations of air entering your nostrils, your chest and belly gently rising with each inhalation and falling with each inhalation, as the air flows back out of the nostrils. Allow yourself to experience all the sensations of your breath, and let them be just as they are.

Now gently scan your body for the sensations of pain. Notice where in your body you feel pain most strongly. Once you've located the pain, notice how its texture feels to you. Does it feel tight, or heavy, or pressured? How does it look in your mind's eye? Does it appear dark, or black, or cloudy? Get a feel for the pain, and label it with a short, nonjudgmental label. You can call it "pain" or "pressure" or "tightness" or "discomfort."

Allow yourself to be with the pain sensations, attending to them with kindness, compassion, and curiosity. Make space for all the sensations, without holding on to them or trying to make them go away. Simple allow them to be just as they are. Notice how the sensations change from moment to moment, sometimes becoming stronger and more intense, sometimes staying the same, sometimes becoming weaker and less noticeable. Let your attention stay with the changing patterns of sensation, observing, allowing, with curiosity and kindness. Remember that the intention is not to make you feel better but to get better at feeling.

If you notice that the sensations of pain are becoming overwhelming, let go of the focus on the pain and shift your attention back to your breath, staying with the rhythmic movements of your breath coming in and going out until the difficult feelings subside and you are able to return to observing the sensations of pain.

When your mind wanders away from the sensations in your body, notice where the mind has been and then gently guide it back to the body, observing the sensations once again with kindness and compassion. Gently redirect your attention to the discomfort and stay with them no matter how bad it seems. Take a look at it—what does it really feel like?

Notice any temptation to get up or stop this practice. Notice where it the body you feel it most strongly. Bring all your attention to that urge, that temptation. Notice all of the sensations that come with it. See how the urge to get up or stop is distinct from the sensations of pain. Notice how the urge to get up or stop is also changing from moment to moment, rising and subsiding. Observe those changes, and allow yourself to stay with this practice, returning your attention to the sensations of discomfort, observing them, and allowing them to stay.

As you do this, you may notice your mind coming up with judgments of your experience—"this is really bad" or "dangerous." You may notice your mind coming up with predictions of what will happen next or questions about when this experience might end. When you notice judgments, predictions, or questions, acknowledge them and let them go, returning your attention to your experience just as it is. Allow all the sensations to stay, making room for them, observing them with kindness and curiosity.

As this time for formal practice comes to an end, gradually widen your attention to take in the sounds around you. Now slowly open your eyes, notice your surroundings, and allow the awareness of the present moment to stay with you throughout the day.

Mindfulness of Sound Meditation

(adapted with permission from The Mindful Path to Self-Compassion *by Christopher Germer)*

Find a reasonably quiet place (no TV or people talking), sit in a comfortable position, and settle into your seat. Let your eyes close, either fully or partially. Begin with several calm breaths, paying attention to each breath as it comes in and goes out. . . .

Now, bring your awareness to the sounds all around you. Just listen. . . . What do you hear? What do you feel as you listen? Just sit and let your ears pick up sounds near and far, all around, in all directions. Let yourself sit and receive the sound vibrations.

You don't need to label the sounds, you don't need to interpret the sounds, you don't need to seek out the sounds, you don't even need to like the sounds. Just sit in the middle of the sound environment, let the sound come to you, let it present itself to you. . . . Just listen and take in every sound. . . .

You might find your mind latching on to a sound and going down the path of interpretation, thinking about the sound or its meaning. You might notice thoughts or feelings rising in response to the sound. You might find yourself judging the sound or your reaction to it. All of that is OK. If you notice your mind wandering off from the vibrations of the sound, notice where it's been and then gently bring your attention back to the sound, just as it is.

Listen . . . you don't need to pay special attention to any particular sound, just let all sounds come and go as they please. You don't need to name the sounds, you don't need to figure out what they mean, you don't need to like the sounds. Just let the sounds be sounds, just let yourself hear them.

Just listen. . . .

Mindfulness of Breath Meditation

(adapted with permission from The Mindful Path to Self-Compassion *by Christopher Germer)*

Find a quiet comfortable place to sit, so that you can remain in one position, back straight and gently supported, chin gently tucked toward the chest, shoulders dropped. Let your eyes close, fully or partially. Take three easy, slow breaths. Now bring your awareness to the position of your body and to the sensations inside your body. What do you notice? Perhaps you notice vibrations or pulsation, warmth or coolness, ease or tension. Fully feel your body, and just let it be as it is, whatever the sensations are.

Now see where you can discover your breath most strongly and most easily. Where do you feel your breathing? Do you feel it in your nostrils as the air goes in and out of your nose? Do you feel it in your chest as a rising and falling? Do you feel your breathing in your abdomen as expansion and contraction? Where do you notice your breathing most easily and most strongly? If you can feel your breath in many areas, pick one. Allow your attention to stay on that location of your body, where you feel the breath most strongly. Allow yourself to feel the breath. Feel the breath and its sensations in your body.

As you breathe, you will notice that your mind wanders from time to time. This is what human minds do. Your mind wandering off is just part of the process. All you have to do is gently return your attention back to the breath when you notice that it has wandered off. It does not matter how many times your mind wanders, just bring it back with kindness, back to your breath, every time, letting go of any thoughts or judgments that may come along the way. Gently return your attention back to your breath, feeling the sensations of your breath in your body. Just feel the breath.

Now bring your attention to the sensations of the inhalation. Notice what the sensations of the inhalation are in the part of your body where you feel your breath most strongly and most easily. Then notice the sensations of the exhalation. Notice what the sensations of the exhalation are in the part of your body where you feel your breath most strongly and most easily. Take a moment to wait until your body inhales again. Don't rush the inhalation. Let yourself exhale fully, and let the inhalation happen all on its own. There is no need to make the inhalation happen. Your body will do that for you all on its own.

Notice any thoughts or feelings that come to you during the transition from the exhalation into the inhalation or from the inhalation into the exhalation. Acknowledge those thoughts and feelings without engaging with them, letting them be, gently returning your attention to your breath.

Allow your breath to move from the inhalation into an exhalation, and from the exhalation into an inhalation. Let your experience between the breaths be just as it is, without attempting to change it. Just feel the breath. Feel the inhalation and the exhalation, and allow whatever may arise during the pause after the exhalation to be just as it is, and then feel the breath again. Notice any urge to rush, and let it go. Keep breathing in and out, gently, smoothly, paying attention to the sensations of the breath.

As you do this, your mind will naturally wander, and often. It will wander off, perhaps distracted by a sound, or a thought, or a feeling, or a sensation. Sooner or later, you'll notice that your mind has wandered, and when you notice that, gently bring your attention back to the breath. . . . Feel the air. . . . When you mind wanders, notice that and gently go back to feeling your breath. Just feel the breath, and when you notice your mind has wandered, feel your breath again. One breath after the next. Inhalation flowing into an exhalation, and exhalation flowing into an inhalation.

Let your body breathe for you; it knows just what to do. Right now you are simply paying attention to the sensations of the breath in the body, in the place where you feel these sensations most easily. Feel your breath again and again. . . . When your mind wanders, gently guide it back to your breath in the place where you feel it most easily and most strongly.

Now let go of the focus on the particular location where you feel your breath most strongly, and allow yourself to feel your whole body move with each breath, expansion and contraction, the hardly perceptible movement of your whole body as you breathe. Let your body breathe for you, as it knows how to do so well. Feel your body move with the breath, back and forth.

Take as much time as you'd like to pay attention to the sensations of your breath, and then whenever you are ready, open your eyes and once again become aware of the rest of your environment.

Mindfulness of Thoughts, Feelings, and Physiological Sensations

(adapted with permission from Acceptance of Thoughts and Feelings exercise from Mindfulness and Acceptance Workbook for Anxiety, *by John Forsyth and Georg Eifert)*

Get into a comfortable position in your chair. Sit upright, feet flat on the floor, arms and legs uncrossed, hands resting on your lap, palms up or down, as is most comfortable for you. Allow your eyes to close, either fully or partially.

Now bring your awareness to the physical sensations in your body, beginning with the sensations of touch or pressure where your body makes contact with the chair or floor—your back against the back of the chair, your arms on the armrests, and your feet on the floor.

Take a few moments to get in touch with the movement of your breath in your chest and abdomen. Feel the rhythm of your breath in the body, like ocean waves coming in and out. Focus on each inhalation and exhalation, breathing in and out. Notice the changing patterns of sensation in your chest and abdomen as you breathe in and out.

There is no need to control your breathing in any way; simply let your body breathe for you. As best you can, bring an attitude of gentle acceptance and allowing to your breath. There is nothing to be fixed, no particular goal, no particular state to be achieved. Simply allow your experience to be your experience, without needing it to be anything other than what it is.

Sooner or later your mind will wander away from your breath to other thoughts, ideas, worries, concerns, images, daydreams, or it may just drift along. This is what human minds do. When you notice your mind has wandered off is the time when you have once again become aware of your experience. You may want to acknowledge where your mind has been—"there is thinking" or "there is feeling." Then gently guide your attention back to the sensation of the breath coming in and going out. As best you can, bring kindness and compassion to your awareness, perhaps seeing the repeated wanderings of your mind as opportunities to bring patience and gentle curiosity to your experience.

When you become aware of any tension, discomfort, or other physical sensations in a particular part of the body, notice them, acknowledge their presence, and see if you can make space for them. Do not try to hold on to them or make them go away. See if you can make some room for the discomfort or tension, just allowing them to be there. Watch the sensations change from moment to moment. Sometimes they grow stronger, sometimes they grow weaker, and sometimes they stay the same. Notice the changing patterns of sensation and allow them to be, just as they are. Breathe calmly into and out from the sensations of discomfort, gently guiding your breath toward that region of the body. Remember the intention is not to make you feel better but to get better at feeling.

If you notice that you are unable to focus on your breathing, because of intense physical sensation in any part of your body or because of an intense emotion, let go of the focus on the breath and shift your attention to the place of physical discomfort in your body or the place in your body where you feel the emotion most strongly. Gently direct your attention to the discomfort and stay with it no matter how bad it seems. Take a look at it—what does it really feel like? Again, see if you can make room for the discomfort, allow it to be there and be willing to stay with it.

Along with physical sensations in your body, you may also notice thoughts about the sensations and thoughts about the thoughts. You may notice your mind judging your experience, or coming up with evaluations such as dangerous or unpleasant. You may notice your mind coming up with predictions of what will happen next, or questions about how things will turn out. When you notice evaluations, or judgments, predictions, or questions, acknowledge them and return to the present experience as it is, not as your mind says it is, noticing thoughts as thought, physical sensations as physical sensation, feelings as feeling, nothing more, nothing less. If you notice questions, gently answer them with "I don't know" and return to your present experience, just as it is.

To help you bring some distance between yourself and your thoughts and feelings, you can label the thoughts and feelings as you notice them. For example, if you notice yourself worrying, silently say to yourself, "Worry, there is worry." Observe the worry without engaging with it, allowing it to stay. If you find yourself judging, notice that and label it: "Judging, there is judging." Observe the judgment with kindness and compassion. You can do the same with other thoughts and feelings, just naming them: there is planning, or remembering, or wishing, or dreading, or whatever your experience may be. Label your thoughts or emotions and move on. Notice how thoughts and feelings come and go in your mind and body. You are not what those thoughts and feelings say, not matter how intense or persistent they may be.

As this time for formal practice comes to an end, gradually widen your attention to take in the sounds around you. Now slowly open your eyes, notice your surroundings, and allow the awareness of the present moment to stay with you throughout the day.

Mindful Progressive Muscle Relaxation
(adapted with permission from The Clinical Handbook of Biofeedback *by Inna Khazan)*

In this practice, you will purposefully tense individual muscles groups, bringing your attention to the sensations of tense muscles, and then release it and bring your attention to the sensations of relaxed muscles. If anything hurts while you are doing this, gently release the tension—don't hurt yourself.

Start by lifting up your eyebrows and tensing your forehead, holding them up. Notice the tension, where it is, what it feels like. Hold the tension a little longer . . . and now release the tension. Let the muscles loosen. Notice the feeling in the muscle now, notice the difference between the tense and relaxed state.

Now squeeze your eyes tightly as if the sun is too bright. Hold the tension, notice the sensations of tension . . . and now release the tension. Let all the tension flow out, and notice the difference in the sensations around the eyes, the difference between tense and relaxed muscles.

From here, you may keep your eyes open or closed, as you wish. Now put on an artificial smile, like a clown. Hold the tension, notice where you feel the tension, notice every sensation . . . and now release, let go of tension. Let the muscle release and soften, notice the difference between the tense state and the relaxed state.

Tighten the neck by bringing your head back toward your spine—not too much, just enough to feel the tension in your neck. Hold it, notice the sensations of tension . . . and now let your head come up and allow the tension to leave, releasing the neck muscles and appreciating the difference between the tense and relaxed state.

Put both arms out straight. Make a fist and tighten both arms from the hand to the shoulder. Feel the tension in the biceps, in the forearm, in the back of the arm, the elbow, the wrist, fingers. Hold the tension, notice the sensations of tension . . . and release. Let the arms slowly drop back down on your lap and allow all the tension to leave. Let the arms, hands, and fingers loosen and soften.

Now pull your shoulders up toward your ears. Hold them up . . . a little longer. Notice the tension, where is it, what it feels like . . . and now release the shoulders. Let then gently come back down. Notice the difference between the tense and the relaxed state.

Pull your elbows behind your back toward each other. Hold them, notice the tension . . . hold a little longer . . . and now release and gently bring your elbows back to your sides. Let go of the tension in the back and shoulders. Notice the difference between the tense and the relaxed state.

Now tighten your abdomen by pulling it in, as if trying to touch your spine, and hold . . . feel the tension, all the sensations . . . now release, letting the muscles soften and relax.

(Make sure you are sitting or lying down for this step.) Now lift both legs and point your toes back toward your body. Notice the tension in every muscle of your legs. Notice the tension in the thighs, knees, calves, ankles, feet, toes, what it feels like. Now gently allow your feet to drop back down to the floor. Let go of the tension your feet and legs. Notice the difference between the tense and the relaxed muscles.

Now turn your feet toward each other. Curl your toes and gently tighten them. Hold the tension. Feel the tension in the feet, all the sensations . . . now gently allow your feet and toes to relax and return to the normal position on the floor. Again, notice the difference between the tense and the relaxed state.

Finally, tense your whole body. Tense every muscle, as many muscles as you can . . . hold a little longer. Feel the tension, where it is, what it feels like . . . and release, letting the tension leave. Notice the difference between the tense and the relaxed state.

Mountain Meditation

(adapted with permission from The Mindfulness Solution *by Ronald Siegel)*

Get into a comfortable position in your chair. Sit upright, feet flat on the floor, arms and legs uncrossed, hands resting on your lap, palms up or down, as is most comfortable for you. Allow your eyes to close, either fully or partially.

Allow your attention to come to your breath. Observe each inhalation and exhalation, letting go of the need to change anything about your breathing. Just feeling your breath as it is, all the sensations of your breath coming in and going out. Take a few moments to let your body breathe, with no pressure to change or fix anything. . . .

As you breathe, bring to mind an image of a beautiful mountain, a beautiful, solid, proud mountain. Allow your mind to focus on this image, gently holding on to the image. Observe the shape of the mountain, its peak, its large base deeply and firmly rooted in the earth, its slopes, sometimes steep and sometimes gentle. Notice whether your mountain has a snow-covered peak, whether there are trees all over the slopes, or whether some slopes are rocky and smooth. Notice how still, stable, and solid the mountain is. Let your mind stay with this image for a few moments.

Your mind will wander from time to time. As best you can, be kind to yourself when that happens. Notice the thoughts that come into your mind and then gently bring your attention back to the image of the mountain. Allow yourself not to struggle with the wanderings of your mind. Bring kindness and compassion to the wanderings of your mind and to all of your experience.

Now allow yourself to imagine your body as the mountain—your legs and torso as the base of the mountain, solidly rooted into your chair; your spine as its axis, solid and straight; your arms and shoulders as its slopes, and your head as its proud peak.

With each breath, experience yourself as the mountain, centered, unwavering, rooted. Now in your mind's eye, see the sun traveling across the sky, its light reflecting in the smooth surfaces of the mountain, glistening in the snowy peak. See the clouds pass over the peak, enveloping it softly and gently and then moving on. See the day change into night, the sky lighting up with the stars and the moon, the sky so deep, so blue, and the stars so bright. Now the sun comes up again, the morning rays bathing the slopes of the mountain in gentle rosy light. And on and on it goes, day turning into night, night turning into day.

And with all these changes, the mountain just stays, experiencing every moment, every change, yet always staying itself—solid, still, rooted, dependable.

If you notice your mind wandering, acknowledge where the mind has been and then gently escort it back to your image of the mountain, with kindness, letting go of any thoughts or judgments that come along the way.

See your mountain remaining solid and calm, as it's always been, as seasons flow one into another, as the weather changes moment to moment.

In the summer, the snow has melted, except maybe in some deep crevices or highest peaks. The trees form a deep green cover for the slopes. The sun is strong and bright during the day. The clouds continue drifting over the mountain, sometimes bringing warm summer rains. Through those changes, the mountain remains as it is, strong and calm.

In the fall, the mountain is covered in brilliant colors—orange, yellow, red, and green. The wind gets stronger and blows the leaves off the trees. The days are getting shorter and the clouds come over the mountain more often. The rains get colder and more frequent, pelting the slopes of the mountain. And yet, the mountain remains itself, just as its always been, solid and strong. No matter what weather happens on its surface, the mountain remains rooted and solid.

In the winter, the days get really short, and snow and ice cover the mountain. The wind is icy cold now, the clouds are dark, sometimes bringing freezing rain, or fog, or snow. Storms come, with strong winds whistling and screaming in the crevices and all around the peak, snow and ice blanketing the mountain. All through the changes, the mountain remains the same. No matter what the season or the weather on its surface, the mountain remains itself. Its true nature is not changed by the changing of the seasons.

As spring comes, tiny leaves start unfurling on the trees, early flowers bloom, and birds return to the trees. The snow starts melting, with numerous streams flowing down the mountain slopes, clear and fast. The days get longer again. The sun is out more often. The rain comes to wash off remaining snow. As always, the mountain stays the same, unmoving, rooted, unchanged at its core.

See yourself as the mountain, unwavering through the changes of your life, the good times, and the tough times. With all the changes happening on the surface, your core remains steady and calm, through the days, the nights, the changing seasons. Experience each moment as it comes. Experience the constantly changing thoughts, feelings, physiological sensations, sights and sounds around you. Through the periods of light and through the periods of darkness, you remain strong and rooted. You, much like the mountain, experience storms of various intensity, darkness and pain, as well as times of joy and excitement, contentment and peace. See your thoughts, feelings, physiological sensations as the passing weather—they come and go, constantly changing. Just as you cannot control the weather, allow yourself to let go of the temptation to control your thoughts and feelings. Let them come and go, experiencing each moment fully.

Through all the changes, you derive strength and resilience from your mountain, encountering each moment as it comes with mindfulness, steadiness of mind, and clarity. Take as much time as you'd like to reflect on the strength and resilience of the mountain that are a part of you, and whenever you are ready, slowly open your eyes and return to the rest of your experience.

Passive Muscle Relaxation

(adapted with permission from The Clinical Handbook of Biofeedback *by Inna Khazan)*

In this passive muscle relaxation exercise, you'll use the natural abilities of your mind and body to experience a deep sense of comfort and relaxation. Begin by becoming aware of the top of your head and the muscles in the face. Let the muscles in your forehead relax . . . all the muscles becoming smoother and softer. Let the muscles around the eyes soften . . . and the eyelids find a place that is just right for them to rest comfortably. And now allow the feelings of comfort and relaxation to move into the temple area . . . even the ears may have a feeling of letting go . . . the nose relaxes . . . allow the muscles in the jaw to release . . . and the teeth part slightly under the gentle pull of gravity on the face and jaw. Now let the relaxation flow into the back of the neck and shoulders . . . allowing the muscles of the neck and shoulders to become loose and more comfortable . . . settling into the chair more deeply . . . feeling the surface beneath you . . . becoming more and more comfortable. Let the relaxation flow now into the back and the spinal column, letting all the muscles from the top of the neck down to the tailbone loosen and soften . . . feeling gently supported, letting the tension go. Allow the relaxation to flow into the chest and abdomen . . . feeling the muscles becoming smoother and softer . . . becoming more comfortable and at ease. Letting the arms feel heavier . . . letting the tension go . . . feeling the arms and hands becoming more comfortable, relaxed and heavier . . . the relaxation flows into the hands and into each finger . . . the thumb . . . the index finger . . . the middle finger . . . the ring finger and into the little finger . . . a deep sense of comfort . . . delightful and soothing . . . energizing and bringing health and wellbeing. Now allow the relaxation to flow into the hips and down the legs . . . soothing and softening every muscle. Allow the large muscles of the thigh to become soft and comfortable . . . the joints of the knee relax . . . the calves soften . . . and letting the feet release . . . the balls of the feet . . . the heels . . . and each toe. Let your whole body feel a flow of energy and well-being.

Raisin Meditation

(adapted with permission from The Mindfulness
Solution *by Ronald Siegel)*

Hold a raisin in your hand, on your open palm or between two fingers. You will use every one of your senses to observe and examine the raisin. Allow this practice to be very slow, noticing and resisting the urge to rush.

Begin with carefully observing the raisin with your eyes. Notice its shape, its color, the patterns of light reflecting on its surface. Notice some surfaces that are shiny, and others that are not. Pay attention to any thoughts or feelings that arise as you examine the raisin. Notice the thoughts or feelings, acknowledge them, and let them go, gently returning your attention to the raisin.

Now, using your sense of touch, explore the raisin with two fingers. It may be helpful to close your eyes as you do this. Notice the texture of the raisin, places where it feels soft, and places where it feels hard, smooth, and rough. Notice its hills and crevices, the way they feel in your fingers. Again, notice any thoughts or feelings that arise as you explore the texture of the raisin, acknowledge them, and gently return your focus to the raisin.

Lift the raisin to your ear, noticing the sensations of your arm lifting. Hold the raisin just outside your ear (don't put it in your ear) and roll it between two fingers, pressing gently on the raisin, noticing the soft sound the raisin makes under the pressure of your fingers.

If you notice any thoughts or feelings, memories or questions evoked by the raisin, thoughts about the rest of your day, or moments of doubt as to the purpose of what you are doing, or if your mind just wanders off somewhere, notice that and gently bring your attention back to the raisin.

Now slowly bring the raisin to your nose and breathe in its scent. Take a few slow, smooth breaths in. What do you notice? What is your reaction to the aroma you breathe in? If you notice thoughts, feelings, or judgments, notice them and return your attention to the smell of the raisin.

Finally, place the raisin in your mouth, without biting into it. Just let it stay on your tongue for a few moments. Notice the initial taste sensation. Explore the texture of the raisin with your tongue. How does the texture feel to you now? Is it similar or in any way different from the texture you noticed with your fingers? Now take one slow bite into the raisin, just one. Notice the taste of that one bite, the sensations of your teeth biting into the raisin. Notice any urge to continue biting into the raisin, any urge to rush. Now continue exploring the raisin with your tongue. How has it changed since you've bitten into it? Continue to slowly chew the raisin, very, very slowly, noticing all the sensations as you are chewing—taste, texture, shape, the movement of your jaw, any thoughts or feelings that arise. Swallow the raisin once there is nothing left to chew. Stay with the sensations in your mouth. What is different now? Stay with those sensations for as long as you wish, and whenever you are ready, return your awareness to everything else around you.

Thoughts on Leaves Meditation
(adapted with permission from The Clinical Handbook of Biofeedback *by Inna Khazan).*

Find a comfortable spot for you to sit or lie down, gently supported. Allow your breathing to become smooth and regular. Bring your attention into the present moment and to the sensations of your breath, and the sensations of your body, particularly where it is making contact with the chair of floor. Take a few easy, comfortable breaths. And as you breathe, imagine yourself walking through the forest, with green grass under your feet, tall trees around you, blue sky overhead. You know the way around the forest, you are safe and protected. The sun is just right, not too warm.

You feel the gentle breeze on your face. Listen to the birds overhead. Breathe in the fragrance in the air, so crisp and refreshing. Feel every step that you take. As you walk, you come to a meadow, with soft green grass, wildflowers, trees all around it. Notice a shallow, fast stream of water at the edge of the meadow, underneath the trees. Come up to it and find a place to sit comfortably. Take a moment to pay attention to the water as it runs over the rocks on the bottom of the shallow stream.

Listen to the babbling sound of the water. Notice how clean and clear the water is—you can see every grain of sand, every pebble on the bottom. You might even touch the water with your hand, noticing how cool and refreshing it is. And notice how from time to time a leaf falls from a tree, gently floats toward the stream, lands in the water, and is carried away by the current. And another leaf falls from the tree, floats toward the water, and is carried away.

Watch how the leaf slowly descends, twirling slightly toward the water, landing on its surface and floating away, out of sight.

Now pay attention to the thoughts going through your mind right now. Whatever those thoughts are, notice them, pick one, attend to it kindly for a moment, long enough to label the thought as planning, or wishing, or worrying, or predicting, or whatever the thought might be. Now imagine gently taking it out of your mind and placing it on one of those falling leaves, watching it twirl toward the water, land on its surface, and float away, out of sight. Notice another thought, attend to it for a moment with curiosity, label it, place it on a falling leaf, and watch it twirl toward the water and float away, out of sight. There is no need to engage with those thoughts, no need to change them in any way, no need to hold on to them, no need to make them go away. Simply notice a thought, label it, place it on a leaf, and watch it float away.

When you notice your mind engaging with a thought and following it somewhere, acknowledge that, and wherever you find your mind going, gently allow it to return to watching your thoughts, and the leaves, and the stream. Notice a thought, label it, place it on a leaf, and watch it float away, out of sight. You will notice that some thoughts come back, again and again. That is what our thoughts do: they come and go, they come and go. No matter whether you experienced this thought before a moment ago or you haven't seen it in a while, notice it, attend to it for a brief moment with kindness, label it, place it on a leaf, and watch it land on the water and float away. There is no need to engage or argue with the thoughts, no need to change the thoughts, no need to hold on to them or make them go away. Simply attend to the thoughts, coming and going, coming and going.

Notice a thought, label it, place it on a leaf, and watch it float away, out of sight. If you notice yourself judging yourself for having some of those thoughts, or judging the thoughts themselves, notice that, label the judging thought as judgment, place it on a leaf, and watch it twirl toward the stream and float away. Watch thoughts come and go, as they always do. Whatever the thought is, notice it, attend to it with kindness, place it on a leaf, and watch it float away. Now take as much time as you'd like to attend to your thoughts, watching them come and go. Whenever you are ready, open your eyes, and return to the room.

Sample List of Biofeedback Devices

Please keep in mind that technology is constantly evolving. New devices are becoming available all the time. This list is intended to give you an idea of the kinds of devices that are available at the time of the writing of this book. This list is not exhaustive, and I do not endorse any particular device.

Heart Rate Variability Devices

- eVu TPS by Thought Technology: a finger sensor that measures HRV, along with skin conductance and temperature; wirelessly communicates with your mobile device
- iFeel by Somatic Vision: finger sensor that measures HRV and oxygen; wirelessly communicates with your computer or mobile device
- Alive by Somatic Vision: finger sensors that measure HRV and skin conductance; communicates with your computer or mobile device
- MeruHealth app: mobile app designed for comprehensive treatment of depression and anxiety, measures HRV with an external device.
- emWave by Heart Math: finger or ear sensor that measures HRV; can communicate with a PC or a mobile device, depending on the specific sensor
- Unyte: finger sensor that measures HRV; can communicate with a mobile device
- BioForce: chest strap or finger sensor; connects to a mobile device
- Whoop fitness tracker: wrist strap with built-in HRV sensor, connects to a mobile device
- LifeTrak Zoom HRV monitor: wrist strap with built-in HRV sensor, connects to a mobile device
- Biostrap: wrist strap with built-in HRV sensor, connects to a mobile device

- Vitalmonitor: torso strap with built-in HRV sensor, connects to a mobile device
- Polar HRV monitor: torso strap with built-in HRV sensor, connects to a mobile device
- Elite HRV: mobile app that measures HRV using an external heart rate monitor
- HRV4training: mobile app that measures HRV using either an external device or the phone camera
- HeartRate Coherence Pro: mobile app that uses the phone camera to measure HRV
- Camera HRV: mobile app that uses the phone camera to measure HRV

Breath Pacers

Numerous breath-pacing apps are available on iOS and Android mobile devices. I suggest selecting one that allows you to customize not only the breathing rate (which most of them do) but also the duration of inhalation and exhalation (which many do not do). Here are a few suggestions for apps that allow more detailed customization of the breath pacer:

- Breathe, available on both iOS and Android
- Breathe2Relax, available on both iOS and Android
- Paced breathing, available on Android

If you prefer to use your PC, Biofeedback Federation of Europe has a breathing pacer that you can download; look for EZAir at BFE.org

Portable EMG Biofeedback Devices

Below I list a few different biofeedback devices that can provide you with electromyographic (EMG) measurements. I will leave it to you to decide what's best for you.

- Antense antitension device: uses a band around the top of your head to pick up signals from the muscles in your head and face and pro-

vides feedback via sound (a tone that changes depending on your
level of tension)

- MyoTrac portable monitor, by Thought Technology: a one-channel
  EMG device that can be used with any one muscle; provides feedback
  via sound and can be set to sound when tension reaches a certain
  threshold
- MyoTrac Infiniti Dual home trainer, by Thought Technology: similar to
  the MyoTrac portable monitor, except that it has two channels of EMG
  and can monitor two muscle groups
- Resility Muscle Activity Sensor: a one-channel EMG device that connects to a mobile device and provides visual and auditory feedback;
  can be used to monitor or train any one muscle
- Athos and Myontec: two brands of clothing with built-in EMG sensors
  that record data during movement; can later be downloaded to a
  computer or mobile device

Temperature Biofeedback Devices

Temperature biofeedback devices are the easiest to find and the least expensive:

- Alcohol-glass thermometer: a simple inexpensive thermometer with
  a cardboard backing will do just fine. These are often sold in packs of
  several, so you'll have enough to share. Just make sure that the little
  bulb on the end of the thermometer is something that you can hold,
  since that is where the actual temperature sensor is located. These
  thermometers give finger temperature within 2 or 3 degrees, close
  enough for training purposes.
- Digital "stress thermometer": this inexpensive option consists of a
  plastic thermometer body and a long cable with a thermistor (temperature sensor) at the end.
- eVu TPS by Thought Technology: finger sensor that measures temperature, along with skin conductance and HRV; wirelessly communicates with your phone or tablet
- Mindfield eSense temperature sensor: available as an attachment to
  your iOS or Android phone

- Plastic temperature sensors: People often ask me about temperature dots (e.g., Biodots) and those plastic sensor cards that change color depending on your finger temperature. These are OK to use as long as you realize that you are getting a ballpark estimate of your finger temperature, not what your temperature is numerically.

Skin Conductance Devices

Several devices that measure skin conductance are easily accessible and easy to use:

- eVu TPS by Thought Technology: a finger sensor that measures skin conductance, along with temperature and HRV; wirelessly communicates with your phone or tablet
- Pip: a handheld device that wirelessly connects to your phone or tablet
- Alive by Somatic vision: a sensor that measures both HRV and skin conductance; communicates with your PC or mobile device
- Mindfield eSense skin response sensor: an attachment to your Android or iOS phone

Notes

1. Tan, G., Shaffer, F., Lyle, R., & Teo, I. (2016). *Evidence-based practice in biofeedback and neurofeedback*. Association for Aplied Psychophysiology and Biofeedback.
2. Tan, G., Shaffer, F., Lyle, R., & Teo, I. (2016). *Evidence-based practice in biofeedback and neurofeedback*. Association for Aplied Psychophysiology and Biofeedback.
3. Germer, C. (2009). *The mindful path to self-compassion: Freeing yourself from destructive thoughts and emotions*. New York, NY: Guilford Press.
4. Fried, R. (1999). *Breathe well, be well*. New York, NY: Wiley.
5. Litchfield, P. M. (2010). CapnoLearning: Respiratory Fitness and Acid-Base Regulation, *Psychophysiology today*, 7(1), 6–12.
6. Shaffer, F., McCraty, R., & Zerr, C. L. (2014). A healthy heart is not a metronome: An integrative review of the heart's anatomy and heart rate variability. *Frontiers in Psychology, 5,* 1040.
7. Lee, S. T., & Hon, E. H. (1965). The fetal electrocardiogram: IV. Unusual variations in the QRS complex during labor. *American Journal of Obstetrics and Gynecology, 92*(8), 1140–1148.
8. Tsuji, H., Larson, M. G., Venditti, F. J., Manders, E. S., Evans, J. C., Feldman, C. L., & Levy, D. (1996). Impact of reduced heart rate variability on risk for cardiac events: The Framingham Heart Study. *Circulation,* 94(11), 2850–2855.
9. Chalmers, J. A., Quintana, D. S., Abbott, M. J., & Kemp, A. H. (2014). Anxiety disorders are associated with reduced heart rate variability: A meta-analysis. *Frontiers in Psychiatry, 5,* 80.

   Cohen, H., Kotler, M., Matar, M. A., Kaplan, Z., Miodownik, H., & Cassuto, Y. (1997). Power spectral analysis of heart rate variability in posttraumatic stress disorder patients. *Biological Psychiatry, 41*(5), 627–629.

   Dekker, J. M., Crow, R. S., Folsom, A. R., Hannan, P. J., Liao, D., Swenne, C. A., & Schouten, E. G. (2000). Low heart rate variability in a 2-minute rhythm strip predicts risk of coronary heart disease and mortality from several causes: The ARIC study. *Circulation, 102*(11), 1239–1244.

   Garrard, C. S., Seidler, A., McKibben, A., McAlpine, L. E., & Gordon, D. (1992). Spectral analysis of heart rate variability in bronchial asthma. *Clinical Autonomic Research, 2*(2), 105–111.

Kemp, A. H., Quintana, D. S., Gray, M. A., Felmingham, K. L., Brown, K., & Gatt, J. M. (2010). Impact of depression and antidepressant treatment on heart rate variability: A review and meta-analysis. *Biological Psychiatry, 67*(11), 1067–1074.

Lehrer, P., Vaschillo, E., Lu, S. E., Eckberg, D., Vaschillo, B., Scardella, A., & Habib, R. (2006). Heart rate variability biofeedback: Effects of age on heart rate variability, baroreflex gain, and asthma. *Chest, 129*(2), 278–284.

Martínez-Lavín, M., Hermosillo, A. G., Rosas, M., & Soto, M. E. (1998). Circadian studies of autonomic nervous balance in patients with fibromyalgia: A heart rate variability analysis. *Arthritis and Rheumatism, 41*(11), 1966–1971.

Mazurak, N., Seredyuk, N., Sauer, H., Teufel, M., & Enck, P. (2012). Heart rate variability in the irritable bowel syndrome: A review of the literature. *Neurogastroenterology and Motility, 24*(3), 206–216.

Singh, J. P., Larson, M. G., Tsuji, H., Evans, J. C., O'Donnell, C. J., & Levy, D. (1998). Reduced heart rate variability and new-onset hypertension: Insights into pathogenesis of hypertension: The Framingham Heart Study. *Hypertension, 32*(2), 293–297.

Thayer, J. F., Yamamoto, S. S., & Brosschot, J. F. (2010). The relationship of autonomic imbalance, heart rate variability and cardiovascular disease risk factors. *International Journal of Cardiology, 141*(2), 122–131.

Tracy, L. M., Ioannou, L., Baker, K. S., Gibson, S. J., Georgiou-Karistianis, N., & Giummarra, M. J. (2016). Meta-analytic evidence for decreased heart rate variability in chronic pain implicating parasympathetic nervous system dysregulation. *Pain, 157*(1), 7–29.

10. Williams, D. P., Cash, C., Rankin, C., Bernardi, A., Koenig, J., & Thayer, J. F. (2015). Resting heart rate variability predicts self-reported difficulties in emotion regulation: A focus on different facets of emotion regulation. *Frontiers in Psychology, 6*, 261.

11. Holzman, J. B., & Bridgett, D. J. (2017). Heart rate variability indices as bio-markers of top-down self-regulatory mechanisms: A meta-analytic review. *Neuroscience and Biobehavioral Reviews, 74*, 233–255.

12. Lane, R. D., McRae, K., Reiman, E. M., Chen, K., Ahern, G. L., & Thayer, J. F. (2009). Neural correlates of heart rate variability during emotion. *Neuroimage, 44*(1), 213–222.

13. Sakaki, M., Yoo, H. J., Nga, L., Lee, T. H., Thayer, J. F., & Mather, M. (2016). Heart rate variability is associated with amygdala functional connectivity with MPFC across younger and older adults. *Neuroimage, 139*, 44–52.

14. Thayer, J. F., & Lane, R. D. (2000). A model of neurovisceral integration in emotion regulation and dysregulation. *Journal of Affective Disorders, 61*(3), 201–216.

15. Thayer, J. F., Åhs, F., Fredrikson, M., Sollers, J. J., III, & Wager, T. D. (2012). A meta-analysis of heart rate variability and neuroimaging studies: Implications for heart rate variability as a marker of stress and health. *Neuroscience and Biobehavioral Reviews, 36*(2), 747–756.

16. Gillie, B. L., Vasey, M. W., & Thayer, J. F. (2014). Heart rate variability predicts control over memory retrieval. *Psychological Science, 25*(2), 458–465.

Hansen, A. L., Johnsen, B. H., Sollers, J. J., Stenvik, K., & Thayer, J. F. (2004).

Heart rate variability and its relation to prefrontal cognitive function: The effects of training and detraining. *European Journal of Applied Physiology, 93*(3), 263–272.

Hansen, A. L., Johnsen, B. H., & Thayer, J. F. (2003). Vagal influence on working memory and attention. *International Journal of Psychophysiology, 48*(3), 263–274.

Thayer, J. F., Hansen, A. L., Saus-Rose, E., & Johnsen, B. H. (2009). Heart rate variability, prefrontal neural function, and cognitive performance: The neurovisceral integration perspective on self-regulation, adaptation, and health. *Annals of Behavioral Medicine, 37*(2), 141–153.

17. Caldwell, Y. T., & Steffen, P. R. (2018). Adding HRV biofeedback to psychotherapy increases heart rate variability and improves the treatment of major depressive disorder. *International Journal of Psychophysiology, 131,* 96–101.

Del Pozo, J. M., Gevirtz, R. N., Scher, B., & Guarneri, E. (2004). Biofeedback treatment increases heart rate variability in patients with known coronary artery disease. *American Heart Journal, 147*(3), 545.

Giardino, N. D., Chan, L., & Borson, S. (2004). Combined heart rate variability and pulse oximetry biofeedback for chronic obstructive pulmonary disease: Preliminary findings. *Applied Psychophysiology and Biofeedback, 29*(2), 121–133.

Goessl, V. C., Curtiss, J. E., & Hofmann, S. G. (2017). The effect of heart rate variability biofeedback training on stress and anxiety: A meta-analysis. *Psychological Medicine, 47*(15), 2578–2586.

Lehrer, P. M., Vaschillo, E., Vaschillo, B., Lu, S. E., Scardella, A., Siddique, M., & Habib, R. H. (2004). Biofeedback treatment for asthma. *Chest, 126*(2), 352–361.

Lin, G., Xiang, Q., Fu, X., Wang, S., Wang, S., Chen, S., . . . & Wang, T. (2012). Heart rate variability biofeedback decreases blood pressure in prehypertensive subjects by improving autonomic function and baroreflex. *Journal of Alternative and Complementary Medicine, 18*(2), 143–152.

Sielski, R., Rief, W., & Glombiewski, J. A. (2017). Efficacy of biofeedback in chronic back pain: A meta-analysis. *International Journal of Behavioral Medicine, 24*(1), 25–41.

Siepmann, M., Hennig, U. D., Siepmann, T., Nitzsche, K., Mück-Weymann, M., Petrowski, K., & Weidner, K. (2014). The effects of heart rate variability biofeedback in patients with preterm labour. *Applied Psychophysiology and Biofeedback, 39*(1), 27–35.

Sowder, E., Gevirtz, R., Shapiro, W., & Ebert, C. (2010). Restoration of vagal tone: A possible mechanism for functional abdominal pain. *Applied Psychophysiology and Biofeedback, 35*(3), 199–206.

Stern, M. J., Guiles, R. A., & Gevirtz, R. (2014). HRV biofeedback for pediatric irritable bowel syndrome and functional abdominal pain: A clinical replication series. *Applied Psychophysiology and Biofeedback, 39*(3–4), 287–291.

Tan, G., Dao, T. K., Farmer, L., Sutherland, R. J., & Gevirtz, R. (2011). Heart rate variability (HRV) and posttraumatic stress disorder (PTSD): A pilot study. *Applied Psychophysiology and Biofeedback, 36*(1), 27–35.

18. Holden, J. (2006). *Effects of heart-rate variability biofeedback training and emotional reg-*

ulation on music performance anxiety in university students. Ph.D. diss., University of North Texas, Dentin.

Gruzelier, J. H., Thompson, T., Redding, E., Brandt, R., & Steffert, T. (2014). Application of alpha/theta neurofeedback and heart rate variability training to young contemporary dancers: State anxiety and creativity. *International Journal of Psychophysiology, 93*(1), 105–111.

Kiviniemi, A. M., Hautala, A. J., Kinnunen, H., & Tulppo, M. P. (2007). Endurance training guided individually by daily heart rate variability measurements. *European Journal of Applied Physiology, 101*(6), 743–751.

Morgan, S. J., & Mora, J. A. M. (2017). Effect of heart rate variability biofeedback on sport performance, a systematic review. *Applied Psychophysiology and Biofeedback, 42*(3), 235–245.

Paul, M., & Garg, K. (2012). The effect of heart rate variability biofeedback on performance psychology of basketball players. *Applied Psychophysiology and Biofeedback, 37*(2), 131–144.

Perry, F. D. (2018). *Examining the effects of a mindfulness-based biofeedback intervention on self-regulation and sport performance in soccer athletes.* Ph.D. diss., Boston University.

Prinsloo, G. E., Rauch, H. L., & Derman, W. E. (2014). A brief review and clinical application of heart rate variability biofeedback in sports, exercise, and rehabilitation medicine. *Physician and Sportsmedicine, 42*(2), 88–99.

Pusenjak, N., Grad, A., Tusak, M., Leskovsek, M., & Schwarzlin, R. (2015). Can biofeedback training of psychophysiological responses enhance athletes' sport performance? A practitioner's perspective. *Physician and Sportsmedicine, 43*(3), 287–299.

Wells, R., Outhred, T., Heathers, J. A., Quintana, D. S., & Kemp, A. H. (2012). Matter over mind: A randomised-controlled trial of single-session biofeedback training on performance anxiety and heart rate variability in musicians. *PLOS One, 7*(10), e46597.

19. Shaffer, F., & Ginsberg, J. P. (2017). An overview of heart rate variability metrics and norms. *Frontiers in Public Health, 5,* 258. doi: 10.3389/fpubh.2017.00258; https://www.frontiersin.org/articles/10.3389/fpubh.2017.00258/full.

20. Lehrer, P. M., Vaschillo, E., & Vaschillo, B. (2000). Resonant frequency biofeedback training to increase cardiac variability: Rationale and manual for training. *Applied Psychophysiology and Biofeedback, 25*(3), 177–191.

21. Steffen, P. R., Austin, T., DeBarros, A., & Brown, T. (2017). The impact of resonance frequency breathing on measures of heart rate variability, blood pressure, and mood. *Frontiers in Public Health, 5,* 222.

22. Whatmore, G. B., & Kohli, D. R. (1968). Dysponesis: A neurophysiology factor in functional disorders. *Behavioral Science, 13*(2), 102–124.

23. McNulty, W. H., Gevirtz, R. N., Hubbard, D. R., & Berkoff, G. M. (1994). Needle electromyographic evaluation of trigger point response to a psychological stressor. *Psychophysiology, 31*(3), 313–316.

24. Hubbard, D. (1996). Chronic and recurrent muscle pain: Pathophysiology and treatment, a review of pharmocologic studies. *Journal of Musculoskeletal Pain, 4,* 123–143.

25. Gevirtz, R. (2006). The muscle spindle trigger point model of chronic pain. *Biofeedback, 34*(2), 53.

26. Peper, E. & Gibney Amersfort, K. H. (2007). *Muscle biofeedback at the computer: A manual to prevent repetitive strain injury (RSI) by taking the guesswork out of assessment, monitoring, and training.* Amersfoort, The Netherlands:Biofeedback Federation of Europe.

27. Hölzel, B. K., Carmody, J., Evans, K. C., Hoge, E. A., Dusek, J. A., Morgan, L., . . . & Lazar, S. W. (2009). Stress reduction correlates with structural changes in the amygdala. *Social Cognitive and Affective Neuroscience, 5*(1), 11–17.

    Hölzel, B. K., Hoge, E. A., Greve, D. N., Gard, T., Creswell, J. D., Brown, K. W., . . . & Lazar, S. W. (2013). Neural mechanisms of symptom improvements in generalized anxiety disorder following mindfulness training. *Neuroimage: Clinical, 2,* 448–458.

    Hölzel, B. K., Carmody, J., Vangel, M., Congleton, C., Yerramsetti, S. M., Gard, T., & Lazar, S. W. (2011). Mindfulness practice leads to increases in regional brain gray matter density. *Psychiatry Research: Neuroimaging, 191*(1), 36–43.

28. Goyal, M., Singh, S., Sibinga, E. M., Gould, N. F., Rowland-Seymour, A., Sharma, R., . . . & Ranasinghe, P. D. (2014). Meditation programs for psychological stress and well-being: A systematic review and meta-analysis. *JAMA Internal Medicine, 174*(3), 357–368.

    Hofmann, S. G., Sawyer, A. T., Witt, A. A., & Oh, D. (2010). The effect of mindfulness-based therapy on anxiety and depression: A meta-analytic review. *Journal of Consulting and Clinical Psychology, 78*(2), 169.

29. Gotink, R. A., Meijboom, R., Vernooij, M. W., Smits, M., & Hunink, M. M. (2016). Eight-week mindfulness based stress reduction induces brain changes similar to traditional long-term meditation practice—a systematic review. *Brain and Cognition, 108,* 32–41.

30. Lazar, S. W., Kerr, C. E., Wasserman, R. H., Gray, J. R., Greve, D. N., Treadway, M. T., . . . & Rauch, S. L. (2005). Meditation experience is associated with increased cortical thickness. *Neuroreport, 16*(17), 1893.

31. Gard, T., Hölzel, B. K., & Lazar, S. W. (2014). The potential effects of meditation on age-related cognitive decline: A systematic review. *Annals of the New York Academy of Sciences, 1307*(1), 89–103.

32. De Vibe, M. F., Bjørndal, A., Fattah, S., Dyrdal, G. M., Halland, E., & Tanner-Smith, E. E. (2017). Mindfulness-based stress reduction (MBSR) for improving health, quality of life and social functioning in adults: A systematic review and meta-analysis. *Campbell Systematic Reviews, 13*(11).

    Goyal, M., Singh, S., Sibinga, E. M., Gould, N. F., Rowland-Seymour, A., Sharma, R., . . . & Ranasinghe, P. D. (2014). Meditation programs for psychological stress and well-being: A systematic review and meta-analysis. *JAMA Internal Medicine, 174*(3), 357–368.

Khoury, B., Sharma, M., Rush, S. E., & Fournier, C. (2015). Mindfulness-based stress reduction for healthy individuals: A meta-analysis. *Journal of Psychosomatic Research, 78*(6), 519–528.

Olson, K. L., & Emery, C. F. (2015). Mindfulness and weight loss: A systematic review. *Psychosomatic Medicine, 77*(1), 59–67.

Pascoe, M. C., Thompson, D. R., Jenkins, Z. M., & Ski, C. F. (2017). Mindfulness mediates the physiological markers of stress: Systematic review and meta-analysis. *Journal of Psychiatric Research, 95*, 156–178.

Winbush, N. Y., Gross, C. R., & Kreitzer, M. J. (2007). The effects of mindfulness-based stress reduction on sleep disturbance: A systematic review. *EXPLORE: The Journal of Science and Healing, 3*(6), 585–591.

33. Carlson, L. E., Speca, M., Faris, P., & Patel, K. D. (2007). One year pre-post intervention follow-up of psychological, immune, endocrine and blood pressure outcomes of mindfulness-based stress reduction (MBSR) in breast and prostate cancer outpatients. *Brain, Behavior, and Immunity, 21*(8), 1038–1049.

34. Sevinc, G., Hölzel, B. K., Hashmi, J., Greenberg, J., McCallister, A., Treadway, M., . . . & Lazar, S. W. (2018). Common and dissociable neural activity after mindfulness-based stress reduction and relaxation response programs. *Psychosomatic Medicine, 80*(5), 439.

35. Killingsworth, M. A., & Gilbert, D. T. (2010). A wandering mind is an unhappy mind. *Science, 330*(6006), 932–932.

36. Raichle, M. E., MacLeod, A. M., Snyder, A. Z., Powers, W. J., Gusnard, D. A., & Shulman, G. L. (2001). A default mode of brain function. *Proceedings of the National Academy of Sciences of the U.S.A., 98*(2), 676–682.

37. Germer, C. (2009). *The mindful path to self-compassion: Freeing yourself from destructive thoughts and emotions*. New York, NY: Guilford Press.

38. Lindahl, J. R., Fisher, N. E., Cooper, D. J., Rosen, R. K., & Britton, W. B. (2017). The varieties of contemplative experience: A mixed-methods study of meditation-related challenges in Western Buddhists. *PLOS One, 12*(5), e0176239.

39. Leotti, L. A., Iyengar, S. S., & Ochsner, K. N. (2010). Born to choose: The origins and value of the need for control. *Trends in Cognitive Sciences, 14*(10), 457–463.

40. Leotti, L. A., Iyengar, S. S., & Ochsner, K. N. (2010). Born to choose: The origins and value of the need for control. *Trends in Cognitive Sciences, 14*(10), 457–463.

41. Langer, E. J. (1975). The illusion of control. *Journal of Personality and Social Psychology, 32*(2), 311.

42. Whitson, J. A., & Galinsky, A. D. (2008). Lacking control increases illusory pattern perception. *Science, 322*(5898), 115–117.

43. Wegner, D. M., Schneider, D. J., Carter, S. R., & White, T. L. (1987). Paradoxical effects of thought suppression. *Journal of Personality and Social Psychology, 53*(1), 5.

44. Clark, D. M., Ball, S., & Pape, D. (1991). An experimental investigation of thought suppression. *Behaviour Research and Therapy, 29*(3), 253–257.

Lavy, E. H., & Van den Hout, M. A. (1990). Thought suppression induces intrusions. *Behavioural and Cognitive Psychotherapy, 18*(4), 251–258.

45. Cioffi, D., & Holloway, J. (1993). Delayed costs of suppressed pain. *Journal of Personality and Social Psychology, 64*(2), 274.

46. Baumeister, R. F., Vohs, K. D., & Tice, D. M. (2007). The strength model of self-control. *Current Directions in Psychological Science, 16*(6), 351–355.

47. Baumeister, R. F., Bratslavsky, E., & Muraven, M., and Tice, D. M.(1998). Ego depletion: Is the active self a limited resource? *Journal of Personality and Social Psychology, 74*(5), 1252-1

48. Visted, E., Sørensen, L., Osnes, B., Svendsen, J. L., Binder, P. E., & Schanche, E. (2017). The association between self-reported difficulties in emotion regulation and heart rate variability: The salient role of not accepting negative emotions. *Frontiers in Psychology, 8*, 328.

49. Tuck, N. L., Adams, K. S., & Consedine, N. S. (2017). Does the ability to express different emotions predict different indices of physical health? A skill-based study of physical symptoms and heart rate variability. *British Journal of Health Psychology, 22*(3), 502–523.

50. Gailliot, M. T., Baumeister, R. F., DeWall, C. N., Maner, J. K., Plant, E. A., Tice, D. M., . . . & Schmeichel, B. J. (2007). Self-control relies on glucose as a limited energy source: Willpower is more than a metaphor. *Journal of Personality and Social Psychology, 92*(2), 325.

    Tuck, N. L., Grant, R. C., Sollers, J. J., III, Booth, R. J., & Consedine, N. S. (2016). Higher resting heart rate variability predicts skill in expressing some emotions. *Psychophysiology, 53*(12), 1852–1857.

51. Quintana, D. S., Guastella, A. J., Outhred, T., Hickie, I. B., & Kemp, A. H. (2012). Heart rate variability is associated with emotion recognition: Direct evidence for a relationship between the autonomic nervous system and social cognition. *International Journal of Psychophysiology, 86*(2), 168–172.

52. Lieberman, M. D., Eisenberger, N. I., Crockett, M. J., Tom, S. M., Pfeifer, J. H., & Way, B. M. (2007). Putting feelings into words. *Psychological Science, 18*(5), 421–428.

53. Lieberman, M. D., Inagaki, T. K., Tabibnia, G., & Crockett, M. J. (2011). Subjective responses to emotional stimuli during labeling, reappraisal, and distraction. *Emotion, 11*(3), 468.

54. Kircanski, K., Lieberman, M. D., & Craske, M. G. (2012). Feelings into words: Contributions of language to exposure therapy. *Psychological Science, 23*(10), 1086–1091.

55. Creswell, J. D., Way, B. M., Eisenberger, N. I., & Lieberman, M. D. (2007). Neural correlates of dispositional mindfulness during affect labeling. *Psychosomatic Medicine, 69*(6), 560–565.

56. Frankle, V (2006). *A man's search for meaning.* Boston, MA: Beacon Press.

57. Schmeichel, B. J., & Vohs, K. (2009). Self-affirmation and self-control: Affirming core values counteracts ego depletion. *Journal of Personality and Social Psychology, 96*(4), 770.

58. Gilbert, P. (2017). Compassion: Definitions and Controversies. In: P. Gilbert (Ed). *Compassion: Concepts, Research and Applications.* (p. 3–15). London: Routledge.59. Breines, J. G., Thoma, M. V., Gianferante, D., Hanlin, L., Chen, X., & Rohleder, N.

(2014). Self-compassion as a predictor of interleukin-6 response to acute psychosocial stress. *Brain, Behavior, and Immunity, 37,* 109–114.

Homan, K. J., & Sirois, F. M. (2017). Self-compassion and physical health: Exploring the roles of perceived stress and health-promoting behaviors. *Health Psychology Open, 4*(2), 2055102917729542.

MacBeth, A., & Gumley, A. (2012). Exploring compassion: A meta-analysis of the association between self-compassion and psychopathology. *Clinical Psychology Review, 32*(6), 545–552.

Van Dam, N. T., Sheppard, S. C., Forsyth, J. P., & Earleywine, M. (2011). Self-compassion is a better predictor than mindfulness of symptom severity and quality of life in mixed anxiety and depression. *Journal of Anxiety Disorders, 25*(1), 123–130.

60. Homan, K. J., & Sirois, F. M. (2017). Self-compassion and physical health: Exploring the roles of perceived stress and health-promoting behaviors. *Health Psychology Open, 4*(2), 2055102917729542.

61. Kirby, J. N., Tellegen, C. L., & Steindl, S. R. (2017). A meta-analysis of compassion-based interventions: Current state of knowledge and future directions. *Behavior Therapy, 48*(6), 778–792.

62. Germer, C. (2009). *The mindful path to self-compassion: Freeing yourself from destructive thoughts and emotions.* New York, NY: Guilford Press.

63. Germer C. (2018) Mindfulness and Compassion: Meeting Challenges, Staying Safe. Talk presented at Meditation and Psychotherapy Conference, Boston, MA.

64. Atkinson, D. M., Rodman, J. L., Thuras, P. D., Shiroma, P. R., & Lim, K. O. (2017). Examining burnout, depression, and self-compassion in Veterans Affairs mental health staff. *Journal of Alternative and Complementary Medicine, 23*(7), 551–557.

Neff, K. D. & Beretvas, S. N. (2013). The role of self-compassion in romantic relationships. *Self and Identity, 12*(1), 78–98.

Raab, K. (2014). Mindfulness, self-compassion, and empathy among health care professionals: A review of the literature. *Journal of Health Care Chaplaincy, 20*(3), 95–108.

Tandler, N., & Petersen, L. E. (2018). Are self-compassionate partners less jealous? Exploring the mediation effects of anger rumination and willingness to forgive on the association between self-compassion and romantic jealousy. *Current Psychology,* 1–11. doi: 10.1007/s12144-018-9797-7.

65. Friis, A. M., Johnson, M. H., Cutfield, R. G., & Consedine, N. S. (2015). Does kindness matter? Self-compassion buffers the negative impact of diabetes-distress on HbA1c. *Diabetic Medicine, 32*(12), 1634–1640.

Friis, A. M., Johnson, M. H., Cutfield, R. G., & Consedine, N. S. (2016). Kindness matters: A randomized controlled trial of a mindful self-compassion intervention improves depression, distress, and HbA1c among patients with diabetes. *Diabetes Care, 31*(11), 1963–1971. dc160416.

66. Homan, K. J., & Sirois, F. M. (2017). Self-compassion and physical health: Exploring the roles of perceived stress and health-promoting behaviors. *Health Psychology Open, 4*(2), 2055102917729542.

67. Ferreira, C., Pinto-Gouveia, J., & Duarte, C. (2013). Self-compassion in the face of shame and body image dissatisfaction: Implications for eating disorders. *Eating Behaviors, 14*(2), 207–210.

Neff, K. D., Kirkpatrick, K. L., & Rude, S. S. (2007). Self-compassion and adaptive psychological functioning. *Journal of Research in Personality, 41*(1), 139–154.

Van Dam, N. T., Sheppard, S. C., Forsyth, J. P., & Earleywine, M. (2011). Self-compassion is a better predictor than mindfulness of symptom severity and quality of life in mixed anxiety and depression. *Journal of Anxiety Disorders, 25*(1), 123–130.

68. Neff, K. D., Rude, S. S., & Kirkpatrick, K. L. (2007). An examination of self-compassion in relation to positive psychological functioning and personality traits. *Journal of Research in Personality, 41*(4), 908–916.

69. Biber, D. D., & Ellis, R. (2017). The effect of self-compassion on the self-regulation of health behaviors: A systematic review. *Journal of Health Psychology*, 1359105317713361.

Breines, J. G., Thoma, M. V., Gianferante, D., Hanlin, L., Chen, X., & Rohleder, N. (2014). Self-compassion as a predictor of interleukin-6 response to acute psychosocial stress. *Brain, Behavior, and Immunity, 37*, 109–114.

Homan, K. J., & Sirois, F. M. (2017). Self-compassion and physical health: Exploring the roles of perceived stress and health-promoting behaviors. *Health Psychology Open, 4*(2). doi: 10.1177/2055102917729542.

70. Kirby, J. N., Doty, J. R., Petrocchi, N., & Gilbert, P. (2017). The current and future role of heart rate variability for assessing and training compassion. *Frontiers in Public Health, 5*, 40.

71. Eisenberg, N., Fabes, R. A., Miller, P. A., Fultz, J., Shell, R., Mathy, R. M., & Reno, R. R. (1989). Relation of sympathy and personal distress to prosocial behavior: A multimethod study. *Journal of Personality and Social Psychology, 57*(1), 55.

72. Kemp, A. H., Quintana, D. S., Kuhnert, R. L., Griffiths, K., Hickie, I. B., & Guastella, A. J. (2012). Oxytocin increases heart rate variability in humans at rest: Implications for social approach-related motivation and capacity for social engagement. *PLOS One, 7*(8), e44014.

73. Chang, C., Metzger, C. D., Glover, G. H., Duyn, J. H., Heinze, H. J., & Walter, M. (2013). Association between heart rate variability and fluctuations in resting-state functional connectivity. *Neuroimage, 68*, 93–104.

74. Luo, X., Qiao, L., & Che, X. (2018). Self-compassion modulates heart rate variability and negative affect to experimentally induced stress. *Mindfulness,9* (5), 1522-1528 1–7.

75. Svendsen, J. L., Osnes, B., Binder, P. E., Dundas, I., Visted, E., Nordby, H., . . . & Sørensen, L. (2016). Trait self-compassion reflects emotional flexibility through an association with high vagally mediated heart rate variability. *Mindfulness, 7*(5), 1103–1113.

76. Salzberg, S. (2004). *Lovingkindness: The revolutionary art of happiness*. Boston: Shambhala Publications.

77. Germer, C. (2009). *The mindful path to self-compassion: Freeing yourself from destructive thoughts and emotions*. New York, NY: Guilford Press.

78. Singer, T., & Klimecki, O. M. (2014). Empathy and compassion. *Current Biology*, 24(18), R875–R878.

79. Singer, T., & Klimecki, O. M. (2014). Empathy and compassion. *Current Biology*, 24(18), R875–R878

80. Klimecki, O., & Singer, T. (2011). Empathic distress fatigue rather than compassion fatigue? Integrating findings from empathy research in psychology and social neuroscience. In Oakley, B., Knafo, A., Madhavan, G., & Wilson, D. S. (Eds.). *Pathological altruism*. Oxford University Press.

81. Klimecki, O., & Singer, T. (2012). Empathic distress fatigue rather than compassion fatigue? Integrating findings from empathy research in psychology and social neuroscience. In Oakley, B., Knafo, A., Madhavan, G., & Wilson, D. S. (Eds.). *Pathological altruism*. Oxford University Press. *Pathological Altruism*.

82. Klimecki, O. M., Leiberg, S., Ricard, M., & Singer, T. (2013). Differential pattern of functional brain plasticity after compassion and empathy training. *Social Cognitive and Affective Neuroscience*, 9(6), 873–879.

83. Aidman, E., Jackson, S. A., & Kleitman, S. (2018). Effects of sleep deprivation on executive functioning, cognitive abilities, metacognitive confidence, and decision making. *Applied Cognitive Psychology*, 2018, 1–13. doi: 10.1002/acp.3463.

84. Venkatraman, V., Chuah, Y. L., Huettel, S. A., & Chee, M. W. (2007). Sleep deprivation elevates expectation of gains and attenuates response to losses following risky decisions. *Sleep*, 30(5), 603–609.

85. Minkel, J. D., Banks, S., Htaik, O., Moreta, M. C., Jones, C. W., McGlinchey, E. L., . . . & Dinges, D. F. (2012). Sleep deprivation and stressors: Evidence for elevated negative affect in response to mild stressors when sleep deprived. *Emotion*, 12(5), 1015.

86. Yoo, S. S., Gujar, N., Hu, P., Jolesz, F. A., & Walker, M. P. (2007). The human emotional brain without sleep—a prefrontal amygdala disconnect. *Current Biology*, 17(20), R877–R878.

87. West, K. E., Jablonski, M. R., Warfield, B., Cecil, K. S., James, M., Ayers, M. A., . . . & Hanifin, J. P. (2010). Blue light from light-emitting diodes elicits a dose-dependent suppression of melatonin in humans. *Journal of Applied Physiology*, 110(3), 619–626.

88. Ding, M., Satija, A., Bhupathiraju, S. N., Hu, Y., Sun, Q., Han, J., . . . & Hu, F. B. (2015). Association of coffee consumption with total and cause-specific mortality in three large prospective cohorts. *Circulation*, 132, 2305–2315.

89. Cano-Marquina, A., Tarín, J. J., & Cano, A. (2013). The impact of coffee on health. *Maturitas*, 75(1), 7–21.

　　Nkondjock, A. (2009). Coffee consumption and the risk of cancer: An overview. *Cancer Letters*, 277(2), 121–125.

　　van Dam, R. M. (2008). Coffee consumption and risk of type 2 diabetes, cardiovascular diseases, and cancer. *Applied Physiology, Nutrition, and Metabolism*, 33(6), 1269–1283.

90. *Consumer Reports*. (2015). Sleeping pills for insomnia: They may not be the best treatment option.

91. Farina, B., Dittoni, S., Colicchio, S., Testani, E., Losurdo, A., Gnoni, V., . . . & Della Marca, G. (2014). Heart rate and heart rate variability modification in chronic insomnia patients. *Behavioral Sleep Medicine, 12*(4), 290–306.

92. Zucker, T. L., Samuelson, K. W., Muench, F., Greenberg, M. A., & Gevirtz, R. N. (2009). The effects of respiratory sinus arrhythmia biofeedback on heart rate variability and posttraumatic stress disorder symptoms: A pilot study. *Applied Psychophysiology and Biofeedback, 34*(2), 135.

93. Brooks, A. W. (2014). Get excited: Reappraising pre-performance anxiety as excitement. *Journal of Experimental Psychology: General, 143*(3), 1144.

94. Brooks, A. W. (2014). Get excited: Reappraising pre-performance anxiety as excitement. *Journal of Experimental Psychology: General, 143*(3), 1144.

95. Blascovich, J., Seery, M. D., Mugridge, C. A., Norris, R. K., & Weisbuch, M. (2004). Predicting athletic performance from cardiovascular indexes of challenge and threat. *Journal of Experimental Social Psychology, 40*(5), 683–688.

    Tomaka, J., Blascovich, J., Kelsey, R. M., & Leitten, C. L. (1993). Subjective, physiological, and behavioral effects of threat and challenge appraisal. *Journal of Personality and Social Psychology, 65*(2), 248.

96. Jamieson, J. P., Nock, M. K., & Mendes, W. B. (2012). Mind over matter: Reappraising arousal improves cardiovascular and cognitive responses to stress. *Journal of Experimental Psychology: General, 141*(3), 417.

97. Jamieson, J. P., Mendes, W. B., Blackstock, E., & Schmader, T. (2010). Turning the knots in your stomach into bows: Reappraising arousal improves performance on the GRE. *Journal of Experimental Social Psychology, 46*(1), 208–212.

98. Morgan, C. A., III, Rasmusson, A., Pietrzak, R. H., Coric, V., & Southwick, S. M. (2009). Relationships among plasma dehydroepiandrosterone and dehydroepiandrosterone sulfate, cortisol, symptoms of dissociation, and objective performance in humans exposed to underwater navigation stress. *Biological Psychiatry, 66*(4), 334–340.

99. Schachter, S., & Singer, J. (1962). Cognitive, social, and physiological determinants of emotional state. *Psychological Review, 69*(5), 379.

100. Park, J., & Baumeister, R. F. (2017). Meaning in life and adjustment to daily stressors. *Journal of Positive Psychology, 12*(4), 333–341.

101. Hsee, C. K., Yang, A. X., & Wang, L. (2010). Idleness aversion and the need for justifiable busyness. *Psychological Science, 21*(7), 926–930.

102. Britton, A., & Shipley, M. J. (2010). Bored to death? *International Journal of Epidemiology, 39*(2), 370–371.

103. Boyle, P. A., Buchman, A. S., Barnes, L. L., & Bennett, D. A. (2010). Effect of a purpose in life on risk of incident Alzheimer disease and mild cognitive impairment in community-dwelling older persons. *Archives of General Psychiatry, 67*(3), 304–310.

    Cohen, R., Bavishi, C., & Rozanski, A. (2016). Purpose in life and its relationship to all-cause mortality and cardiovascular events: A meta-analysis. *Psychosomatic Medicine, 78*(2), 122–133.

104. Doğru, M. T., Başar, M. M., Yuvanç, E., Simşek, V., & Sahin, O. (2010). The relation-

ship between serum sex steroid levels and heart rate variability parameters in males and the effect of age. *Turk Kardiyol Dern Ars, 38*(7), 459–465.

    Rydlewska, A., Maj, J., Katkowski, B., Biel, B., Ponikowska, B., Banasiak, W., . . . & Jankowska, E. A. (2013). Circulating testosterone and estradiol, autonomic balance and baroreflex sensitivity in middle-aged and elderly men with heart failure. *Aging Male, 16*(2), 58–66.

105. McCraty, R., Barrios-Choplin, B., Rozman, D., Atkinson, M., & Watkins, A. D. (1998). The impact of a new emotional self-management program on stress, emotions, heart rate variability, DHEA and cortisol. *Integrative Physiological and Behavioral Science, 33*(2), 151–170.

106. Chalmers, J. A., Quintana, D. S., Abbott, M. J., & Kemp, A. H. (2014). Anxiety disorders are associated with reduced heart rate variability: A meta-analysis. *Frontiers in Psychiatry, 5*, 80.

107. Chalmers, J. A., Heathers, J. A., Abbott, M. J., Kemp, A. H., & Quintana, D. S. (2016). Worry is associated with robust reductions in heart rate variability: A transdiagnostic study of anxiety psychopathology. *BMC Psychology, 4*(1), 32.

108. Kemp, A. H., Fráguas, R., Brunoni, A. R., Bittencourt, M. S., Nunes, M. A., Dantas, E. M., . . . & Thayer, J. F. (2016). Differential associations of specific selective serotonin reuptake inhibitors with resting-state heart rate and heart rate variability: Implications for health and well-being. *Psychosomatic Medicine, 78*(7), 810–818.

    Kemp, A. H., Quintana, D. S., Gray, M. A., Felmingham, K. L., Brown, K., & Gatt, J. M. (2010). Impact of depression and antidepressant treatment on heart rate variability: A review and meta-analysis. *Biological Psychiatry, 67*(11), 1067–1074.

109. Goessl, V. C., Curtiss, J. E., & Hofmann, S. G. (2017). The effect of heart rate variability biofeedback training on stress and anxiety: A meta-analysis. *Psychological Medicine, 47*(15), 2578–2586.

110. Grassi, M., Caldirola, D., Vanni, G., Guerriero, G., Piccinni, M., Valchera, A., & Perna, G. (2013). Baseline respiratory parameters in panic disorder: A meta-analysis. *Journal of Affective Disorders, 146*(2), 158–173.

111. Davies, C. D., & Craske, M. G. (2014). Low baseline pCO_2 predicts poorer outcome from behavioral treatment: Evidence from a mixed anxiety disorders sample. *Psychiatry Research, 219*(2), 311–315.

112. Tolin, D. F., Billingsley, A. L., Hallion, L. S., & Diefenbach, G. J. (2017). Low pretreatment end-tidal CO_2 predicts dropout from cognitive-behavioral therapy for anxiety and related disorders. *Behaviour Research and Therapy, 90*, 32–40.

113. Meuret, A. E., Simon, E., Bhaskara, L., & Ritz, T. (2017). Ultra-brief behavioral skills trainings for blood injection injury phobia. *Depression and Anxiety, 34*(12), 1096–1105.

    Meuret, A. E., Wilhelm, F. H., Ritz, T., & Roth, W. T. (2008). Feedback of end-tidal pCO_2 as a therapeutic approach for panic disorder. *Journal of Psychiatric Research, 42*(7), 560–568.

    Meuret, A. E., Wilhelm, F. H., & Roth, W. T. (2004). Respiratory feedback for treating panic disorder. *Journal of Clinical Psychology, 60*(2), 197–207.

114. Tolin, D. F., McGrath, P. B., Hale, L. R., Weiner, D. N., & Gueorguieva, R. (2017). A multisite benchmarking trial of capnometry guided respiratory intervention for panic disorder in naturalistic treatment settings. *Applied Psychophysiology and Biofeedback*, *42*(1), 51–58.

115. Mochcovitch, M. D., da Rocha Freire, R. C., Garcia, R. F., & Nardi, A. E. (2014). A systematic review of fMRI studies in generalized anxiety disorder: Evaluating its neural and cognitive basis. *Journal of Affective Disorders*, *167*, 336–342.

116. Nitschke, J. B., Sarinopoulos, I., Oathes, D. J., Johnstone, T., Whalen, P. J., Davidson, R. J., & Kalin, N. H. (2009). Anticipatory activation in the amygdala and anterior cingulate in generalized anxiety disorder and prediction of treatment response. *American Journal of Psychiatry*, *166*(3), 302–310.

117. Etkin, A., Egner, T., Peraza, D. M., Kandel, E. R., & Hirsch, J. (2006). Resolving emotional conflict: A role for the rostral anterior cingulate cortex in modulating activity in the amygdala. *Neuron*, *51*(6), 871–882.

118. Etkin, A., Prater, K. E., Hoeft, F., Menon, V., & Schatzberg, A. F. (2010). Failure of anterior cingulate activation and connectivity with the amygdala during implicit regulation of emotional processing in generalized anxiety disorder. *American Journal of Psychiatry*, *167*(5), 545–554.

119. Zidda, F., Andoh, J., Pohlack, S., Winkelmann, T., Dinu-Biringer, R., Cavalli, J., . . . & Flor, H. (2018). Default mode network connectivity of fear-and anxiety-related cue and context conditioning. *Neuroimage*, *165*, 190–199.

120. Hölzel, B. K., Hoge, E. A., Greve, D. N., Gard, T., Creswell, J. D., Brown, K. W., . . . & Lazar, S. W. (2013). Neural mechanisms of symptom improvements in generalized anxiety disorder following mindfulness training. *Neuroimage: Clinical*, *2*, 448–458.

121. Hofmann, S. G., Sawyer, A. T., Witt, A. A., & Oh, D. (2010). The effect of mindfulness-based therapy on anxiety and depression: A meta-analytic review. *Journal of Consulting and Clinical Psychology*, *78*(2), 169.

122. Vøllestad, J., Nielsen, M. B., & Nielsen, G. H. (2012). Mindfulness-and acceptance-based interventions for anxiety disorders: A systematic review and meta-analysis. *British Journal of Clinical Psychology*, *51*(3), 239–260.

123. DeSteno, D., Lim, D., Duong, F., & Condon, P. (2018). Meditation inhibits aggressive responses to provocations. *Mindfulness*, *9*(4), 1117–1122.

124. Nahin, R. L. (2015). Estimates of pain prevalence and severity in adults: United States, 2012. *Journal of Pain*, *16*(8), 769–780.

125. Oliveira, A., Gevirtz, R., & Hubbard, D. (2006). A psycho-educational video used in the emergency department provides effective treatment for whiplash injuries. *Spine*, *31*(15), 1652–1657.

126. Described in Hurwitz, B. (2017). Narrative constructs in modern clinical case reporting. *Studies in History and Philosophy of Science Part A*, *62*, 65–73.

127. Nail found embedded in construction worker's skull. (2005, January). *USA Today*. Retrieved from https://usatoday30.usatoday.com/news/offbeat/2005-01-16-nail-skull_x .htm

128. Kroll, H. R. (2015). Exercise therapy for chronic pain. *Physical Medicine and Rehabilitation Clinics, 26*(2), 263–281.

McCracken, L. M., & Vowles, K. E. (2008). A prospective analysis of acceptance of pain and values-based action in patients with chronic pain. *Health Psychology, 27*(2), 215.

Sturgeon, J. A., & Zautra, A. J. (2016). Social pain and physical pain: Shared paths to resilience. *Pain Management, 6*(1), 63–74.

129. Siegel, R. D. (2009). *The mindfulness solution: Everyday practices for everyday problems.* New York, NY: Guilford Press.

130. Koenig, J., Falvay, D., Clamor, A., Wagner, J., Jarczok, M. N., Ellis, R. J., . . . & Thayer, J. F. (2016). Pneumogastric (vagus) nerve activity indexed by heart rate variability in chronic pain patients compared to healthy controls: A systematic review and meta-analysis. *Pain Physician, 19*(1), E55–E78.

Tracy, L. M., Ioannou, L., Baker, K. S., Gibson, S. J., Georgiou-Karistianis, N., & Giummarra, M. J. (2016). Meta-analytic evidence for decreased heart rate variability in chronic pain implicating parasympathetic nervous system dysregulation. *Pain, 157*(1), 7–29.

131. Bradley, M. M., Silakowski, T., & Lang, P. J. (2008). Fear of pain and defensive activation. *Pain, 137*(1), 156–163.

132. Gard, T., Hölzel, B. K., Sack, A. T., Hempel, H., Lazar, S. W., Vaitl, D., & Ott, U. (2011). Pain attenuation through mindfulness is associated with decreased cognitive control and increased sensory processing in the brain. *Cerebral Cortex, 22*(11), 2692–2702.

Zeidan, F., Grant, J. A., Brown, C. A., McHaffie, J. G., & Coghill, R. C. (2012). Mindfulness meditation-related pain relief: Evidence for unique brain mechanisms in the regulation of pain. *Neuroscience Letters, 520*(2), 165–173.

133. Grant, J. A., Courtemanche, J., & Rainville, P. (2011). A non-elaborative mental stance and decoupling of executive and pain-related cortices predicts low pain sensitivity in Zen meditators. *Pain, 152*(1), 150–156.

Zeidan, F., Emerson, N. M., Farris, S. R., Ray, J. N., Jung, Y., McHaffie, J. G., & Coghill, R. C. (2015). Mindfulness meditation-based pain relief employs different neural mechanisms than placebo and sham mindfulness meditation-induced analgesia. *Journal of Neuroscience, 35*(46), 15307–15325.

Zeidan, F., Gordon, N. S., Merchant, J., & Goolkasian, P. (2010). The effects of brief mindfulness meditation training on experimentally induced pain. *Journal of Pain, 11*(3), 199–209.

134. Gard, T., Hölzel, B. K., Sack, A. T., Hempel, H., Lazar, S. W., Vaitl, D., & Ott, U. (2011). Pain attenuation through mindfulness is associated with decreased cognitive control and increased sensory processing in the brain. *Cerebral Cortex, 22*(11), 2692–2702.

Lutz, A., McFarlin, D. R., Perlman, D. M., Salomons, T. V., & Davidson, R. J. (2013). Altered anterior insula activation during anticipation and experience of painful stimuli in expert meditators. *Neuroimage, 64*, 538–546.

135. Zeidan, F., Salomons, T., Farris, S. R., Emerson, N. M., Adler-Neal, A., Jung, Y., & Coghill, R. C. (2018). Neural mechanisms supporting the relationship between dispositional mindfulness and pain. *Pain, 159*(12), 2477–2485.

136. Bilevicius, E., Kolesar, T., & Kornelsen, J. (2016). Altered neural activity associated with mindfulness during nociception: A systematic review of functional MRI. *Brain Sciences, 6*(2), 14.

137. Masedo, A. I., & Esteve, M. R. (2007). Effects of suppression, acceptance and spontaneous coping on pain tolerance, pain intensity and distress. *Behavior Research and Therapy, 45*(2), 199–209.

138. Forgas, J. P., Goldenberg, L., & Unkelbach, C. (2009). Can bad weather improve your memory? An unobtrusive field study of natural mood effects on real-life memory. *Journal of Experimental Social Psychology, 45*(1), 254–257.

139. Forgas, J. P. (1998). Happy and mistaken? Mood effects on the fundamental attribution error. *Journal of Personality and Social Psychology, 75*, 318–331.

    Forgas, J. P. (2011). She just doesn't look like a philosopher . . . ? Affective influences on the halo effect in impression formation. *European Journal of Social Psychology, 41*(7), 812–817.

140. Goldenberg, L., & Forgas, J. P. (2012). *Can happiness make us lazy? Hedonistic discounting can reduce perseverance and the motivation to perform.* Sydney, Australia: UNSW Press.

141. Tan, H. B., & Forgas, J. P. (2010). When happiness makes us selfish, but sadness makes us fair: Affective influences on interpersonal strategies in the dictator game. *Journal of Experimental Social Psychology, 46*, 571–576.

142. Tuck, N. L., Grant, R. C., Sollers, J. J., III, Booth, R. J., & Consedine, N. S. (2016). Higher resting heart rate variability predicts skill in expressing some emotions. *Psychophysiology, 53*(12), 1852–1857.

143. Stange, J. P., Hamilton, J. L., Fresco, D. M., & Alloy, L. B. (2017). Flexible parasympathetic responses to sadness facilitate spontaneous affect regulation. *Psychophysiology, 54*(7), 1054–1069.

144. Kemp, A. H., Quintana, D. S., Gray, M. A., Felmingham, K. L., Brown, K., & Gatt, J. M. (2010). Impact of depression and antidepressant treatment on heart rate variability: A review and meta-analysis. *Biological Psychiatry, 67*(11), 1067–1074.

145. Karavidas, M. K., Lehrer, P. M., Vaschillo, E., Vaschillo, B., Marin, H., Buyske, S., . . . & Hassett, A. (2007). Preliminary results of an open label study of heart rate variability biofeedback for the treatment of major depression. *Applied Psychophysiology and Biofeedback, 32*(1), 19–30.

146. Siepmann, M., Aykac, V., Unterdörfer, J., Petrowski, K., & Mueck-Weymann, M. (2008). A pilot study on the effects of heart rate variability biofeedback in patients with depression and in healthy subjects. *Applied Psychophysiology and Biofeedback, 33*(4), 195–201.

147. Zucker, T. L., Samuelson, K. W., Muench, F., Greenberg, M. A., & Gevirtz, R. N. (2009). The effects of respiratory sinus arrhythmia biofeedback on heart rate variability and

posttraumatic stress disorder symptoms: A pilot study. *Applied Psychophysiology and Biofeedback, 34*(2), 135.

148. Caldwell, Y. T., & Steffen, P. R. (2018). Adding HRV biofeedback to psychotherapy increases heart rate variability and improves the treatment of major depressive disorder. *International Journal of Psychophysiology, 131,* 96–101.

149. Strauss, C., Cavanagh, K., Oliver, A., & Pettman, D. (2014). Mindfulness-based interventions for people diagnosed with a current episode of an anxiety or depressive disorder: A meta-analysis of randomised controlled trials. *PLOS One, 9*(4), e96110.

150. Gotink, R. A., Chu, P., Busschbach, J. J., Benson, H., Fricchione, G. L., & Hunink, M. M. (2015). Standardised mindfulness-based interventions in healthcare: An overview of systematic reviews and meta-analyses of RCTs. *PLOS One, 10*(4), e0124344.

151. Goldberg, S. B., Tucker, R. P., Greene, P. A., Davidson, R. J., Wampold, B. E., Kearney, D. J., & Simpson, T. L. (2018). Mindfulness-based interventions for psychiatric disorders: A systematic review and meta-analysis. *Clinical Psychology Review, 59,* 52–60.

152. Blanck, P., Perleth, S., Heidenreich, T., Kröger, P., Ditzen, B., Bents, H., & Mander, J. (2018). Effects of mindfulness exercises as stand-alone intervention on symptoms of anxiety and depression: Systematic review and meta-analysis. *Behaviour Research and Therapy, 102,* 25–35.

153. Vignaud, P., Donde, C., Sadki, T., Poulet, E., & Brunelin, J. (2018). Neural effects of mindfulness-based interventions on patients with major depressive disorder: A systematic review. *Neuroscience and Biobehavioral Reviews, 88,* 98–105.

154. Zhu, X., Zhu, Q., Shen, H., Liao, W., & Yuan, F. (2017). Rumination and default mode network subsystems connectivity in first-episode, drug-naive young patients with major depressive disorder. *Scientific Reports, 7,* 43105.

155. Aldao, A., Nolen-Hoeksema, S., & Schweizer, S. (2010). Emotion-regulation strategies across psychopathology: A meta-analytic review. *Clinical Psychology Review, 30*(2), 217–237.

156. Piver, Susan (2011). The importance of sadness. *Mindful.org,* April 20, 2011

157. Freed, S., & D'Andrea, W. (2015). Autonomic arousal and emotion in victims of interpersonal violence: Shame proneness but not anxiety predicts vagal tone. *Journal of Trauma and Dissociation, 16*(4), 367–383.

Index